Ethics and Character

To Rudy —

a good colleague and a great friend.

— with warm regards,

Mike, 24 June 1999

ETHICS AND CHARACTER
THE PURSUIT OF DEMOCRATIC VIRTUES

EDITED BY

William D. Richardson
J. Michael Martinez
Kerry R. Stewart

CAROLINA ACADEMIC PRESS
Durham, North Carolina

Copyright © 1998 William D. Richardson,
J. Michael Martinez, and Kerry R. Stewart
All Rights Reserved.

Library of Congress Cataloging-in-Publication Data

Ethics and character : the pursuit of democratic virtues / edited by
　William D. Richardson, J. Michael Martinez, and Kerry R. Stewart.
　　p.　cm.
　Includes bibliographical references and index.
　ISBN 0-89089-909-6
　1. Ethics—United States. 2. Democracy—United States.
3. Political ethics—United States. I. Richardson, William D.
(William Donald)　II. Martinez, J. Michael (James Michael)
III. Stewart, Kerry R., 1951– 　.
BJ55.E8　1998
172'.1—dc21　　　　　　　　　　　　　　　　　　　98-42285
　　　　　　　　　　　　　　　　　　　　　　　　　　CIP

Cover illustration: Detail of "School of Athens" by Raphael.
Reprinted with permission of Monumenti Musei e Gallerie Pontificie,
Vatican City, Rome, Italy.

CAROLINA ACADEMIC PRESS
700 Kent Street
Durham, North Carolina 27701
Telephone (919) 489-7486
Fax (919) 493-5668
E-mail: cap@cap-press.com
www.cap-press.com

Printed in the United States of America

*To William C. Sawyer, Laura M. Martinez, and
William C. and Margaret M. Stewart*

Contents

Acknowledgments — ix

Part I Morality and the Ethical Tradition

Chapter One · Introduction
  William D. Richardson and J. Michael Martinez — 5

Chapter Two · Ethics, Virtue, and Character Development
  J. Michael Martinez and Kerry R. Stewart — 19

Chapter Three · Plain Persons and Moral Philosophy:
Rules, Virtues, and Goods
  Alasdair MacIntyre — 47

Part II Law, Lawyers, and Ethics

Chapter Four · Constitutional Correctives for Democratic Vices
  William D. Richardson and Lloyd G. Nigro — 69

Chapter Five · The Tension Between Law and Ethics
  William D. Richardson — 91

Chapter Six · Law Versus Ethics: Reconciling Two Concepts
of Public Service Ethics
  J. Michael Martinez — 107

Chapter Seven · Temperance, Passions, and Lawyers
in the American Democratic Regime
  John C. Koritansky — 141

Part III Private Virtues, Public Vices

Chapter Eight · Ethics and Politics: The American Way
  Martin Diamond — 171

Chapter Nine · Democracy's Quiet Virtues
  Sarah R. Adkins — 203

Chapter Ten · The Rediscovery of Character: Private
Virtue and Public Policy
  James Q. Wilson — 225

Part IV Leadership and Virtue

Chapter Eleven · Military Ethics: An Aristotelian Tradition
in a Democratic Society
Anthony J. Giasi   241

Chapter Twelve · Administrators in a Democratic Republic:
A Multivalent View of American Civil Religion
Ralph Clark Chandler   263

Chapter Thirteen · Moral Realism Versus Therapeutic Elitism:
Christopher Lasch's Populist Defense of American Character
Peter Augustine Lawler   289

References   311
Contributors   327
Index   331

Acknowledgments

Several of the contributions to this collection originally appeared elsewhere. The editors wish to express their appreciation for permission to reprint the following: Martin Diamond, "Ethics and Politics: The American Way," in Robert Horwitz, ed., *The Moral Foundations of the American Republic*, 3rd ed. (Charlottesville, Virginia: University Press of Virginia, 1986), reprinted by permission of Kenyon College; Alasdair MacIntyre, "Plain Persons and Moral Philosophy: Rules, Virtues, and Goods," *American Catholic Philosophical Quarterly*, Vol. 66, No. 1 (Winter 1992), pp. 3-19; and James Q. Wilson, "The Rediscovery of Character: Private Virtue and Public Policy," *The Public Interest*, No. 81 (Fall 1985), pp. 3-16. Additionally, versions of some other chapters originally appeared in other forums. The editors similarly express their appreciation for permission to reprint various portions of the following: J. Michael Martinez, "Law Versus Ethics: Reconciling Two Concepts of Public Service Ethics," *Administration & Society*, Vol. 29, No. 6, January 1998: 690-722; William D. Richardson and Lloyd G. Nigro, "Administrative Ethics and Founding Thought: Constitutional Correctives, Honor, and Education," *Public Administration Review*, 47, No. 5 (September/October 1987): 367-76; and William D. Richardson, "Law versus Ethics," in Phillip J. Cooper and Chester I. Newland, eds., *Handbook of Public Law and Public Administration* (San Francisco, CA: Jossey-Bass, 1997), pp. 361-375.

Finally, the editors wish to express their individual and collective appreciation to the various people who directly or indirectly helped to make this collection possible. We especially thank Carol Nigro for her expert proofreading assistance in this manuscript, and Cheryl Hovorka for her efficient secretarial services. William Richardson has been amply indulged by his wife and children throughout the protracted process of shepherding this book to completion. As they have often remarked, he is deeply indebted to them for making it possible for him to work at times that were all too often unusual and inconvenient to the family. He also wants to express his appreciation to William C. Sawyer, whose exemplary life—combat pilot, football player, Lockean entrepreneur, small town mayor, devoted husband and father, steadfast friend—personifies the best of what is meant by the American character. The book is appropriately dedicated to him. J. Michael Martinez expresses appreciation to all friends, family and colleagues who endured numerous long-winded monologues about esoteric ethical theory on occasions when a dialogue would have been the preferred form of communication. Especially deserving of thanks are Paula, Shane, Shelby, Laura, and Hortense, all of whom knowingly or unknowingly made sacrifices so that this project might come to fruition. He dedicates this work to his mother, Laura M. Martinez. Kerry R. Stewart wishes to thank Professors Gary Dean Best and Larry Heintz of the University of Hawaii at Hilo for the encouragement and firm hands that pushed him beyond his own expectations. Had it not been for the two of them, he might still be just a very good carpenter. He adds to the dedication the names of his father, William C. Stewart, and mother, Margaret M. Stewart.

Ethics and Character

PART I

Morality and the Ethical Tradition

Chapter One

Introduction

William D. Richardson
J. Michael Martinez

Since the demise of the former Union of Soviet Socialist Republics after 1989, America has seen variants of its democratic government blossom throughout the world. In a remarkably short time, some few of these have even achieved a degree of stability (El Salvador, Nicaragua, Haiti, South Africa), but far too many others that flirted with democratic processes all too easily reverted to the oldest method of settling disagreements: force. To its credit, America has not stood idly by while its political cousins have struggled. In some places (Angola, Somalia, Bosnia), it has put its troops on the line in an effort to stop the fighting. In regions that are less strife-torn, a host of private and public organizations—such as the National Endowment for Democracy, the Foundation for Education for Democracy, the Institute for Democracy in Eastern Europe—have undertaken the longer term tasks of trying to assure that the economic, political, and administrative infrastructures so essential to democratic health are properly established.

But, as America itself coincidentally reaffirms all too frequently, there are some critical ingredients for the successful founding and maintaining of a democracy that cannot readily be taught or emulated. Perhaps the most important of these concerns the character or "ethos" of the regime's citizens and leaders. For a democracy to thrive, both rulers and ruled must have a respect—in ideal circumstances, even a reverence— for laws rather than for the far more transitory whims of men (no matter how popular they may be). At a minimum, their law-abidingness must be bolstered not just by the processes or methods of democracy (important though they may be), but by such difficult "qualities" or "traits" as tolerance and moderate passions for contending persons, opinions, and beliefs. Without these, there is no firm basis for the critical Aristotelian principle of "rule and be ruled" in turn that is a fundamental promise of modern democratic political arrangements. That is, there can be no willingness to accept electoral defeat with the democratic equivalent of a Gallic shrug and an exasperated sigh of "Next time."

The terms "qualities" or "traits" may strike some contemporary ears as awkward or even inaccurate. They are the products of a debate that began with the works of the Florentine Machiavelli and, in one form or another, animated any serious discussion of ethics on through to the present time. Indeed, for one long dry spell within living memory Machiavelli's project of altering the way in which we even thought about the purposes of politics had been so overwhelmingly successful that public discussions almost ceased to mention the terms "virtue" or "vice." A contemporary variant of Machiavelli's "virtú," the deliberately encompassing and vague "values," became the dominant substitute. As intended, this term minimized if not erased the distinctions that, even in a democracy such as ours, form the essence of the regime. By helping to obfuscate and retard the fundamental purpose of politics—debating and deciding what actions, arguments, and, yes, even thoughts shall be praised and blamed—it advanced the Machiavellian-inspired march towards the goal of relevance in which there are no set or absolute standards, only mutually equivalent preferences.

Of course, discussion of "virtues" and "vices" never really ceased during this time; it simply became far less visibly a part of public life. While he was certainly not one of the first to join the battles being waged over various moral issues, a coincidence of timing and subject matter combined to make a minor public figure a major actor in this particular debate. William J. Bennett, the former Secretary of Education under Reagan, Drug Czar under Bush, and presidential candidate, performed one indisputable public service when he edited two best-selling collections about time-honored virtues.[1] The astounding popularity of these books helped to restore the traditional language of the debates over contemporary morals. Where a few years back the word "virtue" had been made to seem quaint and antiquated, it now boldly reappeared in public discourse and gave no indication that it would be leaving anytime soon.

While Bennett's part in this transformation is important, the critical ingredient was the subject matter of his collections. His first one was targeted at the Baby Boomers, the contemporary generation that had dwelled long and all too comfortably with the Machiavellian relativism of "values." It introduced—perhaps for the first time to a substantial portion of his audience—some of the classical "beast fables" of Aesop as well as appropriate selections from Shakespeare, Dickens, Tolstoy and Baldwin. Intended as much for adult edification as for being read aloud to the progeny of the Boomers, these tales adroitly trumpeted the importance of non-relativistic virtues that were once considered essential for the citizens of well-governed regimes—most especially democratic ones.

---

1. William J. Bennett, *The Book of Virtues: A Treasury of Great Moral Stories*.(New York: Simon and Schuster, 1993); *The Children's Book of Virtues* (New York: Simon and Schuster, 1995).

In the enticing literary world of *The Book of Virtues*, decent citizens of decent regimes regularly practiced compassion, honesty, courage, friendship and faith. These moral lessons were reinforced when Bennett subsequently issued a fulsomely illustrated collection containing selections aimed directly at the regime's younger children.

While the clarity of public debates about morals may have benefitted from readmitting terminology about "virtues" and "vices," that doesn't mean that there has been sweeping agreement on either precisely what "virtues" are appropriate or on their place in the regime. For illustration of this aspect of the battle, one need look no further than the lingering moral scandals that dog the Clinton administration. While many Americans may support the inculcation of Aesopian virtues in their children and praise their possession by adults in their private lives, there appears to be some disagreement about how important such virtues are for the rulers of democracy—at least ones who fortuitously possess collorary virtues of agreeableness, empathy and charm to the degree manifested by Bill Clinton. (In one of those marvelous ironies that periodically arise in the more important public debates, President Clinton's main legal defender in the Paula Jones civil case is none other than Bill Bennett's brother. While the one brother promoted virtue in the citizenry's private lives, his sibling defended the Chief Citizen against accusations of private vice in public office. A richer illustration of the regime's quandary in this debate would be harder to find.)

However painful and disruptive the focus on the respective virtues or vices of democratic leaders may be, it serves at least one highly useful purpose: it shoulders aside the political and economic questions of the moment and ushers in the fundamental issue of *ethos* or *character*. The various combinations of virtues and vices that collectively distinguish the citizens of one regime from those of another—and some citizens of the same regime from each other—reveal the strengths and weaknesses of regimes. If a regime is united and well-governed, the character of its citizens will reflect and may even embody the ends for which it was established. In the early years of our democratic regime, Tocqueville took clear note of this inter-connection between character and ends:

> What do you expect from society and its government? We must be clear about that.... [I]f you think it profitable to turn man's intellectual and moral activity toward the necessities of physical life and use them to produce well-being, if you think that reason is more use to men than genius, if your object is not to create heroic virtues but rather tranquil habits, if you would rather contemplate vices than crimes and prefer fewer transgressions at the cost of fewer splendid deeds, if in place of a brilliant society you are content to live in one that is prosperous, and finally, if in your view the main object of government is not to achieve the

greatest strength or glory for the nation as a whole but to provide for every individual therein the utmost well-being, protecting him as far as possible from all afflictions, then it is good to make conditions equal and to establish a democratic government.[2]

The study of those virtues and vices that comprise the particular character of America and its citizens is important not just for what it reveals about our fundamental ends or the ones that could or should be pursued by those attempting to establish new democracies. It apprises us of the character choices we may have rejected or discarded and, more immediately, suggests the daunting extent of the efforts that may be required to assimilate non-democrats into our own or other regimes. From this perspective, character becomes *the* standard by which one judges past human behavior and predicts future actions.

> Traits of character...play an important part in our understanding of human behavior and in our evaluation of individuals and their actions. These ideas are rich and complex. They can be made to yield the most subtle and profound insights about human beings by wise and skilled novelists, historians, and playwrights. A philosophical study of character traits must deal with the most fundamental aspects of human life: value and education—human goodness, merit, and responsibility; practical reason—action, desires, motives, reasons, reasoning, and judgment; and relations among people—community, convention, and shared ideals.[3]

The intent of this collection is to provide the attentive reader with a thorough introduction to the delightfully rich debate over the *ethos* or *character* that is appropriate to a democratic regime and its citizens. It assumes that the reader will come to the book with some degree of familiarity in one or another aspect of the ongoing debate. However, it could not presume that very many of the likely readers would be predictably conversant with the full depth and breadth of that debate. Accordingly, the contributions to the collection are grouped into four major sections that reflect their respective subject matters: "Morality and the Ethical Tradition"; "Law, Lawyers, and Ethics"; "Private Virtues, Public Policies"; and "Leadership and Virtue." This organization is intended to permit readers to select both the areas of greatest interest to them as well as those in which they may want to acquire more perspective and understanding.

Thus, the first major contribution to the section on "Morality and the Ethical Tradition" is Chapter 2, entitled "Ethics, Virtue and Character

---

2. Tocqueville, Alexis de, *Democracy in America*, ed. J.P. Mayer. (Garden City: Anchor Books, 1969), p. 243

3. Wallace, James D., *Virtues & Vices* (Ithaca: Cornell University Press, 1978), 10.

Development." Here J. Michael Martinez and Kerry R. Stewart summarize the ongoing debate between deontologists and utilitarians stretching across twenty-five centuries of western thought about the appropriate source, nature and scope of ethics. Although some thinkers and schools of thought are not covered (most notably the Medieval philosophies of Skepticism, Stoicism, Epicureanism, Neoplatonism, and some later works, including Spinoza's advances in ethics and the individualism of nineteenth century Transcendentalism, for example), the chapter provides "an introduction to major issues and thinkers that have contributed to the current understanding of character." Beginning with Plato and moving through Aristotle, the Medieval period, Hobbes, Locke, Hume, Kant, the English Utilitarians, and ultimately postmodernism, the authors explore changing conceptions of ethical theory. Should ethics be grounded on absolute values, as Plato posited, or are notions of "ethics" and "character" quaint, antiquated concepts that have no place in a system that requires persons to balance competing interests based on complex calculations of happiness and the public good (as the English Utilitarians suggested)? Perhaps, as the postmodernists observed, the philosophical quest for ethical standards is irrelevant at the outset because it seeks answers to questions that need not, and should not, be asked.

In Chapter 3, "Plain Persons and Moral Philosophy: Rules, Virtues and Goods," the acclaimed Scottish philosopher Alasdair MacIntyre addresses questions raised in Chapter 2 by suggesting that postmodernists, existentialists and other proto-Nietzschean relativists fail to appreciate the importance of the philosophical quest owing to their impoverished assessment of human nature. By arguing that character and ethics are matters of will, perspective or social convention, postmodern thinkers place individual interiority above shared ethical values that everyone, even "plain persons" who know little or nothing of moral philosophy, consciously or unconsciously accepts.

Reiterating a point he made in his influential book *After Virtue*, MacIntyre implies that relativists are correct in their assessments of man's dark side, that is, he has the ability to act as a brute. Yet this pessimistic view of human nature does not obviate the need for philosophy. Just because he can act brutishly in some circumstances does not preclude the possibility of man acting honorably on other occasions. MacIntyre asks that we consider the possibility of man acting on his most enlightened and noble impulses, for it is when he acts according to those impulses that we witness his essential nature, when he is most like a man and least like an animal. He takes the argument one step further. Despite postmodern philosophers' assertions to the contrary, in MacIntyre's view everyone has some intuitive sense of the Aristotelian concept of an essential person or *telos*. Plain persons know good character when they encounter it, although they may not be able to provide a philosophical defense of their position.

To illustrate his thesis, MacIntyre examines plain persons in some detail and asks the rhetorical question: how much of a moral philosopher must such a person become? Clearly, few plain persons will acquaint themselves with great works of philosophy to answer the specific questions they encounter in their lives. Instead, plain persons begin their lives practicing habituation. As they mature, they learn their place in the family, a trade or profession, and the community. Plain persons live each day as a dramatic narrative, a series of vignettes in which ethical choices are made, stands are taken, and consequences are handled. Eventually, plain persons develop a sense of when to honor the letter of the rules, and when to move beyond them to the spirit of the rules, so that virtues and goods, and not the rules themselves, are the paramount consideration. Plain persons need only enough philosophy to help them identify and weigh alternatives and understand why and how past choices were or were not mistakes. Thus, although plain persons may never revel in the Aristotelian or Thomistic traditions or study other great works of philosophy, they are intuitively followers of Aristotle and Aquinas.

This raises one final question. If plain persons don't need philosophy to act ethically, why engage in philosophical inquiry in the first place? The answer is that philosophy enriches our understanding of ourselves. We learn about the human condition in universal terms so that we can marvel at the possibility, indeed the likelihood, that Aristotle, Aquinas or other long-dead theorists experienced problems similar to, or the same as, our own. Moreover, philosophy provides an explanation of the reasons behind the virtues already embraced by plain people of good character throughout their lives.

Because plain persons act virtuously without a knowledge of moral philosophy and because plain persons have it within themselves to act virtuously in their day-to-day lives, they progress toward an ultimate goal (*telos*). By implication, if the universe is teleologically ordered, it is therefore intelligible only when it is understood in the appropriate teleological (and, for that matter, theological) light. For MacIntyre, then, postmodern theory presents a nonsensical alternative to the Aristotelian emphasis on *telos* because it stresses the interiority of the individual as the highest good in lieu of a communal notion of personal identity so apparent in the narrative lives of plain persons.

MacIntyre's concern with the development of character in plain persons implicitly raises the question of how, and to what extent, a regime should encourage its citizens to behave ethically. Because laws are the means by which most well-governed regimes—and especially democratic ones—seek to form the habits that make up their respective characters, it seemed eminently reasonable to have the next section be concerned with "Laws, Lawyers, and Ethics." Not surprisingly, the importance of the relationship between laws and ethics became manifest in the size of this section, which is appropriately the largest of the collection. In Chapter 4, the first contribution to this section is concerned with "Constitutional Correctives for Democratic Vices." Here William Richardson and Lloyd Nigro discuss the special difficulties of governing a democratic regime that is founded in the American manner, that is, with a dependence on human nature "as it is" rather than as it should be. In putting such emphasis on the private interests of its citizenry, the regime may have considerable difficulty defining—much less competently pursuing—its "public interest." Whatever special burdens this emphasis might put upon the nation's governors would be offset by the strength of the institutional structures that were intended to keep the behavior of the self-interested citizenry comparatively restrained and focused on wealth-producing endeavors. The attendant virtues of such a citizenry wouldn't be predictably elevated or heroic. But there is still much to be said for the lower virtues—honesty, hard work, agreeableness—that put "comfortable self-preservation" within the reach of almost the whole of the democracy. In so orienting the regime, the Founders placed its foundation on a bedrock—self-interest—that was far more stable than those "chimerical" ones requiring the regular application of "extraordinary virtue."

In Chapter 5, William Richardson explores the proper relation between law and character in "Law versus Ethics." The "rule of law" may not inspire the magisterial awe that it once did and that quite properly may be its due. Law, after all, is the substitute for the oft-times whimsical rule of men or the use of force to accomplish one's purposes. Even more importantly, it is law that provides the elementary conditions that determine what kind of culture will be present and how well it will flourish. For a democratic regime in which the citizens are intended to have a role in the affairs of state, the inter-relationship between law and culture is critical, for the "character of these citizens is...largely a cultural product resulting from the interaction of a complex array of forces, including family, education, religion, and the leadership of public servants." The quality of the culture and, hence, that of the citizenry's character is affected not just by the quality of the laws, but also by the way in which those laws are applied. Because public servants exercise varying degrees of discretion in the course of applying the laws, the goodness of the latter is in crucial ways dependent upon the goodness of the former.

J. Michael Martinez elaborates on the relationship between external legal rules and internal ethical precepts in Chapter 6, "Law Versus Ethics: Reconciling Two Concepts of Public Service Ethics." He agrees with Richardson's observation that the proper development of individual character is related to the quality and application of laws within a regime; however, Martinez argues that something other than reliance on law alone is required to ensure that democratic values thrive in a republic. A system of ethical rules must be developed separate and apart from the law so that public servants can rely on ethical precepts as well as external legal rules. Unfortunately, it is difficult to develop a workable system of ethics for public servants because a fundamental tension exists between law (public duties) and ethics (private duties). Individuals living under a democratic regime may be educated to appreciate core values, but disputes will still occasionally arise concerning fundamental ethical precepts and democratic virtues owing to confusion, ambiguity, dishonesty, or a simple disagreement among and between reasonable people.

In an effort to assist public service professionals in developing, understanding, and living by a system of ethical rules, Chapter 6 surveys the literature on legal ethics to observe how a relatively well-developed public service profession has reconciled the tension between law and ethics, to some extent, through the adoption of a "legalized" code of ethics, the Model Rules of Professional Conduct. The Model Rules allow a professional to assume a flexible "recourse role" and step from behind a prescribed system of legal prohibitions and engage his or her individual ethical sense in appropriate instances. In essence, a lawyer can follow his or her conscience (internal controls) if circumstances so require. At the same time, he or she can be punished for failing to adhere to professional standards (external controls).

This desire to examine the rules of the legal profession may strike non-lawyers as odd owing to the public's mistrust of elitist, non-democratic power. As one influential commentator has observed, because lawyers often have served as "mitigators of the destructive tendencies of democracy" by counterbalancing the primacy of private property interests with the populist sentiments of the masses, the legal profession has been subject to much scorn and derision. Yet, despite the public's antipathy toward the profession, individual lawyers generally have been held in high regard as shrewd, intelligent professionals, possessors of enviable legal acumen. In the face of this conflicting image of lawyers, the profession has tried to encourage practitioners to practice "better ethics" by providing members of the bar with a means to rely on their individual ethical precepts. Yet the profession also has promulgated a system of inviolable, external rules that serve as the basis for enforceable sanctions in egregious cases where lawyers fail to live up to professional standards.[4]

---

4. M. Christine Cagle, J. Michael Martinez, and William D. Richardson, "Professional Licensing Boards: Self-Governance or Self-Interest?" *Administration & Society*, Vol. 30, no. 6 (January 1999): 734-770.

After discussing the key attributes of the Model Rules, Chapter 6 surveys the literature on administrative ethics and concludes that recent calls for deprofessionalizing American public administration consists of "smoke-and-mirror innovations" that will not necessarily ensure that persons of good character act in an ethical manner. On the contrary, greater professionalization of public service occupations will ensure greater accountability because public servants can be controlled through a gatekeeping organization that closely supervises its members. In lieu of divesting public administrators of their ability to influence democratic virtues, public servants should be subject to a system of ethical rules patterned after the Model Rules of Professional Conduct. Only through a combination of activities—educating citizens in a regime on appropriate democratic virtues, adopting a code of ethics that provides for a recourse role, and ensuring that effective external controls exist—can the continued health and prosperity of a democratic regime be ensured, or at least advanced.

In Chapter 7, John Koritansky addresses the issue of who conducts the ongoing business of our government, but he does so by focusing on lawyers, the intentions of the Founders and the commentary of that marvelous observer of their handiwork, Alexis de Tocqueville. In "Temperance, Passions, and Lawyers in the American Regime," he carefully details the great problem of democratic regimes, namely, majoritarian tyranny, and the ways in which the Founders sought to minimize its effects. The resultant survey takes the reader through the reasons why federalism was chosen and the ways in which its administrative decentralization and the local jury system serve to temper majority factions. In the multitude of local courts where the citizenry would be habituated to seek redress of their grievances, lawyers were expected to perform an indispensable public service for the democratic republic. By the nature of their training, practices and professional inclinations, they would serve as a temporizing brake on the passions of the disputants. The formulation and administration of the law would be their special province—so much so that they would form a "kind of aristocracy" within the very bosom of the democratic republic. Properly constituted, such lawyers would restrain some of the more egregious effects of the egalitarian impulses to which democracies are inclined (which is a point also made in Chapter 6). How well they did so, however, was in turn dependent on the quality of their training and their own characters.

The third section of the collection is entitled "Private Virtues, Public Policies" and seeks to explore the ways in which democratic character is reflected in the kinds of public policies pursued by the regime. Understandably, both the private virtues and the policies are ultimately the products of the kinds of laws (and the ways in which they are administered) that were the focus of the preceding section. The first contribution is by Martin Diamond in Chapter 8 where "Ethics and Politics: The American Way" discusses the "new science of politics" that guided the Founders in establishing the regime. Much of the discussion is drawn from the intricacies of Madison's argument in *Federalist* 10 where he explains the ways in which the new regime will dampen passions in favor of interests. Attachments based on strong passions—such as love and even hate—may well be the "means by which great virtues—courage, eloquence, rectitude, wisdom—communicate their political force and charm to human beings who might otherwise never be drawn upward to such qualities of character." But the costs of these high virtues may be far more than the regime can bear; far better to entrust the future of the nation to lesser but safer virtues and leaders in return for far greater stability. The solution was to focus the citizenry on the pursuit of their individual economic interests which would advance not only their own material well-being but, indirectly and unbidden, that of the nation as well. The result may have features of "private vice, public good"; it may even appear to pave the way for the flourishing of an American way that is more than a little vulgar and narrow. But the disadvantages of "better motives" is more than compensated for by the comparative mildness of a political system animated by "various and interfering interests." This system still incorporated a deference to certain enduring excellences; it just denied that certain classes or segments of the regime would possess them as a matter of right. In short, it firmly "popularized" a meritocracy that recognized the unequal distribution of virtues and abilities and encouraged their nurturing in the private sphere. Indeed, unlike historical aristocracies that greatly restricted rights and privileges to a small minority that may or may not have possessed the necessary excellences, Madison's formulation provided ample opportunity for the (naturally) gifted of each generation to be rewarded with public office.

In Chapter 9, Sarah Adkins looks at those virtues arising out of the Madisonian project that Tocqueville thought to be particularly significant to the regime's development. In "Democracy's Quiet Virtues," she explores the effects that "equality of conditions" has on the citizenry's manners and character. One of the more prominent is a general compassion or empathy for the human race as a whole. In addition to such compassion, "[a]ll those quiet virtues that tend to give a regular movement to the community and to encourage business will therefore be held in peculiar honor.... All the more turbulent virtues, which often dazzle, but more frequently disturb society, will, on the contrary, occupy a subordinate rank in the estimation of this same people."[5] As befits their Madis-

---

5. Tocqueville, Alexis de, *Democracy in America*, II, ed. Henry Reeve, (New York: Vintage Books, 1990), p. 235.

onian origins, all the "quiet virtues" esteemed in America are related to the production of material well-being. Thus, a certain degree of "courage," required to undertake and withstand the risks of commerce, is joined by such commercially useful virtues as "strictly regular habits" and "uniform acts." But it is "the purity of morals" that provides a most distinctive cast to the peculiar American character. Because "a laxity of morals... diverts the human mind from the pursuit of well-being and disturbs the internal order of domestic life,"[6] Tocqueville elects to focus special attention on the contribution of women to the formation of the American character. While he considers women to be socially inferior to men in this democratic regime, Tocqueville considers women to be morally superior. Indeed, he goes further: he attributes the favorable prospects for continued improvement of "the American condition" directly to the "strength of character and purity of morals" of the women.

In Chapter 10, "The Rediscovery of Character: Private Virtue and Public Policy," James Q. Wilson discusses how the sorts of private virtues that were so appreciated by Tocqueville are too often under-appreciated by contemporary policy analysts accustomed to explaining human behavior almost exclusively by reference to the costs and benefits of various actions. What such analysts fail to understand—or too readily discount—is that some of the human behavior one wishes to change with this or that public policy may not be responsive to economic incentives. Some humans may not have the right "tastes" ("what non-economists would call values and beliefs, as well as interests") or they may lack foresight, that is, they may "discount the future too heavily." Stated bluntly, they may lack "character." Wilson then embarks on an exploration of the influence that character has on four major public policies: schooling, welfare, finance, and crime. Since government—and, nowadays, when we discuss these kinds of problems, we are more and more referring to the national government—defines the problems these policies are intended to correct, it implicitly "acknowledges that human character is, in some degree, defective and that it intends to alter it." The decentralized local governments had always recognized this "because they always had responsibility for shaping character." If we see the major public concerns in proper perspective—ultimately, we are really attempting to "induce persons to act virtuously"—there really isn't a "conflict between economic thought and moral philosophy." Both are really engaged in an attempt to form decent character. Analyzing a policy solely in terms of its cost-effectiveness fails to take account of the consequences for character. If a public policy promotes a given course—and

---

6. *Ibid.*, p. 237

that course is repeated "often and regularly enough" — those who follow it are being taught what the society praises and blames. In short, their characters are being formed.

The inter-connection between public policies and character formation logically leads to a treatment of the kinds of leaders a democratic regime is likely to produce. The three chapters in the final section, "Leadership and Virtue," choose to focus on similar problems but from the perspective of different leaders. In Chapter 11, Lieutenant Colonel Anthony Giasi (U.S. Army, ret.) discusses contemporary soldiers—especially officers—who awake every day knowing that they may well be asked to do something that is explicitly expected of no other public officials: to die for the regime. However, the Lockean principles of enlightened self-interest that undergird our (civilian) democracy may be inadequate to the task of persuading soldiers to sacrifice their lives for the greater good. In place of the utilitarian ethical code of the civilian sphere, therefore, the military attempts to embrace an Aristotelian code of absolute virtues that habituate the soldier to do the "harder right rather than the easier wrong." In a regime where the civilians have a more relativistic approach to ethics, the military sees itself as morally superior to the society it serves. Such a relationship of moral inequality would be fraught with tension in almost any circumstances. When one of the parties to the relationship is also the only one that is deliberately trained to "kill and break things," the difficulties are magnified many times over. Giasi persuasively argues about how integrity, loyalty, traditions and Constitutional oaths, in alliance with the critical Aristotelian code of honor, keep the American military outward-looking. However, he worries that the very things that make the military safe for our democracy may render it ineffective in combating the New Warrior Class that is likely to dominate future low-intensity conflicts. As the French experience in Algiers so vividly demonstrated, the brutality of such opponents may make the Aristotelian code of honor into a democracy's inescapable weakness.

In Chapter 12, Ralph Chandler initially takes the reader back to the Roman state in quest of an appropriate standard for assessing the character of our contemporary leaders and the civil-religious relations that so heavily influence the regime. In "Administrators in a Democratic Republic: A Multivalent View of American Civil Religion," he stresses how the Roman civic religion de-emphasized the individual and elevated the community. The other-worldly emphasis of Christianity, however, encouraged a preoccupation with the self at "the expense of the general welfare." While the Roman leaders conducted civic affairs without regard to the prospect of reward or punishment in another life, the Christian religion made such a standard a fundamental focal point for its adherents. In so doing, it undermined the civic virtue of the Romans and made the citizens "contemptuous of their present existence." In the 1990s, some adherents of Christianity are again opposed to certain policies of the state and bring to discussions about moral issues "a kind of incivility and disdain for the opinions of others that the Roman policy of tolerance was designed to counteract." These adherents attempt to "make a Christian state of one carefully designed both to avoid an establishment of religion and to encourage the free exercise of it." Because the character of the republic "envisioned by the founders and based on classical models of toleration and administrative integrity is being challenged by influential citizens unfamiliar with the art of politics and the managerial usefulness of a civil religion," Chandler explores the sometimes ambiguous tenets of that American civil religion and what it demanded in the way of virtues from leaders and citizens, past and present.

Chapter 13, the final contribution to this section and to the book, presents a distinctly different perspective on the relationship of contemporary American leaders to civic virtue. In "Moral Realism Versus Therapeutic Elitism: Christopher Lasch's Populist Defense of American Character," Peter Augustine Lawler draws from Christopher Lasch's extensive work to argue that human beings, in moments of clarity, understand the limitations imposed upon them by their bodies. As self-conscious beings, their own mortality is apparent—to a certain extent, death haunts them. Accordingly, the need for "character or virtue to live well with what we really know is ineradicable." Lasch's unique contribution was to connect a class analysis of American life with psychoanalysis. In championing populism, Lasch expressed his view that "one class is more admirable and lived more in light of the truth." He understood the "true goal of populism" to be "'universal competence'" or a "'whole world of heroes.'" The appropriate populist aim is to make "every human being an aristocrat of character." However, this "'strenuous and morally demanding" goal is opposed by elites intent on making "'a society of supremely contented consumers'" whose contentment is "unmoved by the truth about their existence." While the Founders turned subjects into citizens, the subsequent history of the American regime reflects a "rather extreme separation of mental and physical laborers." The elites—the mental laborers—have restored a class system that "returns most citizens to subjects." While these elites may have compassion for the physical laborers and seek to alleviate their suffering, they cannot respect them. True respect results from "'admirable achievements, admirably formed characters, natural gifts put to good use.'" A regime that does not expect all its members to be admirable citizens "is not a democracy."

Chapter Two

Ethics, Virtue, and Character Development

J. Michael Martinez
Kerry R. Stewart

> So our virtues
> Lie in the interpretation of the time;
> And power, unto itself most commendable,
> Hath not a tomb so evident as a chair
> T'extol what it hath done.
> —William Shakespeare, *Coriolanus*, Act IV, Scene vii[1]

The idea that character is an integral component of ethics has been an important, yet contentious, concept in the western intellectual tradition since Plato and Aristotle penned their landmark works more than two millennia ago. Enlightenment and post-Enlightenment philosophers such as Hobbes, Locke, Hume, Kant, and the English Utilitarians—arguably the quintessential ethical theorists of the western tradition—also devoted considerable attention to the importance of character, although their conclusions differed markedly from the theories advanced by the ancient Greeks. Even twentieth century postmodern thinkers, despite inconsistencies arising from limitations inherent in their relativism, have embraced implicit assumptions about character.

For the ancient Greeks, the term "character" generally referred to the combination of qualities and attributes that comprise the personality of an individual. Thus, if one accepted the view of the ancients, a person exhibited good character when he or she acted in ways that reflected virtue, that is, when an individual tried to become a fully actualized human being by engaging in "right conduct" in accordance with certain recognizable standards.[2] Because the western understanding of what

---

1. William Shakespeare, *Coriolanus*, 4.7, in *The Works of William Shakespeare* (New York: Oxford University Press, 1904), p. 999.
2. One commentator explains the importance of character to the study of ethics: "Traits of character...play an important part in our understanding of human behavior and in our evaluation of individuals and their actions. These ideas are rich and complex.

constitutes virtue and what makes someone an individual of good character has varied throughout history, this definition falls short when one moves beyond the ancient Greek perspective. Accordingly, in an effort to illustrate the evolving conception of character in western ethics, this chapter will explore different ideas about ethics, virtue and character development from the time of the ancients to the postmodern era. Without a doubt, such an endeavor is too large and ambitious to complete within the confines of a single chapter; consequently, the purpose here is to introduce major issues and theorists that have contributed to current thinking. The chapters that follow delve into this issue in greater detail.

The Tradition of Athens

Plato

It is no exaggeration to posit that the works of the Greek philosopher Plato provided the foundation for western philosophy in general, and ethics in particular.[3] In searching for an objective source of virtue, Plato defied the skepticism of the Sophists, the wandering teachers prevalent in his day, to insist on the existence of immutable human qualities. Much to Plato's chagrin, the Sophists preached that virtue consisted of instructing pupils on the techniques of oratory and debating skills in lieu of teaching them to appreciate time-honored qualities such as courage, loyalty, personal honor, and moderation.[4] The Sophists' technique of emphasizing style over substance was aimed at achieving success in a pluralistic, democratic political system. Their teachings were a prescription for "how to win friends and influence people" through pandering and what today might be labeled "public relations wizardry."

Plato contended that if acting virtuously involved nothing more than mastering and applying a series of techniques for appearing to be good,

---

They can be made to yield the most subtle and profound insights about human beings by wise and skilled novelists, historians, and playwrights. A philosophical study of character traits must deal with the most fundamental aspects of human life: value and education—human goodness, merit, and responsibility; practical reason—action, desires, motives, reasons, reasoning, and judgment; and relations among people—community, convention, and shared ideals." James D. Wallace, *Virtues & Vices* (Ithaca: Cornell University Press, 1978), p. 10.

3. W.T. Jones, *The Classical Mind: A History of Western Philosophy*, 2nd. ed. (New York: Harcourt Brace Jovanovich, 1970), pp. 108; 215.

4. In Greek, "virtue" is *arete*, which also can be translated as "excellence." David E. Cooper, *World Philosophies: An Historical Introduction* (Cambridge, MA: Blackwell, 1996), p. 123.

virtue could only serve as the foundation for a situational ethic where standards depended on appearances that were applicable only to the time and place in which they were developed. Sophistry, then, was a base education—no less than intellectual prostitution—an invitation to cultivate whatever tastes and appetites a person chose to satisfy.[5] In modern parlance, "if it feels good, do it," the Sophists would say.

To countermand the relativism of the Sophists, Plato developed and refined his famous theory of forms. According to the theory, all matter is created from "forms," that is, a series of unseen, nonphysical, nonspatial, and nontemporal blueprints. Theologians today might label Plato's forms "spirit," while physical scientists might use terms such as "subatomic particles" or "DNA" to explain the concept.[6] Whatever terms might be used in subsequent years, Plato viewed the forms as the unchanging, eternal, objective "urstuff" that underlay all matter. Without the generality allowed by the existence of an underlying, invisible urstuff, the particularity of the world encountered by mankind through his senses could not exist.[7]

For Plato, then, the existence of the forms was a necessary condition for everything that existed or could exist, whether the thing was concrete and physical, like a horse, or an abstract concept such as justice, love or

---

5. Perhaps nowhere is Plato's point about the perils of an improper education better illustrated than in his description of the myth of Gyges's ring in Book II of *The Republic*. The shepherd who finds a ring that can make him invisible understands that he can act unjustly, while still *appearing* just, and thereby avoid the negative consequences of his unjust acts. Because he favors appearances over reality, the shepherd represents the educational ethic of the Sophists. Much of Plato's task in *The Republic* is to show, through his teacher and mentor, Socrates, why justice—a virtue—is good in and of itself, not simply for its utilitarian value—its payoff.

6. In his classic work, *Confessions*, St. Augustine recognized the similarities between the concepts expressed by Neo-Platonism, which was influential at the end of the Fourth Century CE, and the Christian understanding of God. By substituting "Word" for "forms" and describing an active, benevolent God in lieu of the indifferent universe envisioned by Plato, Augustine demonstrated how important Plato's theory of forms was in later religious works: "So you made use of a man, one who was bloated with the most outrageous pride, to procure me some of the books of the Platonists translated from the Greek into Latin. In them I read—not, of course, word for word, though the sense was the same and it was supported by all kinds of different arguments—that *at the beginning of time the Word already was; and God had the Word abiding with him, and the word was God. It was through him that all things came into being, and without him came nothing that has come to be.*" (Emphasis in the original.) St. Augustine, *Confessions*, R.S. Pine-Coffin, trans. (New York: Penguin Books, 1961), p. 144.

7. Jones, *The Classical Mind: A History of Western Philosophy*, 2nd. ed., op. cit., pp. 124-126.

ethics. Moreover, it followed that without a notion of virtue based on recognized, absolute forms, or standards, a man could not say with confidence that one act was superior to another act. In the world of the Sophists, ethical concepts such as "good," "bad," "right," or "wrong" depended on the time, place, and circumstances of the act. Absent immutable standards, the human condition became mired in a swamp of relativism and, ultimately, humanity was engulfed in despair. It would be two thousand years before Nietzsche reinvigorated the Sophists' position by urging the ubermensch to go "beyond good and evil" into a new world of unbridled perspectivalism that was not limited by the petty, sentimental moral values of an indoctrinated, hence dysfunctional, society. For Nietzsche and his progeny, the Sophists were correct and it was Plato, the great dogmatist, who spoke in error.[8]

Despite epistemological difficulties inherent in Plato's theory, the existence of immutable qualities allowed for the possibility of absolute, or formal, knowledge, which was valuable in grounding ethics in a universal standard of conduct. Absolute knowledge resulted from experiential knowledge acquired through day-to-day living coupled with reflection and a proper education. The quest to attain absolute knowledge (the "good") was the goal of all men of good character (or, as Plato put it, men with "well-ordered souls") and, by extension, it was the goal of the well-ordered regime. Thus, a man of good character lived an orderly life with other well-educated, like-minded individuals in a community that reflected the characteristics of its citizens. Throughout his major works, Plato explored the form of the good as well as the connection between virtue and character. Accordingly, the initial link between virtue, character, and ethics was already evident in the western tradition as early as the Fourth Century BCE.[9]

Although the ultimate goal (*telos*) for man was to live a good life, Plato understood that many attributes contributed to the good life, de-

---

8. Nietzsche's work is often impenetrable to the novice owing to his propensity to write pithy aphorisms which, when taken out of context, are easily misinterpreted. Nonetheless, his objection to Plato's philosophy was clear in the preface to *Beyond Good and Evil*: "[I]t must certainly be conceded that the worst, more durable, and most dangerous of all errors so far was a dogmatist's error—namely, Plato's invention of the pure spirit and the good as such. But now that it is overcome, now that Europe is breathing freely again after the nightmare and at least can enjoy a healthier—sleep, we, *whose task is wakefulness itself*, are the heirs of all that strength which has been fostered by the fight against this error. To be sure, it meant standing truth on her head and denying *perspective*, the basic condition of all life, when one spoke of spirit and the good as Plato did." (Emphasis in the original.) Friedrich Nietzsche, *Beyond Good and Evil*, Walter Kaufmann, trans. (New York: Vintage Books, 1966), p. 3.

9. See, for example: Plato, *The Republic of Plato*, trans. Allan Bloom, (New York: Basic Books, 1968), pp. 184-192.

pending on the abilities and interests of the people seeking the good. He listed positive human qualities such as courage,[10] friendship,[11] honor,[12] justice,[13] and wisdom[14] as examples of those qualities, although this list was not exhaustive.

For all of his idealism in developing the theory of forms, Plato recognized that absolute knowledge—the ultimate good—was unattainable. The good was perfect, but man lacked perfection. Thus, he could never fully know the good. Nonetheless, a person must strive to live a good life to the best of his abilities. Experience shows, however, that some individuals possess greater abilities than others because natural inequalities exist among men. Accordingly, those persons who naturally possessed greater abilities had to assist the less fortunate in realizing virtues such as responsibility, self-discipline and courage. Only persons who possessed superior abilities—"souls of gold"—were fit to be rulers (philosopher-kings), while other persons who lacked abilities to govern themselves without assistance from a philosopher-king were either auxiliaries (souls of silver) or workers (souls of bronze).[15]

As Plato discussed in the "Gorgias,"[16] before a person was fit to rule the polis as a philosopher-king, he had to govern himself. Plato used the analogy of a leaking vessel to illustrate the need for self-governance. Some persons have souls, like sieves, that will never be filled; they are the intemperate and undisciplined. Their appetites are insatiable and uncon-

---

10. Ibid., pp. 52; 58; 74; 81.
11. Plato, "Gorgias," trans. W.D. Woodhead, *The Collected Dialogues of Plato*, ed. Edith Hamilton and Huntington Cairns, (Princeton: Princeton University Press, 1961), pp. 290-292. See also: Plato, "Laws," trans. A.E. Taylor, *The Collected Dialogues of Plato*, ed. Edith Hamilton and Huntington Cairns, (Princeton: Princeton University Press, 1961), pp. 1323-24.
12. Plato, "Laws," op. cit., pp. 1315-16. See also: Plato, *The Republic*, op. cit., pp. 598; 807-808.
13. Plato, "Protagoras," trans. W.K.C. Guthrie, *The Collected Dialogues of Plato*, ed. Edith Hamilton and Huntington Cairns (Princeton: Princeton University Press, 1961), pp. 319-20. See also Plato, *The Republic*, op. cit., pp. 585; 597-598; 601-602; 604; and Plato, "Meno," trans. W.K.C. Guthrie, *The Collected Dialogues of Plato*, ed. Edith Hamilton and Huntington Cairns, (Princeton: Princeton University Press, 1961), p. 356.
14. Plato, "Phaedo," trans. Hugh Tredennick, *The Collected Dialogues of Plato*, ed. Edith Hamilton and Huntington Cairns, (Princeton: Princeton University Press, 1961), p. 50; Plato, "Meno," op. cit., pp. 373-74; Plato, *The Republic*, op. cit., pp. 684-685; Plato, "Laws," op. cit., pp. 1232-33; Plato, "Protagoras," op. cit., pp. 324-25.
15. Jones, *The Classical Mind: A History of Western Philosophy*, 2nd. ed., op. cit., pp. 168-169.
16. Plato, "Gorgias," op. cit., pp. 274-275.

trolled. Those persons who are best at governing themselves, however, are those who have learned to control their appetites. The philosopher-king learns to control himself and develop the self-discipline to distinguish between what is good for himself and what is good for the polis, or city-state. Thus, a philosopher-king possesses an ordered soul that is just and temperate. When he can control himself—that is, when he can live a virtuous life without being enslaved by his appetites—then he can assist those who do not exhibit a similar measure of self-control. This is the first step in developing a system of ethics for the individual as well as a political hierarchy for the polis. The most virtuous man in the polis is the ethical man. Owing to his ability to live a good life, he can legitimately lead others as well.[17] Therefore, Plato's republic, a "city in speech," is a meritocracy where the most virtuous persons rule because they possess superior abilities and wisdom. In other words, a man of good character is also a man of good intellect. Moreover, Plato linked the well-ordered soul of the ethical man to the well-ordered soul of the polis. Ethics and polis were inextricably intertwined.

Aristotle

If Plato provided the framework for the western ethical tradition, the details were left to his most famous student, Aristotle, to develop. Aristotle began his career emulating his teacher, as students often do, yet his views changed markedly during the course of his life. The change was evident, for example, in his most influential work on ethical theory, *The Nicomachean Ethics*.[18] Some scholars contend that *The Nicomachean Ethics* "is the greatest work ever written on practical philosophy."[19] By arguing that ethical standards are not purely questions of interiority—despite Nietzsche's subsequent assertions to the contrary—nor the result of the universality championed by Plato, Aristotle established a tradition of seeking the intermediate position, that is, the mean between two extremes.[20] This emphasis on moderation as the key to "living well or doing well" in accordance with the practices and traditions of one's soci-

---

17. Ibid., pp. 286-288.
18. Aristotle, *The Nicomachean Ethics*, trans. David Ross, (New York: Oxford University Press, 1980).
19. See, for example: Cooper, *World Philosophies: An Historical Introduction*, op. cit., p. 122.
20. Aristotle wrote: "By the intermediate in the object I mean that which is equidistant from each of the extremes, which is one and the same for all men; by the intermediate relatively to us that which is neither too much nor too little—and this is not one, nor the same for all." Aristotle, *The Nicomachean Ethics*, op. cit., p. 37.

ety led Aristotle to examine the virtues important to the denizens of ancient Greece.[21]

In Book I of *The Nicomachean Ethics*, Aristotle began his discussion of the virtues by first distinguishing his moral theory from Plato's theory of forms. According to Aristotle, a single, ideal good does not exist, despite Plato's contentions.[22] "Good" is not a singular noun; it is plural. Accordingly, "goods" are chosen not because they are valuable in and of themselves, but because they create the conditions for man's happiness (*eudaimonia*).[23] Owing, in part, to his interest in scientific classification, Aristotle posited that different categories of happiness exist. For the masses, happiness is linked to sensual pleasure. Men of affairs, on the other hand, identify happiness with honor. Still other persons view wealth as a source of happiness. Whatever its source, happiness does not exist absent the virtues. Any study of the behavior of men, therefore, must examine the nature of the virtues and their relationship to happiness.[24]

Virtues—qualities of excellence—are divided into two categories, according to Aristotle. The "ethical" virtues occupy one category, while the "intellectual" virtues occupy the second.[25] Much of *The Nico-*

---

21. For a more detailed discussion of this point, see, for example: Alasdair MacIntyre, *After Virtue: A Study in Moral Theory* (London: Duckworth, 1982).

22. Aristotle wrote: "Further, since 'good' has as many senses as 'being'...clearly it cannot be something universally present in all cases and single; for then it could not have been predicated in all the categories, but in one only." Aristotle, *The Nicomachean Ethics*, op. cit., p. 8.

23. Ibid., pp. 11-12. "Happiness," as the term is used today, often refers to amusements or sensual pleasures. Yet, as Aristotle explained throughout *The Nicomachean Ethics*, his shorthand reference to happiness is not the precise connotation of *eudaimonia*. "The happy life is thought to be virtuous; now a virtuous life requires exertion, and does not consist in amusement," he wrote. "[T]he activity of this in accordance with its proper virtue will be perfect happiness. That this activity is contemplative we have already said." Ibid., p. 263. Thus, *eudaimonia* more appropriately refers to certain deliberative activities that may lead to the happiness of the contemplative man, for he is less like an animal and more like a thinking, self-actualizing being than the non-contemplative man. If the contemplative man is happier than the non-contemplative man, happiness is not a psychological state. It is the result of living a life devoted to thinking and reason.

24. Aristotle described the need for examining virtue as follows: "Since happiness is an activity of the soul in accordance with perfect virtue, we must consider the nature of virtue; for perhaps we shall thus see better the nature of happiness.... But clearly the virtue we must study is human virtue; for the good we were seeking was human good and the happiness human happiness." Ibid., pp. 24-25.

25. The term "ethical" should not be confused with "morals." The ancient Greeks did not confuse "virtue" with what political scientist Martin Diamond called "Puritani-

machean Ethics is devoted to discussing the ethical virtues as the mean between extreme qualities. In addition to his treatment of the Platonic virtues of courage (Book III), temperance (Book III) and justice (Book V), Aristotle added liberality (Book IV), magnificence (Book IV), wit (Book IV) and, most notably, friendship (Book VIII), among others.

For moral philosophers who counsel that moderation is the key to a happy, successful life, Aristotle's view of ethical virtues resonates with much authority. Yet *The Nicomachean Ethics* failed in one respect: it did not provide an explanation for the connection between ethical and intellectual virtues, as Plato had tried to explain in his dialogues. The majority of *The Nicomachean Ethics* analyzed the ethical virtues. Then, in Book X, Aristotle suddenly asserted that contemplation, an intellectual virtue, was necessary for man to know perfect happiness.[26] Yet he never directly answered the question of how ethical and intellectual virtues were related. He suggested that man's will was guided by desire and controlled through a proper education in ethical virtues. Beyond that, contemplation provided the final ingredient in establishing the grounds for ethical behavior and responsibility. Because he did not include an extended discussion of the relationship between intellectual and ethical virtues, however, the question of whether, or to what extent, man exercises free will or is driven by his nature to act in certain ways was left for later philosophers to consider. This made Aristotle's understanding of character difficult to grasp, especially for modern students.

Nonetheless, some general conclusions can be drawn. Aristotle theorized that all human beings possess an *ergon*, or a characteristic "work." A person of good character is someone who performs his work well, in accordance with the excellences befitting the work. Thus, a carpenter labors to build the best fence he possibly can. When children are instructed properly, they try to perform work to the best of their abilities and, over the course of their lives, they adopt habits that lead to excellence. Eventually, as they grow to maturity, their habits become solidified as character traits. Good character traits ensure that adults will strive to

---

cal or Victorian 'no-no's." See: Martin Diamond, "Ethics and Politics: The American Way," reprinted in Chapter Eight of this collection. As referenced earlier, virtue referred to "excellences of character," or the propensity of men to behave in ways that maximize human rationality. Cooper, *World Philosophies: An Historical Introduction*, op. cit., p. 124.

26. Aristotle wrote: "Happiness extends, then, just so far as contemplation does, and those to whom contemplation more fully belongs are more truly happy, not as a mere concomitant but in virtue of the contemplation; for this is in itself precious. Happiness, therefore, must be some form of contemplation." Aristotle, *The Nicomachean Ethics*, op. cit., p. 268.

do the best work possible absent the inducements of childhood. In Aristotle's view, a well-ordered life where people always reach for excellence in their endeavors leads to happiness. In other words, good character leads to a good, happy, fulfilling life.

The Transition from Ancient to Modern Ethics

Any extended discussion of the period from the Aristotle's death in 322 BCE to the Enlightenment would necessarily address the philosophical positions of Skepticism, Stoicism, Epicureanism, and Neoplatonism in some detail. Such an extended discussion is beyond the scope of this chapter. Although these philosophies differed in their underlying assumptions about human nature and the appropriate goals of mankind, they shared a common link to religious, quasi-mystical thinking that eventually led to the ascendancy of Christianity during the Medieval period. For more than a thousand years, western philosophers and theologians (who often were one and the same) rarely distinguished between philosophy and theology in their works.[27]

Christian thought was important for the future of western ethics because it presented an alternative to the anthropocentric focus of Athenian philosophy. Whereas ancient Greek philosophy had established the standards for applying a rational approach to the problems of man, Christianity shifted the focus to God and His perfection. Faith became a paramount concern for the Christian. The Greeks, on the other hand, lived in a world where a virtuous man worked to live in harmony with others in an orderly regime. Reason was the most important tool for Athens. Christian thinkers, however, struggled to reconcile the perfection of God in heaven with the corruption and depravity of man on earth. Their goal was to find a way for man to return to the transcendent creator who had created the universe.[28]

Expressing his frustration with the influence of Greek metaphysical abstractions on the development of Christianity, Tertullian, the second century jurist-turned-theologian, wrote, "what indeed has Athens to do with Jerusalem? Away with all attempts to produce a Stoic, Platonic, and dialectical Christianity."[29] It was not the mystical nature of Greek philosophical thinking that frustrated the early church father, but the insistence on imposing the rules of rational inquiry on questions that defied

---

27. Cooper, *World Philosophies: An Historical Introduction*, op. cit., pp. 145-154.
28. Ibid., pp. 162-164.
29. Quoted in Terence Irwin, *Classical Thought* (Oxford: Oxford University Press, 1989), p. 203.

definitive, systematic conclusions. The Platonic theory of forms and the subsequent systematic treatment of the virtues championed by Aristotle and his progeny suggested that eternal questions were the domain of philosophy, hence subject to the dogmatic rules of rational discourse. Tertullian and other early Christians believed that the Athenian philosophical tradition represented a threat to religious faith. They contended that theology was superior to philosophy not despite its logical inconsistencies, but precisely *because* it was beyond the realm of reason. Reflecting on Christ's resurrection, for example, Tertullian insisted that "the fact is certain, because it is impossible."[30]

As the Medieval period stretched past the first millennium, the faith-reason debate intensified. It was the twelfth century thinker Peter Abelard and, to an even greater extent, the thirteenth century philosopher St. Thomas Aquinas who began to insist that rationality was integral to developing, among other things, a philosophy of ethics. Aquinas's objective was no less than an attempt to reconcile the tradition of Athens (reason) with the tradition of Jerusalem (faith). The success or failure of his enterprise depends on how one views the scholasticism of his two greatest works, *Summa Theologica* and *Summa Contra Gentiles*.[31]

Aquinas agreed with Aristotle that happiness is the ultimate goal for man, although in Aquinas's view, the pagan Greek philosopher failed to understand that man had a higher purpose than becoming a self-actualized, physical being. Moreover, unlike Christian thinkers who were essentially Neoplatonists in their disregard for "natural" man and his life on earth, Aquinas divided ethical issues into two domains, "natural" and "theological." The natural virtues discussed by Aristotle in *The Nicomachean Ethics* could be attained owing to proper training and practical reason. Thus, Aristotle's view of ethics, insofar as it covered natural virtues, was adequate. On the other hand, theological virtues such as faith, hope, and love required divine grace—concepts that were not part of Aristotelian philosophy.

The same perspective informed Aquinas's view of the highest goods of man. Worldly happiness could be achieved through natural virtues, but eternal beatitude could be achieved only through the church and its sacraments. Aquinas thus fused, to the extent possible, naturalistic Greek ethics with monotheistic theology, albeit the latter was clearly su-

---

30. Quoted in H.A. Wolfson, *The Philosophy of the Church Fathers*, vol. 1 (Cambridge, MA: Harvard University Press, 1956), p. 103. For more detail on the development of medieval philosophy, see also: W.T. Jones, *The Medieval Mind: A History of Western Philosophy*, 2nd. ed. (New York: Harcourt Brace Jovanovich, 1970).

31. Jones, *The Medieval Mind: A History of Western Philosophy*, 2nd. ed., op. cit., pp. 190-286.

perior in achieving the ultimate end of man, which was to know God. In articulating a philosophy that allowed for the coexistence of both religion and natural science, Aquinas became the towering figure of Medieval philosophy. Indeed, he served as a bridge between the Hellenistic and Roman ethics of the ancient world and the modern, "scientific" ethics of the Enlightenment.[32]

The Medieval period ended in the sixteenth and seventeenth centuries with the demise of feudalism and the decline of the church as a religious, ethical and political power in the wake of the Reformation, the Copernican and Galilean revolutions in science, and the ascent of secular governments. During these two centuries of rapid social transformation, a crisis developed in philosophy, namely, the need for new ethical standards to govern the behavior of men in this newly constructed world.[33] The crisis was exacerbated by the Italian Niccolo Machiavelli, whose landmark work, *The Prince*, focused on practical questions necessary to sustain a ruler in lieu of expressing philosophical ideals on virtue, as Aristotle and Aquinas had discussed.

According to Machiavelli, society is an artificial construction designed to ensure that individuals satisfy their base desires with minimal civil strife. Thus, for Machiavelli, a system of ethics becomes a function of efficiency and effectiveness divorced from ruminations on how one *ought* to behave. If a course of action worked to achieve a ruler's objectives, then it *was* the "right" course of action. Philosophical reflections on virtue were of no use to a prince in his quest to consolidate political power.[34]

---

32. Ibid., pp. 257-272. See also: Ernest L. Fortin, "St. Thomas Aquinas," in *History of Political Philosophy*, 2nd. ed., ed. Leo Strauss and Joseph Cropsey, (Chicago: The University of Chicago Press, 1972), pp. 223-250.

33. Cooper, *World Philosophies: An Historical Introduction*, op. cit., pp. 226-235.

34. Much of *The Prince* was devoted to describing the conditions necessary for a ruler to establish and maintain his power. It was a curious work for a man known to harbor republican tendencies, as evidenced by his work *Discourses on Livy*. Cooper, *World Philosophies: An Historical Introduction*, op. cit., p. 232. Nonetheless, Machiavelli was able to forgo an extended treatment of virtue in *The Prince* except to say that a virtuous man was effective in achieving his political goals (in accordance with the more "manly" concept of "virtú." He defined the central problem of ethics and politics facing a ruler as follows: "We have said above that a Prince must have strong foundations, otherwise his downfall is inevitable. The main foundations of all states, new, old, or mixed, are good laws and good arms; and since there cannot be good laws where there are not good arms and likewise where there are good arms the laws must be good too, I shall omit discussion of laws and speak only of arms." Niccolo Machiavelli, *The Prince*, Thomas G. Bergin, trans. and ed. (Arlington Heights, IL: AHM Publishing, 1947), p. 34. This emphasis on the coercive power of the state as the foundation for a legitimate

Thomas Hobbes

The seventeenth century English philosopher Thomas Hobbes took up the mantle from Machiavelli by emphasizing practical matters in lieu of only constructing esoteric theories based on the elaborate metaphysical concepts that characterized pre-Enlightenment philosophy. Living in a time of tremendous political instability, Hobbes despised the theoretical pretensions of the ancient Greeks as well as the scholastic system-building of Medieval theologians because they did not recognize the paramount consideration in a human life, namely, the principle of self-preservation. Owing to recent advances in Galilean science, he conceived of man as material that could be understood according to scientific principles. Thus, developing an effective ethical theory required a philosopher to understand the scientific, mechanistic principles of nature as well as the psychology of human behavior.[35]

Owing to man's concern with ensuring his own self-preservation as well as his eminent rationality, he will attempt to create the conditions necessary to preserve peace and social harmony or, failing in that endeavor, he will aggressively seek to dominate other men so that he himself cannot be dominated. In *Leviathan*, Hobbes labeled these two insights "fundamental laws of nature."[36] A man will determine which law applies to his situation depending on whether he finds himself in a "state of nature" or in an organized, civil society. In the former, man is in a precarious position because he cannot prevent other men from threatening his life or property. Thus, man living in a state of nature is subject to natural conditions of war.[37] Human existence in a state of nature, as Hobbes observed in a famous passage, consists of "continual fear and danger of violent death," which means that "the life of man [is] solitary,

---

regime would have been anathema to earlier philosophers owing to its "might makes right" ethic.

35. In the opening of Hobbes's most influential work, *Leviathan*, he explained his objections to metaphysics and theology in no uncertain terms: "Nor are we therefore to give that name [truth] to any false conclusions, for he that reasons aright in words he understands can never conclude an error; Nor to that which any man knows by supernatural revelation, because it is not acquired by reasoning; Nor that which is gotten by reasoning from the authority of books, because it is not by reasoning from the cause to the effect nor from the effect to the cause, and is not knowledge, but faith." Thomas Hobbes, *Leviathan*, ed. Herbert W. Schneider, (New York: Bobbs-Merrill Co., Inc., 1958), pp. 3-4.

36. Ibid., p. 110.

37. Hobbes wrote: "Hereby it is manifest that, during the time men live without a common power to keep them all in awe, they are in that condition which is called war, and such a war as is of every man against every man." Ibid., p. 107.

poor, nasty, brutish, and short."[38] To insulate themselves from the natural condition of war, men agree to surrender part of their natural liberty in exchange for a measure of security. In other words, they voluntarily covenant with each other to create a commonwealth, or a civil government, which enforces the law through the power of the newly created sovereign.[39]

In light of Hobbes's insistence that laws promulgated by the sovereign are always superior to the conditions of war found in a state of nature, it logically follows that moral virtue consists of obedience to laws and customs of the commonwealth. In lieu of distinguishing between individual conscience and the laws of the sovereign, therefore, Hobbes considered law and ethics little more than a single concept. "For moral philosophy is nothing else but the science of what is *good* and *evil* in the conversation and society of mankind," he wrote.[40]

Hobbes profoundly influenced the development of western ethical philosophy, although his writings were hardly free of controversy. For example, his materialist view of mankind presented intractable problems concerning free will. He never completely resolved the question of how man could act as a free, rational, independent causal agent if he were but the sum and substance of his materiality. In other words, if man's behavior is attributable solely to physical laws, he cannot be held morally responsible for actions he is compelled to undertake owing to his material needs and limitations.

According to Hobbes, voluntary motion is "endeavor," which consists of "appetite" or "aversion."[41] Voluntary actions, therefore, are the result of a mechanical movement toward pleasure and away from displeasure. Pleasure itself is only a physical reaction to external stimuli.[42] Hobbes's work created difficult philosophical problems because it posited that morally neutral mechanical processes were the paramount consideration of natural philosophy, yet ethical theory was a subjective series of rules

---

38. Ibid., p. 107.

39. Hobbes concluded: "A *commonwealth* is said to be *instituted* when a *multitude* of men do agree and *covenant, every one with every one*, that to whatsoever *man or assembly of men* shall be given by the major part the *right* to *present* the person of them all—that is to say, to be their *representative*—every one, as well he that *voted for it* as he that *voted against it*, shall *authorize* all the actions and judgments of that man or assembly of men in the same manner as if they were his own, to the end to live peaceably among themselves and be protected against other men." (Emphasis in the original.) Ibid., pp. 143-144.

40. Ibid., p. 131. (Emphasis in the original.)

41. Ibid., pp. 52-53.

42. Ibid., p. 54.

created by man to govern behavior.[43] This controversy between the external world (phusis) and the internal world (nomos) had plagued philosophy since the days of the ancients, and it plagued Hobbes as well.[44]

Despite the limits of Hobbes's materialism, however, he overcame many of the metaphysical problems presented by earlier philosophers. In insisting on rational discourse as the hard currency of philosophical inquiry, he retreated from the increasingly theoretical, anthropomorphic view of man that was prevalent during the Medieval period.[45] In so doing, Hobbes brought philosophy back to the practical issues facing man. Tradition, sentiment and church authority were deposed and seventeenth century scientific method took their place. Hobbes did not seek to make man a nobler, more "ethical," creature. He sought to apply a mechanistic psychology to mankind and discover the iron principles of human behavior.[46] As a result of his preoccupation with scientific principles, Hobbes's philosophy coincided with many tenets of the Enlightenment and influenced the development of ethical theory in the centuries that followed.

John Locke

In the wake of Hobbes's mechanistic ethics, the seventeenth century English philosopher John Locke attempted to show that "moral knowledge is as capable of real certainty as mathematics."[47] Despite his emphasis on the importance of reflection prior to experience, Locke nonetheless posited that ethical concepts are based on experiences of pleasure and pain. His belief in the necessity of combining experience and reflection led him to distinguish between "speculative" and "practical" epistemological principles in an effort to reconcile these seemingly

---

43. David Gauthier, "Thomas Hobbes: Moral Theorist," *The Journal of Philosophy* 22 (1979): 547.

44. See also: David Gauthier, "Morality and Advantage," *Philosophical Review* 76 (1967): 460-475.

45. Unlike many philosophers who obscured their heretical views in their work, Hobbes boldly stated his premises in *Leviathan*: "With the introduction of false, we may join also the suppression of true philosophy by such men as neither by lawful authority nor sufficient study are competent judges of the truth.... For whatsoever power ecclesiastics take upon themselves (in any place where they are subject to the state) in their own right, though they call it God's right, is but usurpation." Hobbes, *Leviathan*, op. cit., p. 20.

46. Daniel M. Farrell, "Hobbes as Moralist," *Philosophical Studies* 48 (1985): 259-260.

47. John Locke, *An Essay Concerning Human Understanding*, Peter H. Nidditch, ed. (Oxford: Clarendon Press, 1975), p. 565.

contradictory positions. Thus, speculative knowledge was independent of action, while practical knowledge—including ethics—was useful insofar as it was acted upon in the course of daily life.[48]

As was the case with his predecessors, Locke recognized that virtue was necessary if a human being was to become fully actualized. Like Hobbes, he contended that moral virtue required man to conform to custom and law, although Locke was careful to distinguish positive law promulgated by an authoritative governmental body from more fundamental concepts, such as natural law and natural rights. (In egregious cases when the two types of laws conflicted, Locke provided an outlet for the right of revolution in his political theory.)[49]

Unlike Hobbes, Locke viewed the state of nature not as a condition of constant war or a desperate quest for self-preservation, but an "ill condition" that was difficult for man owing to the vagaries of natural conditions. Accordingly, man seeks to enter into a more pleasurable condition—a civil society—which will provide him with comforts and guarantees that he will be treated in an equitable manner. It is little wonder that some historians and philosophers call Locke the founder of Utilitarianism. A virtuous man, according to Locke, recognizes the practical utility of obeying laws and customs, although he does not view them as inviolable in extreme cases.[50]

David Hume

The eighteenth century Scottish philosopher David Hume has been called the "great skeptic" and "a thoroughgoing critic of human reason" because he rejected metaphysical explanations for experiential phenomena, much as Hobbes had rejected them in the preceding century.[51] According to Hume, skepticism is the only logical response for man owing

---

48. See, for example: John Locke, *Some Thoughts Concerning Education and Of the Conduct of Understanding*, eds. Ruth W. Grant and Nathan Tarcov, (Cambridge: Hackett Publishing Company, 1996).

49. John Locke, *Two Treatises of Government*, ed. Thomas I. Cook (New York: Hafner, 1947), p. 228-247.

50. While both Hobbes and Locke grounded their philosophical writings in analyses of a hypothetical "state of nature," Locke recognized that some principles of natural law take precedence over the laws of the state. Robert A. Goldwin, "John Locke," in *History of Political Philosophy*, 2nd. ed, ed. Leo Strauss and Joseph Cropsey (Chicago: The University of Chicago Press, 1972), pp. 459-460.

51. Robert S. Hill, "David Hume," in *History of Political Philosophy*, 2nd. ed., ed. Leo Strauss and Joseph Cropsey (Chicago: The University of Chicago Press, 1972), pp. 509-531. See also: Gottfried Dietze, *The Federalist: A Classic on Federalism and Free Government* (Westport, CT: Greenwood Press, 1960), p. 516.

to the "narrow capacity of human understanding" in considering questions that go beyond his limited sense perception.[52] Because man cannot objectively know metaphysical concepts with any reasonable degree of certainty, he cannot trust those concepts to guide human life. Except for mathematics and "experimental reasoning concerning matters of fact and existence," everything else is "sophistry and illusion" and must be "committed to the flames."[53]

Despite his skepticism, Hume recognized that it was necessary to distinguish among and between judgments of "good" and "bad," "right" and "wrong" to construct a well-ordered society. Accordingly, he searched for the practical meaning of ethical terms and the value of ethics for human life despite a lack of universal application. In rejecting the metaethical teachings of the ancient Greeks and the dual conceptions of mind and body as separate and qualitatively different from each other (as the French philosopher and mathematician Rene Descartes had asserted), Hume supplanted the notion of absolute virtue with a utilitarian understanding of ethical values. "The inner and outer aspects of human life are unified in morality," he observed.[54]

In Hume's view, an abstract bifurcation between the mind and body could not be tested using the tools of science, namely observation and replication. Rules governing man's behavior had to be grounded in something apart from faith in the innate powers of the mind to conceive of universal standards of conduct. Accordingly, Hume argued that ethical decisions could not be understood except insofar as they served man's purposes. A thing was judged to be beautiful because the person who called a thing beautiful found it agreeable. Similarly, a thing was "good" if it served man's purposes and "bad" if it did not.

In light of Hume's skeptical approach to epistemology, virtues could not be absolute because absolutes were beyond the parameters of human cognition. Instead, virtues were qualities that made a person or a thing useful in realizing pleasure. Standards changed as their utility changed. Qualities that were useful for the ancient Greeks probably would not be useful or agreeable for modern man. Man's code of conduct must be adapted to different circumstances.

For Hume, this base utilitarian calculation of usefulness was necessary, but insufficient, to ground ethics. Feeling, or taste, also was necessary because rational knowledge alone could not allow a person to assign moral blame or approbation. Therefore, utility and feeling, when combined, al-

---

52. David Hume, *An Enquiry Concerning Human Understanding* (Indianapolis: Hackett Publishing, 1977), pp. 111-112.
53. Ibid., p. 114.
54. Ibid., p. 4.

lowed man to make ethical judgments.[55] As was the case with Hobbes and Locke, Hume recognized that men are often driven to "do the right thing" owing to a fear of punishment; nonetheless, they also possess benevolent affections, which compel them to behave ethically. If men were not naturally benevolent—if they did not exhibit sympathy—they would not make ethical judgments because they would have no interest in making such judgments or in behaving ethically. Consequently, according to Hume, moral virtue is similar to the artificial quality of justice.[56] As one commentator has concluded, Hume's view of ethics can be summarized as a philosophy of "modified self-interest and a confined benevolence."[57]

His refusal to embrace metaphysics did not prevent Hume from identifying qualities that underlie man's natural benevolence and contribute to the development of his character. He identified four qualities of virtue. First, some qualities, such as justice, generosity, beneficence, and honesty, are useful to other people. Other qualities, including prudence, frugality, industry, and temperance, are useful to the person who possesses them. A third category of qualities—which includes modesty, wit and decency—is agreeable to other people. A final category is agreeable to one who possesses those qualities and includes proper self-esteem, love of glory, and magnanimity.[58]

Because of his attempts to ground ethics in usefulness, Hume's philosophy of ethics suffers from the same deficiencies that all utilitarian-based ethical systems face. The inherent difficulty of calculating utility and the relative value of concepts such as "useful" and "agreeable" ensure that Hume's work remains mired in controversy and confusion. One commentator summarized the problems of this philosophy as a failure to explore the full consequences of skepticism by discussing what makes a trait virtuous:

> With all respect to David Hume, the fact that a trait is generally useful and agreeable to the possessor and to others is not sufficient to make it a virtue. Amiability, cleanliness, and wit are beneficial in these ways, but these traits do not tend to make one a good person. In order for a trait to be a virtue, it must tend to foster good human life in extensive and fundamental ways. It must be the perfection of a tendency or capacity

---

55. Cooper, *World Philosophies: An Historical Introduction*, op. cit., p. 250.

56. Justice is artificial because it serves only to protect property rights in a civil society. As is the case with all philosophical abstractions, it does not exhibit characteristics in and of itself "which fit it for the nourishment of a human body." Hume, *An Enquiry Concerning Human Understanding*, op. cit., p. 21.

57. Knud Haakonssen, "Introduction," in David Hume, *Political Essays*, ed. Knud Haakonssen (Cambridge: Cambridge University Press, 1994), p. xxvi.

58. Hill, "David Hume," op. cit., p. 518.

that connects and interlocks with a variety of human goods in such a way that its removal from our lives would endanger the whole structure.[59]

The Kantian Revolution

With the failure of Hume's skepticism to address all questions concerning the relationship between character, virtue and ethics, later philosophers searched once again for an absolute set of ethical standards—in short, standards that were not possible in Hume's philosophy. A product of the eighteenth-century German Enlightenment, Immanuel Kant sought to reconcile Christian religious beliefs with the intellectual state of western culture in the wake of Hume's skepticism and the relativism of the age, which was occasioned in no small measure by the success of Newtonian science in capturing the European imagination. In arguing that human beings were obligated to develop their natural capacity for rational thought and translate it into rational, autonomous and moral action, Kant set the stage for nineteenth century ethics and philosophy.[60]

Kant wrote that he had been awakened from his "dogmatic slumbers" by Hume's skepticism and its repercussions. He was especially disturbed by the Scotsman's insistence on morals as a matter of opinion, accepted or rejected on the basis of practical utility. The logical implications of Hume's "hypothetical imperative," in Kant's view, were to reduce standards of conduct to an ever-changing, relative series of rules with limited applicability, merely a hypothetical discussion of the behavior expected to bring about happiness. Hume's ethical theory, therefore, seemed to be a moral sophistry that allowed individuals to rationalize their behavior according to the situation. Yet, in Kant's view, if man is to be free to act as a rational, moral agent, he must have immutable rules of conduct to guide him. In a world where a hypothetical imperative exists, anyone can avoid moral responsibility for his actions by asserting that he acted in accordance with the exigencies of time and place. Such a utilitarian notion of moral law reduced man to little more than an animal because it posited that men undertake actions, just as lower animals do, to fulfill

---

59. Wallace, *Virtues & Vices*, op. cit., p. 153.
60. Cooper, *World Philosophies: An Historical Introduction*, op. cit., p. 295. See also: Pierre Hassner, "Immanuel Kant," in *History of Political Philosophy*, 2nd. ed., ed. Leo Strauss and Joseph Cropsey (Chicago: The University of Chicago Press, 1972), pp. 554-593.

basic physical needs. Hume's skeptical philosophy foreclosed the possibility of critical self-analysis or a sense of absolute moral duty.[61]

In *Fundamental Principles of the Metaphysics of Morals*, Kant rejected Hume's utilitarian understanding of ethics and, in its stead, proposed a universal moral law that established a standard of conduct by free, rational, moral agents under all circumstances without respect to space and time.[62] He called this standard the "categorical imperative." "Act only on that maxim whereby thou canst at the same time will that it should become a universal law," he wrote.[63] Kant's imperative was a modified version of the Golden Rule where a person should do unto others as he would have them do unto him. If, in undertaking a certain action, a person presupposed that everyone else would perform exactly the same act, this insight forces the actor to consider the consequences of his action. Accordingly, if a person chooses to commit a random act of violence, he should ask himself a question—"would I want to live in a society where everyone commits random acts of violence?" If the answer is "no, because I might be harmed by someone else's random act of violence" (which would be the response of anyone who agreed with Hobbes that rational beings will seek to avoid violent death whenever possible), the person could not undertake the act without violating the categorical imperative.[64]

The categorical imperative applies not only to persons, but to nations as well. Kant's ethical theory thus serves as the foundation for a theory

---

61. Cooper, *World Philosophies: An Historical Introduction*, op. cit. p. 303. Kant observed: "Each thing in nature works according to laws. Only a rational being has the faculty to act *according to the conception* of laws, that is, according to principles, in other words, has a will." Immanuel Kant, "The Categorical Imperative," in *Combating Corruption/Encouraging Ethics: A Sourcebook for Public Service Ethics*, ed. William L. Richter, Francis Burke, and Jameson W. Doig, (Washington, D.C.: The American Society for Public Administration, 1990), p. 27.

62. Immanuel Kant, *Fundamental Principles of the Metaphysics of Morals*, trans. T. Abbott (New York: Prometheus, 1987).

63. Ibid., p. 49.

64. From a twentieth century perspective, Kant's categorical imperative seems intuitive. Parents all over the world instruct their children on the proper method of fulfilling the categorical imperative on a daily basis. "Johnny, don't hit your sister," they command. It is an absolute command, never modified with the addendum "unless your calculations indicate that such an act brings you pleasure and is generally agreeable to others." For Kant, such an addendum leads to a slippery slope, for once moral laws are subject to bargaining, negotiation and rationalization, they lose their moral force. A concomitant formulation of this absolute value is expressed by Kant when he insists that a rational being should be treated "never as a means only," but always "as an end in itself." Ibid., p. 303.

of international affairs. The state of nature, in his view, is pure heteronomy, or desire. Accordingly, we become more rational, hence more human, when we move away from the state of nature into a political association. Nations, which contain a large number of persons, are moral agents, just as individuals are moral agents. As a result, civil laws in national and international arenas are subject to the same categorical imperative governing persons.[65]

Kant was attacked by critics who found his ethical theory in general, and his expression of the categorical imperative in particular, idealistic and naive. Just as Plato's republic was assaulted because it was based on idealistic concepts that did not, and could not, exist apart from a "city in speech," critics contended that Kant's articulation of an *a priori* categorical imperative begs the question of whether ethical precepts are immutable. Admonitions such as "always keep your promises" may advance the cause of a well-ordered society that desires to produce citizens who can cooperate with each other, but it does not explain how human beings can be persuaded to step beyond calculations of self-interestedness and "do the right thing," whatever that might be. Nietzsche was especially vociferous in his criticism of Kant's assertion that synthetic *a priori* concepts are possible. According to Nietzsche, "old Kant's" assertion of absolute truths not only missed the mark in the quest for philosophical answers, it wasn't even the correct philosophical question.[66]

Utilitarianism

As an alternative to Kant's assertion that absolute, *a priori* standards exist, Utilitarianism has profoundly influenced the development of west-

---

65. Woodrow Wilson's proposal for creating a league of nations in the aftermath of World War I was a Kantian view of international relations. In Wilson's view, nations, like men, should act according to the categorical imperative. Hassner, "Immanuel Kant," op. cit., pp. 580-581.

66. Nietzsche wrote: "...[I]t is high time to replace the Kantian question, 'How are synthetic judgments *a priori* possible?' by another question, 'Why is belief in such judgments *necessary*?'—and to comprehend that such judgments must be *believed* to be true, for the sake of the preservation of creatures like ourselves; though they might, of course, be *false* judgments for all that! Or to speak more clearly and coarsely: synthetic judgments *a priori* should not 'be possible' at all; we have no right to them; in our mouths they are nothing but false judgments. Only, of course, the belief in their truth is necessary, as a foreground belief and visual evidence belonging to the perspective optics of life." Nietzsche, *Beyond Good and Evil*, op. cit., p. 19.

ern ethical and political philosophy owing to its emphasis on pragmatic, "real-world" considerations. Although Hume had relied on utilitarian calculations a century earlier, the modern doctrine was developed by the nineteenth century English Utilitarians, Jeremy Bentham, James Mill, and John Stuart Mill. The English Utilitarians contended that men make rational decisions about their lives according to the principle of utility, which dictates that people will always seek the greatest happiness, that is, the greatest pleasure, from a choice among competing courses of action. Bentham originally developed this philosophy from Hume's theory of moral sentiments, which posited that human beings have an instinctive understanding of utility, that is, of liking or not liking an act.[67]

Bentham's godson, John Stuart Mill, writing in the mid-nineteenth century, took up the mantle from Bentham in defending what some critics saw as an "unethical ethics." In moving away from "intuition" or "innate moral sense" as the grounds for ethics, Mill embraced a more pragmatic, positivist understanding of ethical conduct. He refused to engage in "armchair reasoning," that is, the Kantian enterprise of seeking objective proof for the principle of utility. Instead, he pointed to the propensity of human beings to seek pleasure in their day-to-day lives as a "real world" illustration that such a principle exists.[68]

Mill also relied on the principle of utility as a philosophical justification for maximizing individual freedom in a democratic regime.[69] It is a fact of human psychology that people make choices based on their desire to maximize happiness, he asserted. The wisdom of those choices is dictated by the character of the people who make the decisions. In some cases, according to Mill, people forgo their own short-term happiness to advance a larger goal, such as their future happiness (for example, when

---

67. The natural human tendency to engage in tasks that increase pleasure and avoid tasks that decrease pleasure "placed mankind under the governance of two sovereign masters, *pain* and *pleasure*," Bentham observed. (Emphasis in the original.) Jeremy Bentham, *An Introduction to the Principles of Morals and Legislation* (New York: Hafner, 1948), p. 462.
68. Cooper, *World Philosophies: An Historical Introduction*, op. cit., pp. 348-349.
69. In his influential work, *On Liberty*, Mill wrote: "The object of this Essay is to assert one very simple principle, as entitled to govern absolutely the dealings of society with the individual in the way of compulsion and control, whether the means used be physical force in the form of legal penalties, or the moral coercion of public opinion. That principle is, that the sole end for which mankind are warranted, individually or collectively, in interfering with the liberty of action or any of their number, is self-protection. That the only purpose for which power can be rightfully exercised over any member of a civilized community, against his will, is to prevent harm to others." John Stuart Mill, *On Liberty* (Arlington Heights, IL: AHM Publishing, 1947), p. 9.

a person chooses to save money for retirement in lieu of spending it on consumer goods today). As a result, a person of good character sometimes chooses a course of action that may not be immediately recognizable as pleasurable. He chooses "higher" pleasures based on his past experiences with different forms of pleasure and pain.[70]

An opponent of Utilitarianism might argue that ethics based on maximizing a person's selfish desires is base and presents fundamental problems for a society filled with such appetite-driven human beings. On the contrary, Mill suggested that a proper Utilitarian considers not only his own happiness, but the happiness of other persons—the greatest amount of happiness in society. Thus, Utilitarianism requires persons to calculate happiness based not simply on their own selfish interests and desires, but on an impartial judgment divorced from self-interest. In some cases, therefore, a utilitarian calculation may require someone to sacrifice his own happiness in consideration of the higher good, namely the happiness of the majority. This becomes Mill's philosophical basis for democratic government and majority rule. Public policy is made by calculating the greatest good for the greatest number of people and acting in accordance with that good.[71]

Despite its prominence in the western liberal tradition, Utilitarianism has been subject to intense criticism that has never been adequately rebutted by its adherents. In the first place, Mill's insistence on an ethical empiricism raises problems that go to the core of democratic government, namely, the tension between the individual and the collectivity. Simply because a person seeks pleasure, this base desire alone does not justify every action. If a majority of individuals desires something, the group may adopt policies allowing the majority to tyrannize a minority. In other words, Utilitarianism assumes that ethical choices are a matter of calculating costs and benefits and choosing actions where benefits outweigh costs. Yet this calculation assumes that ethical choices can be identified and quantified. Moreover, it assumes that choices can and will be made on a rational, orderly basis. But questions remain about whether people will always rely on reason in decision-making and whether they will set aside their own self-interest in favor of the collective good.[72]

---

70. Mortimer J. Adler and Seymour Cain, *Ethics: The Study of Moral Values* (Chicago: Encyclopedia Britannica, Inc., 1962), p. 261.

71. Ibid., pp. 262-263.

72. In his landmark work, *A Theory of Justice*, John Rawls observed that Utilitarianism does not distinguish between persons or between the worth of their preferences. He wrote: "This means, as Mill remarks, that one person's happiness assumed to be equal in degree to another person's happiness is to be counted exactly the same. The weights in the additive function that represents the utility principle are identical for all individuals, and it is natural to take them as one. The principle of utility, one might say, treats per-

Individuals make decisions based on a variety of factors that may have no rational basis. History abounds with examples of political, economic, religious, and ethical decisions based on prejudice, misinformation, fear, madness or spite. Understanding the many factors that influenced an individual's or a group of individuals' actions is extremely problematic. One need only peruse a basic psychology text to discern the difficulties inherent in attempting to understand cause and effect relationships in decision-making. In an ethical and political system based solely on quantitative calculations, it is possible that persons would surrender their liberty on the altar of the greatest good, that is, they would maximize their short-term pleasure with little regard for their long-term interests. Accordingly, the Utilitarians' faith in the nobility of men who possess good character may not fully consider the depravity of human nature, nor the permutations and combinations possible when groups of individuals forge public policy.

Postmodernism

If Utilitarianism, one of the foundations of western ethical and political thought, contains fundamental problems in structuring its ethical system, the question of reasonable alternatives naturally arises. Of all the western philosophies that have attempted to address this question, perhaps the most disturbing for the future of ethics is the response of the postmodernists. Their solution to the problems inherent in articulating a workable ethical theory has been to reject the legitimacy of the philosophical inquiry at the outset.

The term "postmodernism" has become a trite, over-used buzzword that describes an eclectic group of philosophers writing at the end of the twentieth century. The thinkers most often identified by the label "post-

---

sons both as ends and means. It treats them as ends by assigning the same (positive) weight to the welfare of each; it treats them as means by allowing higher life prospects for some to counterbalance lower life prospects for others who are already less favorably situated." John Rawls, *A Theory of Justice* (Cambridge, MA: Belknap Press, 1971), pp. 182-183. Therefore, a scenario might develop where a majority of people would prefer to purchase, for example, pornographic books from the library's limited budget and a minority of people would choose to purchase folios of Shakespeare's works for the library. If Utilitarianism is taken at face value, the preference of the majority would dictate the appropriate course of action. In other words, the principle of utility does not acknowledge that the worth of a course of action may depend on factors in addition to the preference of the majority.

modern" include Michel Foucault,[73] Jacques Derrida,[74] Jean-Francois Lyotard,[75] and Richard Rorty,[76] although occasionally writers such as Willard Quine,[77] Jurgen Habermas,[78] Roland Barthes,[79] and Ludwig Wittgenstein (especially his latter work)[80] are included as well. The writings of these theorists are so diverse that labels seem woefully inadequate and, in some cases, misleading. Richard Rorty, for example, is more properly called a "neopragmatist," while Habermas is probably the last great modern philosopher in the Kantian tradition, not strictly a postmodernist. Wittgenstein's work also seems remarkably resistant to labeling because of differences between his early linguistic analyses and his later efforts to revise his thinking about the nature of language.

What seems to unite most of the members of this diverse, idiosyncratic group of thinkers is their insistence that, in advanced capitalist societies, the modern paradigm of knowledge (to borrow a phrase from Thomas Kuhn) has broken down.[81] For postmodernists, the "totalizing metadiscourses" of earlier philosophers are no longer a valid and reliable method of discussing human life. In the search for a grand narrative to explain how human beings should live and think, nineteenth and twentieth century thinkers have disconnected philosophy from human life.

---

73. See, for example: Michael Foucault, *The Archaeology of Knowledge*, trans. A. Sheridan (New York: Harper, 1972); and Michel Foucault, *The Order of Things: An Archaeology of the Human Sciences* (London: Tavistock, 1980).

74. As the putative father of deconstructionism, Derrida has produced a number of important works, including *Of Grammatology*, trans. G. Spivak, (Baltimore: Johns Hopkins University Press, 1976); *Writing and Difference*, trans. A. Bass (London: Routledge & Kegan Paul, 1978); and *Margins of Philosophy*, trans. A. Bass (Chicago: University of Chicago Press, 1982).

75. Lyotard is often credited (or blamed, depending on one's point of view) with coining the term "postmodernism" in his book *The Postmodern Condition: A Report on Knowledge* (Manchester: Manchester University Press, 1986).

76. The American "neopragmatist" Richard Rorty is noted for several works, including *Consequences of Pragmatism: Essays 1972-1980* (Brighton: Harvester, 1982) and *Contingency, Irony, and Solidarity* (Cambridge: Cambridge University Press, 1989).

77. See, for example: Willard V. O. Quine, *Ontological Relativity and Other Essays* (New York: Columbia University Press, 1969).

78. See, for example: Jurgen Habermas, *The Philosophical Discourse of Modernity* (Cambridge: Polity, 1987).

79. See, for example, Roland Barthes, *Mythologies* (New York: Hill and Wang, 1957).

80. See especially: Ludwig Wittgenstein, *Philosophical Investigations*, 3rd. ed., trans. G.E.M. Anscombe, (New York: Macmillan, 1953).

81. Thomas S. Kuhn, *The Structure of Scientific Revolutions*, 2nd. ed. (Chicago: University of Chicago Press, 1970).

Thus, according to postmodernists, the structuralism of previous philosophies has become restrictive, allowing stodgy traditionalists to impose their will on others. This triumph of rule-bound thinking has stifled human creativity.

The postmodern view of man accepts Nietzsche's insight that perspective is the only liberating and important condition. Attempts to know the "self" through grandiose system-building, a la Hegel, or through absurd, logically sterile games, such as Descartes's analysis of the cogito, bear no relation to human life. Postmodernists, therefore, seek to overcome oppressive, dogmatic rules found in traditional metaphysics in favor of what Barthes called "the death of the author," that is, an end to the quest for truth that western philosophy has pursued since the time of the ancient Greeks.[82]

In light of the postmodern condition, "character" is not an objective fact—a collection of traits to be developed in accordance with the mores of society. The search for objective qualities of character is but an illusion, a fool's errand—evidence that someone has been duped by the unyielding dogmatists of ages past. The only absolute in the relative world of postmodernism, ironically, is the realization that there are no absolutes. Because postmodernists relish word-play and irony, however, even this seeming contradiction is not cause for undue concern.

The difficult feature of postmodernism, of course, is that it destroys the structures of philosophy, yet it offers no workable alternatives. If "perspective" is the only absolute value, how do human beings engage in philosophical discourse? Are they not rendered silent by their inability to communicate? Postmodernists would answer "yes." Philosophy has ended and man is liberated from self-delusion. As one commentator has recognized, in the wake of postmodernism, "[w]hat political theory most certainly cannot do, it seems, is to fulfill the promise of the Enlightenment. It is unable, among other things, to divine the rational principles necessary to reinvigorate or reestablish a political and ethical culture where certain limited shared values provide a basis for universally respected rights and a rational and humane politics."[83]

Good character for postmodernists, to the extent that such a thing exists after the self has been exiled from rational discourse, is exhibited by someone who does not subscribe to the metanarratives of long-dead dogmatists. In other words, creativity and perspective are the foundational principles of these antifoundationalist critics of the Enlightenment. In a

---

82. Cooper, *World Philosophies: An Historical Introduction*, op. cit., pp. 465-468.

83. Lawrence J. Biskowski, "Political Theory in the 1990s: Antifoundationalist Critics and Democratic Prospects," *Southeastern Political Review* 20 (Spring 1992): 62.

sense, then, with the rise of postmodernism, the western intellectual tradition has come full circle since the days when Plato attacked the Sophists for their relativistic views. Postmodernism is the ultimate reinvigoration of Sophistry. According to postmodernism, it was those ancient champions of ever-changing virtue, and not Plato, who were the true heroes of the western tradition. In short, Plato was the oppressor and the Sophists were his victims.

No matter how one approaches the issues raised by postmodernism, the analysis falls into a ruthless tautology. By using philosophical discourse to call for an end to philosophical discourse, the postmodern thinker attacks the entire idea of a status quo only to find that, after he has succeeded in his assault, he has become the new status quo—the very thing he hated. Postmodernists would dispute this last insight, of course, but an observer schooled in rational inquiry cannot help but reject an anti-philosophy philosophy that revels in its own contradictions and seems to embrace nihilism. The postmodernists, in effect, recall Tertullian's comment that a concept is believable precisely because it is beyond the realm of reason. Postmodernism may provide philosophical food for thought, but as a contribution to western theory, it fails to provide a workable alternative basis for grounding ethics. Postmodern thinkers proved adept at destroying metastructures, but their ability to offer alternatives has been far less effective.

Conclusion

Virtue and character have been important concepts in the development of ethical theory. From the time of the ancient Greeks until the postmodern era, theorists have attempted to identify appropriate character traits as well as methods for inculcating appropriate virtues in the young. The ongoing conversation between idealists and realists—which eventually led the postmodernists to reject the idea of engaging in philosophical conversation in the first place—has propelled the western tradition away from the absolute virtues and rational discourse of Athens toward the faith of Jerusalem during the Medieval period, into the rationality of the Enlightenment, the skepticism of the post-Enlightenment and the eclecticism of the postmodern period. The next steps in ethical theory seem unclear in light of the twentieth century's call for an end to philosophy and the abolition of the self.

Despite recent developments in ethical theory, an appreciation of shared character traits based on a sense of virtue has been a time-honored practice in the western tradition. Most societies have been based on a sense of civic duty, individual responsibility and personal honor as virtues that ensure the well-being of the ethical man in a well-ordered political regime. It remains to be seen whether the tradition of a new millennium will yield to postmodernism's claims that the philosophical enterprise is irrelevant or if, as in ages past, ethics and politics will continue to evolve.

Chapter Three

Plain Persons and Moral Philosophy: Rules, Virtues, and Goods[1]

Alasdair MacIntyre

What is the relationship between the moral philosopher's judgments about the life of practice and the everyday plain person's moral questions and judgments? Moral philosophers are of course themselves in most of their lives everyday plain persons, but on some views what they do and judge *qua* moral philosopher is very different from what they do and judge *qua* plain person. Some analytic philosophers, for example, have envisaged the relationship between moral philosophy and everyday moral judgments and activity as analogous to that between the philosophy of science and the judgments and activity of the natural scientist or that between the philosophy of law and legal practice. In each such case the philosophy is to be understood as detached second-order commentary upon first-order judgments and activity. But for moral philosophers at work in the Aristotelian Thomistic tradition this is not at all how that relationship is to be conceived.

For, on an Aristotelian view, the questions posed by the moral philosopher and the questions posed by the plain person are to an important degree inseparable. And it is with questions that each begins, for each is engaged in enquiry, the plain person often unsystematically asking: "What is my good?" and "What actions will achieve it?" and the moral philosopher systematically enquiring "What is *the* good for human beings?" and "What kinds of actions will achieve the good?" Any persistent attempt to answer either of these sets of questions soon leads to asking the other. The moral philosopher has to recognize that

---

1. This chapter was originally published as "Plain Persons and Moral Philosophy: Rules, Virtues, and Goods," *American Catholic Philosophical Quarterly* vol. 66, no. 1 (1992): 3-19. It was delivered as the 1991 Aquinas Lecture at the University of Dallas. The author wishes to express his gratitude to four constructive critics of earlier drafts: Stanley Hauerwas, David K. O'Connor, Janet Smith and David Solomon. Reprinted by permission.

any true account of the human good is incomplete and inadequate, unless and until it enables us to understand how particular plain persons, including her or himself, are able to move towards their particular goods. And if I, as a plain person, ask persistently what good it is that is at stake for me here and now in particular situations, I will soon have to ask the further, already philosophical question "What in general is the good for my kind of person with my kind of history in this kind of situation?" and that in turn will lead to a fundamental philosophical question "What is the good as such for human beings as such?"

A plain person who begins to understand her or his life as an uneven progress towards the achievement of her or his good is thus to some significant extent transformed into a moral philosopher, asking and answering the same questions posed by Aristotle in the *Nichomachean Ethics* and by Aquinas in his commentary on the *Ethics* and elsewhere. Often enough, such a plain person will not recognize how far she or he has been transformed in this direction, but insofar as a plain person fails to recognize her or himself as a moral philosopher, to that extent that plain person is the more likely to be less competent as a moral philosopher than she or he needs to be and is able to be. So the question to which this lecture is addressed is: just how much of a moral philosopher does the plain person need to become?

At once it may be objected that I already seem to be assuming by my references to Aristotle and Aquinas that, insofar as the plain person becomes a moral philosopher, she or he will at least tend towards becoming an Aristotelian. And this may seem to be question-begging. For I am, it may be said, highhandedly usurping the role of the plain person and putting my philosophical words, or rather Aristotle's and Aquinas's philosophical words, into her or his prephilosophical mouth. But surely the plain person must be allowed to speak for her or himself and to become whatever kind of philosopher she or he chooses to be. Yet this at first sight plausible objection is in fact misleading.

Consider the image of the plain person which this objection presents: that of someone who initially is a stranger to all moral philosophies and therefore wholly unequipped with the resources provided by any particular philosophical standpoint. Such a plain person therefore begins from a position of philosophical neutrality, taking her or his first steps in the direction of this or that philosophical standpoint without the guidance of any reasons which presuppose same philosophical commitment. But this is to leave the plain person bereft of philosophically relevant reasoning. The counterpart of the neutrality of the plain person thus conceived is therefore a rationally unguided arbitrariness in that person's initial choice of which philosophical direction to take. And at this point we experience a shock of recognition. For we have met this particular plain person before, not in the street or on the farm, but in the pages of a number of philosophers since Kierkegaard, especially those of the Sartre of the late nineteen forties. This is a human being constructed by existentialist philosophical theory, disguised as a plain person; this image of the plain person is itself a philosophical artefact.

When I say this, I do not mean to deny that there are and have been real human beings in the condition represented by this image, human beings, that is, lacking the resources to make fundamental choices in any but a criterionless way. But the question is whether this type of human being is not her or himself a social artefact, someone who has undergone a process of social and moral deprivation, not a plain person as such, but someone who somehow or other has been stripped of the ability to understand her or himself aright. So this attempt to replace my apparently question-begging image of the plain person as someone who is from the very beginning on the verge of becoming a Thomistic Aristotelian by a philosophically untainted image of the plain person has failed. And it could not but have failed. For every conception of the plain person is at home in some particular philosophical standpoint and there is no way of thinking realistically about the plain person except as someone who is from the outset potentially a moral philosopher of one distinctive kind rather than another.

The history of philosophy confirms this. Immanuel Kant's plain person, who possesses what Kant calls an "ordinary rational knowledge of morality," is already a proto-Kantian. Thomas Reid's plain person does not possess mere common sense, but common sense as articulated philosophically by Reid. And when Henry Sidgwick appeals to "common moral opinion," its deliverances turn out to furnish a very Sidgwickian point of entry into Sidgwickian theory. So we have good reason to believe that attempts to portray the plain person as initially completely innocent of philosophy in her or his attitudes, presuppositions, beliefs and questionings are bound to fail. Let us then recognize instead that the plain person must always be conceived as already somehow or other engaged with philosophy in some determinate way, and that we need to ask what particular philosophical standpoint it is which is already implicit in her or his initial attitudes, presuppositions, beliefs and questionings. Is she or he perhaps a proto-Kantian or a potential follower of Reid? Or do plain persons vary a good deal in their initial philosophical allegiance? I want to answer these questions by defending the following theses: that plain persons are in fact generally and to a significant degree proto-Aristotelians, and that, insofar as they are not, it is from the standpoint of a Thomistic Aristotelianism that we can most adequately explain why they are not, and why they have become whatever it is instead that they are.

Characteristically and generally, individuals come to ask the question, 'What is my good?' in social contexts in which different aspects of human activity combine to make it difficult not at some point to raise that question explicitly, and impossible, whether one raises it explicitly or not, not to presuppose some answer to it by the way in which one comes to live out one's life. The first of these aspects is the goal-directedness which from a relatively early age one discovers in different types of norm-informed activity in which one has become involved. Some goals are biologically given, some are social. But in activities as elementary as those which sustain and preserve one's own life, as universal among human beings as those which arise from kin, familial and household relationships, and as open-ended as those which provide one's first education into productive, practical and theoretical arts, one inescapably discovers oneself as a being in norm-governed direction towards goals which are thereby recognized as goods. These norm-governed directednesses are what Aquinas calls *inclinationes*[2] in a passage in which he says that it is in virtue of our relationship to these *inclinationes,* partially defining as they do our nature as human agents, that the precepts of the natural law are so-called.

The connection between *inclinationes* and such precepts I take to be as follows. When I discover that my life is, as a matter of biological and social fact, partially ordered by regularities which give expression to these primary tendencies towards particular ends, I have it in my power to make these ends mine in a new and secondary way by self-consciously directing my activities to these ends and, insofar as I have rightly understood my own nature, it will be rational for me to do so. The rules to which I will have to conform, if I am so to direct my activities, are those expressed by the precepts of the natural law. What was mere regularity becomes rule-governedness.

If this is how Aquinas understood matters, then it is not difficult to respond to a charge levelled by T. H. Irwin that Aquinas entangles himself in contradiction in his account of the relationship between the virtues, inclination towards right ends, and deliberation.[3] Irwin correctly ascribes to Aquinas the theses that what is in our power depends on our deliberative capacities and that ends are fixed non-deliberatively, and Irwin concludes that Aquinas is therefore committed to holding that what our ends are to be is not in our power. But Aquinas also asserts that an inclination towards right ends distinguishes virtue and vice and that to be virtuous rather than vicious is in our power, so that Aquinas is also com-

---

2. *Summa Theologiae* Ia-IIae 94, 2
3. "A Conflict in Aquinas" *Review of Metaphysics* 14 (1990): 21-42

mitted to holding that what our ends are to be must be in our power. Hence, Irwin further concludes that Aquinas is guilty of inconsistency.

What Irwin has failed to distinguish are two distinct ways in which, on Aquinas's view, someone may have an end. We human beings are indeed by our specific nature directed towards certain hierarchically ordered ends, and it is not in our power to have a nature other than that which we have, and so not in our power to have ends other than these. But it is in our power whether or not in our rational decision-making to direct our activities towards the achievements of those ends. It is open to us to move in quite other directions. So, according to Aquinas, in one way our ends are in our power and in another way they are not, and there is no inconsistency in the conclusions to which he is committed. Irwin, however, has done us a service by compelling us to raise the questions: how does the plain person make of the ends which are her or his by nature ends actually and rationally directive of her or his activities? And in what social contexts do plain persons learn how to order ends rightly and to recognize their mistakes when they have failed to do so?

Such learning is generally achieved only through involvement in a type of activity which raises for individuals the question, "What is my good?" in a manner that is complementary to that in which that question is posed by *inclinationes*; a type of activity characteristic of practices, those cooperative forms of activity whose participants jointly pursue the goods internal to those forms of activity and jointly value excellence in achieving those goods. Such practices are of very different kinds. The activities of members of string-quartets, of the crews of fishing fleets, of architects and construction workers jointly engaged in developing good housing, of members of families making and sustaining the familial community, of farmers and of physicists — to name only a few — are all practice-based and practice-structured. It is through initiation into the ordered relationships of some particular practice or practices, through education into the skills and virtues which it or they require, and through an understanding of the relationship of those skills and virtues to the achievement of the goods internal to that practice or those practices that we first find application in everyday life for just such a teleological scheme of understanding as that which Aristotle presents at a very different level of philosophical sophistication in the *Nicomachean Ethics*. It is by our finding application for this scheme in our practical activities, a scheme which provides the directedness of our *inclinationes* with a further rationale, that we first become evidently, even if unwittingly, Aristotelians. It is in doing so that we also acquire a capacity for becoming reflective about norms and goals.

This capacity is expressed in our learning how to apply two closely related distinctions. The first is that between what I would do, if I did what would please me most here and now, and what I would do if, in the light of the best instruction available to me, I were to do what would make me excellent in the pursuit of the goods internal to the particular practice or practices in which I am engaged. Failure in making this first distinction is characteristically a sign of failure in ordering the appetites and passions. A second distinction is that between what it would be to achieve what is good and best unqualifiedly and what is good and best here and now for me, at my stage in the education of my capacities, to do. Failure in making this second distinction is characteristically a sign of failure in evaluating how far I have progressed in ordering my appetites and passions. How to make these distinctions is something that each person has to learn, and what has to be learned always can be mislearned. So that through a process of learning, making mistakes, correcting those mistakes and so moving towards the achievement of excellence, the individual comes to understand her or himself as *in via*, in the middle of a journey. And as she or he also comes to understand how each practice in which she or he is engaged itself has a history in the course of which goals, skills and virtues have been variously identified, misunderstood and reconceived, so she or he comes to understand her or his own history of progress within that particular practice as embedded in the history of the practice. But no individual lives her or his life wholly within the confines of any one practice. She or he always pursues the goods of more than one practice, as well as goods external to all practices, and so cannot escape posing and answering the question, even if only by the way in which she or he lives, of how these goods are to be ordered, of which part each is to play within the structures of a whole life. The recurrent and rival claims of pleasure, of the pursuit of wealth, of power, of honor and prestige to be the ordering principle of human lives will each have to be responded to in turn; and in so responding, an individual will be defining her or his attitudes to those considerations which Aristotle rehearses in Book I of the *Nicomachean Ethics* and which Aquinas reconsiders in the opening questions of the Ia-IIae of the *Summa Theologiae*, in the course of their extended dialectical arguments on the nature of the supreme good.

Characteristically, the plain person responds to these claims not so much through explicit arguments, although these may always play a part, as by shaping his or her life in one way rather then another. When from time to time, the plain person retrospectively examines what her or his life amounts to as a whole, often enough with a view to choice between alternative futures, characteristically what she or he is in effect asking is, "To what conception of my overall good have I so far committed myself? And, do I now have reason to put it in question?" The unity of her or her life about which each human being thus enquires is the unity of a dramatic narrative, of a story whose outcome can be success or failure for each protagonist. Were it otherwise, the notion of an overall good for that life, one which provides that life with its standards of success and failure, would lack application. When someone writes the narrative either of her or his own or of someone else's life, its adequacy can be judged by the extent to which it provides answers to such questions as: What did the person whose life has been thus narrated take to be her or his good? Did she or he misconceive that good? What obstacles and frustrations confronted that person and did she or he possess the qualities of mind and character necessary to overcome them? The conception of a *telos* of human life is generally first comprehended in terms of the outcomes of particular narratives about particular lives.

So when we as readers or spectators put such questions to a narrative, we look for the universal in the particular. Both plot and character have significance for us in so far as we can understand them in terms of universal conceptions of the good and of the virtues and vices which transcend, but inform, the particularities of this narrative. When however in the examination of our own past lives we proceed from the narrative structure of those lives, as they have been lived so far, to enquiry about what from now on we are now to make of ourselves, we are compelled instead to ask of the universal how it may be particularized, how certain conceptions of *the* good and of the virtues may take on embodied form through our realization of this possibility rather than that, posing these questions in terms of the specifics of the narratives of our lives. In so doing, we characteristically draw upon resources provided by some stock of stories from which we had earlier learned to understand both our own lives and the lives of others in narrative terms, the oral and written literature of whatever particular culture it is that we happen to inhabit.

An ability to put ourselves to the question philosophically thus in key part depends upon the prior possession of some measure of narrative understanding, but this ability transcends the limitations of such understanding. For in stories, as contrasted with theories, we encounter the universal *only* in and through the particular. What we need are stories which provoke us to move beyond stories—although everything then turns upon what direction it is that our movement takes. Narratives which point beyond themselves towards the theories that we in fact need are to be found in many places: in some folk-tales, in Sophoclean and Shakespearean drama, and above all in Dante's *Commedia,* which directs us beyond itself towards the kind of theoretical understanding provided by Aquinas's commentaries on the *Ethics* and *Politics.*

One of the things that we most need to learn, first from narrative and then from theory, is that it is one of the marks of someone who develops bad character that, as it develops, she or he becomes progressively less and less able to understand what it is that she or he has mislearned and how it was that she or he fell into error. Part of the badness of bad character is intellectual blindness on moral questions. It is important therefore at an early stage to possess resources for right judgment and action, which include resources for explaining how we may come to fail and have come to fail and what we have to do to avoid failure. We need, that is, an extended, practically usable answer to the question "What is my good" and "How is it to be achieved?", which will both direct us in present and future action and also evaluate and explain past action.

Such an answer will have to supply not only an account of goods and virtues, but also of rules, and of how goods, virtues and rules relate to one another. It will be an account which will answer not only the plain person's practical questions about how to achieve her or his good, but also the central question of this lecture, that of how much of a moral philosopher the plain person needs to become. For the plain person, so it has turned out, must become at least enough of a moral philosopher to understand her or himself, in all her or his particularities, as exemplifying the universal concepts of a theory which is not only both explanatorily and prescriptively powerful, but which also is able to justify a claim to be superior to such rival theories as may present themselves in one guise or another as claimants for the plain person's allegiance. What kind of theory then does the plain person need?

Let us begin with the place, in such a theory, of fundamental rules, of those precepts of the natural law whose evidentness to the plain person who aspires to direct her or himself towards her or his good in the company of other rational persons it is hard to disguise, even although it has often enough been denied. For to violate these rules in one's relationships with other persons is bound to deprive one of their cooperation in the achievement of a good about which one still has much to learn from them. In the search for our good, everyone is a potential teacher and has therefore to be treated as one from whom I still may have to learn. So the rules governing my fundamental relationships with others are not affirmed as conclusions from some yet more fundamental set of premises. Allegiance to those rules cannot depend upon the outcome of theorizing. For suppose someone were to deny this and to embark upon the project of cooperating with others in conducting a theory designed to provide them with a rational justification. In order to do so successfully, she or he would first have to enter into cooperative relationships already informed by allegiance to just those rules for which she or he aspired to provide a justification. Hence, allegiance to these particular rules has to precede any set of arguments, any theorizing.

The same rules have another part to play in the plain person's initial education into the moral life. For a first primitive conception of each of the virtues that we need to acquire, if we are to achieve our good, can be articulated only through a set of rules which turn out to be another application of the primary precepts of the natural law. We can only learn what it is to be courageous or temperate or truthful by first leaning that certain types of action are always and exceptionlessly such as we must refrain from if we are to exemplify those virtues. The disposition which we need to acquire by habituation in the case of each virtue is of course a disposition not merely to act in certain rule-governed ways, but also to do more than the rules require. What more is required varies with time, place and circumstance. And knowing how to go beyond the rules in order to judge appropriately in particular circumstances is itself impossible without the virtue of *phronesis*. So the order of learning is such that we first have to learn in certain initial situations what is *always* enjoined or always prohibited, in order that later we may become able to extrapolate in a non- rule-governed way to other types of situations in which what courage or justice or truthfulness, together with prudence, demand is more than conformity to the universal rule. Learning what the virtues require of us in a wide range of different situations is inseparable from learning which, out of the multiplicity of goods, more is at stake in any given situation. So we go on to learn more than we initially could learn from the rules, but part of what we then learn is that we can never dispense with the rules. And that this is as is integral to our understanding of goods and of virtues as well as of the rules themselves. Consider how those rules relate to our supreme good.

It has to be of the nature of whatever is genuinely the supreme good that it makes no sense to think of weighing it against other goods. The supreme good is not a good that just happens on some particular occasions, or even on every particular occasion, to outweigh other goods. It must be that it *cannot* be outweighed. Otherwise its status as supreme good would be contingent and therefore very possibly temporary. It would be vulnerable to displacement. Moreover, the rules, observance of which is required if *our* final good is to be achieved—that is, if we are to achieve whatever relationship to the supreme good it is in which our own final good consists—must define what is necessarily true of that relationship. Those rules, then, cannot be such as to bind us only so long as certain contingent circumstances obtain, that is, conditionally. So that if someone entertained the thought, as many of course have done, that we perhaps ought on some particular occasion, for the sake of achieving what is taken to be some other good only thus obtainable, temporarily to suspend the requirement of obedience to one or more of those rules, if, that is, we treated them as open to exceptions, we would have misconceived both the nature and function of those rules and the nature of the good and of our good. And in so misconceiving them we would have exhibited a defect both in our possession of and in our understanding of one or more of the intellectual and moral virtues. Virtues, rules and goods, so it turns out, have to be understood in their interrelationship or not at all.

Consider as an analogy the relationship of the rules governing activities of enquiry in mathematics or the natural sciences to the goal of those activities, that of attaining truth: for example, the rule that one should be scrupulous in laying out one's theses and putative proofs so that they are maximally vulnerable to objection and refutation. Suppose that someone were to propose that in the interests of obtaining some nonmathematical and nonscientific good, this rule should, from time to time, be suspended. Such a proposal, ignoring as it does the internal relation between truth and ability to withstand refutation, would make no sense, insofar as it was proposed as a rule for mathematicians qua mathematicians or scientists qua scientists. And a proposal temporarily to suspend the application of the precepts of the natural law, ignoring, as it would, the internal relation between the conception of the supreme good and those precepts, would similarly make no sense insofar as it was proposed as a rule for rational beings qua rational beings. Yet on many occasions, such proposals are made with great seriousness. The benefits of violating some requirement of the natural law are compared with the benefit of conformity. And that is to say that some good or set of goods is being weighed against the supreme good, as if in relation to it any question of weighing could arise. How does such a mistake come to be made?

Characteristically, it is the outcome of fragmenting into independent parts the conceptual scheme in terms of which the plain person had at first organized her or his moral understanding. Goods, rules and virtues are as a result of such fragmentation reconceived as isolable from one another, so that the problem is not that of how to articulate a preexisting relationship, but to construct a relationship apparently not yet established between the disparate parts of one's moral scheme. And the difficulty for the plain person in this situation is that once the different elements in her or his moral conceptual scheme have been thus torn apart, each of them thereby assumes a somewhat different character. Rules, conceived apart from virtues and goods, are not the same as rules conceived in dependence upon virtues and goods; and so it is also with virtues apart from rules and goods and goods apart from rules and virtues.

Observe now that in making these theoretical remarks I have already resorted to the narrative mode. I have begun to tell a story, the story of the decline and fall of the plain person. It is a story in four episodes, a story of a failed quest for what proves in the end to be an illusory grail. In the first of these, the protagonist sets out to discover what the final good for beings such as her or himself is and finds that, in asking 'What is my good?' and 'What is the good?' in any way that is well-designed to secure helpful answers, she or he has to define that quest in a way which already presupposes to a significant degree a particular kind of answer to those questions. For those rules and virtues which alone guide one reliably in the earliest stages of fruitful moral enquiry are structured, so that they already presuppose a great deal about the existence and nature of that same good about which one has only begun to enquire.

The circularity in which the protagonist is thereby involved is one which requires of her or him an asceticism or at least a temperateness about certain classes of less than supreme goods, which she or he will only be able to justify fully at some future time in the light later to be afforded by a more adequate conception of the good. Yet should she or he, solicited by a variety of such goods, physical, aesthetic and intellectual, fail in this temperateness, not only will she or he debar her or himself from ever reaching the point at which such rational justification would become possible, but she or he will, in according independent recognition to a multiplicity of more or less immediate goods, have adopted a set of standards of justification very different from that towards an understanding of which she or he had originally been moving. As a result in this second type of episode a radical discrepancy begins to appear between the rules in obedience to which the quest was originally to have been conducted and the multiplicity of goods now envisaged, possibly as rival candidates for the status of supreme good, possibly as by their very multiplicity excluding the notion of a single supreme good. And already any conception of a good that not only is not but could not be outweighed by other goods has disappeared from view.

In a third type of episode this discrepancy is resolved in either of two incompatible ways. *Either,* the authority of rules is made independent of all relationship to goods, so that obedience to rules is valued for its own sake, *or* the rules are reconceived so that they are authoritative only if and insofar as obedience to them is causally effective in attaining what are taken to be goods.

Whichever of these two resolutions is adopted, new problems are engendered. If conformity to moral rules is now to be valued only for its own sake, as Kant, for example, held, then the question inescapably arises of why and how a rational person should be moved to value such conformity. If rules are only a means to the achievement of goods, and a multiplicity of competing goods are acknowledged, as they are by utilitarians, then it will be necessary to decide how to respond on those occasions when the actions necessary for the attainment of some one particular good violate the rule or rules necessary for the attainment of some other good.

During this third type of episode, therefore, the protagonist of our story discovers not only that she or he must take sides on these issues, but that other similar persons take opposing sides. The protagonist consequently confronts one or more antagonists and becomes involved in intellectual and moral conflict. And this conflict may extend beyond the initial opposition, in which the upholder of rules independent of goods confronted the upholder of rules as nothing more than a means to the achievement of goods, to further questions about what place the virtues are to have in each of these rival schemes and how the problems internal to each scheme are to be resolved. Our protagonist therefore now confronts a variety of antagonists and perhaps her or himself with a divided mind on these divisive issues.

A fourth and final type of episode opens with the protagonist's discovery that the major issues over which conflict has been joined are not rationally resolvable. It is not that each of the contending parties does not have arguments to deploy, but rather that each gives a different weight to different types of consideration, and that there are no rational criteria, shared between the contending parties, to which appeal can be made in deciding what weight should be so given. Fundamental disagreement turns out to be ineliminable. There is more than one way in which our protagonist might respond to this discovery, perhaps by acting out the part of a wholly prephilosophical and now cynical plain person, standing outside and pouring scorn upon all philosophical points of view, or perhaps by becoming a plain person's version of a proto-Nietzschean, one devoted to unmasking a will to power disguised by the proponents of each contending moral standpoint.

I have told this story of the transformations of the plain person only in bare and skeletal outline. But I hope that I have said enough at least to suggest that this story could be told with sufficient detail to explain both how those changing portraits of the plain person which decorate the history of moral philosophy do in fact correspond to social realities — hence the immense plausibility in one time and place of Kant's portrait of the plain person, in another of Reid's, in a third of Sidgwick's, and in a fourth of Sartre's — and how, nonetheless, the plain person is fundamentally a proto-Aristotelian. What is the force of 'fundamentally' here? What it conveys can be expressed in three claims, first that every human being *either* lives out her or his life in a narrative form which is structured in terms of a *telos,* of virtues and of roles in an Aristotelian mode or has disrupted that narrative by committing her or himself to some other way of life, which is best understood as an alternative designed to avoid or escape from an Aristotelian mode of life, so that the lives of those who understand themselves, explicitly or much more probably implicitly, in terms set by Kant or Reid or Sidgwick or Sartre, are still informed by this rejected alternative. Secondly, I have told the story of the decline and fall of the plain person as the narrative of a single life. But the story could have been told, and I have told it elsewhere (in *After Virtue*), as a claim about the narrative history of a set of successive periods in Western culture from the sixteenth to the twentieth century. This partial mirroring of the fate of individuals in the history of the larger social order and of the fate of that larger order in the narratives of individual lives testifies to the inseparability of the two stories.

Thirdly, as these first two claims imply, I am also committed to holding that every human being is potentially a fully-fledged and not merely a proto-Aristotelian and that the frustration of that potentiality is among his or her morally important characteristics. We should therefore expect to find, within those who have not been allowed to develop, or have not themselves allowed their lives to develop, an Aristotelian form, a crucial and ineliminable tension between that in them which is and that which is not, Aristotelian The standard modern anti-Aristotelian self will be a particular kind of divided self, exhibiting that complexity so characteristic of and so prized by modernity.

We can now say something more not only about how much of a moral philosopher the plain person has to be, but also about what kind of a moral philosopher the plain person has to be and how this may differ from situation to situation. The plain person needs as much of a theory as will enable her or him to identify what the significant alternatives are which now confront her or him, and to understand why and how it was in the past that she or he did or did not make mistakes in acting in one way rather than another. That need may not be met, not only if the plain person is insufficiently a theorist, but also if the theory which is made available to her or him, even if true and adequate *qua* theory, is stated in too much abstraction from the specificities and particularities of her or his historical and autobiographical situation.

This is why we would not meet the practical needs of contemporary plain persons by simply providing them with copies of the *Nichomachean Ethics* and of Aquinas's commentary, nor even of the *Ia-IIae* of the *Summa*. What such persons would still lack is a capacity for reading or hearing what is written in such texts as providing answers to their own specific and particular questions. Such texts may be theoretically powerful, but still remain practically idle, for they do no work for us, until and unless we learn how to read them in such a way as to generate specific and particular answers to the practical questions of all of us, moral philosophers and plain persons alike, since in her or his practical life a moral philosopher is just one more type of plain person. But those texts do, if we read them aright, meet us, so to speak, half way. They are responsive to this kind of practical reading, because their authors' expectations of this kind of reader already inform those texts. The reader still, however, has the work to do of constructing her or his own specific and particular reading of the text at the points at which her or his practical questions and the text intersect. What form do such specific and particular readings take?

A practical reader can only approach a text with the resources for questioning it which are afforded by her or his social contest and relationships. Such resources always limit as well as focus our initial questioning, and an effective practical test begins by subordinating our questions to its own. It responds to our interrogation by interrogating us. So it is at the outset in the *Nicomachean Ethics*. So it is at the beginning of the *Ia-IIae*, a work designed for teachers, confessors and other intermediaries between its text and the readings of the practical reader or hearer. Such a reader is forced back upon questions to which her or his own questioning has to be subordinated and by which it is likely to be transformed.

Consider the sequence of questioning as expounded in the *Ia-IIae* and its shadow counterpart in the sequence of questioning of some particular practical reader. Where Aquinas asks what the ultimate end is towards which the activities of any human being qua rational person are directed and explains why wealth, honor, pleasure, power, the goods of the body and the goods of the soul cannot be that end, the practical reader will be concerned with these particular pleasures, with that particular opportunity for enriching her or himself, with the attractions of this or that specific type of power, as these present themselves as the ends of possible courses of action. Where Aquinas presents the most powerful arguments against his own conclusions through a wide range of earlier voices, including those of Plato, Aristotle, Cicero, Boethius, and Augustine, the contemporary practical reader cannot but also hear the practical advice of the major voices of her or his own time, those of, say, Diderot, Rousseau and Kant in the eighteenth century or of Hegel and Mill in the nineteenth, often perhaps in vulgarized and diminished form, presented in the conversation of one's neighbors, rather than in philosophical texts, but not necessarily the less powerful for that. Such a reader needs to learn what Aquinas has to teach us in each of his dialectical responses about how to respond to these contending voices. She or he needs to learn through this process of argumentative debate to identify in concrete terms what here and now she or he must do, if she or he is not to confuse the supreme good with some lesser good.

It was precisely at this point and over this question that the protagonist in my earlier story of the decline and fall of the plain person made a large initial mistake, and the practical reader of the *Ia-IIae* will be able to avoid this same error only by learning how to arrive, in practice, at those conclusions which Aquinas reaches theoretically, in moving from his answer to Question 5 about where happiness is to be found, through the conclusions of Questions 18-21 about what makes an act good and evil, to Questions 24-48 about the function of the passions in making her or him act well and badly, and on to Questions 49-66 about the habits which have to be developed as virtues, so that her or his passions are ordered and transformed, so that she or he, in consequence, acts well rather than badly, so that she or he, in further consequence, is directed towards her or his true final end. But if such a person moves successfully through this process of practical enquiry, embodying in the dramatic sequences of her or his life a highly particularized counterpart of the ordered sequences of moral teaming presented in the questions and answers of those parts of the *Ia-IIae,* she or he is bound to discover the very same circularity that was evident also in the story of the decline and fall of the plain person.

Such a person, that is, will have to recognize that the point in her or his practical enquiry at which recognition of the nature of and the need for the virtues has been achieved could not have been reached, if she or he had not already at a much earlier stage possessed and valued those same virtues to some significant, even if less than perfect degree. Unless the activities in which her or his initial questioning was embodied had been in appropriate measure courageous — both patient, when necessary, and daring, when necessary, just in giving what was due to other participants in those activities, temperate in restraining desires, so that a multiplicity of solicitations liable to distract the course of enquiry were put aside for the sake of a good thereby already implicitly judged to be supreme, and always prudent in the ordering of these activities, she or he could not have achieved any adequate understanding of why without courage, justice, temperateness and prudence her or his enquiry was bound to fail. So a reader making her or his way through the *Ia-IIae* will learn only later what it was in her or his earlier relationship to the text which enabled her or him to make of the narrative of her or his own life a particularized version of the progress of Aquinas's argument. How the text is read depends, that is to say, in key part on the incipient virtues of the practical reader and on what incipient virtues the reader is able to bring to her or his reading depends in turn on the resources on which that reader can draw in and from the particular social context. What kind of resources are these?

In order to answer this question it is worth considering two important objections that may be advanced against my argument so far. The first of these might begin by pointing out that many plain persons have fared very well morally without ever encountering philosophy. With the moral resources afforded by sound, plain, practical teaching, by the cultivation of the virtues and by an instructed conscience, what need is there for philosophy? It may be thought that it is part of the arrogance of an intellectual to project onto plain persons a need for theory. It is however no part of my case that the plain person needs to become anything like a professional theorist. It is central to my argument that the practice of the moral life by plain persons always presupposes the truth of some particular theoretical standpoint and that, when confronted by rival claims to her or his moral allegiance, the plain person's reflective practical choices will implicitly at least be a choice between theoretical standpoints. In our own society common plain persons who have never heard of John Stuart Mill offer as the deliverances of what they take to be their common sense maxims of hedonistic utilitarianism. Other such plain persons, equally ignorant of Kant, will insist on the irrelevance of consequences to the rightness of their actions. A good deal of ordinary conversation and debate bears out the epigram that common sense is a graveyard of past philosophies.

Plain persons then exhibit their allegiances in their actions and in their reasons for action, not in their theorizing. But this does not deprive those allegiances of a philosophical dimension. It might however be objected that those allegiances could never rightly be described as Aristotelian or even proto-Aristotelian. For Aristotle himself took plain persons to be incapable of philosophical reflection. Aristotle's exclusions of not only barbarians, but also women[4] and productive workers[5] from the life of citizenship and of the virtues is surely enough to show that he could not have taken plain persons to be proto-Aristotelians. But Aristotle has of course no worthwhile arguments to support these exclusions, and the Thomistic Aristotelianism of a Maritain or a Simon rightly ignored them. And so do I.

What the first of these objections does draw to our attention is the danger to someone holding my position of too easy an assimilation of the theoretical to the practical life and therefore of the preoccupations of the philosopher to those of the plain person. I have, for example, emphasized how the plain person's moral understanding is of goods, rules and virtues in his or her interrelationships. And the practical need to understand these together, although real, is very different from the philosopher's need to develop a theoretical understanding of each of these in its own terms. So that often enough, if we are to make what philosophers say relevant to the practical concerns of plain persons, including philosophers in their own practical lives, we need first to reorganize and rethink the philosophers' arguments. Some topics which were, for good analytical and didactic reasons, treated separately in Aristotle and Aquinas need in contexts of practice to be treated together. Aristotle considers the ac-

---

4. *(Politics* 1259b21-1260a33)
5. *(Politics* 1328b33-1329a2)

quisition of the virtues in one set of passages and the nature of practical reasoning in another; and Aquinas, in the *Summa,* not only considers these separately, but discusses the character of the natural law in yet a third set of passages. Both provide in their discussions much that suggests the importance of the relationships between them. But subsequent teaching about practical recoding, virtues and natural law has often enforced a separation of topics which has obscured the fact that at the level of practice, especially initial practice, the ability to judge and to act in accordance with the precepts of the natural law, the ability to acquire an increasing set of dispositions to act virtuously, and the ability to judge rightly about goods are all exercised as aspects of one and the same complex ability, the ability to engage in sound practical reasoning. How is this so?

To reason practically, I must always set in front of myself some good which will be specified in the major premise of my practical reasoning and, if my practical reasoning is in any particular instance not to obstruct my attempt to answer the question 'What is my ultimate good?' alternative immediate goods must from the outset be ordered so that no lesser, but more immediate good can be thought to outweigh my ultimate good. My ultimate good, that is to say, will have to be conceived from the outset as a good than which no greater can be pursued by me, in order to ensure the integrity of my practical reasoning.

At the same time, the various relationships into which I will have to enter, in order to achieve the kind of understanding of myself and others without which I will be unable to learn what the human good is, will themselves have to be informed by those virtues and governed by those rules without which the activities of enquiry will be barren. Any ordering of goods which involves my conceiving of my ultimate good as a good than which no greater can be pursued will have to be matched by an ordering of my life in terms of virtues and rules which is consistent with the affirmation of the true nature of the good and the best as the first premise of my practical reasoning. The movement from that first premise to a conclusion which is right action requires from me correspondingly ordered character and a correspondingly ordered set of social relationships. This connection between what kind of person I have to become in order to achieve a given end and what the character of that given end is is of course not peculiar to this kind of enquiry. It is a connection embodied in the structure and reasoning of all practice-based activity; what the need for it in enquiry by particular human beings designed to answer the questions "What is my good?" and "What *is the* good?" confirms is that such enquiry is itself a practice.

So it is not just that, as I said earlier, practices have an Aristotelian structure. It is also that in engaging in the practice of asking seriously and systematically the question "What is my good?" plain persons engage in a reflective practice with an Aristotelian content as well as an Aristotelian structure, a practice in which both Aristotle and Aquinas preceded them. So it is less surprising than we may have thought that those who first come to a reading of the *Nicomachean Ethics* or Aquinas's commentary or the *Ia-IIae* of the *Summa* may already exhibit the cardinal virtues without as yet knowing the reasons for needing them, and it is not after all paradoxical to assert that we must already have those virtues at least to some degree if we are to understand why we need to have them. The *Nichomachean Ethics* and Aquinas's commentary upon it and the *Ia-IIae* are texts in which readers are able to discover themselves as characters, or rather to discover types of character which to some significant degree they already exemplify. And they may also discover that what they are now able to learn about themselves in universal terms from such texts, in beginning to comprehend a philosophical theory of the moral life, is what they had already learned in part through practice-informed activities concerning the particularities of their own lives. If their subsequent practice becomes informed and enriched by philosophical theory, they may feel that they have transcended certain limitations of that past learning, limitations rooted in the relative inarticulacy of the merely practical. But they need never disown, indeed they could not without incoherence disown, the first stages of the enacted narrative of their lives. We are thus able to set beside the fable of the decline and fall of the plain person the story of the plain person who does not go astray, or rather who finds the resources for correcting her or his errors as she or he proceeds towards both an understanding of, and the achievement of, her or his good.

Those stories, it needs finally to be remarked, have genuine application to human lives only if and because certain metaphysical as well as moral claims can be sustained within philosophy. For those stories not only draw explicitly and obviously upon concepts and theses having to do with rules, regularities, passions, dispositions and ends, but also, if less obviously, upon rules and concepts having to do with substances, essential and accidental properties, potentiality and act, form and matter. They involve explanations of what it is for someone to succeed in progressing towards or to fail in progressing towards their ultimate end, and such explanations are of interest only if and insofar as we have good reason to believe that they are true. But such explanations will be true if and only if the universe itself is teleologically ordered, and the only type of teleologically ordered universe in which we have good reason to believe is a theistic universe. Hence, the moral progress of the plain person towards her or her ultimate good is always a matter of more than morality. And the enacted narrative of that progress will only become fully intelligible when it is understood not only in terms of metaphysics but in an adequate theological light, when, that is, the particularities of that narrative are understood to embody what is said about sin and about grace in the *Ia-IIae* of the *Summa* as well as what is said about law and the virtues. The moral progress of the plain person is always the beginnings of a pilgrim's progress.

PART II

Law, Lawyers, and Ethics

Chapter Four

Constitutional Correctives for Democratic Vices[1]

William D. Richardson
Lloyd G. Nigro

> [The American regime] has its foundations in the willing use of human passions and interests, but it has also certain enduring excellences necessary to its fulfillment. Preserving that foundation and, at the same time, nurturing the appropriate excellences is the task of enlightened American citizenship and statesmanship. It is easy to fail; easy to indulge a preference for liberty that exults only in the free play of the passions and interests and easy to make utopian demands for universal excellences which ignore the limiting requisites of the American political system.[2]

Introduction

A regime deliberately built upon a foundation in which behavior is expected to be motivated by self-interests and passions makes special demands on both the competence and character of its governors. Recognizing this, the American regime included some unique structures that were intended to minimize the effects of these demands. Because they represent the most numerous segment of our "governors," public administrators prove to be especially appropriate subjects for examining the ways in which these demands affect character and competence.[3] But the role of

---

1. The present chapter is a revised version of an article that originally appeared as "Administrative Ethics and Founding Thought: Constitutional Correctives, Honor, and Education," *Public Administration Review*, 47, No. 5 (September/October 1987): 367–76. Reprinted by permission.
2. Martin Diamond, "The American Idea of Man: The View From the Founding," in *The Americans 1976, Critical Choices for Americans*, vol. 2, Irving Kristol and Paul Weaver, eds. (Lexington, MA: Lexington Books; Washington: Heath and Co., 1976), pp. 21-22.
3. While public administrators are loathe to accept the title of "governors," their exercise of that portion of political power known as "discretion" amply distinguishes

administrators in the governance of the regime is important not just because of their numbers, but because they routinely exercise broad discretionary powers. Hence, to a considerable extent the proper governing of this self-interested and passionate regime is dependent on the "character" of those administrators whose discretionary decisions can affect the citizenry in so many different ways.[4] That this is not a novel insight can be seen from Woodrow Wilson's own early study on administration, wherein he asked a question concerning the character of the American public administrator that is as salient today as it was in 1887.

> ...The question for us is, how shall our series of governments within governments be so administered that it shall always be to the interest of the public officer to serve, not his superior alone but the community also, with the best efforts of his talents and the soberest service of his conscience? How shall such service be made to his commonest interest by contributing abundantly to his sustenance, to his dearest interest by furthering his ambition, and to his highest interests by advancing his honor and establishing his character?...[5]

In the more than a century that has passed since Wilson posed this question, students of American public administration have worked to provide answers. Government and civil service reform, professionalism, codes of ethics, legislative oversight, judicial review, and citizen participation have been put forward as ways to improve the chances that public administrators will consistently serve the public interest.[6] However,

---

them from the ordinary citizens. While there may be valid questions about the legitimacy of their possessing such power, its existence is indisputable. Add to that possession the fact that administrators constitute the most numerous of our governors (the combined total of federal and state "civil servants" approaches 15 million), and their collective importance to the proper governance of the regime becomes strikingly clear.

4. A fuller development of this theme is to be found in William D. Richardson, *Democracy, Bureaucracy, and Character: Founding Thought* (Lawrence, Kansas: University of Kansas Press, 1997).

5. Woodrow Wilson, "The Study of Administration, " in Dean L. Yarwood, ed., *Public Administration: Politics and the People* (White Plains, NY: Longman, 1987), p. 29.

6. The literature on these and related topics is extensive. For example, see Martin J. Schiesl, *The Politics of Efficiency: Municipal Administration and Reform in America* (Berkeley: University of California Press, 1977); Dwight Waldo, *The Administrative State* (New York: Ronald Press, 1948); Emmette S. Redford, *Democracy in the Administrative State* (New York: Oxford University Press, 1969); Barry Karl, *Executive Reorganization and Reform in the New Deal* (Cambridge, MA: Harvard University Press, 1963); Paul H. Appleby, *Big Democracy* (New York: Alfred A. Knopf, 1949); Vincent Ostrom, *The Intellectual Crisis in American Public Administration* (University, AL: University of Alabama Press, 1974); Paul Van Riper, *History of the United States Civil Ser-*

the explicit attention to the character of the public administrator called for by Wilson has received far less attention than his desire for a "science" of administration.[7] At least in regard to the ethical content of public administration, Wilson framed the issue in a manner that placed it squarely in the Founding tradition. The very language used reveals an attempt to link 1787 and 1887 and, in so doing, to clearly connect the science of administration with the ideas that form the foundations of the American regime.

Recognizing and encouraging the development of those virtues or excellences needed to sustain the American regime was of concern to those who established the United States. A close look at the thoughts of some participants in the Founding, therefore, offers a partial answer to the question asked by Wilson in the essay that is generally considered to have launched Public Administration as a self-conscious field of study.[8] Accordingly, the focus here is on the potential contributions of Founding thought to current efforts to define and establish a public administration that is ethically excellent.

Citizen Character and Founding Thought

The "black letter text" of the Constitution of the United States offers little if any explicit assistance to those seeking to understand the role of citizen character in the thinking of the Founders. Since Article II and related parts of the document do not go beyond general references to the powers, duties, and requirements of the executive branch, it is not surprising that there is equal vagueness regarding the character required of those who would administer the affairs of the new national government.[9]

---

vice (Chicago: Row, Peterson, 1958); Theodore Lowi, *The End of Liberalism*, 2nd ed. (New York: W. W. Norton and Co., 1979); and Laurence J. O'Toole, Jr., "American Public Administration and the Idea of Reform," *Administration and Society*, vol. 16 (August 1984): 141-166.

7. Dwight Waldo, "The Perdurability of the Politics - Administration Dichotomy: Woodrow Wilson and the Identity Crisis in Public Administration," in *Politics and Administration: Woodrow Wilson and American Public Administration*, Jack S. Rabin and James S. Bowman, eds. (New York: Dekker, 1984), p. 231; and Gerald E. Caiden, "In Search of an Apolitical Science of American Public Administration," in *Politics and Administration*, Rabin and Bowman, eds., pp. 51-76.

8. Dwight Waldo, *The Enterprise of Public Administration* (Novato, CA: Chandler and Sharp Publishers, 1980), pp. 10-12, 67-69.

9. *Ibid.*, pp. 66-67.

The Constitution's silence on these matters, of course, is deceptive. The historical record, including the written works of those who were delegates to the Constitutional Convention, reveals that their expectations, fears, and aspirations concerning citizen character were central to their deliberations over the powers and form of the new government.[10] While interpretations differ, students of American political thought agree on the point that the Constitution establishes a form of government designed to rest on what the Founders understood to be the bedrock realities of human nature. To sustain the new republic, they also sought to encourage the development of certain "appropriate excellences" or virtues.

Clearly related, but less closely examined, are the implications of Founding thought on these matters for that group of citizens who would be public administrators.[11] *The Federalist Papers* provides perhaps the clearest evidence that public administration was of great concern to several of the Founders, most notably James Madison and Alexander Hamilton. Publius argued that the federal executive should be energetic, competent, and govern in the public interest, and these attributes require that public administrators have certain appropriate character traits.[12] Public administration also had an important role to play in cultivating citizen character. Rejecting the Anti-Federalists' argument for small and administratively weak governments, Hamilton in particular asserted that a strong and competent public administration would command public support and "...promote private and public morality by providing them with effective protection."[13]

Public Virtue and the American Regime

There is, in short, ample reason to conclude that many of the most influential delegates to the Constitutional Convention believed that the character of public administrators was an important part of the founda-

---

10. *The American Founding: Politics, Statesmanship, and the Constitution*, Ralph A. Rossum and Gary L. McDowell, eds., (Port Washington, NY: Kennikat Press, 1981).

11. For example, see Robert A. Goldwin, ed., *Bureaucrats, Policy Analysts, Statesmen: Who Leads?* (Washington: American Enterprise Institute, 1980).

12. Alexander Hamilton, James Madison, and John Jay, *The Federalist Papers* (New York: New American Library, 1961), Numbers 1-4.

13. Herbert J. Storing, *What the Anti-Federalists Were For: The Political Thought of the Opponents of the Constitution* (Chicago: The University of Chicago Press, 1981), pp. 42-43.

tion upon which they hoped the American regime would securely rest.[14] A common theme that cuts across the well-documented disagreements among these delegates is their conviction that the survival of the new regime would depend heavily on the public virtue of those who governed and on the extent to which those governors could reliably be expected to serve the public interest. Often their debates revolved around the questions of what constituted public virtue and of how best to achieve it. Some contemplated a regime designed to produce an elevated form of public virtue involving "...firmness, courage, endurance, industry, frugal living, strength, and above all, unremitting devotion to the weal of the public's corporate self, the community of virtuous men...[E]very man gave himself totally to the good of the public as a whole."[15] Others urged constitutional arrangements predicated on the assumption that public virtue of this kind would be a rare commodity. Since a democratic republic of some kind was contemplated, there was also disagreement over the extent to which its citizens would be able to select virtuous governors. If ambitious, self-interested governors were to be the norm, what was necessary to assure that the consequences would not be fatal to the regime?

In one crucial area of dispute, that concerning which constitutional arrangement would be proposed for ratification by the states, the Federalists' position set forth by Publius in *The Federalist Papers* prevailed. The constitutional framework advocated by Publius accepted the premise that the American character would be self-interested to the point that the private sphere should normally be more important than the general welfare as a guide to action. In Publius's eyes, people were in the main ambitious and self-interested, and they should be expected to make the improvement of their own conditions the basis for political choices. Those who *govern* a free people, therefore, must seek to use and channel the motive of self-interest.[16] Alexander Hamilton bluntly made this point in the following terms:

---

14. As used in this chapter, the term "Founders" is intended to include both "Federalists" and "Anti-Federalists." In short, we are drawing on the works of those individuals who could be perceived as having had a significant influence on the issues discussed at the Constitutional Convention, regardless of whether they were on the "winning" (Federalist) side or not. For a treatment of the significance of this approach, see Herbert J. Storing, *What the Anti-Federalists Were For: The Political Thought of the Opponents of the Constitution, Ibid.*

15. Forrest McDonald, *Novus Ordo Seclorum: The Intellectual Origins of the Constitution* (Lawrence: University Press of Kansas, 1985), pp. 70-71.

16. Martin Diamond, "Ethics and Politics: The American Way," in *The Moral Foundations of the American Republic*, 3rd ed., Robert Horwitz, ed. (Charlottesville: University of Virginia Press, 1986), p. 83. Reprinted as Chapter Eight in the present collection.

> Take mankind as they are, and what are they governed by? Their passions. There may be in every government a few choice spirits, who may act from more worthy motives.... Our prevailing passions are ambition and interest; and it will ever be the duty of a wise government to avail itself of these passions, in order to make them subservient to the public good....[17]

Led by Madison and Hamilton, the Federalists sought to establish a regime in which "choice spirits" need not be the norm. They were emphatically unwilling to write a constitution based on the assumption that virtuous governors would always be available and in office. Since these governors were to be drawn from the ranks of the governed, Publius argued that they realistically could be expected to resemble their fellow citizens in that they too would usually be self-interested. Thus, according to Martin Diamond, their objective was "a durable regime whose perpetuation require[d] nothing like the wisdom and virtue necessary for its creation."[18] Robert Horwitz uses even stronger language: "Pushing questions of virtue aside, they sought to develop political arrangements and institutions that would insure 'the existence and security of the government, *even in the absence of political virtue*'.... The guiding and energizing principle of the community would be the vigorous pursuit of individual self-interest."[19] Diamond, however, goes on to ask: "But does not the intensity and kind of our modern problems seem to require of us a greater degree of reflection and public-spiritedness than the Founders thought sufficient for the men who came after them?"[20]

This is the issue that Woodrow Wilson recognized and that, more recently, other students of American public administration have raised in a variety of contexts.[21] Does Founding thought offer any guidance to those

---

17. *The Records of the Federal Convention of 1787*, vol. 1 Max Farrand, ed. (New Haven: Yale University Press, 1937) p. 82; also, see McDonald, *Novus Ordo Seclorum*, Ibid., pp. 188-189.

18. Martin Diamond, "The Federalist," in *American Political Thought: The Philosophic Dimension of American Statesmanship*, 2nd ed., Morton J. Frisch and Richard G. Stevens, eds. (Itasca, IL: F. E. Peacock, 1983), p. 69.

19. Robert H. Horwitz, "John Locke and the Preservation of Liberty: A Perennial Problem of Civic Education," in his *The Moral Foundations of the American Republic*, op. cit., pp. 139–140.

20. Diamond, "The Federalist," op. cit., p. 88.

21. For example, see Brian J. Cook, "The Representative Function of Bureaucracy: Public Administration in Constitutive Perspective," *Administration and Society* (February 1992): 403–429; J. Patrick Dobel, "Integrity in the Public Service," *Public Administration Review* (May/June 1990): 354–366; H. George Frederickson, "Toward a Theory of the Public for Public Administration," *Administration and Society* (February 1991): 395–417; H. G. Frederickson and David K. Hart, "The Public Service and the Patriotism of Benevolence," *Public Administration Review*, vol. 45 (September/October

seeking ways in which the public-spiritedness or civic virtue of public administrators might be enhanced? We will argue here that it does have a great deal to offer because the Founders did not simply jettison the idea of public virtue. They gave the term a distinctly modern definition, one stressing the compatibility of self-interest, moderation, and service to the community.[22] Working from this perspective, the Founders reasoned that the American regime would be capable of producing a steady stream of people dedicated to public service.[23] Thus, Publius said in No. 57:

> The aim of every political constitution is, or ought to be, first to obtain for rulers men who possess most wisdom to discern, and most virtue to pursue, the common good of the society; and, in the next place, to take the most effectual precautions for keeping them virtuous whilst they continue to hold their public trust.[24]

The writings of several delegates to the Constitutional Convention strongly indicate they shared the belief that those excellences of character needed to sustain the American regime would have their origins in one or more of three mutually reinforcing sources: constitutional correctives, a concern for reputation or honor, and education. These writings substantially increase our understanding of how the Founders proposed to enhance the probability that Americans would be served by *publicly virtuous governors* (a term which would include Wilson's public administrators).

1985): 547-553; Louis C. Gawthrop, "Civas, Civitas, and Civilitas: A New Focus for the Year 2000," *Public Administration Review*, vol. 44 (March 1984): 101-107; David K. Hart, "A Partnership in Virtue Among All Citizens: The Public Service and Civic Humanism," *Public Administration Review* (March/April 1989): 101-105; David K. Hart, "The Virtuous Citizen, the Honorable Bureaucrat, and 'Public' Administration," in *Public Administration Review*, vol. 44 (March 1984): 111-120; David K. Hart, "The Honorable Bureaucrat Among the Philistines," *Administration and Society*, vol. 15 (May 1983): 43-48; Larry M. Lane, "Individualism, Civic Virtue, and Public Administration," *Administration and Society* (May 1988): 30-45; John A. Rohr, "Ethical Issues in French Public Administration: A Comparative Study," *Public Administration Review* (July/August 1991): 283-297, and his *Ethics for Bureaucrats: An Essay on Law and Values* (New York: Dekker, 1978); Camilla Stivers, "The Public Agency as Polis: Active Citizenship in the Administrative State," *Administration and Society* (May 1990): 86-105, and William D. Richardson, *Democracy, Bureaucracy, and Character: Founding Thought* (Lawrence, KS: University Press of Kansas, 1997).

22. Diamond, "Ethics and Politics: The American Way," in *Moral Foundations of the American Republic*, op. cit., p. 99ff.
23. McDonald, *Novus Ordo Seclorum*, op. cit., pp. 188-191.
24. *The Federalist Papers*, op. cit., p. 350.

Public Virtue and Constitutional Correctives in Founding Thought

As a group, the Founders were painfully aware of the administrative failings of the Confederation, but they were divided over a series of questions relating to the jurisdiction and powers of its contemplated successor. All concerned recognized, at least in general terms, that these questions had serious administrative implications since the new government—whatever form it took—would have to be capable of fulfilling its domestic as well as its international responsibilities. Citizen character was a centerpiece of the debate, in part because of disagreement between those advocates of institutional arrangements that depended on high levels of public virtue in the citizenry and those who believed, in John Adams' words, "...that all projects of government, founded in the supposition or expectation of extraordinary degrees of virtue, are evidently chimerical."[25] There was, however, general agreement with the idea that constitutional arrangements should reflect certain assumptions about citizen character.

The Anti-Federalists argued that relatively small, homogeneous, and highly democratic states offered the best opportunity to *form* citizen character around public virtues that would nurture and protect republican government.[26] In their view, the long-term survival of the new Republic would depend on the citizens' adherence to community as opposed to individual or minority interests. They believed that a primary function of government should be the cultivation of public or civic virtue because: "Republican government depends on civic virtue, on a devotion to fellow citizens and to country so deeply instilled as to be almost as automatic and powerful as the natural devotion to self-interest."[27] Here the Anti-Federalists tended to mirror the classical conception of the regime as a comprehensive system for the formation of character in which the governors are to be judged by their commitment to the ethical purposes of the regime and their capacity to instill (and enforce) public virtues in the citizenry.[28]

Leaning heavily on the classical tradition, the Anti-Federalists opposed the extended commercial republic contemplated by the Federalists in part because they saw it as a threat to public virtue and, therefore, to

---

25. John Adams to Samuel Adams (1790), in *Political Thought in America: An Anthology*, Michael B. Levy, ed. (Homewood, IL: Dorsey Press, 1982), p. 73.
26. Storing, *What the Anti-Federalists Were For*, op. cit., p. 8.
27. *Ibid.*, pp. 15-23.
28. *Ibid.*, p. 21.

a truly republican form of government.[29] They saw the small homogeneous republic as a school of citizenship, a school that could not survive in the large, heterogeneous, and factionalized republic advocated by the Federalists.[30] If citizenship declined, they feared that popular control would be replaced by aristocratic rule. Accordingly, their arguments in opposition to ratification of the Constitution typically expressed the following sentiments:

> A republican, or free government can only exist where the body of the people are virtuous, and where property is pretty equally divided. In such a government the people are the sovereign and their sense or opinion is the criterion of every public measure; for when this ceases to be the case, the nature of the government is changed, and an aristocracy, monarchy or despotism will rise on its ruin.[31]

As expressed by Publius, the Federalist point of view maintained that a constitution applying a "composition" of federal and national principles to an extended republic was necessary because people were not "angels" and, left to their own devices, could not reliably be expected to select virtuous leaders. Publius's forceful criticism of classical republican approaches to public virtue—particularly their inability to homogenize the opinions, passions, and interests of a naturally diverse citizenry without destroying liberty—is well known. Publius's treatment of the causes of factional politics and the corrective functions of an extended commercial republic still stands as the clearest, most powerful statement of this perspective on the connections between citizen character and the American regime.[32] In this view, the belief that democratic citizens and governors would possess superior virtues simply *could not be relied upon as the foundation of the regime*. Accordingly, the alternative was to accept as the "bedrock" of the regime that character trait most commonly in evidence, namely, self-interest.

---

29. *Ibid*. To understand the arguments over "virtue" in the new regime, it helps to clarify the distinction between "virtue" per se and "public" (or "political") "virtue." The former is understood to mean the actual possession of a particular laudable attribute such as moderation. The crucial aspect of such a possession is that one acts moderately *because* one values moderation for itself. "Public virtue" is different in that while one may act moderately, one does so primarily because of the public honor or reputation attached to such a display.

30. *Ibid.*, p. 20.

31. Samuel Bryan, "Letter of Centinel, No. 1" (1787), in *Political Thought in America*, op. cit., p. 115.

32. *The Federalist Papers*, Number 10, esp. pp. 78-79. See also Martin Diamond, "Ethics and Politics: The American Way," in *The Moral Foundations of the American Republic*, op. cit., pp. 75–108.

In *Federalist* No. 51, Publius applied this point of view to the "interior structure of the government" in order to see to it that ambition counteracted ambition and that the "...interest of the man [was] connected to the constitutional rights of the place."³³ Robert Goldwin observes that ambition and self-interest are so fundamental to Publius's design that, "...if officials in one part of the government should be insufficiently moved by ambition and self-interest, a necessary balancing restraint would be lacking.... As fundamental as separation of powers is as a principle in the Constitution, that office holders must be ambitious and self-interested is even more fundamental."³⁴

The argument between the Federalists and Anti-Federalists over the proper constitutional approach to citizen character was resolved largely in favor of the Federalists' position. For those such as Madison and Hamilton, effectively to channel human passions and interests was the most important goal.

> ...because character formation was no longer the direct end of politics, the new science of politics could dispense with those laws [by means of which the ancient philosophers had sought to "high tone" human character] and, for the achievement of its lowered ends, could rely largely instead upon shrewd institutional arrangements of the powerful human passions and interests. Not to instruct and to transcend these passions and interests, but rather to channel them became the hallmark of modern politics.³⁵

The Federalists recognized that self-interest was, by itself, an inadequate foundation for the regime they contemplated. Restraints were needed. They did not, however, choose to rely on an aristocracy of virtuous governors to achieve that restraint: citizens, elected governors, and administrators were to be restrained by constitutional correctives. In this regard, Herbert J. Storing has clearly described the need for citizens both to understand and to support these constitutional devices. His words suggest that public administrators have "special" responsibilities.

> ...This government is popular but not simply popular. It does not, however, rely on mystery or myth to check the fundamental popular impulse. "Nondemocratic" "elements" are at work...but they are out in the open. This government is like a glass-enclosed clock. Its "works" are visible to all and must be understood and accepted by all in order to function

---

33. *The Federalist Papers*, op. cit., Number 51, p. 322.
34. Robert A. Goldwin, "Of Men and Angels: A Search for Morality in the Constitution," in *The Moral Foundations of the American Republic*, op. cit., p. 33.
35. Diamond, "Ethics and Politics: The American Way," in *The Moral Foundations of the American Republic*, op. cit., p. 83.

properly... [T]he government... [the Framers] constructed was nevertheless understood by them all to be unusual in the relatively small demands it placed on a political aristocracy and in the relatively great demands it placed on the people.[36]

The Founders' system of constitutional correctives requires public administrators who both appreciate and actively support it. John Rohr, for example, argues that ethical standards "derived" from regime values should apply to bureaucrats because they are sworn to defend the regime. In this context, he turns to the character-forming role of the Supreme Court. He points out that Supreme Court procedures and opinions often "teach" enduring principles, offer insightful interpretations of American values, have direct applicability to administrative actions, and raise questions "that are useful for reflection on fundamental values."[37]

Another constitutional corrective, the extended commercial republic with its multiplicity of interests (which Publius called "a republican remedy for the diseases most incident to republican government"), is seen by Stephen Bailey as a source of administrative obligation.

> A large part of the art of public service is in the capacity to harness private and personal interests to public interest causes. Those who will not traffic in personal and private interests (if such interests are themselves within the law) to the point of engaging their support on behalf of causes in which both public and private interests are served, are, in terms of moral temperament, unfit for public responsibility.[38]

The diffusion of powers among the branches of government established by the Constitution also guides the public administrator. Rohr concludes that upholding the Constitution "... means that public administrators should use their discretionary power in order to maintain the constitutional balance of powers in support of individual liberty."[39] Since public administration often applies the three powers of government, it has been placed in the position of being able to influence events by favoring one branch or another. According to Rohr, this imposes a formidable responsibility: public administrators, as constitutional trustees, "... must learn to think like judges, as well as like legislators and executives, be-

---

36. Herbert J. Storing, "American Statesmanship: Old and New," in *Bureaucrats, Policy Analysts, Statesmen: Who Leads?*, op. cit., pp. 92-93.
37. John A. Rohr, *Ethics for Bureaucrats*, op. cit., especially pp. 59, and 64-74.
38. Stephen K. Bailey, "Ethics and the Public Service," in *Public Administration and Democracy*, Roscoe C. Martin, ed. (Syracuse: Syracuse University Press, 1965), pp. 283-298.
39. John A. Rohr, *To Run A Constitution: The Legitimacy of the Administrative State* (Lawrence: University Press of Kansas, 1986), p. 181.

cause they are all three of these. In a regime of separation of powers, administrators must do the work of statesmen."[40]

The Constitution makes a "politics-administration dichotomy" a literal impossibility. The Weberian bureaucrat who, unlike the politician, finds honor in the energetic and competent carrying-out of a superior's orders (whether or not one agrees with them) does not fit comfortably into the Founding scheme.[41] While Publius emphasized the need for ability as well as virtue on the federal level, he saw it as a means to a political end: building popular support for a new national government that, in certain important respects, would be in perpetual competition with the several states for the loyalties of the people. For Publius, the conduct of a national public administration deserving of public *confidence* was an enterprise essential to the vitality of the regime.[42] This line of reasoning leads to the conclusion that American public administrators are more than Weberian bureaucrats. They are constitutional representatives who find honor through service to the regime and the values it represents. This is far more than "neutral" competence; it is a profoundly political role demanding a "...*devotion* to public duty and an *understanding* of the principles of governmental structure and operation of the broadest and deepest kind."[43]

Public Virtue and Honor in Founding Thought

The Founders sought ways in which the passions of those who govern might be so channeled as to result in publicly virtuous behavior. Federalists such as Madison and Hamilton thought it only prudent to assume that the most reliable of passions would be self-interest and ambition. However, in Forrest McDonald's words, they "...expected something better, for men are driven by a variety of passions, and many of these—love of fame, of glory, of country, for example, are noble. When any such

---

40. *Ibid.*, p. 185. See also Dwight Waldo, *The Administrative State*, 2nd ed. (New York: Holmes and Meier Publishers, 1984), pp. 104-127.
41. Max Weber, *Economy and Society*, G. Roth and C. Wittich, eds. (Berkeley, CA: University of California Press, 1978), p. 1404.
42. John A. Rohr, *To Run A Constitution*, op. cit., pp. 1-11; *The Federalist Papers*, op. cit., Numbers 3, 17, 27, 46, 68; and Laurence J. O'Toole, Jr., "Doctrines and Developments: Separation of Powers, the Politics-Administration Dichotomy, and the Rise of the Administrative State," *Public Administration Review*, vol. 47, (January/February 1987): p. 17-25.
43. Herbert J. Storing, "American Statesmanship: Old and New," in *Bureaucrats, Policy Analysts, Statesmen: Who Leads?* Robert A. Goldwin, ed., op. cit., p. 98 (emphasis added).

passion becomes a man's ruling passion, he must necessarily live his life in virtuous service to the public; and it was such men whom the nationalists counted on to govern others through their baser passions."[44] For the statesmanlike governor, self-interest requires public virtue.[45]

McDonald, citing George Washington's example, suggests that the Federalists subscribed to the idea that "...public persons are and should be governed mainly 'by the law of *honour* or *outward esteem*'...."[46] A desire for the esteem of those of high reputation should be the guiding standard of individuals in public life: "To others be true, seek the esteem of the wise and the virtuous, and it follows that thou cannot then be false to thyself—or to the republic."[47]

John Locke, who was widely read in the American colonies, also emphasized the individual's concern with reputation and its social uses. He argued that the "law of public opinion" was a powerful (indeed socially necessary) element in controlling behavior. He reasoned that the law of public opinion is so effective because people have a strong need to be held in high esteem and greatly fear public shame or disgrace.[48]

This sentiment was subsequently reflected in the influential works of Adam Smith, who assigned priority to the love of "praise-worthiness." His interpretation of the relationship between self-approbation and the approbation of others seems particularly relevant to the situation of the contemporary American public administrator:

> The love and admiration which we naturally conceive for those whose character and conduct we approve of, necessarily dispose us to desire to become ourselves the objects of the like agreeable sentiments....Neither can we be satisfied with being merely admired for what other people are admired. We must at least believe ourselves to be admirable for what they are admirable....Their approbation necessarily confirms our own sense of our own praise-worthiness.[49]

The significance of Woodrow Wilson's previously mentioned reference to the connection between advancing the honor of public servants and

---

44. Forrest McDonald, *Novus Ordo Seclorum*, op. cit., p. 189.
45. *Ibid.*, p. 223.
46. *Ibid.*, p. 198.
47. *Ibid.*, pp. 198-99.
48. Robert H. Horwitz, "John Locke and the Preservation of Liberty: A Perennial Problem of Civic Education," in *The Moral Foundations of the American Republic*, op. cit., p. 146ff.
49. Adam Smith, *The Theory of Moral Sentiments*, (Indianapolis: Liberty Classics, 1976), pp. 208-209. A related discussion of this issue is found in David K. Hart and P. Artell Smith, "Fame, Fame-Worthiness, and the Public Service," *Administration and Society* (August 1988): 131–151.

their service to the community becomes clear if it is understood in the context of the Founders' effort to utilize what they saw to be a basic human concern for reputation and love of praise-worthiness. Their constitutional design is one intended to channel these private passions into those public excellences appropriate to (and needed by) the American regime. However, if this channeling is in fact fundamental to the regime's capacity to produce publicly virtuous or excellent public administrators, how can it be achieved in a regime that is now considerably more democratic than that contemplated by most of the Founders?

With regard to reputation, it has been a long time since civil servants have been held in high esteem by the general citizenry. Recently, public scorn, often fueled by the words and actions of elected officials, has reached the point where some in the community of public administrators have seen the need to publish "polemical" defenses of bureaucracy.[50] Efforts also have been made to provide (or at least to revive) constitutionally-grounded justifications of the "administrative state."[51] Others have been content to warn of an erosion of morale and of competence as government loses (as well as fails to attract) qualified personnel.[52] None of this is unique to the present time. Complaints about tyrannical, incompetent, and self-interested officials date from the colonial period, and the constitutional framework provides no explicit legitimation of bureaucratic power, however real that power may be. In short, in the United States, civil service has never been an easy road to honor and high levels of public approbation.

To whom do contemporary public administrators look for approbation and, hence, whom do they seek to emulate? Clearly, the Founders intended that, within limits, "public opinion" be heard and heeded in a democratic republic. As Storing points out, they saw no need for an administrative aristocracy operating according to its own idea of the public interest and independent of the formative influence of majority public opinion. If they were correct in believing that public virtue is closely connected to reputation and approbation, must it necessarily suffer when those who want to be praised and to see themselves as praiseworthy are not reinforced by public approval?

In "The Study of Administration," Wilson recognized this issue. In the course of his argument for a highly professionalized corps of civil servants having extensive discretion, he asked:

---

50. Charles T. Goodsell, *The Case for Bureaucracy: A Public Administration Polemic* (Chatham, NJ: Chatham House Publishers, 1983).

51. John A. Rohr, *To Run A Constitution*, op. cit.

52. Bruce Adams, "The Frustrations of Government Service," *Public Administration Review*, vol. 44 (January/February 1984): 5.

> To whom is official trustworthiness to be disclosed, and by who is it to be rewarded? Is the official to look to the public for his meed of praise and his push of promotion, or only to his superior in office?....These questions evidently find their root in what is undoubtedly the fundamental problem of this whole study. That problem is: What part shall public opinion take in the conduct of administration?[53]

Wilson's answer placed the public in the role of "superintending" the legislative and executive policy-making processes while leaving the day-to-day public administration in the hands of specially schooled and efficiently organized civil servants. In reply to those who might complain that he was advocating the creation of an "offensive official class," Wilson stated that "...administration in the United States must be at all points sensitive to public opinion" and earn its praise through "hearty allegiance to the policy of the government."[54] Since the American regime rests solidly on the principle of majority rule, Wilson understood that any fundamental solution to the "problem" of public approbation would have to be grounded in that majority's opinion. His solution included a call for civil service reform and professionalism: "If we are to improve public opinion, which is the motive power of government, we must prepare better officials as the *apparatus* of government."[55]

Between 1887 and the present, Wilson's call for merit systems and a technically trained civil service has been in large measure answered affirmatively. However, the anticipated improvement in public opinion has apparently not materialized. Charles Goodsell has colorfully described the current climate in the following terms.

> Bureaucracy...is despised and disparaged. It is attacked in the press, popular magazines, and best sellers....It is assaulted by molders of culture and professors of academia....It is charged with a wide array of crimes...failure to perform; abuse of political power; and repression of employees, clients, and people in general. In short, bureaucracy stands as a splendid hate object.[56]

Under these conditions, the Founding strategy would appear to stand a better chance of success if the range of those to whom public administrators look for approval were severely narrowed. Along these lines, a favored approach in the United States has been to attempt to build a foundation for public virtue through professionalization and codes of ethics

---

53. Woodrow Wilson, "The Study of Administration," in *Public Administration: Politics and the People*, Dean Yarwood, ed., op. cit., p. 26.
54. *Ibid.*, p. 27.
55. *Ibid.*(emphasis added).
56. Charles T. Goodsell, *The Case for Bureaucracy*, op. cit., p. 11.

for public administrators. While the public service is now highly professionalized in the sense that it is staffed by a wide variety of experts, most students of the field believe that *public administration* itself still has not achieved the status of a recognized profession. The desirability of such a profession, of course, has been the subject of lively debate since Wilson's essay.[57] Despite these difficulties, many academics and practitioners have urged that "professional" standards be adopted and applied uniformly for all administrators.[58] In part, the aim is to provide a reference group of professional peers to guide and evaluate behavior. What remains unresolved is the possibility that substantial differences between public opinion and professional norms could arise—even to the point that what Wilson called "an offensive administrative class" could emerge.

Stephen Bailey and Frederick Mosher are perhaps the best known commentators on the tensions between professional standards and democratic norms.[59] Both accept the inevitability of a government dominated by professionals who exert significant influence on public policies. The problem may be that these same individuals see little or no honor in serving democratic norms or constitutional principles. If professional peers are to be the primary points of reference for public administrators, education may be the most effective way of orienting them to these standards.

> For better or worse—or better *and* worse—much of our government is now in the hands of professionals (including scientists). The choice of these professionals, the determination of their skills, and the content of their work are now principally determined, not by general governmental agencies, but by their own professional elites, professional organizations, and the institutions and faculties of higher education.... The need for broadening, for humanizing, and in some fields, for lengthening pro-

---

57. Dwight Waldo, *The Enterprise of Public Administration*, op. cit., pp. 61-62, 77-78.

58. *American Society for Public Administration Code of Ethics and Implementation Guidelines*, Supplement to *P.A. Times* (May 1, 1985); John A. Rohr, "The Study of Ethics in the P.A. Curriculum," *Public Administration Review*, vol. 36 (July/August 1976): 398-406; *Public Duties: The Moral Obligations of Government Officials*, Joel L. Fleishman, Lance Liebman, and Mark H. Moore, eds. (Cambridge, MA: Harvard University Press, 1981); John A. Rohr, *Ethics for Bureaucrats*, op. cit., pp. 50-51; and Ralph Clark Chandler, "The Problem of Moral Reasoning in American Public Administration: The Case for a Code of Ethics," *Public Administration Review*, vol. 43 (January/February 1983): 32-39.

59. Stephen K. Bailey, "Ethics and the Public Service," in *Public Administration: Concepts and Cases*, 3rd ed., Richard J. Stillman II, ed. (Boston: Houghton Mifflin, 1984), pp. 480-489; and Frederick C. Mosher, "The Professional State," in *Public Administration: Politics and the People*, Dean L. Yarwood, ed. (White Plains, NY: Longman, Inc. 1987).

fessional education programs may in the long run prove more crucial to governmental response to societal problems than any amount of civil service reform.[60]

Public Virtue and Education in Founding Thought

The importance of a "proper" education for those who would govern in the American regime was a central concern of the Founders. In addition to expressing their belief that the small republic was itself a school of citizenship, a number of the Anti-Federalists proposed the establishment of schools or seminaries where youth could be educated in the habits of public virtue. Citizens, they argued, should be broadly educated in morality and the useful arts and sciences. Such education would form virtuous citizens who "...instead of abusing, would wade up to their knees in blood, to defend their governments."[61]

The Federalists were no less interested in the education of the regime's future leaders. Several among them, including Madison and Washington, proposed the establishment of a national university for this purpose. They hoped to foster the habits of public virtue through a combination of public and private sources of education. At least indirectly, certain aspects of John Locke's commentaries on education are reflected in the Federalists' thinking. Locke, who wrote extensively on the subject of education, stressed the character-forming functions of the family and urged the class of "gentlemen" to use certain methods to instill public virtues during the childhood years.

While civil law and religion have roles to play in morality, Locke thought that the socially derived standards of public opinion more powerfully affected individual conduct, including one's choice of occupations. Therefore, he stressed the need to "educate" children in the standards or opinions of the community. This early socialization teaches not only standards but also the idea of rewards or penalties associated with actions that uphold or violate them. In Locke's scheme, a successful education of this sort would control even those who might otherwise casually break religious and civil law in the pursuit of self-interest:[62]

---

60. Frederick C. Mosher, "The Professional State," ibid, p. 198.
61. Herbert J. Storing quoting Maryland Farmer VI, 5.I.82, in *What the Anti-Federalists Were For*, op. cit., p. 21.
62. Robert H. Horwitz, "John Locke and the Preservation of Liberty," in his *Moral Foundations*, op. cit., p. 148ff. See also *The Educational Writings of John Locke*, James L. Axtell, ed. (Cambridge: Cambridge University Press, 1968); and John Locke, *Some*

[I]t follows that governments, even though they are legitimately constituted by Lockian standards, will be ineffective unless they rest on a foundation of sound opinion. That in turn can be accomplished only if the content of public opinion is established through the proper education of those citizens on whom the proper functioning of the commonwealth depends.[63]

Locke's argument relies on the assumption that people are by nature acquisitive, ambitious, and self-interested. The task of a proper education, therefore, is not to change human nature, but to help channel it in socially beneficial directions.[64] Accordingly, education should be a process devoted to demonstrating the connections between public virtues and personal rewards. The pursuit of self-interest *properly understood* is a hallmark of Locke's well-educated gentleman.[65] Not surprisingly, the Federalists shared Locke's goals for the education of the citizenry:

[T]he major thrust of their activities would be toward the acquisition of property, whether through the careful management of land or through trade, commerce, or such professions as law, medicine, or the like.... They would be "men of business," in the broad seventeenth-century meaning of that term.[66]

Thomas Jefferson's influence on public administration thought has also received considerable attention, particularly in the "new public administration" literature.[67] His ideas regarding education are particularly significant in part because they are based on a treatment of self-interest that is somewhat at odds with that of Locke and the Federalists. In his *Notes on the State of Virginia*, Jefferson considers his law establishing an

---

Thoughts Concerning Education (Woodbury, NY: Barron's Educational Series, Inc., 1964).

63. Robert H. Horwitz, "John Locke and the Preservation of Liberty," *Ibid.*, pp. 148–149.

64. *Ibid.*

65. Locke's approach to the connections between self-interest and public virtue also found expression in Alexis De Tocqueville's concept of self-interest properly understood: "...that by serving his fellows man serves himself in that doing good is to his private advantage.... [I]f it does not lead the will directly to virtue, it establishes habits which unconsciously turn it that way." Alexis De Tocqueville, *Democracy in America*, J. P. Mayer, ed. (Garden City, NY: Anchor Books, 1969), pp. 525 and 527.

66. Horwitz, "John Locke and the Preservation of Liberty," op. cit., p. 163.

67. H. George Frederickson and David K. Hart, "The Public Service and the Patriotism of Benevolence," *Public Administration Review*, vol. 45, (September/October 1985); H. George Frederickson, *New Public Administration* (University, AL: University of Alabama Press, 1980); and Richard J. Stillman II, "The Changing Patterns of Public Administration Theory in America," in *Public Administration: Concepts and Cases*, 3rd ed., Richard J. Stillman, ed. (Boston, MA: Houghton-Mifflin, 1984), pp. 5-24.

educational system in the state to be one his most important contributions because of the "need" for a public education that would prepare the people to defend their liberty against those who would seek to establish a new form of monarchy.[68] As a defense against ambitious despots, the government should provide for the basic education of the people.[69]

Contending that "...people will be happiest whose laws are best, and are best administered, and that laws will be wisely formed, and honestly administered, in proportion as those who form and administer them are wise and honest...," Jefferson set forth a plan to discover those "fitly formed" children "whom nature had endowed with genius and virtue."[70] After a selection process which grew progressively more rigorous as the students advanced in their studies, those few students possessing the most superior "parts and disposition" were to be sent on for three years of studying science at William and Mary College. It was these college students who were to serve the state.[71]

---

68. David Tucker, "The Political Thought of Thomas Jefferson's *Notes on the State of Virginia*," in *The American Founding: Politics, Statesmanship, and the Constitution*, Ralph A. Rossum and Gary L. McDowell, eds. (Port Washington, NY: Kennikat Press, 1981), p. 116.

69. Lynton K. Caldwell, *The Administrative Theories of Hamilton and Jefferson: Their Contribution to Thought on Public Administration* (Chicago: University of Chicago Press, 1944), p. 110.

70. "Bill 79 of 1779 for the 'More General Diffusion of Knowledge,'" in *Thomas Jefferson and the Development of American Public Education*, James B. Conant, ed. (Berkeley, CA: University of California Press, 1962), pp. 88-93.

Some contemporary commentators have also discussed the role of public administration in terms reminiscent of Jefferson. For example, H. George Frederickson and David K. Hart set forth a distinctly Jeffersonian point of view in their discussion of the moral obligations of American public administrators: We "define the primary moral obligation of the public service in this nation as the patriotism of benevolence...[T]he primary duty of public servants is to be the *guardians* and *guarantors* of the regime values for the American public." H. George Frederickson and David K. Hart, "The Public Service and the Patriotism of Benevolence," *Public Administration Review*, vol. 45 (September/October 1985): 549 and 551 (emphasis added). A related discussion of the role of public administration is found in Charles J. Fox and Clarke E. Cochran, "Discretion Advocacy in Public Administration: Toward a Platonic Guarding Class?" *Administration and Society* (August 1990): 249-271.

71. Thomas Jefferson, *Notes on the State of Virginia*, William Peden, ed. (New York: W.W. Norton & Co., 1972), pp.146-149.

For an argument that the *Notes* represent an Aristotelian-like detailing of the proper requisites for the new regime, see William D. Richardson, "Thomas Jefferson and Race: The Declaration and *Notes on the State of Virginia*," *Polity*, vol. 16 (Spring 1984): 447-466.

Thus, like constitutional correctives and honor, education was an important part of the Founders' thinking with regard to the goal of assuring that the American regime would be served by publicly virtuous governors. One hundred years later, Wilson made the connection between education and virtue in public administration a key element of his essay. Of course, he *did not* believe that "universal political education" would in itself create competent public administrators. In 1887, conducting government required technical training as well: "It will be necessary to organize democracy by sending up to the competitive examinations for the civil service men definitely prepared for standing liberal tests as to technical knowledge. A technically schooled civil service will presently become indispensable."[72] Dwight Waldo observes that Wilson "...saw everything through a political lens...and was highly motivated to make the republican-democratic [experiment] succeed."[73] Wilson's lecture notes reveal that he had no intention of restricting public administration education to purely instrumental or technical matters. Constitutional principles, history, comparative government, practical politics, public law, *and* management were essential to a proper curriculum.[74] It is against this background that Wilson made the following statement:

> The ideal for us is a civil service cultured and self-sufficient enough to act with sense and vigor, and yet so intimately connected with the popular thought, by means of elections and constant public counsel, as to find arbitrariness or class spirit quite out of the question.[75]

Conclusion

We suspect that the Founders would not have disapproved of the post-Wilson preoccupation with public administration as an instrumental field. But they likely would have considered it to be incomplete because it neglected the development of desirable public virtues. The contemporary interest in ethics for public administrators in reality is consistent with the Founders' view that, left to itself, the citizenry (of whom public administrators are a part) would act in a self-interested manner. The problem, however, is that the regime requires public administrators who can be reliably expected to act in the public's behalf.

---

72. Woodrow Wilson, "The Study of Administration," in Yarwood, op. cit., p. 27.
73. Dwight Waldo, "The Perdurability of the Politics - Administration Dichotomy: Woodrow Wilson and the Identity Crisis in Public Administration," op. cit., p. 225.
74. *Ibid.*, pp. 230-231.
75. Woodrow Wilson, in Yarwood, op. cit., p.27.

The Founders understood that the new nation required "certain enduring excellences." While there is no reason to believe that the Founders anticipated the size, scope, and complexity of today's administrative state, they did anticipate that the quality of public administration under the Constitution would play a major role in determining the success of their experiment in republican-democratic government. "Nurturing the appropriate excellences," therefore, is a challenge of particular importance to American public administration.

Our reading to Founding intentions reveals a heavy reliance on the *interaction* of constitutional correctives, honor, and education to produce virtuous public officials who would serve the regime "with the best efforts of [their] talents and the soberest service of [their] conscience." Seen in this light, Woodrow Wilson's oft-quoted assertion that "It is getting harder to *run* a constitution than to frame one" becomes far more than a call for rational organization and efficiency—it is also a reaffirmation of the Founders' belief that the promise of the American regime could be fulfilled only if those who govern are committed to preserving and strengthening the foundations upon which it rests.

Public administrators should understand the importance and function of the constitutional correctives discussed above. As Wilson understood, this clearly means that their education must encompass far more than a simple description of the Constitution. The public administrator is well-served by a thorough grounding in American political thought and constitutional history and law.[76] Public administration is an imprecisely defined field, open to many prescriptions regarding the preparation of its practitioners; however, in the American setting, we can see no definition that could sensibly exclude these topics and an examination of their applications to the administrative enterprise.

The study of the Constitution and the ideas that underpin it should, hopefully, provide a major element of public administrators' understanding of the duties and obligations that flow from a commitment to the regime. However, as Wilson wrote, particular attention must be paid to the problem of how best to integrate the *self-interest* of the public administrator with service to the community or public interest. (With the possible exception of Jefferson, the Founders had little confidence in *noblesse oblige* as the moral foundation of the Republic.)

---

76. On these and related topics, see Dwight Waldo, *The Administrative State*, 2nd ed., op. cit., pp. ix-lxiv; Dwight Waldo, *The Enterprise of Public Administration*, op. cit., pp. 49-64; H. George Frederickson, *New Public Administration*, op. cit., pp. 93-111; and Phillip J. Cooper, "The Wilsonian Dichotomy in Administrative Law," in *Politics and Administration: Woodrow Wilson and American Public Administration*, Rabin and Bowman, eds., op. cit., pp. 79-94.

As we have pointed out, concern for reputation—the desire for approbation or honor—is fundamental to the Founders' design. For those who govern, to be well-educated meant a proper orientation to the "law of public opinion" or to the standards and judgments of those we are taught to admire. In contemporary terminology, public virtue is the result of orienting oneself to a reference group which values service to the regime, community, and others. On the one hand, it is to this group that the individual looks for guidance and approbation. On the other, it is their disapproval that is most feared and, therefore, to be avoided.

> Is it then unethical somehow to want to be honored by the public, to seek the esteem of one's peers? Clearly not. But...the relevant distinction is between doing right, helping people who need help, preserving democratic government, achieving some measure of excellence, on the one hand, and being honored for its own sake, on the other. In the end, then, the desire for honor, which is inherently selfish, can be redeemed only by seeking to satisfy it through service to others.[77]

The greatest irony of public administration since Wilson's essay may lie in the success of policies and practices designed to avoid the creation of anything resembling an American "administrative class." In combination with the emphasis on technical expertise or public management, the lack of any identifiable community of public administrators may have seriously eroded the foundations upon which the Founders relied to assure that the regime would be served by publicly virtuous administrators capable of being effectively superintended by public opinion. At the very least, this is a matter that should be of considerable concern to those who care about the proper governance of the American regime.

---

77. Joel L. Fleishman, "Self-Interest and Political Integrity," in *Public Duties: The Moral Obligations of Government Officials*, Fleishman, Liebman, and Moore, eds., op. cit., pp. 70-71.

Chapter Five

The Tension Between Law and Ethics[1]

William D. Richardson

Introduction

"The rule of law" is such an oft-used phrase nowadays that it no longer inspires the awe that is quite properly its due. In the world's oldest democratic republic, perhaps Americans should not even pretend to be surprised at this. After all, a regime founded on a base but "new science of politics" comes into being with an inherent suspicion about ancient ways and ideas.[2] Nevertheless, it takes little observation of the contemporary world since 1989 to realize that our recent political kin, those many fragile new democracies and republics on every continent, are struggling so mightily precisely because one of their key deficiencies is any kind of tradition in which law (rather than men or force) truly rules. Lacking that particular tradition, it is hardly surprising that the complementary one of "law-abidingness" is similarly absent among those who not so very long ago were subjects rather than citizens.

It is law that establishes the foundation that permits a culture to flourish. This is especially the case with democratic republics in which the citizens are intended to play a role in affairs of the regime. The character of these citizens is, in turn, largely a cultural product resulting from the interaction of a complex array of forces, including family, education, religion, and the leadership of public servants. Because a large portion of public servants must of necessity exercise varying degrees of discretion in the course of implementing the laws of the regime, the goodness of those laws is in many

---

1. A slightly different version of this chapter originally appeared as "Law versus Ethics," in Phillip J. Cooper and Chester I. Newland, eds., *Handbook of Public Law and Public Administration* (San Francisco, CA: Jossey-Bass, 1997), pp. 361–375. Reprinted by permission.

2. Alexander Hamilton, James Madison, and John Jay, *The Federalist Papers*. Edited by Clinton Rossiter (New York: New American Library, 1961).

crucial ways dependent on the goodness of those who are applying them. It is this linkage between law and ethics that is the focus of this chapter.

Legitimacy: Who Says?

Before law can become the awe-inspiring "rule of law" that is accepted and obeyed by members of a regime, it must first be promulgated. And before that can occur, lawmakers must be prepared to give a definitive answer to a rather irreverent but most fundamental question: "Who says?" That is, why should I or anyone else voluntary defer to the laws? The answer to this question is politically all important and, not surprisingly, varies both over time and from regime to regime. Among other important consequences, the source of one's power over another determines whether a lawgiver is a legitimate or illegitimate ruler (or just a wielder of power).

Historically, one of the most obvious sources of such power has been force: obey because the ruler is clearly more powerful than the ruled and their lives hang in the balance.[3] But once having conquered, the ruler generally discovers that the extent of acquiescence is directly proportional to the visibility of the threat of force. Fear may be a powerful motivator, but it needs to be continually nourished.

If the ruler is extraordinarily successful at maintaining the force that is the foundation of such rule, rather soon he or she may find that advancing age dictates a search for a successor. Historically, the search has often gone no farther than the ruler's eldest son, who assumes the mantle of ruler by virtue of heredity. If he, in turn, is similarly adept at ruling by the sword, there may well come a time when the originally illegitimate rule by force comes to be seen as a legitimate hereditary power passed down from generation to generation. From a regime's standpoint, a major advantage of such hereditary rule may lie in its peaceful transfer of power from father to son or daughter. The ranks of the claimants here are few and, because of blood ties, indisputable.

At times it has helped to cement a claim to rule by assuming a level of unchallengeable superiority. For mere human beings, what could be better than claiming that the entitlement to rule rests on Divine Right, that is, on the fact that God has determined who shall rule? Indeed, such claims have an ancient lineage at least partly because the very nature of the assertion is so difficult to deny. Despite the fundamental difficulties of establishing its bonafides, up until just three hundred years ago Divine Right was the ultimate source of almost every monarchial claim to rule.

---

3. Locke, John, *Two Trestises of Government*. (New York: Hafner Press, 1947).

Indeed, as the theocratic regime established by Ayatollah Khomeini and his successors attests, its allure sometimes seems irresistible even today.

While there are other credible but less persuasive ways of securing the voluntary deference of others (such as the demonstrated superiority of virtue possessed by a Mother Teresa), the longevity and prominence of the American regime in the world has certainly helped to ensure the supremacy of today's democratic alternative: the selection of rulers by majoritarian elections. From rule by the strongest sword, the nearest in blood, and the closest to God, contemporary claims of legitimacy have come to be grounded on the approval of the greatest number. Hence, now all but the most entrenched of tyrants eventually find it prudent from an international if not domestic standpoint to hold elections in order to demonstrate their standing with the ruled. These elections do not necessarily have to be competitive or even "fair"; in the basest sense of the word, it is the *process* that is important.

Who Rules and For What Ends

As the dominant means of conferring legitimacy, elections reflect the late twentieth century triumph of one kind of regime: democracy. While it is possible to maintain a non-democratic regime while submitting to the democratic process of elections—Iran being an obvious case in point—the very fact that rulers feel compelled to utilize them represents a powerful concession to democracy's potent allure. Having conceded that their legitimacy is dependent upon at least the appearance of democratic means, such regimes are probably not good candidates for resisting the other democratic pressures that may be brought to bear against them over the long term. However, in very fundamental ways, both the rulers and the elections by which they are chosen are still mere *means*. In other words, the majority's selection of certain rulers reflects a perception that those individuals will better pursue certain *ends*. The triumph of the democratic regime, though, is unquestionably one of ends, for, unlike other regimes, it properly pursues the greatest good of the greatest number. While the greatest good of *the whole* is the grandest of ideals—and is the fullest meaning of the "common good"—the lesser mark of the greatest good of the greatest number seems to be the best of which human beings are really capable.

Within such a regime, the electorate is rather continually challenged to select as a ruler one of several potential contenders who hold forth with different ideas or policies for achieving the desired end. Under different conditions, these claimants might have used the very basis of their claim—virtue, wisdom, etc.—as a source of legitimacy. The triumph of majoritarian elections, however, currently reduces them to mere contenders for the electorate's favor. One such claim is made by the Wise, whose justification for being given political power rests on the quite undemocratic principle of inequality—in this case, their possession of superior or expert knowledge that sets them apart from ordinary citizens. Well ingrained within the American regime, this claim, of course, also became a fundamental defense for the powers wielded by non-elected administrators. Indeed, the claims of "meritocracy" were rather proudly stressed by large numbers of public administrators from the time of the debates over the Pendleton Act on through to the era of the "Best and the Brightest" in FDR's New Deal and JFK's Camelot. From one perspective, though, the somewhat hubristic appropriation of the name of the grandest of aristocracies was probably not the wisest of tactics in the grandest of democracies.

Competing and somewhat intertwined claims to rule on behalf of the electorate are also advanced in democratic regimes by the wealthy. Having amassed a great deal of a scarce good that is widely admired within the contemporary regime, the wealthy reasonably contend that they alone best know how to improve everyone's earthly lot. That such claims resonate with the electorate as readily today as they did at the time of the Founding seems obvious in an era when Ross Perot and Steve Forbes have been able to generate impressive followings by, among other things, spending copious quantities of their own money.

Additional claims are advanced by still others, such as military heroes; the poor who, relatively speaking, comprise the largest portion of the regime; and even advocates of various virtues who propose to save either secular lives or immortal souls. It becomes readily apparent how easily a democratic regime can be wafted about by one or another of the competing claimants. With their intimate understanding of the peril that such claimants can pose to the long-term health of a democratic regime, prudent Founders promote the claim of one additional potential ruler over all others, namely, that of the law.

Law and Ethics

In a very fundamental way, democracies are among the best suited of regimes to the rule of law and, paradoxically, least able to do without it. In such regimes, the rule of law is chosen as much for what it does as for what it prevents. First, a law by definition is universal rather than particular, that is, it is designed to encompass as many members of the regime as possible. Ideally, a law should exclude no one, applying as readily to the behavior of the *lawmakers* as it does to the *lawabiders*. Second, a law, by definition, embodies an understanding of the principles undergirding the regime and should advance them.[4] Thus, since a democracy has as one of its most important principles the general preference of equality over inequality (especially in public matters), democratic laws cannot stray too far from that principle without coming into conflict with it. Third, a properly crafted law helps to assure uniformity of treatment across time, connecting the previous generations to the present and future. This, in turn, serves as an obvious restraint on what can be done in the present. Fourth, and perhaps most important, a law fulfilling the previous three requirements serves as a substitute for the rule of men. While it is possible that a ruler could be chosen who is just, temperate, courageous and wise, such an individual would rule for only a relatively short time. With such individuals, perhaps no laws are needed, for their word could be the law and it would be just. But what about after their rule? History teaches that such rulers are extraordinarily rare. Indeed, the ruler whose word is constrained by no higher law historically has proven to be a source of the greatest tyranny. Among the advantages of living in the twentieth century is that one does not have to cast about very much in search of illustrative cases. Stalin, Hitler, Mao, Castro, Idi Amin, and Saddam Hussein come readily to the fore as examples of totalitarians unconstrained by the existing laws of their regimes.

While law has all of these powerful reasons to recommend it, there are some troubling deficiencies in its actual rule. Perhaps the greatest of these arises from that all-encompassing universality that makes it such a powerful constraint on both the ruled *and the rulers*. The greater the number and variety of citizens that a law is intended to encompass, the more general it must be in its language. (Ponder for a moment the succinctness of that great Divine Law, "Thou shalt not steal!") Conversely, the smaller the number and the greater the similarity of the citizens who are intended to be affected, the more specific and particular a law can be. Such precision matters not only because it limits the interference with liberty by making clear just what the ruler seeks to prohibit and then leaves other behavior unrestrained. Clarity also allows adequate notice so that those affected can bring themselves into compliance. Indeed, America's Founders were so concerned about this aspect of law that they devised a constitutional prohibition against bills of attainder, which are aimed at only one person.

The problem, however, is that human behavior, far from being universal, is wondrously and even maddeningly particular. The universal law

---

4. Rohr, John, *To Run a Constitution: The Legitimacy of the Administrative State.* (Lawrence: University Press of Kansas, 1986), and "Bureaucratic Morality in the United States." *International Political Science Review* 1988: 167-178.

cannot possibly provide in its black letter text for every imaginable variant of human conduct that conceivably would come within its purview. For this reason, laws are intended to be interpreted by the law-abiding citizen, the law-enforcer, and especially the judge who attempts to determine if this particular behavior was contemplated by this particular law. At every stage, numerous opportunities arise for a seemingly universal law to be applied differently according to the particularities of the circumstances. Accordingly, the rule of law focuses chiefly on processes that are essential to justice rather than on fixed substance.

It is at this point that the importance of the *character or "ethos"* of the individuals applying the law becomes obvious. Because the application of the law to a particular case requires disciplined *discretion*, opportunities exist for even a well-crafted law to be judiciously or injudiciously enforced. Thus, the child welfare caseworker who personally shepherds a heartrending case out of the queue and expedites it is exercising discretion. There has even been a backlash against officials for failing to use discretion in such situations.[5] Similarly, the regulatory agency that decides not to launch an investigation and enforcement action is exercising discretion.[6] However impractical the expectation, an ideal persists about who should be wielding these unavoidable discretionary powers, namely, individuals whose character is at least faintly reminiscent of the just, temperate, prudent, and wise philosopher-king. It is this mix of universal law, particular applications, discretionary power, and the quest for exemplary characters to exercise those powers that has brought the regime to its contemporary emphasis on ethics.

The Higher Law of the Constitution

As well read, even classically educated individuals, the Founders of the American regime understood that one of the greatest causes of earthly unhappiness had been the persistent attempts to create good human beings by formally linking the political entities of this world with the precepts of one or another of the world's religions.[7] The succession of political failures that resulted convinced the Founders that there was one indispensable foundation for their contemplated democratic republic: take human beings as they *really are*, not as one might wish them to *become*. This meant preparing a regime that was institutionally and con-

---

5. See *DeShaney v. Winnebago Department of Social Services*, 489 U.S. 189 (1989).
6. See *Heckler v. Chaney*, 470 U.S. 821 (1985).
7. Locke, op. c.t. and Jefferson, Thomas, *Notes on the State of Virginia*. Edited by William Peeler (New York: W.W. Norton and Company, 1972).

stitutionally able to endure in the face of the baser aspects of human behavior.

To accomplish this feat, the Founders made the *channeling* of the baser elements of human nature one of the bedrock foundations of the new regime. Since self-interested behavior was an inevitable ingredient in the motivation of most people most of the time, they decided to *encourage* it! They fostered a commercial regime that would multiply the opportunities for such behavior (by vastly increasing the "kinds and degrees" of property that is the focus of citizen self-interest) so that the self-interest of one political faction would serve to check that of another.[8] Then, in direct opposition to those Anti-Federalists who wanted to nurture character in the then traditional democratic way (by utilizing "shame" to habituate appropriate conduct in relatively small, homogeneous, self-sufficient farming communities), the Founders encouraged the dispersion of these self-interested citizens throughout a large land area.[9] By so doing, they hoped to retard their ability not only to come together in any one place, but even to identify easily those who had similar interests. Finally, the channeling devices of a large land area and a commercial regime were married to a particular kind of democracy: a republic which would *re*-present the self-interested views of the citizenry through the filtered medium of elected officials. These same officials were, in turn, subdivided *horizontally* into three separate branches and *vertically* into three levels of distinct governments. The incorporation of these and other channeling mechanisms into the Constitution of 1787 provided the new regime with its highest secular law, one which was intended to guide and govern the establishment of all future laws.

The multiplicity of governments, branches and offices created or ultimately required by this new Constitution was animated by a number of additional principles. First, there was the presupposition that the protection of individual liberties was far more important than efficiency in operations. Indeed, the new Constitution was calculated to ensure inefficiencies precisely because these would help impede the potential abuses of political power by the rulers. At the very same time, it provided more opportunities for the citizenry actually to learn about their liberties by vigilantly having to protect them. Second, while the Founders did not premise the proper operation of the new regime on the continual presence of virtuous rulers, they did have reason to expect that the multiple government offices would encourage the isolation and checking of overly ambitious rulers. Indeed, it was even hoped that these diverse offices

---

8. Hamilton, op. cit.
9. Hamilton, op. cit., Jefferson op. cit.

would help nurture the appropriate skills and habits in each succeeding generation's crop of new office holders. Some influential members of that era even contemplated a careful culling of the young in hopes of identifying those deemed most fit by character, temperament, and education for potential rule.[10]

The Preparation of Democratic Citizens

The constitutional plan of the late eighteenth century thus envisioned a regime of numerous divided governments which were balanced and checked both internally and externally. The citizens, in turn, were to be divided in numerous informal and formal ways in the expectation that they would more often than not effectively check themselves before one faction could come to wield too much political power. Accordingly, it was realistic for the Founders to expect that the great bane of democracies, a tyrannical faction wielding dominant political power, would be reduced to the status of a minor threat.[11] Divided by self-interest, it was likely that the only proposals that could bridge the self-interests and unite a substantial number of the individualistic citizens would be temperate ones. Obviously, there would always be a small number of broad, common interests—war against outsiders, increases or decreases in national taxes, limitations on new immigration—that could still serve to unite the divided citizenry into dominant factions. Absent these issues, though, the likelihood was that rulers seeking majoritarian approval would have to make moderate, centrist proposals.

This encouragement of centrist proposals from the rulers had its counterpart among the citizens as well. The channeling of self-interested behavior was intended to nurture a concern for one's private affairs. This preoccupation worked best if one was not distracted by passionate attention to the affairs, political views, or religious beliefs of one's fellow-citizens. In other words, a certain *tolerance* went a long way toward facilitating domestic harmony. Indeed, it is sometimes useful to recall that tolerance was not readily present at the Founding or summoned forth at the stroke of a pen on parchment. The Constitution's expectations regarding this political virtue required many precursor events, including the proliferation of religious sects to dampen the historical source of factional strife from that quarter and the culling out of ambitious demagogues—the traditional de-

---

10. See Jefferson, *Ibid.*, and Pangle, Lorraine, and Thomas Pangle, *The Learning of Liberty: The Educational Ideas of the American Founders.* (Lawrence: University Press of Kansas, 1993).

11. Hamilton, op. cit.

stroyers of republics—through, among other things, the multiple governments.[12] Only when one's private interests were threatened—as when there was a proposed widening of the road in front of one's home—or an unusual common interest was formed—wars and taxes—was the ordinary citizen most likely to become politically aroused.

However, because the Constitution established a regime with so many different offices, office holders, and overlapping or even conflicting powers, it also succeeded in creating one of the world's greatest incubators of democratic citizenship. From one perspective, the opportunities to hone the skills necessary for effective self-governance have increased in some ways during the past two hundred plus years. This development would undoubtedly please Tocqueville, who thought that an increase in the number of those wielding political power—especially at the local level—would multiply the opportunities for citizens to have disputes over the implementation of laws and regulations. These disputes, in turn, would force the citizens to be concerned with something other than their own private self-interests.[13] A glance at the regime's current 86,743 political jurisdictions—which, interestingly, are actually little more than half the number of jurisdictions in existence fifty years ago—reveals 511,034 elective offices.[14] Even under the influence of "reinventing government,"[15] total civilian employment in the public sector has crept past 18,745,000.[16] Together, these elected and appointed public servants officially wield all of the political power permitted under the Constitution. In the process of so doing, they inevitably provide innumerable opportunities for citizens to learn the critical requisites of self-governance.

Indeed, because of the generally agitated and reactive state of American political affairs, observers such as Tocqueville long understood that a fair number of the laws and regulations promulgated each year would be "retrievable mistakes," that is, flawed instruments which, after having been critiqued by those adversely affected by unintended consequences, could be corrected or withdrawn. For instance, the legislation issuing from the various state legislatures pertaining to intrastate speed limits certainly has all the earmarks of this Tocquevillian phenomenon. The laws are likely to be experiments in which the proper resolution of two

---

12. *Ibid.*
13. Tocqueville, op. cit.
14. U.S. Department of Commerce, *Statistical Abstract of the United States: 1995* (Washington, D.C.: U.S. Government Printing Office, 1995).
15. Osborne, David and Ted Gaebler. *Reinventing Government: How the Entrepreneurial Spirit is Transforming the Public Sector From the Schoolhouse to the Statehouse, City Hall to the Pentagon.* (New York: Addison-Wesley Publishing Company, 1992).
16. U.S. Department of Commerce, op. cit.

conflicting principles—the efficiency of swift transportation and the safety of those being transported—is subjected to empirical tests.

In the American design, the self-interested citizen of the regime is expected to be relatively isolated from his or her fellow-citizens. In order to be effective in challenging the substance or application of a law or regulation, though, this same citizen must engage in some of the very behavior that the regime structurally discouraged because of the potential political dangers it could pose. Thus, the citizen who is politically aroused for the first time may not only have to master the intricacies of making his or her views known throughout the elected and administrative hierarchies, but may also have to learn how to mobilize like-minded fellow-citizens. These are not easy skills to master but, once possessed, they paradoxically make for a more vigilant, public minded citizen (who may well come to serve as another in a myriad number of regime checks on potential abusers of political power).

The Importance of Character in Public Administration

If the Tocquevillian prescription for inculcating the skills of democratic citizenship continues to be of fundamental importance for the political health of the regime, some of the reforms of the past few years may be beneficial. At a minimum, the impetus to reinvent, redirect, or otherwise devolve power from the national government to the states and localities seems likely to increase the opportunities for citizens to become more acquainted with affairs of the public world.

In the face of contemporary reactions against large government programs and the agencies that implement them, public servants may find their exercise of discretion to be (once again) a subject of debate. Now, thoughtful administrators have long realized that an exceedingly troubling paradox is attached to discretion. On the one hand, the inherent universalism of laws required someone to have and wield discretion in order to make the transition to the particularities of the ordinary citizen's behavior. On the other hand, though, the mere possession of discretion—and its clear potential for abuse—in a regime recognizing elections as the primary source of political power all but invited the asking of that irreverent question: "Who says?" Since giving that early (and decidedly self-serving) answer of a "politics/administration dichotomy" that "innunized" them against the republican disease of self-interest, public administrators have struggled to present a more candid response that would be convincing to the democratic citizenry. Given the nature of their responsibilities in this regime, perhaps it was inevitable that most of their major answers would involve claims of some form of superiority. While occasionally a bit muted, this has even been the response when the subject of "ethics" became the focus of citizen concerns.[17] In all fairness, the ethics is at the very heart of questions about the exercise of administrative discretion, for here the "Who says?" question thinly veils a related query: "Why should they be trusted?"

External Restraints

Even a casual observer of the contemporary American regime is aware that professional associations and governments at all levels have been busily devising "codes of ethics" intended to guide their respective members in the use of their discretionary powers. Prominently featured in professional journals, printed in employee manuals and even emblazoned in artful script in public lobbies, these codes typically have ranged from the "Thou Shalt Not" variety to almost inspirational exhortations about the primary importance of the citizen. This flurry of activity, however, tends to overshadow the realization that governments have long been indirectly involved in superintending ethical conduct, especially on state and local levels where officials are tasked with the issuance of licenses to certain practitioners. Professional associations, such as the International City/County Management Association (ICMA), have also exercised a more direct supervision through the establishment of rules of conduct for public employees.

Indeed, it is this last area that has seen some of the more prominent reforms. These reforms have consistently focused on the area with the most visible potential for abuse: financial conflicts of interest. On the national level, one of the most visible reforms has been the establishment of the U.S. Office of Government Ethics (OGE), which arose from the 1978 *Ethics in Government Act*. Severed from OPM in 1989 and made an independent agency, OGE today issues *Standards of Ethical Conduct for Employees of the Executive Branch*, an eighty-five page manual intended to guide the conduct of the nearly three million executive branch employees. While a substantial portion of this manual is understandably concerned with financial impropriety, the OGE also has assumed broader responsibilities, such as that of coordinating and facilitating ethics education within the executive branch.[18] Similarly, state ethics enforcement offices and commissions often assume similar responsibilities.

---

17. Frederickson, H. George and David K. Hart, "The Public Service and the Patriotism of Benevolence," *Public Administration Review* 45 (1985): 547-553.

18. U.S. Office of Government Ethics, 1994. *Third Biennial Report to Congress*. (Washington D.C.: U.S. Government Printing Office, 1994), pp. 15, 36.

As devices for moderating and guiding the use of discretion, codes of ethics seldom do harm. They may even do a bit of good. A public organization, after all, is composed of numerous people, some of whom may well be exceptionally wise, virtuous, and temperate, and some others who may be otherwise. The extent to which the best succeed in setting the tone for the whole unit is largely dependent on the quality of the organization's leadership. For example, if the leaders are unstintingly observant of the law as well as scrupulously attentive to both fiscal austerity and their responsibilities to the citizenry and their elected representatives, this attitude insinuates itself throughout the organization. Under the best of circumstances, such leadership can inspire an emulation that leavens the whole unit. It can also serve as a standard that makes quite clear what is considered shameful and unacceptable behavior. Conversely, if the leaders become known as skirters of the law or fiscal profligates, those within the organization who are disposed to ignore ethical standards might well conclude that they now have an informal license to do so.

Internal Restraints

Despite the Founders' expectation that practical self-interested behavior would dominate, America has long had an admiration for an education steeped in the liberal arts. As some commentators well recognized, one of the explanations for this view derived from an ancient association of wisdom with virtue.[19] Whether it was the result of a natural culling in which only those with an innate predisposition for learning went on to acquire it, or a salutary effect produced by the slow accumulation of a certain kind of knowledge, both experience and political theory suggested that merit exists in a proper education. Aristotle is undoubtedly the most renowned proponent of producing the appropriate kinds of moral and intellectual virtues in both the citizenry and their rulers by means of careful habituation.[20] In other words, the preponderance of character is culturally derived. To greatly simplify, the expectation was that an individual with a proper nature might actually come to "possess" the desired virtues if a diligent regimen of praise and blame constantly served to reinforce their acquisition. For the admiring democrat, however, there was a major difficulty: this system of praise and blame had little tolerance for a democracy's distinctions between public and private

---

19. Pangle, op. cit.; Richardson, William D., *Democracy, Bureaucracy and Character: Founding Thought*. (Lawrence: University Press of Kansas, 1997).

20. Aristotle, *Nicomachean Ethics* Trans. H. Rackham. (Cambridge: Harvard University Press, 1975).

lives (much less for its attachment to material well-being). An Aristotelian approach might well inculcate the desired virtues, but at such a cost to liberties and rights that it might be ill-suited to a democratic regime.

The allure of such culturally-induced character formation was not easily relinquished, though. Influential thinkers such as Jefferson, Franklin and Washington long entertained ideas about making a special place within the regime for a "sort of aristocracy" whose members would be educated from the earliest of ages for the rigors of rule.[21] This education would focus on the acquisition of knowledge appropriate to future republican rulers (such as law, history, engineering, and the works of John Locke). Not surprisingly, it was quite consistently linked with the establishment of a special academy.

For good or for ill, the establishment of such an academy has never come to pass. In one of its most idealized forms, this academy was intended to emulate the military service academies in prestige and purpose. In more recent times, one of the main inspirations for this has been the aristocratic French National Academy of Public Administration. Such an aristocratic model has little chance of being implanted within this mature democratic republic. However, the goal of more directly cementing the linkage between technical competence and ethical fitness as important determinants of one's qualifications to rule never seems to stray too far from the horizon. While unwilling to emulate the now-modified British practices, which traditionally approached civil service staffing with the Aristotelian view that an excellent liberal arts education alone is the primary prerequisite, Americans should still be able to take some small comfort from the willingness of commentators to suggest the kinds of ethical knowledge that should be taught to pre-service and in-service public servants.[22]

---

21. Jefferson, op. cit.; Pangle, op. cit.; Richardson, op. cit.

22. Catron, Bayard L. and Kathryn G. Denhardt, "Ethics Education in Public Administration," in Terry L. Cooper, ed., *Handbook of Administrative Ethics* (New York: Marcel Dekker, 1994), pp. 49-61; Hejka-Ekins, April, "Ethics in Inservice Training," in Cooper, *Ibid.*, pp. 63-80, and "Teaching Ethics in Public Administration," *Public Administration Review*, 48 (September/October 1988): 885-891; Kavathatzopoulos, I., "Training Professional Managers in Decision-Making About Real Life Business Ethics Problems: The Acquisition of the Autonomous Problem Solving Skill," *Journal of Business Ethics*, 13 (1994): 379-386; Marini, Frank, "The Uses of Literature in the Exploration of Public Administration Ethics: The Example of *Antigone*," *Public Administration Review*, 52 (September/October 1992): 420-426: Pratt, C.B., "Critique of the Classical Theory of Situational Ethics in U.S. Public Relations," Public Relations Review, 19 (1993): 219-234; Rohr, John, *Ethics for Bureaucrats: An Essay on Law and Values* (New York: Marcel Dekker, 1986); Taylor, Sir Henry, *The Statesman*, ed. David Schaefer

Conclusion

An understanding of the intertwined relationship between the rule of law and ethics in America is admittedly difficult, for it is complicated by issues of legitimacy, competing claims to rule, discretion, and moral fitness to rule. The vivid prospect of a realignment in the current powers of the various governments is likely to increase, not decrease, both the importance of the rule of law and the attention given to ethics. At state and local levels, elected and appointed officials may well be wielding more (visible) political powers that will increase the potential for clashes with the citizenry of the regime. While such clashes may inspire a sense of real civic responsibility among the affected citizens and advance the task of teaching them important political skills, it also will almost certainly redirect attention to the uses and abuses of administrative discretion. The historical justifications for this power—a politics/administration dichotomy, efficiencies, superiority of wisdom—were not overly persuasive in the past. They will be even less so in the shadow of the present view that majoritarian elections are *the* indisputable source of political legitimacy.

The issue of the *character* of those wielding administrative discretion will continue to be an appropriate subject for inquiry. While the proliferation of codes of ethics and ethical training is unlikely to do harm from the standpoint of one's character—aside from the possibility that certain ethically-challenged individuals might become more clever through their training in situational ethics—there is currently little persuasive evidence to demonstrate that it does a great deal of good in terms of improving ethical behavior. The prospects for such training are further complicated by the fact that it is expensive, for among existing public servants it usually takes place during the normal workday. In times of fiscal austerity, this approach will have to demonstrate that it is accomplishing its "mission" (which, to date, it has been hard pressed to do).

Given both the nature of the regime itself and the contemporary emphasis on the dominance of majoritarian approval, there may be more appropriate ways of bolstering the interdependent relationship of law, character, and discretion. For instance, among the more fruitful of such approaches is the resurgence of discussion about the roles to be played in the regime by citizen boards. While there are potentially significant differences between boards whose members are appointed by elected officials, those filled by administrators, and others that are community based or staffed by volunteers, they may be effective devices for advising

---

and Roberta Scaefer (Westport, CN: Praeger, 1992); and Torp, Kenneth H., "Ethics for Public Administrators," *National Civic Review*, 83 (Winter 1994): 70-73.

administrative units and, yes, even reviewing their actions. On the local level, citizen bodies composed of self-interested parents are blossoming in school districts as a way of checking and guiding the power of professional educators. Such entities have long served as politically important checks on controversial actions by local police. Now they are also being extended into the realm of child welfare as the critical but politically volatile actions of state agencies for children and family services find themselves under progressively greater scrutiny. Under these conditions, the necessary exercise of administrative discretion can be bolstered and, if need be, checked by its direct linkage to the ultimate source of democratic power, the citizenry. Furthermore, citizens participating in these ways have opportunities to hone the skills so admired by Tocqueville. At the same time, fellow-citizens observing and being served by affected administrative units are given some democratic reassurance about the ways in which discretionary powers may be wielded.

Whatever the long-term merits of such forms of citizen participation, they are but the most recent manifestations in a long line of attempts that have sought to lessen the inherent tensions between democratic and undemocratic elements of the regime. However, if such forms of citizen involvement are successful in more firmly linking the undemocratic necessity of administrative discretion with the democratic foundations of majoritarian political power, regime virtues such as temperance and law-abidingness may prove to have been well served.

Chapter Six

Law Versus Ethics: Reconciling Two Concepts of Public Service Ethics[1]

J. Michael Martinez

I. Introduction

The title of this chapter, "Law *Versus* Ethics," highlights a tension between law and ethics that has been recognized in the western intellectual tradition since the time of the Ancient Greeks.[2] Articulating the tension is relatively straightforward; developing a workable, consistent system of public service ethics in the face of such tension, however, is an exceedingly difficult matter. What makes the endeavor so difficult is that an individual public servant (in this context, any private individual, such as a lawyer or public administrator, who engages in professional and policy-making activities that affect the political values and traditions of the regime) has developed, during the course of a lifetime, a private sense of ethics based on many particularized factors, including education, habits, and experience. In some instances, a public servant's social role as someone charged with a duty to uphold and, to some extent, to legitimize the shared democratic values of the regime (including, but not limited to, adherence to political pluralism and a belief in the primacy of "one-man, one vote" representativeness, for example) may conflict with his or her private sense of ethics.[3] When an individual public servant's public and

---

1. A slightly revised version of the present chapter originally appeared as "Law Versus Ethics: Reconciling Two Concepts of Public Service Ethics," *Administration & Society*, vol. 29, no. 6 (January 1998): 690-722. Reprinted by permission.

2. See, for example: Aristotle, *The Nicomachean Ethics*, trans. David Ross (Oxford: Oxford University Press, 1980); W.T. Jones, *The Classical Mind: A History of Western Philosophy*, 2nd. ed. (New York: Harcourt Brace Jovanovich, 1980); and Plato, *The Republic*, trans. and ed. Raymond Larson (Arlington Heights, IL: Harlan Davidson, Inc., 1979).

3. See, for example, William D. Richardson, *Democracy, Bureaucracy, & Character: Founding Thought* (Lawrence: University Press of Kansas, 1997).

private ethical precepts conflict, this clash of values reflects the tension between law and ethics, that is, the tension between public and private duties.

In an effort to reconcile the tension between law (public duties) and ethics (private duties) for public servants seeking to develop a system of ethics, this chapter will, first, survey the literature on legal ethics to observe how a relatively well-defined public service profession has dealt with this tension and, second, suggest ways in which lessons from the legal profession can be applied to the field of public administration. At its conclusion, the chapter will argue in favor of a system of public service ethics where "legalistic" rules of conduct are a necessary, but insufficient, component of such a system. Similarly, an individual's sense of ethics alone is insufficient. A combination of the two, however uneasy the marriage, allows for the development of a system of public service ethics that, while not wholly satisfactory, is an improvement over an either-or approach. Moreover, to achieve the goal of fusing codified rules of conduct with an individual sense of ethics, the chapter will suggest ways in which public administrators can be made to respond more like members of a distinct profession, arguably a necessary first step in establishing a workable system of public service ethics.

II. Distinguishing Law from Ethics

It is axiomatic that law is, or should be, universally applied within a democratic regime. Even common law rules that regulate private transactions, such as contracts, torts, and family law, are universal since the rules governing those situations apply to everyone in more or less the same manner. Thus, under the rule of law, like cases are to be treated alike based on a known and knowable system of rules. This modern notion of law, which encompasses at least a rudimentary concept of equity, depends upon the application of general legal principles to specific factual situations without regard to a particular person's wealth, social status, or family position. Classifications are made only on the basis of reasons that can be articulated and defended against a charge of capriciousness or, in egregious cases, invidiousness.[4]

In addition to the modern fusion of legal and equitable principles, law is defined in the western tradition as "[t]hat which must be obeyed and followed by citizens subject to sanctions or legal consequences."[5] In

---

4. For a definition of "equity," see Henry Campbell Black, *Black's Law Dictionary*, 5th ed. (St. Paul: West Publishing Company, 1979), pp. 484-485.

5. Ibid., p. 795.

Blackstone's parlance, law is the result of society's contractual obligation to citizens "in exchange for which every individual has resigned a part of his natural liberty."⁶ Recognizing the power of law to command citizens to behave in ways deemed "right" by the sovereign, Hobbes defined positivist law as "to every subject those rules which the commonwealth has commanded him, by word, writing, or other sufficient sign of the will, to make use of for the distinction of right and wrong...."⁷ With some exceptions, Locke concurred with Hobbes's definition, adding that law is the result of democratic processes: "in assemblies impowered to act by positive laws, where no number is set by that positive law which impowers them, the act of the majority passes for the act of the whole...."⁸ In his landmark work *Taking Rights Seriously*, Ronald Dworkin defined the positivist view of law predominant in modern democratic regimes as special rules enforced through the use of public power, which are distinct from rules that dictate acceptable social interaction, that is, "moral" rules that a community follows but does not enforce through the use of public power.⁹

Dworkin's distinction between legal and social (or moral) rules highlights the difficulty in reconciling law and ethics: under a strictly positivist sense of legal rules, "public power" generally is not used to sanction lapses of a purely "moral," or private, nature. How could it be otherwise? If public servants acted solely upon their own often ill-defined, perhaps inarticulable, private ethical precepts, society would lose the great virtue of positivist legal rules, namely their well-defined, explicated characteristics. Moreover, private ethical lapses by public servants would be difficult or impossible to identify or, for that matter, rectify.¹⁰

---

6. William Blackstone, *Commentaries on the Laws of England*, vol. 1, ed. David Christian (Boston: T.B. Wait and Sons, 1818), p. 34.

7. Thomas Hobbes, *Leviathan*, ed. Herbert W. Schneider (Indianapolis: Bobbs Merrill, 1958), p. 210.

8. John Locke, *Two Treatises of Government*, ed. Thomas I. Cook (New York: Hafner Press, 1947), p. 169.

9. Ronald Dworkin, *Taking Rights Seriously* (Cambridge, MA: Harvard University Press, 1978), p. 17.

10. Implicit in Dworkin's definition is the notion of ethics as involving purely private concerns since an ethical standard is an individual's *particular* code of conduct separate from society's enforceable rules of *universal* conduct. In its modern sense, divorced with Aristotle's understanding of ethics as virtue, the term "ethics" often refers to individual morality, what Martin Diamond called " 'thou shall nots'...Puritanical or Victorian 'no-no's'." Martin Diamond, "Ethics and Politics: The American Way," in *The Quest for Justice: Readings in Political Ethics*, 3rd. ed., ed. Leslie G. Rubin and Charles T. Rubin (Needham Heights, MA: Ginn Press, 1992), p. 296. The terms "ethics" and "morals" often have been used interchangeably, although "[m]odern usage might distinguish the

As for the differences between law and ethics/morality, Mark Lilla observed that an ethical system is not an abstract justification for actions or a series of propositions that can be applied with legal precision to fact situations that arise. A system of ethics—an ethos—is something that is lived and practiced. An individual's sense of ethics is "anthropological... a way of learning virtue which is time-tested and subtly complex," developed through a life-long association with families, churches, peers, and schools.[11]

Thus, in contrast to the clearly-defined, generally-accepted characteristics of positivist or "black letter" law designed to cover analogous factual situations, a system of ethics envisions the particular, context-specific dilemmas that confront individuals, who must respond in part based on "virtues and habits." One commentator further highlights the differences between law and ethics:

> Whereas, moral decisions are value-based decisions that are content- and context-specific, legal decisions are just the opposite: procedure-based decisions that are dependent upon historical precedent. Generally, a law is born as a response to a peculiar (atypical) behavior that exceeds the bounds of social acceptability, even where those bounds might not be representative of the society as a whole. Thus, the specific exception gives rise to the general rule, which thereafter provides the basis for countering comparable exceptions. This process of codification and standardization serves to define situations that the moralist would view as unique according to some generic structure. The ultimate effect is to reduce environmental uncertainty, to narrow the gauge of interpretation, by delimiting the number of unique situations possible.[12]

Owing to a lack of "legal precision" and the absence of a "process of codification and standardization" in all areas of public service, as well as the possibly irrational features of ethics, the question arises: can the tension between law and ethics be resolved, perhaps by asking recognized leaders employed in public service to articulate an agreed-upon concept of private ethics and, afterwards, codify the resultant list so that all pub-

---

two in that 'ethics' has become associated with both philosophical inquiry and professional standards, while morals continue to hold the connotation of 'right rules of conduct'." Kathryn G. Denhardt, *The Ethics of Public Service: Resolving Moral Dilemmas in Public Organizations* (Westport, CT: Greenwood Press, 1988), p. 31. However the terms "ethics" and "morals" might be distinguished technically, the terms often are used synonymously or in conjunction with one another.

11. Mark T. Lilla, "Ethos, 'Ethics,' and Public Service," *The Public Interest* 63 (Spring 1981): 14.

12. Gregory D. Foster, "Law, Morality, and the Public Servant," *Public Administration Review* 41 (January/February 1981): 31.

lic servants will have a guide by which to judge their actions? This leads to a second question: if it is desirable, how would this codified system of rules be implemented since public administrators—unlike the legal profession, for example—are not members of a clearly-defined profession regulated by an occupational or licensure organization that exercises a gatekeeping function and commands the power to impose sanctions?

The answer to the first question suggested herein is that such a codification of rules is desirable. Indeed, it is a necessary, albeit insufficient, component in developing a system of public service ethics. The codification, although not perfect, would be a compromise embodying the best features of both worlds: a list of ethical precepts would retain the redeeming features of positivist law (it would be agreed-upon, written down, known and knowable, taught to students of the profession) while also incorporating a sense of private morality at its core. The "moral distance" between law and ethics would be minimized, although not completely abolished.[13]

The second question is more difficult to address since the literature on whether a profession of public administration currently exists—or is even possible—is varied and inconclusive.[14] Suffice it to say that the argument here is in favor of both the possibility and desirability of developing a stronger professional public administration. Much can be learned, for example, from the legal profession's quest to develop professional rules of conduct while concomitantly leaving room for lawyers to rely on their private ethical precepts to augment their professional responsibility.

Generally, lawyers have focused their efforts on incorporating ethical concepts into codified standards of conduct for all members of the Bar. Because lawyers traditionally have been cast in the role of protectors of the regime, the public has expected lawyers to practice "better" ethics. The legal profession has responded to such expectations by adopting stricter rules governing lawyers' behavior, instituting more comprehensive professional responsibility requirements in many jurisdictions, and providing enforcement mechanisms such as formalized grievance procedures and rules for undertaking disciplinary hearings. At the same time, however, recent efforts to reform legal ethics have recognized the importance of combining codified rules of professional conduct with individual ethical precepts.[15]

---

13. Gerald J. Postema, "Moral Responsibility in Professional Ethics," *New York University Law Review* 55 (April 1980): 65.

14. See, for example: Gregory Streib, "Ethics and Expertise in the Public Service: Maintaining Democracy in an Era of Professionalism," *Southeastern Political Review* 20 (Spring 1992): 122-143.

15. Geoffrey C. Hazard, Jr., "The Future of Legal Ethics," *Yale Law Journal* 100 (1991): 1240.

III. Lawyers and the Legal Profession: An Immoral Universe?

A. The Practical Nature of Legal-Rational Authority

Of the three types of governmental authority identified by Max Weber, the "legal-rational" tradition, or the rule of law, is the generally accepted basis for legitimizing power in stable, ongoing democratic regimes.[16] According to this view, the rule of law operates through the existence of a body of clearly-defined, generally-accepted rules characteristically found in bureaucratic states.[17] Authority attaches to the political office, not to the individual, hence the maxim "a government of laws and not of men."[18]

Lawyers, purveyors of law in democratic regimes such as the United States, understand their duties from a predominantly legal-rational perspective, sometimes with little regard for philosophical abstractions divorced from practical applications. One respected commentator on legal ethics, Professor L. Ray Patterson, has explained the perspective of the American Bar as a preference for rules of professional conduct that are pragmatic rules of law, not merely philosophical ruminations on behavior that ought to be encouraged.[19] By considering rules of professional responsibility as legal rules with clearly prescribed sanctions for persons who engage in prohibited behavior, the Bar has established a means for controlling the conduct of members of the profession that falls below a certain standard. While this may seem to be a base approach to ethics since it focuses only on negative behavior, it reflects a fundamental concept in American government, namely a mistrust of power exercised by persons, such as lawyers, in positions of authority. Perhaps the most famous example of this concern with potential abuses of power was articulated in "Federalist Number 51," when Publius observed that "[i]f men were angels, no government would be necessary. If angels were to govern

---

16. Max Weber, "Selections from *Politics as a Vocation*," in *The Quest for Justice: Readings in Political Ethics*, 3rd. ed., ed. Leslie G. Rubin and Charles T. Rubin (Needham Heights, MA: Ginn Press, 1992), p. 274.

17. See, for example: H.L.A. Hart, *The Concept of Law* (Oxford: Oxford University Press, 1963), and H.L.A. Hart, *Law, Liberty, and Morality* (New York: Vintage Books, 1961).

18. Quoted in Andrew Heywood, *Political Ideas and Concepts: An Introduction* (New York: St. Martin's Press, 1994), p. 108.

19. L. Ray Patterson, *Legal Ethics: The Law of Professional Responsibility*, 2nd. ed. (New York: Matthew Bender, 1984), p. 11.

men, neither external nor internal controls on government would be necessary."[20] Because divine intervention cannot be counted upon to control human behavior, ethical rules of conduct must "have teeth," such as enforceable sanctions, if they are to serve as an effective means of regulating professional behavior.

The Bar's perspective that ethical rules are legally enforceable external controls first and foremost may strike non-lawyers as troubling owing to the positivist approach to questions that initially appear to be normative. But the approach should not be surprising since lawyers analyze factual situations in relation to their duties to their clients and to the legal profession. As one commentator has observed, "[i]nsofar as lawyers design the rules of legal ethics to protect themselves from *legal* mishaps, 'defensive ethics' is a species of legalism."[21] Patterson has defended the reasons for this pragmatic focus as an understanding of the lawyer's duty as a professional. Ethical analysis, according to this perspective, is an analysis of a person's duty to himself as a private individual: how should I behave? What are my rights and obligations to myself in relation to the rest of society? Since lawyers are concerned with their duty not just to themselves, but to their clients and the courts as well, they must look beyond rules that encourage *individual* ethical behavior. They must look to rules that encourage — and, if necessary, punish — an individual's performance of his or her duty *as a professional*. In other words, a professional code of ethics is concerned with a professional's performance as someone who, by virtue of his or her role, affects other people within the regime. Rules of professional conduct for lawyers are not concerned with individuals acting as private citizens; they are concerned with lawyers acting as public servants.[22]

The emphasis on a lawyer's legal, or fiduciary, duty to the client has led, first, to the development of canons of ethics and, later, to the adoption of disciplinary rules and model codes of conduct which specify permissible and impermissible behavior and provide sanctions for the latter.[23] In the wake of adopting legalized codes of conduct, lawyers sometimes have found themselves, ironically, representing clients and causes they believe to be morally objectionable. This paradoxical posi-

---

20. Alexander Hamilton, James Madison, and John Jay, *The Federalist Papers*, ed. Clinton Rossiter (New York: New American Library, 1961), p. 322.
21. Ted Schneyer, "Professionalism as Bar Politics: The Making of the Model Rules of Professional Conduct," *Law and Social Inquiry* 14 (1989): 725.
22. Patterson, *Legal Ethics: The Law of Professional Responsibility*, 2nd. ed., op. cit., p. 11.
23. American Bar Association, *Model Rules of Professional Conduct and Code of Judicial Conduct* (Chicago: The American Bar Association, 1983).

tion—the lawyer entertains ethical qualms but is bound by codified rules of legal ethics to provide zealous representation for the client—illustrates the occasional divergence of law and ethics and contributes to the popular image of a lawyer as a "hired gun." As commentator Richard Wasserstrom has observed, "at best the lawyer's world is a simplified moral world; often it is an amoral one; and more than occasionally, perhaps, an overtly immoral one."[24]

B. Conceptions of Legal Ethics

If legal-rational authority, which is universally applied within a regime, occasionally is insufficient to guide the particular conduct of individuals, ethical guidance is needed. Judging by the available literature, the legal profession long-ago recognized the need for integrating ethics into the profession.[25] The question remains, however, by what method, and to what extent, legal ethics should be understood, taught, and applied.

Two approaches readily come to mind. First, lawyers might seek a casuistry for ethical problems facing them and then incorporate general principles into ethical canons, codes, and rules. This approach, which describes the standard conception of ethics integrated into legal-rational authority, requires an understanding of the lawyer's role morality, discussed *infra*. The second approach is to develop to an understanding of general ethical principles and use this understanding systematically as a

---

24. Richard Wasserstrom, "Lawyers as Professionals: Some Moral Issues," *Human Rights* 5 (1975): 2.
25. See, for example: Richard Abel, "Why Does the ABA Promulgate Ethical Rules?" *Texas Law Review* 59 (1981): 639-688; Owen Fiss, "The Varieties of Positivism," *Yale Law Journal* 90 (1981): 1007-1016; George P. Fletcher, "Two Modes of Legal Thought," *Yale Law Journal* 90 (1981): 970-1006; Charles Fried, "The Lawyer as Friend: The Moral Foundations of the Lawyer-Client Relation," *Yale Law Journal* 85 (1976): 1060-1089; David Luban, *Lawyers and Justice: An Ethical Study* (Princeton, NJ: Princeton University Press, 1988); Thomas Lumbard, "Setting Standards: The Courts, the Bar, and the Lawyers' Code of Conduct," *Catholic University Law Review* 30 (1981): 249-271; Thomas D. Morgan, "The Evolving Concept of Professional Responsibility," *Harvard Law Review* 90 (1977): 702-743; Thomas L. Shaffer and Mary Shaffer, *American Lawyers and Their Communities* (Notre Dame, IN: University of Notre Dame Press, 1991); Philip Shuchman, "Ethics and Legal Ethics: The Propriety of the Canons as a Group Moral Code," *George Washington Law Review* 37 (1968): 244-269; William Simon, "The Ideology of Advocacy: Procedural Justice and Professional Ethics," *Wisconsin Law Review* 1:29-143; and Charles W. Wolfram, "Barriers to Effective Public Participation in Regulation of the Legal Profession," *Minnesota Law Review* 62 (1978): 619-647.

guide for resolving particular situations as they arise (general moral philosophy).

Each of these approaches has severe drawbacks. Casuistry provides answers if the particular ethical difficulty can be placed into a category covered by the canon, code or rule. If the difficulty is unique or ambiguous, a codified rule may be only of limited use. The second approach, relying on general moral philosophy, may be even more difficult since the body of work on ethical philosophy spans the entire scope of western civilization and often is open to a variety of conflicting meanings and interpretations.[26]

This does not mean, of course, that the legal profession has not tried to develop ethical rules through both methods, especially the former. As early as the late nineteenth century, for example, legal scholars and members of the Bar called for canons to guide the conduct of practitioners, albeit canons were not seen as enforceable legal standards, but as "admonitions emanating from a merely private organization" that "had no direct legal effect, either in grievance proceedings against lawyer misconduct or in civil actions for legal practice."[27] The first Canons of Professional Ethics were adopted by the American Bar Association on August 27, 1908. They had their origins in the Alabama Association's 1887 *Code of Ethics* as well as Judge George Sharswood's lectures, entitled *Professional Ethics* (1854), and David Hoffman's *A Course of Legal Study* (2nd ed., 1836).[28] In time, however, the Bar transformed the canons into a series of disciplinary rules. This transformation was accomplished, in large measure, with the adoption of the American Bar Association's Code of Professional Responsibility in 1970. The "legalization" of the Bar's ethical precepts continued after 1970 and later resulted in the adoption of the Model Rules of Professional Conduct in 1983.[29]

1. Role Morality

Before lawyers are condemned as "hired guns," immoral and utterly unredeemable, as in Wasserstrom's ruminations, their functional role in society should be considered. As advocates of their client's interests, regardless of their personal opinion of the client or the client's cause, lawyers perform a valuable service to society by standing in the client's stead. A lawyer's representation "does not constitute an endorsement of the client's political, economic, social or moral views or activities."[30]

---

26. Postema, "Moral Responsibility in Professional Ethics," op. cit., p. 67.
27. Hazard, "The Future of Legal Ethics," op. cit., p. 1250.
28. American Bar Association, *Model Rules of Professional Conduct and Code of Judicial Conduct*, op. cit., p. ix.
29. Ibid.
30. Ibid., p. 16.

Thus, a lawyer must separate personal feelings from professional responsibility when and if a conflict exists. This bifurcation of the lawyer's personal opinions and the client's interests ensures that even unpopular causes are championed and controversial cases receive their day in court.[31] While a particular individual may feel uncomfortable divorcing his or her individual feelings from the role he or she plays as a public servant, society benefits from the division of legal and moral duties. Social institutions within a democratic regime are designed so that individuals who interact with those institutions promote social values. If an individual working within an institutional setting decides to promote his or her personal values above the values of the institution, this circumvents the democratic processes that created, or at least championed, those social values.

An individual is free, for example, to oppose the death penalty on ethical grounds as long as he or she is acting as a private individual. If that same individual holds a position within a prosecutor's office that has responsibility for prosecuting death penalty cases, this will not necessarily change the individual's personal objections to the death penalty; however, it does require that the individual refrain from refusing to carry out the prosecutor's mission of prosecuting death penalty cases. If the individual cannot reconcile his or her personal objections to the death penalty with the prosecutor's public responsibility for prosecuting death penalty cases, the individual must leave the prosecutor's office, where he or she is then free to object to the death penalty without fear of compromising his or her public duties. As one commentator has observed, "social and professional roles" create a special duty for individuals serving in those roles. The individual has, in effect, become a public servant owing to the division of labor between private individuals and individuals acting as decisionmakers within the regime. This social role requires that the individual consider his or her duty as a public servant above his or her individual feelings, except in rare instances, discussed *infra*.[32]

In addition to the role of lawyers as defenders of democratic social values within an institutional setting, private lawyers often serve an important role as "mitigators of the destructive tendencies of democracy." Geoffrey C. Hazard, Jr., a University of Pennsylvania law professor and a frequent commentator on legal ethics, has written that the legal profession serves society in another useful, albeit often unpopular, manner. The public generally hates lawyers, often ridiculing the profession with jokes and rating lawyers in public opinion polls next to used-car salesmen in

---

31. Fried, "The Lawyer as Friend: The Moral Foundations of the Lawyer-Client Relation," op. cit.

32. Postema, "Moral Responsibility in Professional Ethics," op. cit., p. 72.

terms of honesty and social utility. Hazard has suggested that much of this scorn and derision can be attributed to the profession's historical role in "counterbalancing the vagaries of popular government with the pressures of the market."[33] Because lawyers often assist the business community and established political leaders through litigation, the contract process, corporate law, and political maneuvering, the public views the profession as protectors of the status quo, anti-democratic defenders of elite privilege. In Hazard's view, this image of lawyers as "unpopular and morally suspect" is an understandable perspective in light of the populist sentiments shared by large segments of the population. Nonetheless, by aiding "the development and protection of business property within a political system committed both to popular government and constitutional restraints on government," lawyers have allowed the regime to function, to some extent, as a check on the destructive nature of unfettered democracies. This view of democratic government as potentially destructive was Publius's concern when he observed in "Federalist Number 10" that "democracies have ever been spectacles of turbulence and contention; have ever been found incompatible with personal security or the rights of property; and have in general been as short in their lives as they have been violent in their deaths."[34] By protecting personal security and rights of property from a tyrannical majority or a destructive minority faction, lawyers have served an important social function, in Hazard's estimation, although they have been paid for their service with a tarnished image.[35]

Lest one think the lawyer a hapless victim in the public relations wars, it is good to remember that the negative image of a "hired gun," inhabitant of a singularly immoral universe, has been mitigated in the popular consciousness by a contrary view: the heroic narrative of a courageous lawyer standing up for unpopular causes at great personal sacrifice. This view is reflected throughout the American experience: fictional Atticus Finch in *To Kill a Mockingbird*[36] readily springs to mind, as do historical examples, including Clarence Darrow at the Scopes "Monkey Trial" of 1925[37]; the courageous lawyers who finally defended the infamous "Scottsboro Boys" in *Powell v. Alabama* (1932)[38]; the American prosecutors at the Nuremberg Trials, led by United States Supreme Court Jus-

---

33. Hazard, "The Future of Legal Ethics," op. cit., p. 1241.
34. Hamilton, Madison and Jay, *The Federalist Papers*, op. cit., p. 81.
35. Hazard, "The Future of Legal Ethics," op. cit., p. 1241.
36. Harper Lee, *To Kill a Mockingbird* (New York: Warner Books, 1960).
37. Alan M. Dershowitz, ed., *The World's Most Famous Court Trial: Tennessee Evolution Case* (Birmingham, AL: The Notable Trials Library, 1990).
38. 287 U.S. 45 (1932).

tice Robert Jackson[39]; Joseph Welch's attack on the scare tactics of Senator Joseph McCarthy in the 1950s[40]; and Abe Fortas's defense of Clarence Earl Gideon in *Gideon v. Wainwright* (1963),[41] to name a few. Arguably, these examples illustrate the positive features of a lawyer's role morality. Advocates in those cases may have harbored personal reservations about the rightness of the cause, but they set aside those reservations and advanced their clients' interests, nonetheless. Even Shakespeare's famous line "[t]he first thing we do, let's kill all the lawyers" is not the anti-lawyer invective it initially appears to be since the words are spoken by one co-conspirator to another as they plot to undermine the stability of an existing regime by disposing of the guardians of justice.[42]

This emphasis on role morality, however, is not without its critics. The problem with recognizing the existence of a role morality is that it requires lawyers to compartmentalize their private and public personas, to ignore their "off-the-job values," which may have the unintended effect of blocking "the cross-fertilization of moral experience necessary for personal and professional growth."[43] Because rational human beings often make decisions based on a variety of factors, including a sense of morality that they might be hard-pressed to articulate, it is questionable whether lawyers can satisfactorily and consistently divorce their private and public selves, even if this act is considered a desirable component of the lawyer's role morality.[44] Critics charge that, by creating a "moral distance" between "ordinary morality" and professional responsibility, the legal profession has diminished the "moral universe" of the lawyer.[45]

Ironically, the perception of a lawyer as "an instrument of both liberty and political justice," as illustrated in the famous cases cited *supra*, is probably no more accurate than the image of a lawyer as an amoral, or immoral, "hired gun."[46] Yet the existence of a role morality has been valuable for another reason. Owing to lawyers' unique role in modern society, the legal profession has always insisted that laypersons should not develop rules of behavior governing lawyers since non-lawyers could

---

39. Ann Tusa and John Tusa, *The Nuremberg Trial* (New York: Atheneum, 1986).
40. Hazard, "The Future of Legal Ethics," op. cit., p. 1243.
41. 372 U.S. 335 (1963). See also: Anthony Lewis, *Gideon's Trumpet* (New York: Random House, 1991).
42. William Shakespeare, *King Henry VI, Part II*, Act IV, Scene 2, in *The Works of William Shakespeare* (New York: Oxford University Press, 1904), p. 55.
43. Postema, "Moral Responsibility in Professional Ethics," op. cit., p. 64.
44. Schneyer, "Professionalism as Bar Politics: The Making of the Model Rules of Professional Conduct," op. cit., p. 731.
45. Postema, "Moral Responsibility in Professional Ethics," op. cit., p. 65.
46. Hazard, "The Future of Legal Ethics," op. cit., p. 1244.

not possibly understand, and therefore could not effectively regulate, the ethical conduct of lawyers facing ethical dilemmas in the course of practicing law.[47] Indeed, in the early years of the American legal profession, the Bar was more or less self-policing. Canons of ethics were not promulgated by third parties, but by lawyers themselves.[48] This fraternal "old boy's club" was based on a simple assumption: leaders of the Bar "presupposed that right-thinking lawyers knew the proper thing to do and that most lawyers were right-thinking." The concept of a special role morality protected lawyers from the vagaries of an interfering, possibly ignorant, laity.[49]

In the ensuing years, however, the call for improved ethical rules was issued in response to several factors: the perceived "litigation explosion" associated with allegedly frivolous claims; the concern for equal access to the judicial system; increased industrialization and advances in technology, which led to increasingly complex conflicts and injuries; newly-recognized "rights," often associated with government largess; and the recognition of lawyers' "great temptations to shoulder aside one's competitors, to cut corners, to ignore the interests of others in the struggle to succeed."[50] This required the development of an improved understanding of the lawyer's role in society. (The public administration field faces similar attacks on its proper role within the regime.)

2. A Recourse Role

Moral philosophers have expressed concern that the standard conception of ethics embodied in a role morality envisions a "fixed role" for lawyers, that is, "as far as the individual practitioner is concerned, the moral universe of his role is an objective fact, to be reckoned with, but not for him to alter." Codes of conduct are outcome determinative; they require practitioners to adopt one particular role according to the situation under consideration and then behave in accordance with codified rules of conduct. By contrast, a "recourse role" allows a lawyer to act, if necessary, apart from the "legalized" duties of his or her role morality.[51]

---

47. See, for example: Lumbard, "Setting Standards: The Courts, the Bar, and the Lawyers' Code of Conduct," op. cit., and Wolfram, "Barriers to Effective Public Participation in Regulation of the Legal Profession," op. cit.

48. See, for example: Hazard, "The Future of Legal Ethics," op. cit., and Schneyer, "Professionalism as Bar Politics: The Making of the Model Rules of Professional Conduct," op. cit.

49. Hazard, "The Future of Legal Ethics," op. cit., p. 1250.

50. Derek C. Bok, "A Flawed System of Law Practice and Training," *Journal of Legal Education* 33 (1983): 570-585.

51. Postema, "Moral Responsibility in Professional Ethics," op. cit., pp. 82-83.

Moral philosophers have pointed to Aristotle to illustrate their point. In *The Nicomachean Ethics*, for example, Aristotle contended that the distance between general theories and action can be bridged by "practical wisdom," which is another way of saying that "[o]ur ability to resolve conflicts on a rational basis often outstrips our ability to enunciate general principles."[52] In Aristotle's words:

> Practical wisdom is the quality of mind concerned with things just and noble and good for man, but these are the things which it is the mark of a *good* man to do, and we are none the more able to act for *knowing* them if the virtues are states of *character*, just as we are none the better able to act for knowing the things that are healthy and sound, in the sense not of producing but of issuing from the state of health....[53]

Ethical action is not the result of good character alone (private morality), just as it is insufficient to know general principles without acting on those principles (casuistry). Practical wisdom allows human beings of good character to exercise judgment in adapting general principles to specific situations. It is the combination of a person's character, knowledge of ethical principles, and his or her exercise of judgment through practical wisdom that results in just acts. Aristotle also observed:

> As we say that some people who do just acts are not necessarily just, i.e., those who do the acts ordained by the laws either unwillingly or owing to ignorance or for some other reason and not for the sake of the acts themselves (though, to be sure, they do what they should and all the things that the good man ought), so it is, it seems, that in order to be good one must be in a certain state when one does the several acts, i.e., one must do them as a result of choice and for the sake of the acts themselves.[54]

Private morality alone is insufficient; knowledge of rules of professional conduct, especially if undertaken owing to a fear of legal sanctions, is insufficient without a method of "bridging the gap" between positivist legal rules and a private sense of ethics. In the Aristotelian sense, a flexible "recourse role" is necessary. Such a recourse role forces the lawyer to step from behind the shield provided by a codified system of rules and engage his or her own system of ethics. In this view, a lawyer cannot claim that he or she was acting merely as a technician or an agent of the client. The lawyer must engage his or her moral judgment in representing a client.[55]

---

52. Ibid., p. 68.
53. Aristotle, *The Nicomachean Ethics*, op. cit., p. 154.
54. Ibid., pp. 155-156.
55. Postema, "Moral Responsibility in Professional Ethics," op. cit., p. 83.

3. The Model Rules of Professional Conduct

Partially in response to continued concerns about the fixed and "legalistic" nature of the 1970 Code of Professional Responsibility, the American Bar Association adopted the Model Rules of Professional Conduct in 1983.[56] The new rules allowed room for a recourse role and were heralded by many commentators within the legal community as a satisfactory compromise between casuistry and general moral philosophy. Indeed, by specifying the appropriate conduct of a lawyer acting as advocate (Rules 3.1-3.9), advisor (Rule 2.1), intermediary (Rule 2.2), and evaluator (Rule 2.3), the Model Rules set forth a series of black-letter rules—certainly an advantage of positivist law—while specifying the myriad circumstances facing the lawyer, depending on his or her role, thus taking into account the difficulties associated with establishing standards of professional conduct from a single perspective. One commentator observed:

> ... [T]he moral philosophers' "hired gun" criticism of the earlier ABA codes seems largely inapplicable to the Model Rules. That criticism asserted that legal ethics rules have forced lawyers into an advocate's role that places client interests above all others, and have done so by forbidding lawyers to let their own values or the interests of third parties affect their decisions about whom to represent and how to represent them. Yet the Model Rules recognize that lawyers play several roles, not just that of advocate. They also invite lawyers in *any* role to take their own values into account. They permit lawyers to refuse on moral grounds to represent would-be clients, authorize lawyers to "limit the objectives" of representation by excluding client aims they find "repugnant or imprudent"; and in a remarkable concession to lawyers' sensibilities allow them to withdraw whenever "a client insists upon pursuing an objective the lawyer considers repugnant or imprudent"—even if the client's interest will be "adversely affected" by the withdrawal! These rules are meant precisely to resolve the "potential conflict between the lawyer's conscience and the lawyer's duty to vigorously represent a client."[57]

With the adoption of the Model Rules, some members of the legal profession were distressed by what they saw as the continued "legalization" of the Bar. For example, the Model Rules no longer used the term "canons" when discussing professional ethics, instead referring to the rules as "authoritative," with accompanying comments "intended as

---

56. Hazard, "The Future of Legal Ethics," op. cit., p. 1251.
57. Schneyer, "Professionalism as Bar Politics: The Making of the Model Rules of Professional Conduct," op. cit., p. 736.

guides to interpretation."[58] The Rules emphasized in a dramatic way that the legal profession was no longer simply an informal, cohesive group of peers who trusted one another to "do the right thing" by honoring a gentleman's agreement with a handshake. In effect, the heroic narrative had been reduced. In Max Weber's parlance, a "traditional" institution had been transformed into a "bureaucratic" institution. As a member of a traditional institution, a lawyer might think immediately in terms of what he or she *could* do as a creative, problem-solving member of the profession. As a member of a bureaucratic institution, a lawyer might be forced to think immediately in terms of what he or she *could not* do as a regulated member of the profession.[59]

Whether the Model Rules entirely bridge the gap between the two conceptions of legal ethics depends upon one's point of view. The rules certainly can, and should, be improved as new circumstances warrant, but in the meantime they represent a marriage of both worlds—a "legalized" approach and a philosophical approach, a joining of public and private duties. They also hold valuable lessons for the field of administrative ethics.

IV. Public Administration: A Work in Progress

A. The Nature of Administrative Ethics

The public administration literature has seen a call for "improved" ethics within the field, especially, although not exclusively, in the wake of government scandals and public concern for integrating ethical precepts into the public service.[60] Some works that delve into public administra-

---

58. American Bar Association, *Model Rules of Professional Conduct and Code of Judicial Conduct*, op. cit., p. 13.
59. Hazard, "The Future of Legal Ethics," op. cit., pp. 1254-1255.
60. See, for example: W.J. Michael Cody and Richardson R. Lynn, *Honest Government: An Ethics Guide for Public Service* (Westport, CT: Praeger Publishers, 1992); Terry L. Cooper, "Hierarchy, Virtue, and the Practice of Public Administration: A Perspective for Normative Ethics," *Public Administration Review* 47 (July/August 1987): 320-328; Terry L. Cooper, *The Responsible Administrator: An Approach to Ethics for the Administrative Role*, 3rd. ed. (San Francisco: Jossey-Bass, 1990); Kenneth Culp Davis, *Discretionary Justice* (Baton Rouge, LA: Louisiana State University Press, 1969); Donald J. Devine, *The Political Culture of the United States* (Boston: Little, Brown & Company, 1972); Carl J. Friedrich, *The Pathology of Politics* (New York: Harper & Row, 1972); Robert T. Golembiewski, *Men, Management and Morality: Toward a New Organizational Ethic* (New York: McGraw-Hill, 1965); Harold F. Gortner, *Ethics for Public Managers* (Westport, CT: Praeger Publishers, 1991); Stephen A. Holmes, "Dick Morris's Behavior, and Why It's Tolerated," *The New York Times*, September 8, 1996,

tion ethics have even been recognized as modern classics in western political thought.⁶¹

As the concern with improving ethics arose, Paul Appleby urged caution in reacting to perceptions of "crude wrongdoing" as the sole motivation for adopting a system of public service ethics. "More complicated and elevated" ethical issues, such as the nature and scope of bureaucratic discretion, should be the focus of ethics in public administration.⁶² The challenge, of course, is in identifying appropriate ethical precepts, especially since the field of public administration is comparatively new, still evolving, and may lack the cohesiveness of many professions, such as law and medicine.⁶³

As in the legal profession, the public administration literature has recognized the bifurcation between the concepts of ethics as a series of codified rules and ethics as general moral philosophy. Nonetheless, the literature has concluded that the necessarily individualistic character of ethics does not preclude teaching public administrators about "regime

---

p. E5; Wayne A.R. Leys, *Ethics for Policy Decisions* (Englewood Cliffs, NJ: Prentice-Hall, 1952; Robert M. MacIver, *The Web of Government* (New York: Macmillan Company, 1947); Frederick C. Mosher, *Democracy and the Public Service* (New York: Oxford University Press, 1982); Arthur M. Okun, *Equality and Efficiency: The Big Tradeoff* (Washington, D.C.: The Brookings Institute, 1975); Emmette S. Redford, *Ideal and Practice in Public Administration* (University, AL: University of Alabama Press, 1958); Glendon A. Schubert, *The Public Interest* (New York: The Free Press, 1960); Patrick J. Sheeran, *Ethics in Public Administration: A Philosophical Approach* (Westport, CT: Praeger Publishers, 1993); Frederick C. Thayer, *An End to Hierarchy! An End to Competitition!* (New York: New Viewpoints, 1973); Edward Weisband and Thomas M. Franck, *Resignation in Protest* (New York: Grossman Publishers, 1975); Aaron Wildavsky, *How to Limit Government Spending* (Berkeley, CA: University of California Press, 1980); James Q. Wilson, "The Rediscovery of Character: Private Virtue and Public Policy," *The Public Interest* (Fall 1985): 3-16 (reprinted in the present collection as Chapter 10); David Wise, *The Politics of Lying: Government, Deception, Secrecy, and Power* (New York: Random House, 1973); and Sheldon S. Wolin, *Politics and Vision: Continuity and Innovation in Western Political Thought* (Boston: Little, Brown & Company, 1960).

61. See, for example: Hannah Arendt, *Crises of the Republic* (New York: Harcourt Brace Jovanovich, 1972); John Dewey, *The Public and Its Problems* (New York: Holt, 1927); Friedrich A. Hayek, *The Road to Serfdom* (Chicago: The University of Chicago Press, 1944); and Dwight Waldo, *The Administrative State* (New York: Ronald Press, 1948).

62. Paul H. Appleby, *Morality and Administration in Democratic Government* (Baton Rouge, LA: Louisiana State University Press, 1952), p. 56.

63. Streib, "Ethics and Expertise in the Public Service: Maintaining Democracy in an Era of Professionalism," op. cit., p. 134.

values" through the case method or through an emphasis on understanding the "higher law" background of American government.[64]

Compared with the materials on legal ethics, the administrative literature has been late in recognizing the need for integrating concepts of ethics into public administration. This may be the result of the different emphases in the legal and public administration fields. As recounted *supra*, the law has been seen as a profession with a unique role morality. The recognition of public administration as a distinct profession where politics and administration are not divided spheres, on the other hand, has been a comparatively recent phenomenon, and not altogether uncontested.[65] Accordingly, issues of ethics and accountability have not been discussed in the public administration literature to the extent that they have been discussed in the literature on the legal profession, although valuable lessons may be learned from the Bar's efforts. Perhaps the most important lesson is the relative clarity of lawyers' general ethical obligations (although their application in individual cases may still give rise to ambiguity). Members of the legal profession share an understanding of what it means to be a legal professional and what makes lawyers differ-

---

64. See, for example: Bayard L. Catron and Kathryn G. Denhardt, "Ethics Education in Public Administration," in *Handbook of Administrative Ethics*, ed.Terry L. Cooper (New York: Marcel Dekker, 1994), pp. 49-61; Edward S. Corwin, "The 'Higher Law' Background of American Constitutional Law," in *American Government: Readings and Cases*, 3rd. ed., ed. Peter Woll (Boston: Little, Brown & Company, 1969), pp. 37-54; April Hejka-Elkins, "Teaching Ethics in Public Administration," *Public Administration Review* 48 (September/October 1988): 885-891; Iordanis Kavathatzopoulos, "Training Professional Managers in Decision-Making About Real Life Business Ethics Problems: The Acquisition of the Autonomous Problem Solving Skill," *Journal of Business Ethics* 13 (May 1994): 379-386; Frank Marini, "The Uses of Literature in the Exploration of Public Administration Ethics: The Example of *Antigone*," *Public Administration Review* 52 (September/October 1992): 420-426; Cornelius B. Pratt, "Critique of the Classical Theory of Situational Ethics in U.S. Public Relations," *Public Relations Review* 19 (Fall 1993): 219-234; William D. Richardson and Lloyd G. Nigro, "Administrative Ethics and Founding Thought: Constitutional Correctives, Honor, and Education," *Public Administration Review* 47 (September/October 1987): 367-376; John A. Rohr, *Ethics for Bureaucrats: An Essay on Law and Values*, 2nd. ed. (New York: Marcel Dekker, 1989); ed. Sir Henry Taylor, *The Statesman*, David L. Schaefer and Roberta R. Shaefer (Westport, CT: Praeger Publishers, 1992); Alexis de Tocqueville, *Democracy in America*, ed. J.P. Mayer (Garden City: Anchor Books, 1969); and Kenneth H. Torp, "Ethics for Public Administrators," *National Civic Review* 83 (Winter 1994): 70-73.

65. See, for example: David H. Rosenbloom, *Public Administration: Understanding Management, Politics, and Law in the Public Sector*, 2nd. ed. (New York: Random House, 1989), and James Q. Wilson, "The Rise of the Bureaucratic State," *The Public Interest* 41 (Fall 1975): 77-103.

ent from non-lawyers. Public administrators, to a large extent, do not share this same understanding of their place in the public sector.[66]

Reflecting, in part, the lack of understanding about what it meant to be a public administrator participating within the realm of public policymaking, the early literature discussed ethics from a practical perspective. Values such as economy and efficiency were considered paramount objectives for (supposedly) politically and morally-neutral public administrators. This perspective gradually changed, especially with the rise of the administrative state in the 1940s and the realization that public administrators exercise a significant policymaking role.[67]

A more sophisticated understanding of public administration's role within the regime developed in the 1930s and 1940s. Gone was the politics and administration dichotomy, and with it the simplistic notion that the only ethical requirement for public administrators was that they implement the will of elected officials with as much economy and efficiency as possible. In its place was a new dilemma: how can public administrators in a large bureaucratic state be held politically accountable given the reality of bureaucratic discretion? Stated another way, how can the polity ensure that public administrators will behave in ways that support democratic principles given the diverse work performed in public agencies and the lack of a centralized profession of public administration?

B. The Friedrich-Finer Debate

The most cogent discourse on this new dilemma occurred in the famous Friedrich-Finer Debate, which originated in the 1930s and focused on the differences between "internal" and "external" bureaucratic controls. In a series of essays, Carl J. Friedrich argued strongly for the development of an individual sense of moral responsibility as an internal control on behavior in addition to the traditional emphasis on placing external controls on public administrators as a means of ensuring accountability to elected leaders. Psychological factors such as the willing-

---

66. Rosenbloom, *Public Administration: Understanding Management, Politics, and Law in the Public Sector*, 2nd. ed., op. cit., p. 483.
67. See, for example: Ralph Clark Chandler, "The Problem of Moral Reasoning in American Public Administration: The Case for a Code of Ethics," *Public Administration Review* 43 (January/February 1983): 32-39; Louis Gawthrop, *Public Management Systems and Ethics* (Bloomington, IN: Indiana University Press, 1984); Theodore Lowi, *The End of Liberalism* (New York: W.W. Norton, 1969); ed. Frank Marini, *Toward a New Public Administration* (Scranton, PA: Chandler Press, 1971); Rosenbloom, *Public Administration: Understanding Management, Politics, and Law in the Public Sector*, 2nd. ed., op. cit., pp. 34-52; and Waldo, *The Administrative State*, op. cit.

ness of individuals to behave responsibly are the paramount considerations in ensuring administrative responsibility, Friedrich contended. In fact, "[r]esponsible conduct of administrative functions is not so much enforced as it is elicited."[68] In other words, the quest for public accountability should not ignore the role of moral or religious responsibility in ensuring that public administrators behave in an ethical manner.

Friedrich was writing at a time when the Wilsonian politics-administration dichotomy was still recognized as axiomatic in the public administration literature.[69] If the exercise of political power and the performance of administrative functions were not separate and distinct endeavors, the ethical implications were enormous. Public administrators did not exercise policymaking authority according to the old school of thought; thus, their ethical duty required only that they achieve technical competence and remain accountable to elected officials who instructed them on the mechanics of implementing policy. Recognizing a changing view of bureaucratic politics, Friedrich was troubled by the suggestion that the actions of public administrators did not hold repercussions for policymaking. He attempted to move away from an artificial distinction between politics and administration in discussing ethics. His argument was similar to F.M. Marx's contemporaneous contention that no matter how detailed statutes and legislative grants of authority to public administrators appeared to be, their implementation was "a creative act, separate and apart from the making of the law itself."[70] In other words, no matter how tight the external controls, public administrators ultimately must rely upon an individual sense of ethics in performing their duties as public servants since they must exercise discretion.

In response to Friedrich's arguments, Herman Finer argued that only external controls such as codes of ethics and legal rules could ensure public accountability. "Moral responsibility is likely to operate in direct proportion to the strictness and efficiency of political responsibility, and

---

68. Carl J. Friedrich, "Public Policy and the Nature of Administrative Responsibility," in *Combating Corruption/Encouraging Ethics: A Sourcebook for Public Service Ethics*, ed. William L. Richter, Francis Burke, and Jameson W. Doig (Washington, D.C.: The American Society for Public Administration, 1990), p. 43.

69. See, for example: Luther Gulick, "Science, Values and Public Administration," in *Papers on the Science of Administration*, ed. Luther Gulick and L. Urwick (New York: Augustus M. Kelley Publishers, 1937), and Woodrow Wilson, "The Study of Administration," *Political Science Quarterly*, June 1887; reprinted in 56 (December 1941): 481-506.

70. F.M. Marx, *Public Management in the New Democracy* (New York: Harper & Row, 1940), p. 237.

to fall away into all sorts of perversions when the latter is weakly enforced," he wrote.[71] Relying on the individual conscience of a particular public administrator, no matter how well-meaning he or she may be in performing his or her duties, will always lead to abuses of power. Individuals will either misunderstand democratic values or they will pursue their own interests. While Finer later acknowledged that public administrators may enhance their accountability by educating themselves to appreciate public opinion and technical and professional standards, the paramount issue in ensuring ethical conduct is to improve external controls to the extent possible.[72] In many ways, Finer was echoing Weber's positivist arguments in *Politics as a Vocation*.[73] Democratic government operates best when behavioral controls are external and ethical behavior is clearly defined in a codified, rule-based system that is known and knowable beforehand.

C. The "New Public Administration"

While the Friedrich-Finer Debate continued to be discussed in subsequent years, it was Friedrich's emphasis on the importance of internal controls that gave birth to the movement often referred to as the "New Public Administration," which initially grew out of the 1968 Minnowbrook Conference.[74] H. George Frederickson is perhaps the most famous adherent of the New Public Administration approach.[75] Proponents of this "new" school argued that the field of public administration had come a long way since the days when Woodrow Wilson insisted that politics and administration could, and should, be separated. New public administrators recognized that they exercised bureaucratic discretion, which invariably meant that they were involved in some aspects of policymaking. They further contended that, while external controls are a valuable means of ensuring political accountability, they can only go so

---

71. Herman Finer, "Administrative Responsibility in Democratic Government," in *Combating Corruption/Encouraging Ethics: A Sourcebook for Public Service Ethics*, William L. Richter, Francis Burke, and Jameson W. Doig, eds. (Washington, D.C.: The American Society for Public Administration, 1990), p. 44.

72. Cooper, *The Responsible Administrator: An Approach to Ethics for the Administrative Role*, 3rd. ed., op. cit., pp. 128-132.

73. Weber, "Selections from *Politics as a Vocation*," in *The Quest for Justice: Readings in Political Ethics*, 3rd. ed., op. cit., pp. 273-283.

74. Cooper, *The Responsible Administrator: An Approach to Ethics for the Administrative Role*, 3rd. ed., op. cit., p. 148.

75. See, for example: H. George Frederickson, *New Public Administration* (University, AL: University of Alabama Press, 1980).

far toward ensuring that public administrators behave ethically and appreciate the importance of "social equity" in making administrative decisions.[76]

Proponents of New Public Administration quickly issued a call for inculcating concepts of social equity into the public administration field to augment traditional goals of efficiency and economy. This appreciation of social equity perhaps reached its apex in the mid-1970s, when one issue of *Public Administration Review* was devoted exclusively to an extended discussion of the topic.[77] In 1976, Susan Wakefield of Brigham Young University, recognizing the variety of means available for teaching ethics and the latent difficulties of incorporating ethics into the curricula, concluded that "[t]here exists a strong case for individual responsibility as both primary and ultimate sources of public service ethics. External controls become a necessary and secondary support system."[78]

The New Public Administration has been criticized for its idealistic goals and its lack of accessibility to most public administrators. Since empirical evidence suggests that some public administrators "lack a commitment to public service" owing, in part, to their failure to recognize themselves as public administration professionals with a duty to uphold the public interest, it is possible that an over-reliance on an individual's private sense of ethics can circumvent democratic values. Gregory Streib, for example, has observed in a different context that government professionals must demonstrate "respect for the democratic process" over and above their "reverence for their own expertise" or secondary considerations such as their individual opinions on social and political issues.[79] In the quest to become champions of social equity, New Public Administrators may consciously or unconsciously substitute their own

---

76. Marini, ed., *Toward a New Public Administration*, op. cit.

77. The issue featured the following articles: Stephen R. Chitwood, "Social Equity and Social Service Productivity," *Public Administration Review* 34 (January/February 1974): 29-35; Michael M. Harmon, "Social Equity and Organizational Man: Motivation and Organizational Democracy," *Public Administration Review* 34 (January/February 1974): 11-18; David K. Hart, "Social Equity, Justice, and the Equitable Administrator," *Public Administration Review* 34 (January/February 1974): 3-11; Eugene B. McGregor, "Social Equity and the Public Service," *Public Administration Review* 34 (January/February 1974): 18-29; David O. Porter and Teddie W. Porter, "Social Equity and Fiscal Federalism," *Public Administration Review* 34 (January/February 1974): 36-43; and Orion White and Bruce L. Gates, "Statistical Theory and Equity in the Delivery of Social Services," *Public Administration Review* 34 (January/February 1974): 43-52.

78. Susan Wakefield, "Ethics and the Public Service: A Case for Individual Responsibility," *Public Administration Review* 36 (November/December 1976): 661-666.

79. Streib, "Ethics and Expertise in the Public Service: Maintaining Democracy in an Era of Professionalism," op. cit., p. 123.

values for the values of the democratic regime. Their zeal to become social reformers may put them ahead of, and out of touch with, the public they ostensibly serve as public servants.

D. Combining Subjective and Objective Approaches to Administrative Ethics

As was the case with the legal profession, public administrators have come to understand that recent debates on developing a workable system of public service ethics necessitate reconciling, to some extent, individual concepts of ethics (a subjective approach) and legalistic ethical codes (an objective approach). Accordingly, recent works on public administration ethics generally have avoided the either/or approach illustrated by the Friedrich-Finer Debate, choosing instead to argue for a reconciliation of the two concepts into a workable, systematic ethical system for the public service. The difficulty for scholars has been in developing an appropriate model that applies to substantially all public administrators.

Recognizing the importance of philosophical and psychological conceptions for ethical foundations, for example, John Rohr concluded in his influential work *Ethics for Bureaucrats* that public administrators will rely upon their individual understanding of ethics in the context of specific, real-world situations. Yet, not surprisingly, they will also need to look to an outside source for guidance on how to exercise individual discretion in accordance with democratic principles. It is simply too much to expect that students and practitioners of public administration will consult great works of philosophy and discern practical information for resolving ethical dilemmas. He wrote that "[a] haphazard perusal of the works of the great philosophers will yield nothing more than a gentleman's veneer."[80] Moreover, even if public administrators want to understand democratic values, it is difficult to find consensus on those values. Thus, he argued in favor of examining "regime values" expressed through opinions of the United States Supreme Court, that is, "the values of that political entity that was brought into being by the ratification of the Constitution that created the present American republic."[81] In Rohr's view, the fusion of an individual's ethical sense and the democratic values of the regime can be accomplished when public administrators enrich their own individual understanding of ethics with an appreciation of the principles of the polity as explicated by an authoritative source, and use their discretion accordingly.

---

80. Rohr, *Ethics for Bureaucrats: An Essay on Law and Values*, 2nd. ed., p. 67.
81. Ibid., p. 68.

Rohr's work may be seen as a search for positivist explications of the regime's moral and legal rules. Unfortunately, in some cases positivist legal rules and underlying regime principles may not be identical. Moreover, Rohr's approach "tends to assume that regime values and morality will coincide. In the past, however, regime values condoned slavery, racial segregation, and the denial of full political rights and equal protection of the law for women, despite opposition on moral grounds from many quarters."[82]

By contrast, Terry L. Cooper discussed the practical ethical challenges that confront public servants on an almost daily basis without consulting an outside authoritative source for "in-the-trenches" guidance. "The central thesis of this book," he wrote in *The Responsible Administrator*, "is that it is through the process of defining professional responsibility in specific, concrete administrative situations that an operational ethic is developed."[83] Cooper thus examined the *process* of ethical decisionmaking in lieu of searching for authoritative regime values or refining the specific content of ethical codes. Although he called Rohr's search for regime values "an excellent example of a treatment of values that a public administrator ought to internalize and reflect upon," Cooper disagreed with Rohr's narrow focus.[84] In *The Responsible Administrator*, for example, Cooper observed that regime values are broader than Rohr's emphasis on constitutional values articulated by the United States Supreme Court:

> Taking this general approach, but extending it beyond Rohr's specific focus on the U.S. Constitution, we might note these regime values associated with the American tradition: the beneficial aspects of pluralism of interests, the creative possibilities in conflict, the sovereignty of the public, the rights of the minority, the importance of citizen participation in government, the societal values of freedom of expression. These are but a few exemplary values that might emerge as important in such a broadened study.[85]

Cooper contended that public administrators do not need a "substantive ethic" to govern their behavior since they will take their cues on ethical behavior from their respective organizations. This is not to suggest that an individual public administrator can avoid individual responsibility for his or her actions by placing blame on the organization. If the organization does not function properly, the public administrator owes a

---

82. Rosenbloom, *Public Administration: Understanding Management, Politics, and Law in the Public Sector*, 2nd. ed., op. cit., p. 483.
83. Cooper, *The Responsible Administrator: An Approach to Ethics for the Administrative Role*, 3rd. ed., op. cit., p. 5.
84. Ibid., p. 166.
85. Ibid., p. 167.

higher duty to the public to act in an ethical manner based on the administrator's private ethical sense. In most cases, however, it is a combination of two concepts—acting in accordance with a properly run organization's central tenets and exercising individual notions of ethical behavior—that results in a responsible administrator. The organization, an external control, sets the standard of behavior and the individual seeks to understand and comply with that standard. If the standard is deficient, in the individual's considered opinion, then he or she has a duty as a citizen, an internal control, to ensure that the organization does not undermine democratic principles.[86]

Other public administration theorists have followed Rohr and Cooper in attempting to fuse subjective and objective approaches, internal and external controls. In *The Ethics of Public Service*, for example, Kathryn G. Denhardt sought to bridge the gap between philosophical and practical ethics based on "a better-developed theoretical framework...more grounded in philosophy, and...ultimately more practical in that it considers and accommodates the exigencies of the environment in which public administrators must practice—the modern public organization."[87] She stopped short of listing the philosophical standards that should be used to ground her system.

Patrick J. Sheeran, on the other hand, chose to reject what he viewed as the "legalistic" approach advocated by Rohr and the duality approach advocated by Cooper and Denhardt, focusing instead on the philosophical aspect of public service ethics:

> The conflict between the objectivist and subjectivist approaches, coupled with the difficulties raised by Rohr and Cooper, is a poor excuse for failing to develop and implement ethics courses in schools of public administration.... This book begins by developing the philosophical "dimension" that Denhardt "left to other works." It marks a departure from Rohr by claiming that ethics, though based on a "smattering of philosophy," is not only important in developing public administration courses in ethics but also in its application to other courses in public administration.... Courses in philosophy, whether complete or partial, are important for not only public administration but, as Denhardt points out, almost every science.[88]

Sheeran raised an interesting point: a grounding in philosophy ensures that public servants will have a sense not simply of the values underlying

---

86. Ibid., pp. 226-232.
87. Kathryn G. Denhardt, *The Ethics of Public Service: Resolving Moral Dilemmas in Public Organizations* (Westport, CT: Greenwood Press, 1988), p. ix.
88. Sheeran, *Ethics in Public Administration: A Philosophical Approach*, op. cit., p. 11.

decisions affecting the public but, perhaps more importantly, the *reasoning* behind those values. A well-developed, philosophically-based, reasoned sense of justice is an important prerequisite for a public servant who will exercise considerable bureaucratic discretion. Many works of philosophy, including the contemporary theories espoused by John Rawls[89] and Robert Nozick,[90] provide the concerned public servant with philosophical food for thought. William K. Frankena's classic work, *Ethics*, also provides a contemporary view on ethical behavior. Sounding remarkably like a modern Utilitarian writing in the language of theology or morality, Frankena posited that human beings need to act with beneficence, "the principle that we ought to do the act or follow the rule which will or will probably bring about *the greatest possible balance of good over evil* in the universe."[91] Unfortunately, the philosophical approach to ethics may be unworkable in practice. The burden of identifying, mastering, and internalizing a consistent philosophy of public service in the fast-paced, ever-changing context of a public organization virtually guarantees that public servants will not develop the necessary skills with which to resolve ethical problems encountered in the course of a long career.

Recognizing the difficulty of requiring that public administrators engage in a broad-reaching philosophical inquiry at the time they enter the public service, William D. Richardson has argued that the search for an appropriate ethical system for public administrators begins at the earliest stages of an individual's moral and intellectual development. Moreover, the quality of a citizen's character within a regime is important in understanding how an individual will incorporate democratic values into his or her activities as a public servant. "[I]f it is to thrive and prosper," Richardson wrote, "a commercially oriented regime must more or less successfully inculcate among its citizenry such traits as rudimentary honesty, a desire for wealth, pacific habits (war consumes wealth), and some respectable degree of what we call the Protestant work ethic."[92] The development of good moral character, with a concomitant appreciation of "civic virtue," can be encouraged, to some extent, by educating individuals in democratic values from infancy. The reliance on good character as an important component in developing civic-minded citizens, which in

---

89. John Rawls, *A Theory of Justice* (Cambridge, MA: Belknap Press of the Harvard University Press, 1971).

90. Robert Nozick, *Anarchy, State, and Utopia* (New York: Basic Books, 1974).

91. William K. Frankena, *Ethics* (New York: Prentice-Hall, Inc., 1963), p. 37 (emphasis in the original).

92. Richardson, *Democracy, Bureaucracy, and Character: Founding Thought*, op. cit., p. 16.

turn leads to a characteristic way of behaving—an *ethos*—is what Martin Diamond meant when he referred to "the American Way" in his famous essay on ethics and politics reprinted in this collection.[93]

The different approaches to ethics in the public administration literature reflect the debate that has occurred in the legal literature, which focuses on two primary questions. First, should ethics be codified as a "legalistic" system of rules that applies to everyone in a given profession or should public servants be left to their own individual senses of morality to resolve ethical questions? Alternatively, can and should the two approaches be combined?

V. Conclusion

A. Reconciling Law and Ethics

Not coincidentally, the literature on legal ethics and public administration ethics presents the same dilemmas. How can the individual nature of ethics be reconciled with the universal requirements of public service? In other words, how can law and ethics be reconciled? If an individual's sense of ethics is championed above codified rules, this leads to definition and enforcement problems. Alternatively, if codified ethical rules are preferred, they can lead to rigid, formalized prescriptions that leave little room for an individual to rely on his or her sense of ethics while acting in various public service roles.

A combination of personal ethics and codified rules is the only marginally satisfactory compromise for what may be an intractable problem. "I contend that a sense of responsibility and sound practical judgment depend not only on the quality of one's professional training, but also on one's ability to draw on the resources of a broader moral experience," one commentator has written.[94] Even if ethical theorists call for a bifurcation of codified rules and private morality, another commentator has observed that, "[t]he fact is that there is no way of avoiding the introduction of personal and private interests into the calculus of public decisions."[95] Stated another way:

> This process of interpreting and applying the specifications of ethics legislation and codes of ethics should be informed by the core values that represent the foundations of the political tradition, sometimes referred to as regime values, as well as by the developed conscience of the adminis-

---

93. Diamond, "Ethics and Politics: The American Way," op. cit.

94. Postema, "Moral Responsibility in Professional Ethics," op. cit., p. 64.

95. Stephen K. Bailey, "Ethics and the Public Service," in *Public Administration and Democracy*, ed. Roscoe C. Martin (Syracuse: Syracuse University Press, 1965), p. 286.

trator. These encourage compliance with the spirit of the law and codes rather than merely the letter. Also, internalized political values and developed conscience provide a check on self-protective and self-serving codes, which professional associations have been known to adopt. They also establish a broader point of reference from which to evaluate the legitimacy of any particular piece of ethics legislation.[96]

It is true that the fusion of codified rules with private concepts of ethics does not completely bridge the gap between law and ethics. The general (law) and the particular (ethics) always will be different, by definition. One might go so far as to say that the gap between the (ethical) spirit and the (positivist) letter of the law will never be closed. Yet, perhaps, the uneasy reconciliation of the two, in Aristotle's words, may be achieved through the exercise of practical wisdom. "It is clear, then, from what has been said," he observed, "that it is not possible to be good in the strict sense without practical wisdom, or practically wise without moral virtue."[97] Thus, while combining the particularity of ethics and the universality of law might complicate efforts to punish those public servants deemed to be "unethical" because the actions undertaken will depend in part on potentially unique circumstances, ultimately such a union allows for a broader concept of public service ethics than is possible in choosing one approach over another.

B. Suggestions for Reconciliation

At the outset, this chapter suggested that it was an exceedingly difficult matter to develop a workable, consistent ethical system from disparate elements of the public service owing to the fundamental tension between law (public duties) and ethics (private duties). To reconcile this tension, to the extent possible, the body of the chapter was devoted to a discussion of the various theories and efforts that were established to harmonize those disparate elements in the legal profession, which culminated in support for a recourse role through the adoption of the Model Rules of Professional Conduct. The chapter concluded that the comparatively new field of public administration could learn much from the efforts of the legal profession in crafting a system of ethics. The question naturally arises at this point: how can this goal be realized? As with implementing any plan of reform, the devil is in the details.

---

96. Cooper, *The Responsible Administrator: An Approach to Ethics for the Administrative Role*, 3rd. ed., op. cit., p. 227.

97. Aristotle, *The Nicomachean Ethics*, op. cit., p. 158.

1. "Rehabilitating" the Image of Public Administration

It is nothing new to call for an improved system of ethics for public administrators. The literature abounds with such calls to action.[98] Unfortunately, this call to action is easier said than done. Yes, educating tomorrow's leaders in the appropriate democratic values today is extremely important.[99] Yes, professional associations such as the American Society for Public Administration (ASPA) can be called upon to lead reform efforts such as sponsoring study committees on revitalizing public service ethics, hosting conferences to discuss the appropriate components of an ethical system, and passing resolutions urging public administrators to comply with ethical standards. These are important first steps and, for the most part, have already been undertaken in the past. Moreover, formalized codes of ethics such as the ASPA Code of Ethics and Guidelines, the International City Management Code of Ethics with Guidelines, the National Contract Management Association Code of Ethics, the United States Code of Ethics of 1980, or any of the state codes of ethics can be touted as precursors to the development of a uniform code of ethics for the field. But these external controls will only have a limited effect until the image of the average public administrator as a nameless, faceless, dispassionate bureaucrat improves.

Use of the term "image" is not meant to imply that the task of improving the public administration field is merely an exercise in public relations. It isn't. The only realistic way to improve the image of the public administrator is to make individual administrators happy to be public servants, to make them proud of telling their fellow men that "yes, I am a public administrator," the way lawyers proudly boast of their courtroom prowess and legal acumen. While it is unlikely that the heroic narrative will ever develop around most public administrators, perhaps the

---

98. See, for example: Chandler, "The Problem of Moral Reasoning in American Public Administration: The Case for a Code of Ethics," op. cit.; Cooper, *The Responsible Administrator: An Approach to Ethics for the Administrative Role*, 3rd. ed., op. cit.; Vincent Ostrom, *The Intellectual Crisis in American Public Administration* (University, AL: University of Alabama Press, 1974); Laurence J. O'Toole, Jr., "American Public Administration and the Idea of Reform," *Administration & Society* 16 (August 1984): 141-166; and Streib, "Ethics and Expertise in the Public Service: Maintaining Democracy in an Era of Professionalism," op. cit.

99. See, for example: Lorraine Smith Pangle and Thomas L. Pangle, *The Learning of Liberty: The Educational Ideas of the Founders* (Lawrence, KS: University Press of Kansas, 1993), and Richardson, *Democracy, Bureaucracy, and Character: Founding Thought*, op. cit.

public will regard the work of bureaucrats with less disdain when, and if, the field is rehabilitated.

In an effort to rehabilitate the field, recent scholars have defended the need for public administration on many grounds.[100] One scholar has suggested that the continued denigration of public administrators may lead to a loss of valuable personnel as individuals flee public service careers in search of more money, honor, and prestige.[101] Encouraging honor and the esteem of fellow men, even more than paying higher wages, is the paramount issue in reinvigorating public administration.[102] This is a crucial first step in transforming the field into a true profession and, afterwards, in establishing a workable code of ethics.

This gargantuan task can be accomplished, if no less an authority than Tocqueville is to be believed, by relying on "self-interest properly understood."[103] In other words, a concerted effort to increase the prestige and approbation of public administrators can be achieved if reformers do more than simply call for reform. First, public administrators must be made to see that it is in their best interests to join a genuine "profession" of public administration, just as lawyers join the legal profession upon passing the bar examination in a particular jurisdiction.

By modeling a new profession of public administration on the legal profession, reformers can ensure that the professionalization of public administrators does not pose a threat to democratic values since the gatekeepers of the profession can insist upon adopting a code of ethics that encourages members of the new profession to act on democratic values as a fiduciary obligation to the public. While the identification of those values will never remain free of controversy, at least the development of an ethical code for a professional group of public servants based on democratic values will resolve some ambiguity that currently exists about appropriate ethical standards.

2. Professionalizing Public Administration

The field of public administration must become a genuine profession. Far-reaching efforts are needed to achieve this goal. It will not be easy. In

---

100. See, for example: Charles T. Goodsell, *The Case for Bureaucracy: A Public Administration Polemic* (Chatham, NJ: Chatham House Publishers, 1983), and John A. Rohr, *To Run a Constitution: The Legitimacy of the Administrative State* (Lawrence, KS: University Press of Kansas, 1986).

101. Bruce Adams, "The Frustrations of Government Service," *Public Administration Review* 44 (January/February 1984): 5-13.

102. Forrest McDonald, *Novus Ordo Seclorum: The Intellectual Origins of the Constitution* (Lawrence, KS: University Press of Kansas, 1985).

103. Tocqueville, *Democracy in America*, op. cit.

addition to educating students about democratic values beginning in infancy, it will require additional incremental steps, first at the federal level and later in states and municipalities. Reformers ideally should lobby Congress to enact legislation creating a new federal class of public administrators. Similar to the Senior Executive Service, but broader, and available at all levels of government, this new class of public administrators would be granted a new title, perhaps "Certified Public Guardian," or something similar. Individuals would enter the profession through a licensing procedure, say, an examination, governed by an independent board of public administrators. The board would serve as gatekeepers of the new profession. (To placate members of the public who undoubtedly would lobby for citizen participation in such a gatekeeping activity as a means of ensuring that the profession would not become too self-serving and elitist, provisions could be adopted to allow for public representation on the board.)

Within a given agency, certified public guardians would be paid a larger salary and assigned greater responsibility than their non-licensed counterparts, who would still work within the agency, but in a lesser capacity. This new class of certified public guardians would be expected to serve the public in a fiduciary capacity, just as lawyers serve clients in their profession, in lieu of slavishly adopting the goals of a particular organization.

Is this a lofty goal with little chance of being implemented? Perhaps. Is the call for greater professionalization within the public administration field contrary to current trends, such as the desire to deprofessionalize public administration by "reinventing government" and engaging in similar smoke-and-mirror "innovations"?[104] Certainly. For the reasons discussed *infra*, greater professionalization of the field, on balance, will ensure greater accountability among public administrators than will efforts to decentralize government operations and parcel them out among private entities, who are not subject to the same controls that apply to the public sector. Deprofessionalizing the field may (or may not) lead to gains in efficiency, but this change will necessitate lesser *governmental* accountability and all the constitutional and operational problems attendant thereto. Is this a price worth paying? Ultimately, this is a question for policymakers considering privatization and similar proposals, al-

---

104. See, for example: Albert Gore, *Report of the National Performance Review: Creating a Government That Works Better and Costs Less* (Washington, D.C.: U.S. Government Printing Office, September 1993), and David Osborne and Ted Gaebler, *Reinventing Government: How the Entrepreneurial Spirit is Transforming the Public Sector From Schoolhouse to Statehouse, City Hall to Pentagon* (New York: Addison-Wesley Publishing Company, 1992).

though the position herein is that the price is too high. In the meantime, the issue remains: how can public administrators be made more accountable? Consider the option of greater, not lesser, professionalization, as discussed *infra*.

3. Implementing Enforceable Codes of Ethics

Voluntary adherence to a code of ethics, while admirable, is not sufficient to ensure that all members of a field are held to the standards contained in the code. Moreover, as long as public administrators generally do not view themselves as guardians of a sacred public trust, they will not look to a voluntary code of ethics as a standard for judging their service to the public. In a best-case scenario, if public administrators see themselves as part of a voluntary paraprofessional group, perhaps some administrators will follow the ethical guidelines of their professional association. Yet the number of participants will be fairly small, as Gregory Streib has indicated.[105] In addition, the consequences of non-compliance with a voluntary code remain largely inconsequential.

What is needed, then, is a code of ethics for this new group of professional public administrators that will *require* group members to follow the codified rules of the profession or risk the imposition of sanctions. Again, this is a lesson learned from the legal profession. Of course, this is not to say that strict codes of ethics can always force individuals to behave ethically if they are predisposed to behave otherwise, but certainly enforceable codes of ethics provide incentives for "correct" behavior in a way that no voluntary code can.

At a minimum, a strong code of ethics must require, with appropriate enforcement mechanisms (private and public letters of reprimand; monetary fines; and expulsion from the profession in rare, egregious circumstances), that public administrators act in accordance with "the public interest" and "democratic values" as those ambiguous terms are defined through codified rules and guidelines published by the independent board of public administrators in consultation with practitioners and scholars. In short, a code of ethics "with teeth" that also allows for a private sense of ethics is the most practicable means of ensuring that public servants behave responsibly.

4. Role Morality and a Recourse Role for Public Administrators

In addition to a "legalized" system of rules, however, the new class of public administrators must recognize its unique role morality within the

---

105. Streib, "Ethics and Expertise in the Public Service: Maintaining Democracy in an Era of Professionalism," op. cit.

regime. This is where life-long education in democratic values is important. Public administrators serve an integral role as guardians of the regime and its values. In adopting a recourse role, administrators are held to the standards of the new public administration profession contained in the code of ethics. Beyond the legalistic standards of the code, an individual public administrator should rely on his or her understanding of democratic values to "fill the gaps" in responding to real-world situations not covered by the code. In the event that an individual public administrator believes that the work he or she is called upon to perform violates a fundamental precept central to the democratic process, he or she will have the right, indeed the duty, to act in the role of public citizen in placing the interests of the regime over and above the interests of the profession or the agency. The fact that this calculation will be made infrequently, even in cases where it should be made, is acknowledged. Nonetheless, the rarity of an individual public administrator acting in his or her recourse role as a public citizen over and above his or her professional role does not obviate the necessity of providing for such a role.

The tension between law and ethics, between general and specific duties, will continue to confound scholars and practitioners owing to fundamental differences in the two concepts. Despite this tension, it is incumbent upon citizens of the regime to seek a marriage of law and ethics, the public and the private. Perhaps it is the effort of continually wrestling with ethical issues, and not the development of a particular code of ethics, that leads to what Aristotle deemed "practical wisdom."

Chapter Seven

Temperance, Passions, and Lawyers in the American Democratic Regime

John C. Koritansky

The View of the Framers Regarding Representation: Their Failure to Acknowledge the True Role to be Played by Lawyers

When we return to the thought of the American framers, and particularly the authors of *The Federalist Papers*, it is surprising and somewhat amusing to see the disparity between their expectations and present day reality regarding the role of lawyers in the American regime. Today lawyers are involved with the regulation of every kind of social intercourse. Other countries (Japan is an oft cited example) rely on people to work out their own problems, or enlist the aid of counselors who focus on the human dynamics and/or practical requirements of a situation. Among ourselves the notion of legal rights weighs more heavily. It is always necessary in seeking to resolve interpersonal tensions and conflicts for us to know what people have the right to expect and demand of one another; often this is taken to be not only the necessary but even the sufficient requirement for resolution. So, even though there are more lawyers *per capita* in America than in any other country, one wonders if we could really do with fewer.[1] In fact there is some truth to the waggish remark that every lawyer who exists constitutes a demand for another one! Lawyers also dominate our public life: nearly all of our elected representatives are lawyers by profession, even though there is some resent-

---

1. By the latest count, there are some 861,000 lawyers currently licenced to practice by the various state bar associations. cf. *U.S. Bureau of the Census, Statistical Abstract: 1995* (115th ed.) (Washington, D.C., 1995): p. 411.

ment of the fact among the general public, their electors. Up to a point this is easy to understand: the training of a lawyer to the business of "fighting with words" is directly relevant to the conduct of public life insofar as public life is constituted by disputes regarding the allocation of goods and also regarding the determination of a common good. Still, we might have reason to feel more comfortable with the prominence of lawyers in our common life if there were any evidence that their education or natural disposition or anything whatever caused them to feel responsibility for the health of the regime or to exercise that responsibility in an intelligent way. There is not, though. Legal education is certainly relevant to the conduct of the business of governing; but it makes no claim and exhibits no feature of an education that would be wished for in a nation's ruling class, were the existence of such a class to be recognized.

To be sure, to speak of a "ruling class" in democratic America is to risk scandal. This is not only or mainly because a democracy insists that it is a "classless" society. We are not speaking of a hereditary aristocracy of lawyers, of course, but even as a meritocratic body of experts in ruling, democratic societies are at least suspicious and more likely hostile to any cadre's making such a claim—lawyers or anyone else. Democracy is hostile to the very idea that there is any expertise or art of rule. Rule should emerge from the bounty of good common sense of the people at large. The standards of common life are clear enough; it is thought that government ought to aim to facilitate the collective needs of individuals in a society whose overall tone is that of a common decency. What, though, of the framers? Did they share the democratic aversion to the idea that rule is an art whose mastery requires rare gifts or exclusionary educational requirements? If we look to the *Federalist Papers* for an answer, we see that Madison's and Hamilton's views, while not identical with the current popular one, nevertheless exhibit certain antipathy towards the issue of an art of rule as well. The authors of *The Federalist* are themselves, to be sure, members of a self-conscious ruling elite. In fact, nearly all of the members of the Constitutional Convention had a political education that included profound study of political history and philosophy, as well as law. Madison is, of course, the outstanding example of the fact that the Constitution was the product of a long study, conducted on behalf of the people, but not "representative" in the fullest sense, as is proved by the secrecy and even the illegality of the deliberations at Philadelphia. When it came to proposing a Constitution, possession of the art of rule was at a premium. But the framers did not expect that the management of the day to day affairs of governing under the Constitution would involve the same high level of intelligence or statesmanship. Broadly speaking, a measure of the success of their project would be precisely the non-reliance of the new regime on the availability of men like themselves.

The question of what sort of person *would* conduct the ongoing business of government did receive attention from the authors of *The Federalist Papers*, most notably in the discussion of the make up of the legislative chambers, the Senate and the House of Representatives. For Madison, the discussion of representation is part of his response to the problem that he sees as generic to democracy, but which he tries to solve "on the level of democracy,"[2] namely, the problem of the factious and potentially tyrannous majority. A well organized *representative* democracy is safeguarded against this danger in two ways. First, Madison thinks that it is reasonable to expect that the representatives of a large population are likely to be at least somewhat superior, intellectually and morally, to those they represent. This is especially important because of the way it serves the second advantage, for a representative democracy is able to take in more territory and a greater variety of persons than a direct one, with the consequence that no one faction is likely to constitute in itself a governing majority. Majorities are still necessary to govern, of course, but they are to be temporary and artificial. They will be shifting coalitions of minor factions (the contemporary term is "interest groups"), formed up on the basis of calculation and compromise over particular policies. This notion of representation clearly puts the demand on legislative representatives that they be both able to reflect the particular interests and attitudes of their particular constituents and that they be sufficiently free of them so as to be able to negotiate and bargain, and thus to formulate the governing majorities in conformity with the requirements of justice. To employ the appropriate technical terminology, Madison's representatives must be both "virtual" as well as "actual" so that minority factions can be the ingredients of the governing majorities.

At first glance Hamilton's remarks concerning representation in the new regime appear only a gloss on what Madison says. In fact, while Hamilton's view is not incompatible with Madison's, there is more than a nuance of difference. Hamilton opens his most extended discussion of the issue with an uncompromising attack on "actual representation" as being completely unworkable. Unless required, it would never take place. Hamilton then insists that there is a need for some specific group to be "virtual" representatives; and this class is provided by merchants.

> "These considerations (cf. the whole paragraph) and many others that might be mentioned prove, and experience confirms it, that arti-

---

2. The useful phrase is Martin Diamond's. He employs it throughout his writings on the founding and *The Federalist Papers* in particular.

sans and manufacturers will commonly be disposed to bestow their votes upon merchants and those whom they recommend. We must therefore consider merchants as the natural representatives of all these classes of the community.[3]

Towards the end of this section, Hamilton mentions that, in contrast to merchants, there is really no other group that could or would perform the role. Among those whose claims Hamilton repudiates are "the learned professions," among whom we must, of course, count lawyers.[4]

Hamilton's and Madison's views regarding the representativeness of the new regime are, thus, not identical but they are broadly compatible; and this compatibility is the result of their deriving from a single source. That source is the whole basis for every conclusion of Hamilton or Madison, or of practically everyone who gave attention to political issues during the period, that is, the Liberalism of the 18th Century, which had been refined and elevated to the elegant formulation that we find in the *Declaration of Independence*. This thought held, in outline, that government is limited as to its legitimate purposes (although not necessarily

---

3. *The Federalist Papers* (New York: The New American Library of World Literature, Inc., 1964), p. 215. All references are to this edition.

4. It should be added that the importance given to merchants in *Federalist #35* regarding representation is only one—not the most important—dimension of the whole question of what sort of person would conduct the affairs of national government for Hamilton. He, in some contrast to Madison, also considers the members of the executive department, that is, the elected officers of president and vice-president and the members of the permanent federal bureaucracy. As Leonard White has shown in his study of the Federalist administration, what Hamilton had in mind was the development of a corps of career officers, serving for good behavior, and distinguished for their competence and high moral character. Government itself, or at least national government, was to be the field for the play of legitimate ambition among "the first characters of the union." This was a necessity for all government but especially for the central administration of a federal system. The great danger in all confederated government that the local units would encroach upon and undermine the authority of the central government had to be overcome by the greater efficiency, effectiveness, and honesty of the central government. In general, to the extent that government enlisted the talents and energies of such persons might it be called good. It is in what he says regarding the executive department and the bureaucracy rather than the legislature that we could recover what Hamilton thinks about the art of rule in American government. It is a relatively truncated form of it, having more in common with contemporary managerialism than with traditional soulcraft. But as regards the issue of this chapter, Hamilton gives no reason for thinking that education in law would be common among the preponderance of governmental bureaucrats or that they would tend to come from the ranks of lawyers.

as to its powers).⁵ Government derives its just powers from a consent of the governed, given in order to facilitate the exercise of their own primary and natural rights to their own lives, liberties, and the pursuit of their own happiness. It is a view which scarcely entails any common good; "justice" is a term that, when it is used by the framers, tends to mean only the absence of arbitrariness, which is the bane of that natural condition from which we sought to escape by consenting to government. This does not mean, though, that legitimate government can only be regulative of private life. There is nothing illegitimate about the people giving their consent to government's performing a number of activities which they might instead do through their own enterprise. The Washington administration undertook several instances of what we might call "positive government," including a program of public roads, canals, postal administration, and territorial administration. Still, all of these activities were related to further facilitating private enterprise and private life.

The Federalist Papers' expectation that lawyers would not play any significant role in the legislature is by no means an insignificant embarrassment for his thought, especially as underscored by Hamilton's confident and explicit prediction. Still, we must be careful not to overestimate it. Despite its shortcomings, *The Federalist Papers* is simply unrivaled as an interpretive text, a source of vital information regarding the intention of the framers. America is unique and uniquely fortunate in having not only records of the deliberations that lie behind the Constitution's text but in having this carefully argued apology to accompany it. The Court, in its exercise of the power of judicial review, cannot but turn to this set of papers when it wishes to buoy up its conclusions regarding the fundamental powers and basic structural features of the regime. Nor has the passage of time rendered it less relevant or authoritative. As long as the country wishes to be guided by a written Constitution which sets the conditions for the legitimate exercise of all governmental authority, even legislative authority, and so long as the particular expressions of that written document pose any ambiguity for immediate practical purposes, it will always be that the question of the actual intentions of the Constitution's framers will be looked to and debated, and this explicit record of those intentions prized. Nevertheless, in a broad way it is not difficult to see the *Federalist Papers'* shortcoming as regards its social philosophy and its expectations for the whole tone and shape of the civil society that America would become. In a word, *neither* Madison nor Hamilton un-

---

5. Hamilton, ibid., p. 207.

derstand the *fully* democratic character of America. To be sure, Madison and Hamilton understand that American civil society will be democratic and that its governmental structures may be called "democratic" along with "republican." This means for them, though, only that the majority of free persons will be authoritative and that procedures will be majoritarian. And, as far as was possible without compromising the principle of majority rule, the framers set themselves the task of resisting the danger inherent in democracy of a leveling spirit inimical to the rights of minorities. Modern readers who are of a democratic disposition cannot help but notice almost immediately what separates the *Federalist Papers* from themselves. *The Federalist Papers'* authors are not enthusiastic for democracy. They do not identify any specifically democratic notion of justice and champion it; and they do not encourage or celebrate any collective egalitarian sentiment. The "love *of* equality" which we take almost for granted as the distinguishing feature of democratic government and society is either passed over in silence by the framers or, in the form of "the leveling spirit," is actually resisted.

The question now naturally arises, how did democracy grow out of the soil of the Liberalism of the American founding? Even today, this remains a question that calls for subtle talents on the part of the historian. Of fundamental relevance to such an account is the fact that the Liberalism of the *Declaration of Independence* is not *essentially* democratic. It cannot be stressed too heavily that the *Declaration* is in fact neutral to the whole question of the comparison of forms of government: democracy as versus aristocracy and so on. What we may call the regime question is just not provided an answer by the *Declaration*. Indeed, we need to carry this point even further. The teaching of the *Declaration* is precisely that *whatever* form of government to which a people may give their consent is, *ipso facto*, legitimate; and that is the whole applicable standard. Even monarchy might be legitimate; that is why the *Declaration* must delineate the long list of particular transgressions that King George committed and why it must interpret them as indications of some still darker, vaguer prospect, which it presumes to be beyond anyone's consent. Moreover, the *Declaration's* neutralism regarding the regime also entails a vacuousness regarding the standards for the formation of public policy in the day to day life of the nation.[6] Nevertheless, *some*

---

6. The clearest and profoundest understanding of the shortcoming of Liberalism is presented by Rousseau, especially in his *The Social Contract*. He attacks Liberalism for its neutralism, saying that the individual's natural right, which Liberalism holds to be the foundation of legitimate government, amounts to no more than the option of submission or hopeless rebellion against the armed might of the state. Rousseau's newer doctrine of the social contract taught that freedom and equality such as we enjoy by right as

sort of standard does have to guide the deliberations about, and conduct of, the nation's business, even if only vaguely and by default, so to speak. There are, then, two closely relatedly consequences, both of which are manifest in America. First, Americans tend to be caught up in debates about which procedures are most representative of all of the various constituencies affected by a decision. As the late Herbert Storing put it, "We are constantly in the business of getting ready to govern." Secondly, we tend to convert Liberalism into a sort of civil religion, unwittingly transforming the very vacuousness of the *Declaration* into a substantive standard for our own individual life and for common life. Equality and freedom thus become more than the conditions upon which we have unalienable, natural rights. They become moral/political principles. Justice comes to mean equality; or at least equality wears the halo of justice.

Democratic Equality and the Prominence of Lawyers in the American Regime: The Observations of Tocqueville

For our framers, freedom and equality were, strictly speaking, only the bases for establishing legitimate political authority. The ends or aims for the exercise of that authority were different, more pedestrian, and ultimately ministerial to the individuals' pursuit of their own happiness. But this was to underestimate the significance of what might be called "political passion" in human psychology. Liberalism produces American liberal democracy when the liberty and equality spoken of in the *Declaration of Independence* become objects of the people's political passion. And with that development, lawyers would come to the fore. The commentator who understands this best is Tocqueville. His observations are made in 1831, during the Jackson administration, as the democratization of our politics and public life was well underway. Tocqueville professes great respect for the framers, but that notwithstanding, he understands the country, its democratic soul, better than they. Indeed, Tocqueville's oft cited acuteness and prescience derive entirely from his central insight as to the democratic character of the American nation, not just its institutional structures and procedures but its sentiments,

---

natural individuals might be reconstituted *in* civil society if each member can be brought to give himself over completely to a *"general will."* We are not Rousseauans, to be sure. It is true, however, that American political history traces a course that parallels the response to the shortcomings of classical Liberalism that Rousseau understood and stated with perfect clarity.

characteristic opinions, and moral habits. And one of Tocqueville's most celebrated and amazing observations concerns the role of lawyers. "There is hardly a political question in the United States which does not sooner or later turn into a judicial one".[7]

Tocqueville's clairvoyance as a commentator on American democracy derives from his knowing just what he is looking for. He had read Rousseau's *Social Contract* and thought about its essentially democratic teaching with great care before coming to America; and his stated intention in coming was to see democracy itself—in its unadulterated state (which is not to say its only possible, or most mature, or best state). Tocqueville puts forth his ultimate judgment of democracy very cautiously, preferring to insist that democracy is simply a soon to be settled fact of at least the Christian world rather than to argue for it from the standpoint of desirability. Probably Tocqueville thought that democracy might more easily achieve the best that is possible for it if he did not court the contentiousness of any explicit argument but rather made a gesture of bowing to its inevitability—even with a certain vague and gentle reluctance. Still, if democracy was to be simply accepted as a "fact," it was not a morally neutral fact. In his "Introduction" to *Democracy in America,* Tocqueville describes democracy as a Providential fact, and explains the meaning of this ambiguous phrase by saying that democracy brings about the revelation of "the natural greatness of man".[8] Much later in the book, but still in the first of the two great volumes, Tocqueville tips his hand further and says that whatever else might be said in detraction, equality causes men to feel a certain instinctive love for freedom; and in his own name he adds that on that account "That is why I cling to it".[9] On the other hand, this favorable judgment of democracy relates only to its healthy, uncorrupted form. Tocqueville is writing not merely a commentary or even an analysis but a book of practical democratic state-

---

7. Tocqueville, Alexis de *Democracy in America,* ed. J. P. Mayer and Max Lerner, trans. George Lawrence (New York: Harper and Row, 1966), vol. I, p. 248. In what follows I will be quoting from this edition of *Democracy in America* with some frequency. All of the quotations except the one to follow, as explained in note 9, are from the first volume, in which Tocqueville deals with the structural features of American and democratic government and society and the psychology of its governing majority. The second volume of the work, published some five years later than the first, was devoted to discussing the opinions, sentiments and *mores* of individuals in democracy. It is less directly related to the argument of this chapter, although it does contain some interesting remarks about lawyers.

8. *Ibid.,* p. 5

9. Tocqueville, op. cit., p. 643. The sentence is the final one from the first chapter of book four, Volume II of *Democracy,* that is, the book in which he presents his summary and conclusion of the extended discussion that has gone before.

craft; and that in turn is necessary because democracy may take a perverse or debased form, where its fundamental love for equality is indistinguishable from low and petty jealousy that is hostile to freedom of all sorts.

> There is indeed a manly and legitimate passion for equality which rouses in all men a desire to be strong and respected. This passion tends to elevate the little man to the rank of the great. But the human heart also nourishes a debased taste for equality, which leads the weak to want to drag the strong down to their level and which induces men to prefer equality in servitude to inequality in freedom.[10]

The examination of America is intended then as a case study in how a democratic society can promote and preserve the noble love of equality. Europeans will not be able to imitate all of the peculiar, successful features of American democracy, but they can take heart from them, understand them, and perhaps find substitutes.

If we are to understand fully just what the practical lessons are that Tocqueville implies for democratic Europe in his examination of America, we have to be careful not to softpeddle his criticisms of American institutions. This is a common error. Tocqueville courts it because he does not want to insult his American audience and because his overall judgment of America *is* favorable. But to speak broadly, his conclusion regarding American institutions is that they are not models worthy of imitation. For example, he criticizes the institution of the presidency as having too much authority—a defect that is masked by the lack of opportunity for the abuse of such authority in America. He criticizes the system of political jurisdiction for making public officers too vulnerable to discharge at the public's whim. And he criticizes the whole federal system for being too weak in the central administration—a defect that is masked by the fact that the nation is not required to meet the demands of foreign policy or war. American institutions do work because of remarkably lucky and unique physical circumstances and even more so because of the laudable public virtues (*mores*) with which he credits Americans—and these factors will themselves require explanation in the latter parts of the book. Suffice it to say that Americans are able to make a bad system work.

In Volume I of *Democracy in America*, the most sweepingly indicting remarks about American democracy that Tocqueville allows himself are to be found in Part II, Ch. 7, which he titles "The Omnipotence of the Majority in the United States and its Effects." Here he asserts that in America practically every aspect of public life is governed by the princi-

---

10. Ibid., p. 49.

ple that the majority rules. He goes on to observe that the rule of the majority is defended, at least in the popular understanding, by a connection with two other ideas: that since all human intellects are relatively equal, there is likely to be the greatest wisdom in the greatest number; and that the interest of the greater number ought to be preferred to the interest of fewer. It is a feature of Tocqueville's style for him to report these observations in a spirit of equanimity, almost deadpan; nevertheless, he does not hide for long his aversion to them. For as to the first of the majority's defenses, can wisdom be added up in such a way that two or three individuals of modest attainments might have more of it than one superior mind? To take that argument seriously, would we not only have to sum the wisdom of the many but also discount it by the greater sum of their folly? Surely there is something thuggishly irrational about appealing to the greater number in an *argument*. Such appeals, where they are at all convincing, are made just at the point where argument, that is, reason and wisdom, fail. And does not the serious case for freedom of thought and expression depend fundamentally on just the assertion that the wisdom of one or a few may be greater than that of a greater number? And as regards the second defense, where is the *justice* in the sacrifice of one person's interest to that of another's or any number of others? Justice is a *common good*; it may, to be sure, require sacrifice, perhaps even from some more than others. If that sacrifice is to be justifiable, however, must it not be in the name of and for the sake of some good in which all have a stake? That *you* must suffer in order that *I* may enjoy greater satisfaction is the rule of tyranny, the very antithesis of justice. And Tocqueville does say in this context that tyranny, even where it may comprise a majority, is still tyranny. It cannot be excused by the "detestable" maxim that the majority has the right to do everything.

So, the American majority does assert, in a somewhat reckless way, the presumptions of tyranny, and even some of its prerogatives. Still one must be very careful about gauging the actual seriousness that Tocqueville attaches to this charge. One relevant question is, just what is the real alternative to tyranny? Some thinkers have answered this question by suggesting that political authority ought not to be exercised by any one person or identifiable faction in civil society, lest that element rule for the sake of its own good at the expense of others. Democracy would, on this view, have to be rejected as soon as one grants that the majority *is* a distinguishable group, as versus the rich, or the intelligentsia for example. Tocqueville, however, insists uncompromisingly that to define the problem this way is simply to give up the game, for the simple reason that *all* governmental power is exercised by some *one* identifiable group. The idea of a *mixed* system, where, for example, different classes are made to cooperate or to check each other's impetus, which had been argued for by Montesquieu and Aristotle, is rejected by Tocqueville as fraudulent.

> I have always considered what is called a mixed government to be a chimera. There is in truth no such thing as a mixed government (in the sense usually given to the words), since in any society one finds in the end some principle of action that dominates all the others.[11]

Tocqueville does not offer much of an argument in support of this important point; it seems that he offers it more as an observation with which he expects we will likely concur. Democracy, *all* democracy, is rule by a faction and we will admit as much as soon as we recognize that the democratic majority has a distinctive, identifiable character in contrast to other potential ruling groups. But Tocqueville argues that rule by a faction is not necessarily invidious or tyrannical. The democratic majority cannot be effectively checked by any counter majoritarian interest but it nevertheless can be rendered more moderate and self-restrained. It could become virtuous—even just.

> But suppose you were to have a legislative body so composed that it represented the majority without being necessarily the slave of its passions, an executive power having a strength of its own, and a judicial power independent of the other two authorities; then you would still have a democratic government, but there would be hardly any remaining risk of tyranny.[12]

Tocqueville's rejection of the possibility of checking the rule of the democratic majority by any counter majoritarian authority and his recommendation for the moderation of the majority might be described as attacking the problem of tyranny only indirectly. The direct effect of such structural safeguards as he proposes would be to require the democratic majority to rule through a complex of procedures and to maintain the formalities of law. That is to say, such a democracy would be less arbitrary or *despotical*, as versus *tyrannical*; and Tocqueville is careful to elucidate the traditional distinction between these two things just at this point of his argument. Tyranny means the unjust rule by one element of civil society at the expense of others. Despotism means arbitrary or lawless government. One could imagine at least a ruler or ruling body that dispensed with legalities and yet still governed in the name of and for the sake of the common good. Tyranny can never be a good thing, but it need not be despotical. A tyrant, especially a many headed tyrant, might employ the formalities of law to its invidious purposes. However, ordi-

---

11. *Ibid.* p. 232
12. *Ibid.*, p. 233.

narily tyrants are not scrupulous about legalities. To arrange things so that a ruling authority is unable to act arbitrarily and therefore despotically has the effect of *tempering* it. If this technique were fully successful it could even overcome the tendency of that ruling body towards tyranny. This, then, is Tocqueville's interpretation of what the American framers attempted to do through their Constitutional arrangements. He quotes the very famous and seminal passage from *Federalist* # 51 to support the contention.

> It is of great importance in a republic not only to guard the society against the oppression of its rulers, but to guard one part of society against the injustice of the other part....
> Justice is the end of government. It is the end of civil society. It ever has been and ever will be pursued until it be obtained, or until liberty be lost in the pursuit. In a society under the forms of which the stronger faction can readily unite and oppress the weaker, anarchy may as truly be said to reign as in a state of nature, where the weaker individual is not secured against the violence of the stronger; and as, in the latter state, even the stronger individuals are prompted, by the uncertainty of their condition, to submit to a government which may protect the weak as well as themselves; so, in the former state, will the more powerful factions or parties be gradually induced, by a like motive, to wish for a government which will protect all parties, the weaker as well as the more powerful.
> It can be little doubted that if the state of Rhode Island was separated from the Confederacy and left to itself, the insecurity of rights under the popular form of government within such narrow limits would be displayed by such reiterated oppressions of factious majorities that some power altogether independent of the people would soon be called for by the voice of the very factions whose misrule had proved the necessity of it.[13]

It is important to note that although Tocqueville quotes this important, extended passage, he does not fully endorse the argument that Madison is making in it. Madison is here returning to the argument that he had made in the even more famous tenth *Federalist*, wherein he cites as critical the advantage of an extended republic as versus a compact direct democracy. In the extended republic there will probably be a sufficient number of factions that no one of them will be able to rule as a majority in its own right. Ruling majorities in the extended republic of the new nation will, therefore, have to be comprised of several factions whose terms of association will have to be subjected to the public's scrutiny. In short, Madison thinks that, as opposed to what he says is the situation in, say, Rhode Island, in the United States factious government will be overcome. But this is precisely what Tocqueville has said is not

---

13. *Ibid.* p. 240.

really possible. The reason for the difference of opinion is that Tocqueville thinks that the democratic majority will inevitably have the character of a faction, one not rooted in the economic interest of its members but rather in the shared and distinctive *political passion* which is the essence of democracy, namely the love of equality. Therefore, when Tocqueville quotes Madison he does so more by way of showing that he shares with Madison a common view of the problem of the potentially despotical and tyrannical character of the rule of the majority than that he shares Madison's confident solution to that problem. In fact, Tocqueville practically ignores the specific, positive aspect of Madison's thought; instead, he holds Madison to have been engaged in an attempt like his own to render the majority less despotic and, as a hopeful consequence, less tyrannical.

Thus interpreted, Tocqueville indicates that Madison's prescriptions had met with rather limited success. He mentions in this context, for example, that there is in truth very limited intellectual freedom in America. It is a theme that Tocqueville will return to in a much more emphatic way in the second Volume of *Democracy in America*, which he would publish five years later. The weight of majoritarian public opinion in American democracy is such that it tends to crush genuinely contrary opinions even before they are generated. Like John Stuart Mill, that other friend of liberty who admired so much of what he found in *Democracy in America*, Tocqueville assaults democracy and specifically American democracy as exhibiting a soft, heavy tyranny over the mind. He then adds to this indictment the observation that in America one sees a revival of something like a courtier spirit among the citizens.[14] Americans inadvertently mock themselves when they speak of the democratic majority and when they address themselves to it in such obsequious tones that one would think they were in the presence of some whimsical and cruel personal despot and tyrant! In sum, Tocqueville's judgment appears to be that, at least by 1831 when his observations were being formed, American democracy was essentially tyrannical, and that it was a tyranny with despotic proclivities. It is, of course, to Tocqueville's great credit that his love of liberty was so keen that it allowed him to recognize the fact of tyranny even when it lacked a face or a voice. His readers, now as then, may be grateful to him especially on this account.

"Tyranny with despotic proclivities" is, to be sure, a condemnatory phrase, and yet despite that Tocqueville applauds much of what he sees in America and holds it up, if not as a model for Europe to emulate, then at least as an example from which it can take heart that the spirit of lib-

---

14. *Ibid.* pp. 238-39.

erty is compatible with egalitarian conditions. In America, it is not only true that the democratic majority rules, we may even say rules absolutely, but that the democratic majority is practically all that exists! Here there are surely not even the remnants of any such anti-democratic elements as the landed aristocracy that had recently been swept aside in Europe. So what we see is a sort of participatory tyranny, in which all or nearly all are involved. Moreover, the spirit of that involvement is appealing to Tocqueville. It is boisterous, aggressive and high-hearted, so that by way of Tocqueville's description we do see in America what he had earlier called the "noble love of equality" which is practically the same as the lust for freedom. It may seem strange and even shockingly offensive to say that any form of freedom and tyranny may be compatible, but this is in fact part of Tocqueville's rich and subtle, and new, political teaching. Tyranny is the opposite of justice, but it may go together with a certain species of freedom—at least for those, who may be a majority, who are enrolled in it. There is little doubt that Tocqueville thinks Americans are a free people and a great people, for he calls them that, and there is hardly a greater doubt that the majority in America has the features of tyranny. As is indicated by the title of the chapter immediately following the one we have just been examining, "What Tempers the Tyranny of the Majority in the United States," Tocqueville concedes the propriety of the term "tyranny" to America; but it is one that is *tempered* up to a certain point. These tempering factors are key to the explanation of how the institutions in America function without being swept away in a tide of egalitarian impatience and zealotry.

It is in the chapter on tempering the tyranny of the majority that Tocqueville makes his memorable statements regarding the role of lawyers in democratic societies and in American democracy particularly. "The legal profession" is cited here as one of three factors that have this effect, the other two being the decentralization of administration in America and the jury system. As for administrative decentralization, Tocqueville's remarks in this specific context are quite brief. He has, after all, already provided an extended discussion of the subject in Part I of the volume and has explained how it serves to provide opportunity for active participation of the common citizenry in the management of their own local affairs—the very meaning of freedom in practice. And he has already addressed the difficulty of maintaining a useful degree of decentralization while preserving the capacity of the central authority to act effectively where the general good requires it. We will have to return to these themes shortly. For the present it is sufficient to note that Tocqueville now asserts another, related advantage: administrative decentralization makes it difficult for a democratic majority to exercise authority despotically, just because each local administrative unit constitutes a brake against it, constantly challenging the legality of its directives. As for the jury system, Tocqueville's point is that it serves to involve and hence educate the general public in the habit and the value of meting out justice according to legal protocol. That is to say, the political benefit that Tocqueville stresses is gained by the members of the jury; he does not argue the case on the basis of its effect for the accused.

Both administrative decentralization and the jury system are said, then, to be a tempering of majoritarian tyranny by way of resisting despotism; and that benefit also, obviously, holds for the central factor that he discusses: the legal profession. Lawyers are *the* anti-despotic element in any society. Their whole training, and the habits natural to their profession, cause them to have an almost instinctively high regard for authority and for law: its institutions, its procedures, and its mode of reasoning. These characteristics are so distinctive and so opposed to the impatience with legal formalities that democratic citizens sometimes feel, that one is tempted to think of lawyers as a kind of aristocracy even within the bosom of democracy; indeed, we see that democratic citizens do in their less generous moods call them just that. But such language is, of course, only a reflection of how little sense democratic citizens have of what a *real* aristocracy would be. In fact, Tocqueville's account of this matter is perfect. Lawyers do exhibit certain qualities of discipline and taste that are aristocratic; but they are not economically or politically independent. They are only hirelings, after all, and so their interest binds them to whoever employs them. In a democracy, lawyers are bound to serve the general citizenry. Moreover, for the most part democratic citizens know, or sense, that lawyers are bound to them through their interest and this moderates the animosity that they might otherwise feel. So, as lawyers make the claim to expertise when it comes to wrangles over the definition of legitimate authority and the administration of justice, democratic citizens can afford to respect those claims, albeit with a certain admixture of begrudgement.

> When the rich, nobles, and kings are excluded from government, the lawyers then step in to their full rights, for they are then the only men both enlightened and skillful, but not of the people, whom the people can choose.[15]
>
> Lawyers, forming the only enlightened class not distrusted by the people, are naturally called on to fill most public functions.[16]

In sum, lawyers exemplify an indirect, partial, but still invaluable exception to the more general pronouncement that there can be no aristocratic element in democratic society that opposes democracy's natural propen-

---

15. *Ibid.* p. 245.
16. *Ibid.*, p. 248.

sities. But for their influence, democracy would be the tyrannical despotism of the mob.

Tocqueville does not need to recommend that lawyers be influential in democratic society; their good effect is practically an automatic consequence of their situation and their natural disposition. There are, however, particular circumstances about American democracy that render this effect more solid and these might be of special interest to a democratic legislator. The American legal system is like England's insofar as it is rooted in common law, that is, a set of precedents which are themselves not necessarily clear or consistent but which have been in force since before any memory or record runs to the contrary. This is contrasted with the situation of France, whose legal *code* stems from the explicit pronouncement of one lawgiver. The result is that, while laws in France may sometimes be hard to understand, every common citizen may read them and draw his own conclusions. A lawyer in France is simply a person of learning; the conclusions he draws from his practical syllogisms are matter for the scrutiny of non-professionals. In England and America, on the other hand, both the meaning and the authority of the law are rooted in the fact that it is hoary with age. So when a lawyer speaks of that meaning and authority it is as if the lawyer is invested with a special sort of knowledge that is hidden from those who are not of the fraternity. Perhaps a people may find some comfort in deferring to a less than scrutable expertise among lawyers in interpreting the vagaries of the terms whereupon they must resolve their civic disputes because it spares them what would be a painful confrontation with the raw fiat of a legislator. But whether this is so or not, the result of the English/American system is clearly to enhance the status of the legal profession more highly than does the French system and, therefore, to derive greater benefit from their natural virtues.

The tradition of common law that America shares with England is, though, only one of the particular, extra-democratic circumstances that serves to enhance the role of lawyers. The other, perhaps even more significant, circumstance is the whole elaborate system of administrative decentralization in a peculiar and complex federal system of government. Tocqueville has spent most of Part I of the first volume of *Democracy in America* explaining the advantages, and the workings, of this system. He has shown us that the advantage of federalism is in the way that it allows for some degree of local self-government through which a people may become directly involved. One cannot stress too much the importance of this point for Tocqueville; it goes to the very meaning of the distinction between the "noble" love of equality, in freedom, as versus the "debased" form of that passion which seeks only to reduce everyone down to the same dead level.

> Local institutions are to liberty what primary schools are to science; they put it within the people's reach; they teach the people to appreciate its peaceful enjoyment and accustom them to make use of it. Without local institutions a nation may give itself a free government, but it has not got the spirit of liberty.[17]

Federalism, in some form, is simply an indispensable condition for democratic freedom.

This being said, the point that has to follow immediately is that the proper structuring of a federal system is a very tricky proposition. There is probably no one right prescription that would hold good for all nations; the arrangements would have to be accommodated to accidental factors in a way that frustrates the attempt to generalize. One can be clear only about the controlling considerations and the practical difficulties. As Tocqueville cannot help but admit, order, even in secondary matters, is sometimes a matter for national concern. But *when* and *how far*? For example, is it a matter of national concern that each school age child have the opportunity to attend an equally well managed and equally funded public school, which would require central administration of the system? Or is this an area of public policy that the nation can afford to have administered at the local level, and to tolerate the disparate results that will inevitably follow, for the sake of the advantages of inducing local community responsibility and involvement? As we see today, this is a very complicated question that depends on a host of subtle and usually speculative factors. What would be the likely actual effect of local administration of school finance on the overall level of spending for education, and what would be the actual disparity among localities? How important would such disparities be in their ultimate effects on the quality of education? How likely is it that the communities will be interested in their local schools if they do have a certain measure of control? Will their influence be to effect a good educational outcome? Will it, among the whole array of local activities, contribute importantly to the development of responsible freedom? What concession ought to be made to prejudice in favor of local prerogatives?

In Tocqueville's America, such questions tend to be answered in a way that is very favorable to local freedom. This is one of the best known features of his description and one of the most frustrating if we wish to apply his recommendations to other circumstances. The reason is that the vitality of American local governmental units depends upon two lucky circumstances that cannot be reproduced elsewhere. In the first place, America's political history is such that the existence of her towns preceded the states and the nation, so people got used to the idea of

---

17. *Ibid.* p. 173.

doing for themselves at that level and conceded only reluctantly powers to the larger jurisdictions. To breathe life into local communities among a people who are already conscious of themselves as a nation would seem to be a much more difficult prospect. Then, in the second place, America simply does not experience the needs and the perils that require constant exercise of central authority. Here the most important consideration is that she is protected from the dangers of foreign relations by her relative physical isolation. This, though, is obviously an advantage not enjoyed by the European democracies that Tocqueville knows and is thinking about, just as it is no longer an advantage of America today.

> No one can appreciate the advantages of a federal system more than I. I hold it to be one of the most powerful combinations favoring human prosperity and freedom. I envy the lot of the nations that have been allowed to adopt it. But yet I refuse to believe that, with equal force on either side, a confederated nation can long fight against a nation with centralized government power.
>
> A nation that divided its sovereignty when faced by the great military monarchies of Europe would seem to me, by that single act, to be abdicating its power, and perhaps its existence and its name.
>
> How wonderful is the position of the New World, where man has no enemies as yet but himself. To be happy and to be free, it is enough to will it to be so.[18]

All this is not quite to say that there are no lessons that other democracies can learn from examining the structure of American federalism. America does exhibit a novel *type* of federalism. In other federal systems it has ordinarily been the case that the central authority had no authority to act directly on individuals. It needed to engage the executive authority of its subordinate units in order to carry out its resolves. This, Tocqueville asserts, made for constant friction and threatened the confederation with dissolution, which was then sometimes prevented through a seizure of power by the central authority. In America the central authority is *plenary*; the nation has all the aspects of political power—legislation, execution and adjudication—to carry into effect its own resolves. So Tocqueville celebrates in the same terms as does Hamilton or Madison that the American form of federalism is something new and improved insofar as the nation is complete within its own sphere. Like them, Tocqueville thinks it is necessary to call it by a novel and more precise term; he calls it an "incomplete national government".[19]

Still, while the *type* of federalism in America may indeed be worthy of general emulation, the issue of the *degree* of federalism a nation can tol-

---

18. *Ibid.* pp. 154-55.
19. *Ibid.* p. 143.

erate is one that depends decisively on circumstances, not all of which will be equally fortuitous. The theme of federalism relates to the whole issue regarding lawyers since this question of *degree*, that is, of the scope of federal power as versus states' reserved power, is thought by Tocqueville to be a Constitutional question, and hence within the provenance of courts and lawyers.[20] Tocqueville would only have to look, as we know he did look, to what were the most prominent cases decided by the courts by 1831 to conclude that the definition of the terms of American federalism was their principal occupation.

That courts in America define and protect the complex and delicate structure of the federal system is of course dependant on another unique American institution, judicial review. It is a cause for wonder, though, why this institution, which is so obviously useful as to seem indispensable to maintaining the legitimacy of the American regime and its laws, should nevertheless not be fully imitated elsewhere. Although the employment of the courts for some form of constitutional review of executive and even legislative decisions is not uncommon, and in fact appears to be growing in popularity, nowhere outside the United States does the court have so broad and so final an authority. In part the explanation must be sought in the very powerful way that the doctrine of legitimacy by consent in the Declaration of Independence is connected with the idea and the fact of written constitutionalism. Americans tend to see their Constitution as establishing the basic terms *of* the consent that they, or their forefathers, explicitly gave to the new national government. When the court interprets the powers of the government, even its implicit powers, or when it upholds the directly proscriptive passages such as are in the Bill of Rights, Americans feel that the legitimating terms of their basic act of consent are being vindicated. Their legally vested rights are felt to be, or at least to reflect, their fundamental natural right not to be subjected to any coercion to which they did not give their consent. This is, at any rate, the "old time religion" of American constitutionalism. And however much it may have been beleaguered over the whole course of our constitutional history, it is probably still necessary to the explanation of the authority that courts exercise in America, and less directly but still fundamentally necessary to the continued authority of the regime itself.

Does not the institution of judicial review, though, pose the problem of too much rigidity in our politics? This has been, at various times in

---

20. The question of how far the issue of the separation of powers and hence the structure of American federalism is a Constitutional question has itself been a question of debate among the Supreme Court justices. Tocqueville's view of this matter is Madison's, endorsed as authoritative by Justice O'Connor in, e.g. *Garcia v. MTA*.

American history, a common complaint, namely, that too strict an adherence to the Constitution's formal terminology gets in the way of public policies that are useful or even necessary in dealing with changing circumstances. The problem can be severe, especially since the distinction between the "legal questions" that the court is charged to answer and the "political questions" of public policy left to the people's representatives is itself somewhat artificial and hence hard to delineate. For his part, Tocqueville shows how keenly he is aware of this whole range of difficulties insofar as he discusses the peculiar attitude that Americans have towards the alteration of the Constitution, and how this helps to sustain judicial review. Americans occupy a position regarding this matter that is a compromise between the French, who hold that their constitution is not changeable, and the English, who allow their largely unwritten constitution to be changed through legislative enactment. The French may be presumed to see the anomaly in allowing that any officer or authoritative procedure could change a constitution which is itself created by that constitution. The constitution can therefore be changed only by the authority or power that created it. When that happens, it is really the case that the regime has perished and been replaced with a new one more or less similar to the old. To deny any of this is simply to fail to think through what it means to be a *constitution* and just how it is superior to all subordinate authority. We can imagine a Frenchman asking an American a rather embarrassing question: suppose there were a constitutional amendment that abolished the House of Representatives or which changed the procedure for making further amendments. Could your system tolerate that? Whatever the cogency of this view, though, Tocqueville knows that it can never be tolerated by a democracy. If there were a special agency charged to speak for the constitution, for example a court, and if it were to resist or rebut the wishes of the popular majority *with no possibility of the majority's changing the text,* it would be swept away, through some despotic act. As it is the French do court this danger; they avoid it insofar as they do not have recourse to the terms of their constitution in dealing with the ongoing problems of political life. In other words, they do not have judicial review. The more pragmatic English are continually reinterpreting the meaning of their constitution as new contingencies and the prudence to deal with them dictate. This is a task, perhaps the highest task, for the members of the legislature. In England the legislature is a sort of "living constitution" unto itself. It is a workable arrangement; however, it is one which has little resistance to the legislative despotism that Tocqueville shows is the natural danger in all democracies. There can be no *judicial* review in England of the American sort that legitimates and moderates government. The English model is suitable for England, as Tocqueville describes it, because, as we must not forget, England is not a fundamentally democratic nation. Her legislature enjoys, and endeavors to merit, a certain measure of deference for exercising aristocratic prerogative. Parliament represents, or at least inherits the legacy, of a class that embodied England.

In sum, the institution of judicial review is the crown of the American democratic faith in *law*. The consequent deference to lawyers in American democracy is a corollary and partial substitute for the deference that a traditional aristocracy claimed for its wisdom and virtue. Some such substitute is necessary lest democracy be condemned to despotism and the tyranny of the mob. The substitute is possible insofar as democracy does not *crave* despotism. It may be brought to believe in, to experience and feel, the rule of law as the mode through which the people rule themselves. Given the delicacy of the rule of law, however, perhaps it is wrong to speak of a *substitute* for living wisdom. Rather, we are bound to hope that lawyers themselves should exercise it, albeit modestly and in keeping with their professionalism.

Conclusion: The Rule of Law and Lawyers in Contemporary Democracy

If we now consider the contemporary situation of American democracy with regard to the role of lawyers in public life, it appears that Tocqueville's observations remain forceful. In fact, if anything the role of lawyers has increased since the early Nineteenth Century. As a percentage of the population as a whole, the number of lawyers has grown considerably. Political offices continue to be held normally by lawyers, such that a legal education is the most common element in an American *cursus honorem* for a political career. What is most important among post-Tocquevillian developments, however, is that public policy has become increasingly determined by courts. This is a development that has, naturally, worried many commentators and even ordinary citizens. Justice Robert Jackson's phrase, "government by lawsuit," marks the danger of the atrophy of the other, more directly representative branches of government, whether as cause or effect.

In view of this development, what may we think of Tocqueville's argument that lawyers tend to preserve democracy against the danger of despotism? Are we still entitled to this charitable interpretation? For the most part the answer surely has to be yes; what Tocqueville said did not turn on any particulars that have eroded over the last 170 years. Nevertheless, if Tocqueville were alive today, he would surely have to take notice of the fact that there have been some more than subtle changes in what he described as the taste and instinct of the profession, changes that he might justifiably attribute to the continuing process of democratization of American society and of the American mind. This change of attitude towards law is something which was pounded home in monographs and in case after case by progressive jurists, and its implications have been subsequently broadened at the hands of "pragmatist" professors and their practicing students. The aim was to bring about a certain weakening of the belief in the formality of the law; and this has been partially effective within the ranks of lawyers and even among the general public. Progressives and pragmatists set out to debunk, even demythologize, what traditionalists claim is an implicit claim of the law to self evident meaning, which lawyers and judges can know and apply impersonally. They argue that all laws, as all words, require interpretation. We human beings simply cannot escape the requirement of figuring out the meaning of what has been said or written in the light of our own current experience. Where the text is a legal command, one must determine what the actual consequences of this or that interpretation would likely be for us in the contemporary situation and then assess those with, it is to be hoped, a deepened understanding of the controlling values at stake, and decide accordingly what the command is.

Thus, for example, the commentator Margaret Jane Radin writes that our notion of "property" in the Constitution's "takings" clause should be read as having any of several different meanings depending upon how each one in various circumstances affects the prospects for what she calls "human flourishing."[21] The word will mean one thing when it operates to resist legal restrictions on selling it, another when it operates to resist legal restrictions on its use. Or, Justice Brennan can express his now famous opinion that the Eighth Amendment's ban of "cruel and unusual punishments" means that the death penalty is unconstitutional even though it was not deemed so by the framers of the Amendment. The Amendment no longer means what it did for its framers, says Brennan, but rather proscribes what is "cruel and unusual" *for us*, given our deepened sense of "human dignity" and the "supreme value of a democracy (as) the presumed worth of each individual."[22]

---

21. Margaret Jane Radin, "The Constitution and the Liberal Conception of Property," quoted in McCann and Houseman, *Judging the Constitution* (Glenview: Scott, Foresman, 1989), p. 221.

22. Cf. Brennan's opinions in *Furman v. Georgia* and *Gregg v. Georgia* especially. Justice Brennan set out the controlling principles of his jurisprudence best in his article, "The Constitution of the United States: Contemporary Ratification," *South Texas Law Review*, vol. 27 (1985–86): 433.

For the detractors of this way of thinking, such pragmatism is a transparent excuse for unprincipledness. In his well known criticism of Brennan, for example, Judge Robert Bork insists that once one abandons the attempt to be guided by the plain meaning of the words of the legal text, as amplified by the explicit intentions of its framers, one is at sea with neither rudder nor compass. It is, in short, judicial despotism.[23] Bork bitterly contests the ironic development that the very agency whose authority derives from the commitment of our society to the rule of law should itself take the law into its own hands. And then brazenly to offer a public defense as well! In response, pragmatists profess bewilderment. Who can deny that the meaning of the words of the law is not always clear or self-evident? Who can deny that the intention of the framers is itself likely also to be unclear, especially insofar as situations diverge? Who can deny that words require interpretation? We must simply do our best with the resources of our own experience. If we do so in broad daylight, so to speak, unencumbered by invidious self-interest, where is the problem? This *is* legal reasoning.[24]

The pragmatist argument would be more politically persuasive than it is if proponents such as Justice Brennan demurred from employing slogans like "(the) sparkling vision of the supremacy of the human dignity of every individual" which are anything but clear or uncontroversial. If we were persuaded that what Brennan and others assert to be a "deepened understanding" of the law's basic text were truly deeper and contained more *understanding*, why then we could afford to be more comfortable with a continual reinterpretation even where it strayed far afield from anything we can plausibly presume its framers had in mind. This is, however, simply not true. For example, to cite what was a key issue for the Justice, there are many sincere and thoughtful people who think and feel that "human dignity" actually requires capital punishment for certain crimes of exceeding heinousness. Brennan himself, though, considered it to be a violation of human dignity. Similarly, human dignity has been employed as grounds for both sides of controversies regarding instances of a legal right to "privacy." As individuals, we are still permitted to ask in all seriousness, "What *is* human dignity?" but as a society we ought to recognize that we are not all of the same mind and heart regarding these profound matters. Where disagreements about these mat-

---

23. Robert H. Bork, "Interpreting the Constitution," reprinted in Peter Augustine Lawler and Robert Martin Schaefer, *Political Rhetoric* (Lanham: Rowman & Littlefield, Publishers. Inc., 1995), pp. 263–5.

24. Cf. Lief H. Carter, *Reason in Law*, fourth edition (New York, HarperCollins College Publishers, 1994).

ters exists, there is the need for *law*. That is to say, there is the need to stand fast with what the law has been held to mean as consistently as we can, from its framing and over the course of its history. Even when the consequences of such steadfastness may seem inconvenient or bizarre, such instances prove that it is not impossible to be aware that the law means something different from what we might like it to mean. Where the inconveniences are significant, the law may be changed. But to preserve a commitment to the rule of law while changing it requires that the changes be made through the procedures that the law itself prescribes. Those procedures preserve and promote the fundamental responsibility of those who make the law. In a democracy, those are the representatives of the people themselves.

Strictly speaking, the pragmatic approach to legal reasoning ought to have neutral or unpredictable consequences regarding just what particular interpretations may be read into the law. This, in fact, is part of the public criticism of it that Judge Bork and others state. In reality, though, the specific outcomes of decisions that avail themselves of a pragmatic approach are rather predictable; one cannot put too fine a point on it but the tendency is towards a progressive egalitarianism. Questions of the definition of legally vested rights remain difficult, of course, but the aim tends to be to answer these with reference to the notion of the equality of basic values and the equal claim to respect among persons holding divergent values. Social equality is by and large taken to be the meaning of social justice. It is held to be the overarching aim of good legislative policy and, as regards the exercise of jurisprudence, it is the guide for the interpretation of existing law. To cite Justice Brennan's "deepened understanding" once more, what he means is not that he or we understand the substance of human dignity more deeply than before except in the respect that, whatever it is, it is something that applies to all human beings equally. For him it is a matter of course that the framers were enamored of democracy because of the "sparkling vision of the supremacy of the human dignity of every individual," which he sees in the Bill of Rights and the Civil War Amendments. This, though, is precisely where the serious *questions* arise, or ought to. These questions become obvious as soon as one begins to think along the lines of political statecraft, to which we are directed by a Tocqueville. *Practically* speaking, among the various sorts of government one might consider, *is* democracy in fact most conducive to the promotion of human dignity, or of those rights that we may think human beings have equally? Which sort of democracy? May not a society commit itself to structuring social relationships in a way that maximizes the *equal* respect or recognition to which all are thought to be entitled but by way of such restrictions on freedom that end up reducing all to a dead level? What, in other words, of the distinction, fundamental to Tocqueville, between the love of equality consonant with nobility as versus the "debased" taste for it which leads the weak to try and drag the strong down to a common level of attainment?

If we are trying to think about the reasons for the egalitarian prejudices of members of the contemporary legal community who are nontraditionalists, we are led back to the issue of the grounds for the fundamental animus towards democracy, with which this chapter began. We need to explicate the profound connection between law and equality which caused democracy to emerge out of classical Liberalism, more particularly out of the incompleteness of classical Liberalism. Such an explication demands in the very first place a clear recognition that democracy is not essentially entailed in the unalienable rights that the *Declaration of Independence* says all men have, Justice Brennan to the contrary not withstanding. For Liberalism, *the* evil to be avoided is the *arbitrary* force to which we are subject in the state of nature. Government negates this evil by establishing *legitimate* authority. Such legitimate authority has two essential features, really two sides of the same coin: it derives from and rests upon the *consent* of those who are subject to it, and it maintains the claim of such universal consent by acting categorically, which is to say by adopting the form of *law* which is "no respecter of persons." That everyone is then entitled to "the equal protection of the law" is a necessary aspect of the foundation for authority thus understood. Those for whom the law is their profession, judges and attorneys, are naturally disposed to honor the idea of equality in *this* sense at least. But what, then, can be the aim of legislation? What can be the *purpose* of law, as distinct from its legitimizing condition? Liberalism does not provide an answer to that question. What is worse, in a way it denies that there can be any rational answer, since consent has to be the whole standard for Liberal government. Whatever the people consent to *ipso facto* meets the test. If this were not so, there would be some forms of consent which a people could not rightfully give. Nevertheless, despite the neutralism of Liberal thought, questions of which policies and laws are good ones have to be answered somehow. The result is unavoidable. The citizens of a Liberal political community cannot help but misunderstand their own public philosophy and, having no other recourse, make the attempt to wring out of Liberalism a substantive answer to the questions about which form of government and of society are *good*. Mere legitimacy tends to take on the meaning of goodness and justice. (We hear the result in our vernacular; the very word "legitimate" tends to take on the meaning of "reasonable," as in "legitimate disagreements," or "legitimate arguments.") So, as the proviso that legitimate authority must treat all persons, however unequal, as equals becomes pressed into serving as the aim of public policy, equality tends to become conflated with justice.

Contemporary egalitarians resonate to a morality that is lodged in what Kant calls "the idea of law itself," which practically means equality.[25] This is what is meant by "deepened understanding" of the text of the Constitution, for example. Understandably, someone who has made the jump from a study of the law's specific provisions to this notion of its deep *moral* meaning would be impatient when its specific provisions, as traditionally interpreted, seemed to be in conflict with its deep moral meaning. Examples would be when a traditionalist might cite the equal protection clause as forbidding "recompensatory" discrimination; or when it is shown that the framers of the Eighth Amendment simply did not think that the death penalty was unconstitutionally cruel and unusual on grounds of repudiating the human dignity of a capital criminal. Pragmatism is then availed of as a mode of legal reasoning that preserves and deepens the true moral meaning of the law. If this is an excuse for despotism, it must feel like the despotism of the law's truest servants, serving to maintain its conscience. Should we not be mistrustful, though, of so partisan a "conscience"?

When Tocqueville makes his famous statement that "in America every question becomes, before long, a legal question and a judicial one," he is reflecting something that only partly results from distinctively American factors. More fundamentally, the tendency to translate questions of our common life into a form for lawyers and courts is connected with Liberalism and democracy in general. Democracy itself is a product of a sort of fetishism of legitimacy, which Liberal society can scarcely avoid. This fetishism is the root of both the burgeoning social and political significance of lawyers and of the attribution of a moral value to democracy. Thus, in *Democracy in America*, Tocqueville declines from making an explicit argument in support of the natural justice of democracy, or relatedly, of the reasons for the irresistible power of the democratic movement which he describes. Instead he does what he can to reconcile his readers to democracy by insisting that it is a "Providential fact." But consider carefully the implications of his remark in a note to his own text, where he remarks that the French Revolution only perfected a taste and movement towards centralization that began "when lawyers came into the government."[26] Tocqueville is generally sanguine about the expected role of lawyers in democracy because, he says, their natural instinct for authority and discipline will tend to temper the tyranny of the majority by making it less despotical than it would otherwise be. It is an observation that remains relevant and profoundly important. However,

---

25. One may observe this Kantianism in, for example, Lawrence Tribe's widely used text, *American Constitutional Law* (Mineola: Foundation Press, 1988).

26. Tocqueville, op. cit., p. 696, note K.

the instinct for authority and discipline may not be as definitive of the legal profession today as Tocqueville observed it to be. As democracy has continued to develop, contemporary lawyers tend more to feel and act as the egalitarian conscience of their nation. Is it not easy to see that the "judicialization of political questions" in America over the last fifty years has gone hand in hand with a more egalitarian interpretation of social justice? This vague morality, however, may now itself operate in the service of what Tocqueville feared most, a tyranny of the lowest common denominator. These considerations point to an obvious conclusion. It behooves us, the nation, to think about the education that is provided to the class of professionals who must necessarily represent us and even rule us. The soft corruptibility of their best instinct, for justice as they may understand it, should be toughened and elevated towards thoughtful, practical statecraft. One modest recommendation would be that during their undergraduate years they might encounter Tocqueville, and be required to consider carefully his political science.

PART III

Private Virtues, Public Vices

Chapter Eight

Ethics and Politics: The American Way[1]

Martin Diamond

All men have some notion of what we may call the universal aspect of the relationship between ethics and politics, a notion of what the relationship would be for men at their very best. The unqualified phrase in the title of this essay — "Ethics and Politics" — points to that universal aspect, to the idea of an ethics proper to man as such and to the political ordering appropriate to that ethics. But the qualification — "The American Way" — reminds that ethics and politics always and everywhere form a particular relationship, a distinctive way in which each people organizes its humanness. The whole title together indicates the intention of this essay: while taking our bearings from the universal relationship of ethics and politics, we will examine the special "American way" in which ethics and politics are related to each other here.

I

The "American way of life" is a familiar phrase that nicely captures the notion that the relationship of ethics and politics has everywhere a unique manifestation. Yet familiar as the phrase is to us, we Americans characteristically overlook that notion when we think about ethics and politics. Instead, more than most other people, we tend to consider the relationship of ethics and politics in universal terms. Perhaps this is because we have been shaped to such a great extent by the principles of the Declaration of Independence, which of course addresses itself to all mankind and conceives political life in terms of rights to which all men are by nature entitled. Our tendency to understand moral principles in universal terms may also be furthered by the lingering influence of the

---

[1] This chapter originally appeared as "Ethics and Politics: The American Way," in Robert Horwitz, ed., *The Moral Foundations of the American Republic*, 3rd ed. (Charlottesville, VA: University Press of Virginia, 1986). Reprinted by permission of Kenyon College.

Biblical heritage, which lays down moral principles applicable to all men in all countries. To the extent that Americans continue to be guided by the Biblical outlook, their disposition to understand the relationship between ethics and politics in universal terms is reinforced. This propensity is perhaps also furthered by a tendency of democracy described by Tocqueville. He observed that democratic people, because of their extreme love of equality, tend to abstract from human differences and thus to think of man with a capital M—that is to say, in generic terms—rather than in terms of the many subtle gradations of human experience. Whatever the reasons, the familiar fact is that Americans generally think about politics in terms of a universal morality and, therefore, to view the relationship of ethics and politics almost exclusively in its universal aspect.

Oddly enough, in always thinking about ethics and politics in terms applicable to all men everywhere, we have in fact narrowed the idea of ethics. Today we think of ethics, not in the broad sense in which it was understood by classical political philosophy, but rather in the much narrower sense now conveyed by the word *morality*. Our word *morality* was originally derived from Cicero's Latin rendering of the Greek word for ethics, but it gradually acquired a quite different and narrower meaning. We think of ethics or morality today primarily in the limited, negative sense of "thou shall nots," as Puritanical or Victorian "no-no's." Ethics or morality thus narrowed down to a number of prohibitions has indeed a universal status; all men *are* under the same obligation not to murder, steal, bear false witness, and the like. Since morality thus conceived applies to all men as men, all regimes are deemed as obliged to honor it; hence the relationship of ethics and politics comes to be seen only in its universal aspect. The same narrowing effect on the idea of ethics is also produced by the modern theory of natural rights. That is, in this view of civil society, the politically relevant aspect of morality or ethics is similarly reduced to negative prohibitions on what governments and men may do. And this narrowing also has the effect of making political morality universally obligatory in the same way upon all regimes.

But morality thus universally conceived hampers our understanding of the particular relationship of ethics and politics within each political order or regime. To recover this understanding and apply it to the American case, we have to recapture something of the original broad meaning of ethics as it presented itself in classic Greek political philosophy. For that purpose Aristotle's *Ethics* will suffice. Aristotle deals of course with such universal prohibitions as those against murder, theft, and lying. However, Aristotle's understanding of ethics is not chiefly concerned with such prohibitions, but, much more importantly, with positive human excellences or virtues in the broadest sense. Notice well: excellences or virtues. Aristotle's word *arete* is usually and properly translated as *virtue*. But because the word *virtue* is now understood in the same narrow and negative sense as morality, it is important to associate with it the positive word, excellence, in order to bring out the positive implications of Aristotle's ethical teaching.

For example, the very first virtue that Aristotle discusses is courage; while late in his discussion he includes as a minor ethical virtue or excellence the quality of affability. Today we would hardly consider either courage (as Aristotle meant it, namely, the kind demanded in military combat) or affability as belonging to a discussion of virtue or morality. They might be regarded as useful or even admirable qualities, but surely not as virtuous or moral qualities; they simply do not fit our modern conception. In contrast to our narrow view, Aristotle meant by the virtues all those qualities required for the full development of humanness, that is, all those qualities that comprise the health or completion of human character. This is the key: the very word *ethics* literally meant *character* to the Greeks, and the idea of character formation is the foundation of the ancient idea of ethics. When ethics is thus understood as being concerned with the formation and perfection of human character, we may more readily understand not only why ethics and politics have a universal relationship proper to man as man, but also why a unique relationship between ethics and politics is necessarily formed within each particular political order.

This necessity is made clearer by reference to a Greek word that is still familiar to us in the English use we make of it—namely, *ethos;* indeed, this is the Greek word from which our word *ethics* derives. A given pattern of ethics forms, as it were, an *ethos*. Like the Greeks, we still mean by ethos that a group or other entity possesses certain fundamental features that form its distinctive character. Something like this is what we mean when we speak, say, of "the ethos of Chaplin's films" or "the ethos of poverty." Ethics understood in this old, broad sense, as forming an ethos, helps to make clear why there is a distinctive relationship of ethics and politics in every regime. In all political communities, humanity manifests itself in some particular way, in the formation of a distinctive character or characters. It is the distinctive human types nurtured in each regime that manifest the ethos of that regime. This is not, of course, to say that any such community is formed of identical human types; much human variety can be found in any complex society. But still we know that something is at work that makes a certain kind of human character more likely to occur in one setting and among one people, rather than another. We would be surprised, for example, to find Cotton Mather fully formed and flourishing in the Berlin of the 1920s. We would be surprised to find a full-fledged, homegrown Oscar Wilde in old Dodge City.

It is likewise most unlikely that George Babbitt would have turned up in the early Roman republic; he belongs to Zenith, the fastest growing town in the Middle West. Such distinctive human characters are the nurture of a particular *ethos*, so to speak.

How can we account for the fact that each country forms its own peculiar ethos? We know that differing physical circumstances have something to do with the matter. The character of a people permanently settled on rich agricultural land and earning its living by farming will differ from that of a tribe of desert nomads who eke out an uncertain existence from their flocks and herds as they move from oasis to oasis. Each people will tend by virtue of its circumstances to value different human qualities and to nurture them. Technological development, "modes of production," and other such factors all have similar effects in the production of modal human types. But greater than the effect of all such material factors is the effect on human development of mores and laws, that is, of the political order or the regime. The difference of human characters in the various regimes is above all the product of the distinctive relationship between ethics and politics within each regime. Each political regime is, so to speak, in the business of handicrafting distinctive human characters. Indeed, each political order is literally constituted by the kind of human character it aims at and tends to form.

We may explore the meaning of this by considering Aristotle's well-known argument regarding the way political communities come into being. The lesser forms of human association—the family, tribe, and village—do not suffice for the fulfillment of man's nature; for that purpose, Aristotle argues, the form of human association must reach to the level of the *polis,* the political community. This is because the prepolitical associations serve largely for the mere preservation of life; they correspond in some respects to the hives or herds through which other social animals, such as bees and elephants, preserve themselves. These primary and rudimentary associations are adequate for bees and elephants because mere preservation of life is all that their beings require.

But the full development of man's being requires something more. He has an ethical need, a need that follows from his possession of *logos,* his unique faculty for speaking-reasoning, the faculty that defines man and distinguishes him from all other creatures. It is this faculty that enables and impels man to ponder "the advantageous and the harmful, and therefore also the just and the unjust."[2] Man's ethical need consists precisely in his capacity to reason out a view of the "advantageous and the

---

2. Aristotle, *Politics,* 1253a15 *et seq.* The translation here, and elsewhere in this essay, is that of Professor Lawrence Berns, who has kindly given permission to quote from a translation of the *Politics* that he is now preparing.

just" and to organize his character and his life upon that basis. Because of this inherent capacity, this need for the formation of his full human character, man is ultimately impelled toward the formation of the polis. The subpolitical associations of the family, the tribe, and the village do not form a sufficient habitat for the full development of humanness. The polis is then, above all, understood by Aristotle as an association for the formation of character. It is a partnership within which the character of citizens is formed in accordance with some shared view of "the advantageous and the harmful" for man.

From this it followed for Aristotle that the very best polis would be that one partnership which, because it was based on the true view of what is "advantageous and just," would generate the highest human character. This idea of the "best regime" in which the best human character would be formed represents the Aristotelian understanding of the universal aspect of the relationship between ethics and politics. In this Aristotle differs, of course, from the modern approach which, as we have seen, makes the universal aspect of the ethics-politics relationship that which can be demanded and actualized everywhere. In contrast, the ancient approach was paradigmatic only; the universal aspect for Aristotle consists in a model of the one best character-forming regime, a model that serves as a standard for understanding and dealing with the enormous variety of actual, imperfect character-forming regimes. As measured against that model of the best regime, all other regimes would be understood as based on varying imperfect views of what is advantageous and just, and all would differ accordingly in the human characters they produced. In this particular regime, courage would be nurtured to a fault, there piety, here the love of honor, there domination, here commercial daring, and so forth through all the shadings and combinations of the possible human qualities. This is the exact sense in which it may be said that each polis actualized human character in a particular way and hence that in each polis there is a unique relationship of ethics and politics.

On the basis of this analysis of the polis as a character-forming association, Aristotle might well have denied that most contemporary "states" are genuine political communities. In any event, he does explicitly deny the status of political community to certain aggregations of people whose arrangements sound suspiciously like our own. That is, he explicitly characterizes as subpolitical those mere alliances or contractual arrangements for the sake of commerce, and even those arrangements that, somewhat more broadly, seek to prevent fellow residents from being "unjust to one another." Societies based on such arrangements may have a thriving commerce, life in them may be secure and tranquil, and they might appear to Americans to be adequate political societies.

But for Aristotle they still would lack the crucial political desideratum—namely, a "concern with what the qualities of the others are," that is, a concern for the development among fellow citizens of certain common ethical excellences and hence a common character.[3]

For Aristotle, the formation of this common character is what makes an association political, and the question of how these character-forming ethical excellences are to be developed in man is what links ethics and politics. Indeed, this is literally the link between Aristotle's two great practical works, the *Ethics* and the *Politics*.[4] At the end of the *Ethics*, when he has finished his account of the excellences that perfect the human character, Aristotle says that it will now be necessary to turn to the study of politics. This is because human nature does not find it readily pleasant to acquire and persist in the character-forming excellences. To say the least, the idea of the good is not of itself sufficiently compelling to regulate behavior. Hence men will not be perfected merely by precept and exhortation, and not even by paternal authority. Human character, Aristotle argues, can be perfected only within a comprehensive system of character-forming conditions and constraints—in short, within the political community. Only within the political community, and through what it alone can supply, namely, good laws "with teeth in them," can men in fact raise their characters above the merely necessitous life, or above a life of mere passional indulgence.

In the ancient view, then, political life had the immensely important ethical function of providing the way through which man could complete or perfect this humanness. No wonder then that the laws, by means of which human character was to be formed, had to have teeth in them. So comprehensive and elevated an end made extraordinarily strenuous demands upon the political art. The classical political teaching took its bearings from the highest potentialities of human nature. Making no egalitarian presuppositions, it did not believe that all human beings or, indeed, even most human beings, could be perfected. But it thought it right and necessary that every resource of the political art be employed to realize the highest potential of the few, while providing as just a political order as was possible for those many others whose potentialities or circumstances precluded the highest development. This helps us to understand something of the harsh demands of the classical teaching: the general sternness of the laws; the emphasis placed on rigorous and comprehensive programs of education; the strict regulation of much that we now deem "private"; the necessity of civic piety; the extremely limited size of the polis; and the severe restrictions on private economic activity.

---

3. *Ibid.*, 1280a34 *et seq.*
4. Aristotle, *Ethics*, 179a33 et seq. (Loeb Classical Library ed.).

These and other stern and strenuous measures were necessitated by the height of the human excellence that the classic political teaching sought to produce. An unceasingly demanding and powerful political art was required if men were to be raised so high against the downward pulls of ease, creature comfort, and the lower pleasures.

II

In the light of all the foregoing, how might Aristotle rank America? Would he characterize it as a genuine political community, one with its own special moral foundation, or only as "an association of place and of not acting unjustly to one another and for the sake of trade"? Would he find it a place where law is only "a compact, just as Lycophron the Sophist said, a guarantor for one another of the just things, but not able to make the citizens good and just"[5]— that is, good and just in the way their characters were formed and not merely in conformity to a compact? Or might he conclude that there is indeed an American political ethos, a unique character-forming mix of ethics and politics? In short, is there an "American way" by which this republic nurtures in its citizens certain ethical excellences upon the basis of some particular view of what is advantageous and just?

If the answer proves to be that somehow America is an authentic political community, that there is in fact an "American way" of political-ethical character formation, it will surely not be in the classical way but in a distinctively modern way. This is because America was formed on the basis of that modern political thought that waged so successful a war against the political outlook of antiquity. The classical understanding of the proper relationship between ethics and politics dominated the Western world for nearly two millennia, as did classical political philosophy generally, albeit modified by Christianity. But the great traditions of classical and Christian political philosophy came under trenchant attack during the sixteenth and seventeenth centuries by such political philosophers as Machiavelli, Bacon, Hobbes, and Locke.[6] These proponents of a "new science of politics" charged that classical and Christian political philosophy had been both misguided and ineffective, in a word, "utopian." They observed that, during some two thousand years of this

---

5. *Politics*, 1280b10 *et seq*.

6. Acknowledgment is gladly made of my indebtedness here and throughout to the late Professor Leo Strauss, whose instructive account of the "battle of the books," ancient and modern, has done so much to restore the meaning of the modern enterprise and to renew our grasp of the ancient alternative.

elevated political and religious teaching, man's lot on this earth had remained miserable; his estate had not been relieved. Greed and vainglory ruled under the guise of virtue or piety, and the religious tyrannies and wars of the sixteenth and seventeenth centuries had but climaxed two millennia of the failure of the old, utopian political science.

Blaming classical and medieval thought for adhering to dangerous illusions regarding the way men *ought* to live, that is, for trying to shape human character by misleading and unachievable standards of perfection, the new, or modern, political philosophers purported to base their views and recommendations upon the character of man "as he actually *is*." In place of the lofty and seemingly unrealistic virtues demanded by classical and Christian political philosophy, the moderns accepted as irremediably dominant in human nature the self-interestedness and passions displayed by men everywhere. But precisely on that realistic basis, they argued, workable solutions could at last be found to hitherto unresolved political problems. This meant, as opposed to ancient and medieval exhortation and compulsion of man to high virtue, a lowering of the aims and expectations of political life, perhaps of human life generally. As it were, the new political science gave a primacy to the efficacy of means rather than to the nobility of ends: The ends of political life were reduced to a commensurability with the human means readily and universally available. In place of the utopian end postulated by the ancients, the forced elevation of human character, the moderns substituted a lowered political end, namely, human comfort and security. This lowered end was more realistic, they argued, because it could be achieved by taking human character much as actually found everywhere, or by molding it on a less demanding model than that of the premodern understanding.

This removal of the task of character formation from its previously preeminent place on the agenda of politics had an immense consequence for the relationship of ethics and politics in modern regimes. The hallmark of the traditional ethics-politics relationship had been those harsh and comprehensive laws by means of which the ancient philosophers had sought to "high-tone" human character. But now, because character formation was no longer the direct end of politics, the new science of politics could dispense with those laws and, for the achievement of its lowered ends, could rely largely instead upon shrewd institutional arrangements of the powerful human passions and interests. Not to instruct and to transcend these passions and interests, but rather to channel and to use them became the hallmark of modern politics. Politics could now concentrate upon the "realistic" task of directing man's passions and interests toward the achievement of those solid goods this earth has to offer: self-preservation and the protection of those individual liberties which are an integral part of that preservation and which make it decent and agreeable.

One has only to call to mind the Declaration of Independence to see that such commodious self-preservation and its corollary individual liberties came to be viewed as the sole legitimate objects of government. In short, whatever the modern perspective may leave of the traditional lofty virtues for men to seek in their private capacities, it drastically reduces or limits the legitimate scope of government. Indeed, the very idea of *government*—as distinguished from the old, more encompassing idea of *polity* or regime—was a response to this restriction in the scope of the political. In the old, broader view, "government" was inextricably linked with "society." Since it was the task of the laws to create a way of life or to nurture among citizens certain qualities of character, then the laws necessarily had to penetrate every aspect of a community's life; there could be no separation of state or government and society, and no limitation of the former with respect to the latter. But under the new liberal doctrine, with its substantive withdrawal of the character-forming function from the domain of the political, it became natural to think of state and society as separated, and of government as limited to the protection of individual life, liberty, property, and the private pursuit of happiness. It became both possible and reasonable to depoliticize political life as previously conceived, and that is precisely what happened wherever the new view came to prevail. Perhaps above all, religion was depoliticized; belief and practice regarding the gods, which classical political philosophy had held to be centrally within the purview of the political community, was largely relegated to private discretion. Similarly depoliticized were many other traditional political matters such as education, poetry and the arts, family mores, and many of the activities we now lump under the term "economics." In the premodern understanding, these were precisely the matters that had to be regulated by "laws with teeth in them," because they were the essential means by which a regime could form human characters in its own particular mold.

With the removal or reduction from political life of what had for two thousand years been regarded as its chief function, namely, ethical character formation based on some elevated view of the "advantageous and just," what, then, became that chief function of politics in the new understanding? A striking and explicit answer to this question is to be found in James Madison's *Federalist* 10, perhaps the most remarkable single American expression of the "improved" or new science of politics. At the end of the famous paragraph in which he argues that the latent causes of faction are ineradicably sown in human nature, Madison sketches the "most common and durable" of those ineradicable causes, namely, the diversity of economic interests. He then states one of the most important conclusions of his essay: "The regulation of these various and interfering interests forms the principal task of modern legislation and involves the spirit of party and faction in the necessary and ordinary operations of government." Notice: "the principal task of *modern* legislation"; Madison is acutely aware of the modernity of his political analyses and solutions. He does not tell us what the premodern principal task was, and we may not put words in his mouth; but we will see how his principal modern task becomes intelligible precisely when contradistinguished from the principal task of the premodern political art as that has been presented in this essay. Bringing that modern task clearly to light may teach us something about the "American way" regarding the relationship of ethics and politics.

III

Madison announces his theoretical intention: "To secure the public good and private rights... and at the same time to preserve the spirit and form of popular government, is then the great object to which our inquiries are directed." Only by a showing that popular government can now avoid committing those injuries to the public good and private rights, which have hitherto proved its undoing, can this form of government "be rescued from the opprobrium under which it has so long labored." Taken as a whole, then, James Madison's "inquiries" provide a comprehensive statement of the way political science should address the pathology of democracy. In *Federalist* 10, Madison outlines that part of his political science upon the basis of which the gravest imperfection of popular government may be guarded against, namely, the propensity of that form of government to "the violence of faction." In examining his argument regarding the problem of faction, we want to pay particular attention to the way Madison deals with the problem of *opinion*. It is through Madison's discussion of the nature of opinion in general and its particular status in American political life, that we will learn most about what is uniquely modern in that "principal task of modern legislation."

Madison argues that all earlier democracies have "been spectacles of turbulence and contention... as short in their lives as they have been violent in their deaths." This was because, as he observes in *Federalist* 14, all earlier democracies had been too small in scale; they had been founded on "the error which limits republican government to a narrow district." Built on the scale of the ancient polis, these republics had been utterly unable to deal with the pathogenic element of democracy, namely, majority faction. Madison's novel but now familiar conclusion was that the hitherto fatal effects of majority factiousness could be controlled only in a republic organized on a sufficiently large scale. In the course of this general argument, Madison is obliged to analyze in detail the various causes of faction, and it is this detailed analysis that brings to the fore his treatment of the problem of opinion.

Madison's first step is to identify the nature of faction. The precise statement of the elements that constitute faction prepares the way, first, for his diagnosis of how different kinds of faction come into being and, later, for his novel solution to the problem. Here is his famous definition: "a number of citizens, whether amounting to a majority or minority of the whole, who are united and actuated by some common impulse of passion, or of interest, adverse to the rights of other citizens, or to the permanent and aggregate interests of the community." We must notice the twofold "normative" character of this definition. The generating impulse to faction is dubious or low; faction is "united and actuated" by passion or interest and not by reason. But this is not enough to denominate a group a faction. After all, not every passion or interest need impel toward policies inimical to society; although motivated by passion or interest, a group might yet seek policies that are perfectly compatible with the rights of others and the interests of the community. It is therefore further necessary that a group be following an oppressive or dangerous course of action. But this is to say in effect, as indeed becomes explicit in the very next step in the argument, that the group is possessed of an oppressive or dangerous opinion. From his definition, then, Madison's task becomes clear: to show how the conjunction of a "common impulse" of passion or interest and an "adverse" opinion in a majority may be averted or rendered unlikely.

Madison turns to the ways this may be done. "There are two methods of curing the mischiefs of faction: the one, by removing its causes; the other by controlling its effects." As to removing the causes, Madison says that there are likewise two possibilities. The first, which is to destroy the liberty essential to the existence of factions, Madison quickly rejects as a remedy worse than the disease. He then examines at length, as we must also, the remaining possible way to remove the causes of faction, which is to give to "every citizen the same opinions, the same passions, and the same interests." Opinion, passion, and interest: Madison's comprehensive theoretical statement of the causes of faction; these are the three independent generating sources of factional behavior. If all citizens have the same impulse of passion or interest, they would have no motivation to divide into oppressive or dangerous factions. And whatever the status of the passional or interested motivations, if all citizens were agreed on the same opinions, there could be no oppressive or dangerous division of the society with respect to public policy. Unanimity of impulse and opinion would of necessity extinguish the possibility of faction.

But Madison, of course, proceeds to demonstrate that such unanimity of opinion, passion, and interest is utterly "impracticable." He deals first with the irreducible diversity of opinion. "As long as the reason of man continues fallible, and he is at liberty to exercise it, different opinions will be formed." Notice: self-originated, self-formed opinion; opinion, so to speak, is an independent variable. That is to say, these are *not* opinions whose content is determined by underlying causes—not opinions as mere rationalization of underlying passion or interest, as we now typically conceive opinions to be—but rather opinions whose content is determined by the *autonomous operation of the opining faculty itself*. Thus, quite apart from the diversity or uniformity of the human passions and interests, political opinions will inevitably vary, simply as a function of man's fallible reasoning, or opining, faculty and his natural need to exercise it on political subjects. In this respect we may say that Madison is at one with Aristotle in recognizing the power and autonomy of the speaking-reasoning or opining capacity of man. But as to what should be done with that capacity, the difference between them, as we shall see, is the difference between modernity and antiquity.

Having demonstrated that all men cannot be given the same opinions, Madison proceeds to demonstrate that the passions and interests of mankind likewise cannot be reduced to uniformity; like opinion, they irremovably exert a divisive factious influence upon political behavior. The details of his argument need not detain us. It suffices here simply to state the conclusion Madison reaches at this stage of his argument: The problem of faction cannot be solved by removing its causes because "the latent causes of faction are...sown in the nature of man."

Still, this is no cause for despair because there remains the possibility of "controlling the effects of faction." Madison reminds us that, while the latent causes of faction are ineradicably universal, particular factions are "brought into different degrees of activity according to the different circumstances of civil society." Which kinds of factions will be brought into a high degree of "activity" and which into a low degree all depends on the circumstances of the particular society. It is in the manipulation of these "different circumstances" that Madison's novel prescription of a "cure" is to be found. By such circumstances Madison clearly includes the extent or scale of the political community and the constitutional structure and processes of government, and also apparently such things as the kind of economy to be fostered and the beliefs citizens are encouraged to hold. All such circumstances affect the operation of the universal "latent causes of faction" and thereby determine what the actual pattern of factionalism will be in any given society.

It is with precisely these circumstances that founders must deal. Armed with the proper science of politics, a founder can choose what kinds of factions to avoid and, since factionalism is inevitable, what kinds to encourage. Accordingly, in order to discover how to do the avoiding and encouraging, Madison elaborates his threefold typology of factions. He again deals first with man's natural inclination to opining, that is, with his "zeal for different opinions concerning religion, concerning government, and many other points, as well of speculation as of practice." These opinions, to repeat, are not merely rationalizations of prior passion or interest, but rather are the autonomous product of the high human need and capacity to opine about such elevated matters as, say, what is advantageous and just. Now, Aristotelian political science, as we noted earlier, takes its bearing from just this high human capacity. From the classic perspective, *the* political task is to refine and improve a regime's opinion of what is advantageous and just and to help thereby to improve the human characters formed by that regime. But Madison instead turns away almost in horror from the human "zeal for different opinions concerning religion, concerning government."[7] He is only too aware that such opining has rendered mankind "much more disposed to vex and oppress each other than to co-operate for their common good." From the perspective of the new political science, it is apparently too risky to rely on refining and improving a society's opinions. The statesmanly task, rather, is to mute as much as possible the force of religious and political opining as a cause of faction. Such opinion is not so much to be improved as tamed or devitalized. If America is to avoid the "violence of faction" that commonly destroyed earlier popular governments, "circumstances" must be so arranged that factionalism deriving from the operation of opinion must not reach to a high "degree of activity."

Madison comes to a similar conclusion regarding factions that derive directly from the human passions. These are factions caused by "an attachment to different leaders ambitiously contending for pre-eminence and power; or to persons of other descriptions whose fortunes have been interesting to the human passions." Notice that these are not the factional passions that build up around a preexisting interest or opinion; that happens commonly enough. Rather, Madison is talking here about those factions that have their genesis directly and solely in the passions themselves. He is talking about passion as an "independent variable," just as he treated opinion as such and will shortly be seen to treat "interest" in the same manner. Moreover, he is not talking about the whole

---

7. As Douglass Adair's essay on Hume and Madison has shown, further light on Madison's view of factionalism may be sought in Hume's essay "Of Parties in General." Hume warns against "parties from principle, especially abstract speculative principle," and warns also that "in modern times parties of religion are more furious and enraged than the most cruel factions that ever arose from interest and ambition." Hume suggests that interest-based faction, low though it may be, is less cruel than faction based on principle or opinion.

range of human passions that affect political behavior. He is talking here only about that single specific passion that by itself can be the direct cause of a faction. He means that particular passion—empathy is a useful word to recall here—by force of which humans have a natural political readiness to love and hate, a kind of spiritedness that is evoked by, or reaches out to, exceptional leaders. By force of this passion, masses of men, without any reason of interest or opinion, simply are "turned on" by dazzlingly attractive leaders.

The attachments based on such loves and hates are by no means contemptible; indeed, they may well be the means by which great virtues—courage, eloquence, rectitude, wisdom—communicate their political force and charm to human beings who might otherwise never be drawn upward to such qualities of character. Nevertheless, Madison concludes that on balance such attachments are too dangerous; they generate factions that torment and destroy society and hence must somehow be avoided. What Madison is in effect saying is: no Savonarolas or Cromwells or extraordinarily "interesting" figures, thank you; what is wanted generally are men of lesser but safer political ambition and religious appeal. The thrust of the American political order must be somehow to diminish the readiness of ordinary Americans to respond to leaders who generate faction, as it were, simply out of their own "charisma."

The bold and novel requirement of Madison's political science and of the American political order, then, is to mute or attenuate the age-old kinds of political behavior that derive from two of the fundamental causes of faction. But there is also the political behavior that derives from the third fundamental cause of faction, namely, interest: "the most common and durable source of factions has been the various and unequal distribution of property." Madison is far from seeking to diminish the efficacy of this cause, as he is of the other two. On the contrary, his intention is precisely the opposite: He wishes to magnify its operation, because therein lies the new cure of the "mischiefs of faction." To anticipate the conclusion of his argument: if Americans can be made to divide themselves according to their narrow and particularized economic interests, they will avoid the fatal factionalism that opinion and passion generate. By contrast, the relatively tranquil kind of factionalism resulting from economic interests makes possible a stable and decent democracy. But this does not mean economic-based faction in general. Madison distinguishes between two kinds of economic faction, one resulting from the "unequal distribution of property" and one from its various distribution. Faction based on property inequality, like faction based on opinion and passion, also leads to the fatal factionalism that destroyed earlier popular governments—specifically, to the perennial struggle of the many poor with the few rich, fighting under the banners of grandly conflicting ideas of justice. The American polity looks to replace this struggle over the *inequality* of property by causing to flourish a new kind of economic faction derived from the *variety* of property. It is on this basis that there can arise a tranquil, modern politics of interest groups, as distinct from a politics of class struggle. This is the meaning and intention of Madison's famous "multiplicity of interests" and of democratic government based upon the "coalition[s] of a majority" that rise out of that multiplicity.

But whence derives the "multiplicity" that makes it all possible? What are the civil "circumstances" that bring the right kind of economic-based faction into a high "degree of activity"? This new, salutary multiplicity of economic factions is uniquely the product of a large modern commercial society. For millennia the mass of men had been poor in but a handful of ways, toilers little differentiated in their class-poverty by the ways they eked out their existences; the rich likewise have gained their wealth in but a handful of ways that little differentiated their common oligarchic impulses and interests. Only the modern commercial spirit flourishing in a large, complex, modern economy can supply the faction-differentiating division of labor and the great economic diversity that directs the attention of all to the moderating private pursuit of individual economic happiness.[8] "Extend the sphere" of a republic, Madison said, "and you take in a greater variety of parties and interests; you make it less probable that a majority of the whole will have a common motive to invade the rights of other citizens." But it is only in an extended *commercial* republic that men are thus moderatingly fragmented into that "greater variety" of economic activities from which alone develops the necessary variety of economic interests. In such a society men will tend to think in terms of their various immediate economic interests, that is, to think as members of an "interest group" rather than of a class or sect. They will then tend to form political opinions in defense of those interests, and then jockey frenetically, but ultimately tamely, for group and party advantage on the basis of those interests.

Madison's search for a solution to the democratic problem thus led him to envisage and help found the extended, commercial, democratic republic. Always before the politics of democracy had flowed naturally

---

8. Cf. Alexander Hamilton in *Federalist* 12 on how the "prosperity of commerce" entices and activates "human avarice and enterprise." But this leads to a result that Hamilton regards with satisfaction. "The assiduous merchant, the laborious husbandman, the active mechanic, and the industrious manufacturer—all orders of men look forward with eager expectation and growing alacrity to this pleasing reward of their toils." We will consider later a passage in Montesquieu, on a "democracy founded on commerce," which makes a similar point. And we will in that context suggest that the "avarice" of which Hamilton speaks may better be understood as "acquisitiveness."

into the fatal factionalism deriving from opinion, passion, and class interest; the democratic mass of men had always turned to opinionated politics (or, as we might say now, to ideology) or to opinionated piety, or had followed some impassioning leader, or had fought the battle of the poor against the rich and had brought their democratic governments down in ruin. Employing the "new science of politics," Madison had discovered in "interest" its latent possibility, that is, a novel way of channeling the stream of politics away from these natural directions and toward that kind of factionalism with which a democracy could cope, namely, a politics of "various and interfering interests." Such is our political world—the modern world, the substratum of which consists of these narrowed, fragmented, unleashed interests—in which the "principal task" does indeed become what Madison stated it to be: "The regulation of these various and interfering interests forms the principal task of modern legislation and involves the spirit of party and faction in the necessary and ordinary operations of government."

IV

The American political order was deliberately tilted to resist, so to speak, the upward gravitational pull of politics toward the grand, dramatic, character-ennobling but society-wracking opinions about justice and virtue. Opinion was now to be ballasted against its dangerous tendency toward destructive zealotry, or, to change the nautical figure, to be moored solidly in the principle of commodious self-preservation and economic self-interest. As much as possible, opinion was to be kept from reaching upward to broad considerations of the advantageous and the just by being made more nearly into a reflection of "the sentiments and views of the respective proprietors" of the various kinds of property. (Is this not precisely what came to be a distinctive aspect of opinion-formation in American political life—indeed, so much so that contemporary American political science has been beguiled, as it were, into forgetting what virile autonomous opinion is really like?) In thus seeking to tame opinion, Madison was following the general tendency of modern political thought to solve the problems of politics by reducing the scope of politics. As we saw earlier, by abstracting from politics the broad ethical function of character formation, modern political thought had begun a kind of depoliticizing of politics in general. Now Madison, as it were, depoliticized political opinion in particular.

Madison's strategy for solving the democratic problem of faction—not by trying to make opinion more disinterestedly virtuous but by reducing it to a safe reflection of diverse interests—helps to illuminate, and may be understood as part of the famous general policy of opposite and rival interests that Madison derived from the new science of politics. His general strategy for moderating democracy and thus making it commendable to the "esteem and adoption of mankind" is nowhere stated more thoughtfully, nor more chillingly, than in *Federalist* 51. He is explaining why the powers formally separated under the Constitution will remain so in practice, despite a despotizing tendency for them to become concentrated in one or another of the branches of government. "The great security against a gradual concentration of the several powers in the same department," he states, "consists in giving to those who administer each department the necessary constitutional means and personal motives to resist the encroachments of the others. Ambition must be made to counteract ambition. The interest of the man must be connected with the constitutional rights of the place." This all sounds sensible, even commonplace, to present-day Americans, who are habituated to the moral horizon of the American political system. But Madison was writing when the new science of politics was still unhackneyed, and he knew that there was something novel and shocking in his acceptance and counterpoised use of ambitious interest as the principal security for the public good; it smacked much of "private vice, public good."

He thus pauses immediately to apologize, in a way, for such a cool recommendation, admitting it to be "a reflection on human nature that such devices should be necessary," but justifying them as necessitated by the weakness of that nature. He then boldly and comprehensively states the general principle underlying such "devices": "This policy of supplying, by opposite and rival interests, the defect of better motives, might be traced through the whole system of human affairs, private as well as public." Restated very plainly, Madison is saying this: Human nature is such that there just are not enough "better motives" to go around, not enough citizens and politicians who will be animated by motives that rise above self-interestedness and the gratification of their own passions so as to get the work of government and society done. But again there is no reason for despair because we can "supply the defect," that is, make up for the insufficiency of "better motives" with "personal motives," that is, by means of a shrewdly arranged system of opposite and rival personal interests. We cannot here trace the "policy" through the whole system of the Constitution; it suffices for our purposes to return to the question of opinion and the problem of faction. As we saw in our analysis of *Federalist* 10, this "policy" was precisely the basis of the scheme whereby the "multiplicity of interests" solves the problem of faction. We may paraphrase Madison's language: the defect of better opinions is supplied by the system of "various and interfering interests."

Now, Aristotle and ancient political science had no illusions about the quantity of "better motives" available; Aristotle thought them to be in as short supply as is supposed by modern political thought. The difference between the ancients and the moderns consists in the way each addressed the problem of the "defect," and the costs of their respective solutions. For the ancients, since improving those motives—or virtues, we may say in this context—was the end of political life, there was no alternative but to try to increase or improve the stock of "better motives" or virtues. These virtues were not merely instrumental in achieving certain governmental or societal goals; they *were* the goals. Hence in the premodern perspective there was no way to conceive that the defect could be supplied by any substitute. But for modern political thought—because making the motives better, that is, forming the human excellences, was no longer the primary end of politics—a different prospect was opened. The chief political end had become commodious self-preservation, with the higher human matters left to the workings of society. It thus became possible to conceive of interested behavior as a general substitute for the too-hard-to-come-by "better motives."

With respect to the quality of opinion in particular, the answer is the same. For the ancients, since the opinions of society so decisively influence the character of citizens, the formation of which was the end of politics, there was no alternative but to arrange the polis so as to "high tone" the opinions of the citizens as much as possible in the circumstances. For the moderns, however, there is no such necessity; indeed, it is not too much to say that opinion must literally be toned down in order that democratic factionalism not rip society apart.

That raises the question of costs. The moderns say, and with some justification, that ancient and medieval political *practice* had not vindicated the high aims and claims of premodern *thought;* the cost of a political philosophy that aimed too high, we have heard them argue, was to perpetuate in practice a vast human misery. But what of the modern costs and, in particular, what of the cost of the "American way"?

In the public realm, as we saw regarding the separation of powers, Madison's policy condones and even encourages hitherto reprobated interests like self-serving political ambition. In the private realm of the "various and interfering interests," this policy not only accepts but also necessarily encourages perspectives and activities that had hitherto been ethically censored and politically constrained, namely, the aggressive private pursuit by all of immediate personal interests. The very qualities that the classical and Christian teachings sought to subdue so that those with "better motives" could be brought to attain their full natural height, the new science of politics emancipates and actively employs. This means nothing less than to whet democratically the appetites of all, to emancipate acquisitiveness and its attendant qualities, and to create the matrix—the large commercial democratic republic—within which such appetites and acquisitive aims can be excited and sufficiently satisfied. Put bluntly, this means that in order to defuse the dangerous factional force of opinion, passion, and class interest, Madison's policy deliberately risks magnifying and multiplying in American life the selfish, the interested, the narrow, the vulgar, and the crassly economic. That is the substratum on which our political system was intended to rest and where it rests still. It is a cost of Madison's policy, the price to be paid in order to enjoy its many blessings.

From the point of view of the generality of mankind, the new policy delivered on its promises. In comparison with the premodern achievement, it raised to unprecedented heights the benefits, the freedom, and the dignity enjoyed by the great many. But the cost must be recognized, precisely in order to continue to enjoy the blessings. Again in comparison with the premodern perspective, that cost is the solid but low foundation of American political life. And *foundation* must be understood quite literally: American institutions rest upon it. Those who wish to improve American life—specifically, those who would improve the relationship between ethics and politics in America—must base such improvement upon the American foundation; and this means to come to terms with the "policy" that is an essential part of that foundation. Revolution or transformation, that is something else. But if the aim is improvement, it must be improvement that accepts the limits imposed by the "genius" of the particular political order; it must be improvement that makes America her better self, but still her own self.

Yet it is just this foundation that has baffled or immoderately repelled many contemporary students of American political life and history. This is the case with what is perhaps the most influential, and very likely the most widely read, scholarly statement on the American Founding, Richard Hofstadter's *The American Political Tradition*. Hofstadter's book is an especially revealing example of a work that cannot abide the Madisonian reliance upon, and deliberate encouragement of, the system of opposite and rival interests. By seeing that system in the light of Hofstadter's rejection of it, we will further our own effort to understand it. Perhaps we will enlarge our understanding of the American political order by seeing how it can be defended from Hofstadter's attack.

In the spirit of Charles Beard, Hofstadter admires the Founders' republican decency and "realism," but at the same time severely rebukes that realism because it antiquatedly restricts the moral possibilities of American democracy. The Founders, he claims, "did not believe in man." They had "a distrust of man [which] was first and foremost a distrust of the common man and democratic rule." Consequently, the political system they devised was aimed at "cribbing and confining the popular spirit." Notice that Hofstadter does not merely make an interpretive claim as to how the Constitution should be understood; most American disputation has been of that sort, a kind of "quarrel among the heirs" as to the precise meaning of the political heritage. Rather, Hofstadter challenges the worth of the heritage itself. He is not concerned with particular shortcomings in American institutions but with the foundation upon which the entire structure of American politics rests. In short, his criticism goes to the Founders' idea of human nature, of its possibilities and limitations with respect to human excellence. Thus Hofstadter's chapter on the Founders opens with a critical characterization of their idea of man as Calvinist in its sense of evil, and as Hobbesian in its view of man as selfish and contentious. The chapter closes with a long final paragraph that strongly condemns this idea of man and his ethical potential. It is a condemnation that is implicit in many other contemporary rejections of the American political-ethical presuppositions and rewards careful examination.

Hofstadter writes that "from a humanistic standpoint there is a serious dilemma in the philosophy of the Fathers, which derives from their conception of man." The dilemma is this: while the founders were not full-blooded Hobbesians, still they had not advanced sufficiently beyond Hobbes to be satisfactory from "a humanistic standpoint." They had at least advanced beyond Hobbes in that, while they accepted his view of man as murderously self-interested, "they were in no mood to follow Hobbes to his conclusion," namely, to the absolute Leviathan state that Hobbes deemed necessary to restrain natural, anarchic man. Rather, despite their Hobbesian view of man, the Founders nonetheless "wanted him to be free—free, in essence, to contend, to be engaged in an umpired strife." But such freedom, while an improvement on Hobbesian absolutism, is still unsatisfactory because it does not succeed in putting an end to "the Hobbesian war of each against all." Indeed, the Founders did not even have such an intention; they wanted "merely to stabilize it and make it less murderous." The crucial defect of the American Founding, then, is that the Founders "had no hope and they offered none for any ultimate organic change in the way men conduct themselves. The result was that while they thought self-interest the most dangerous and unbrookable quality of man, they necessarily underwrote it in trying to control it." And, Hofstadter continues, things have worked out exactly as the founders intended; the American political system has provided just the sort of "stable and acceptable medium" for "grasping and contending interests" that the founders had in mind.

Such a political system, and the ideas that shaped and inspired it, cannot apparently be recommended from the "humanistic standpoint." Especially the Founders' chief idea, the idea of an unchanging human nature characterized by rapacious self-interestedness, is humanistically indefensible: "No man who is as well abreast of modern science as the Fathers were of eighteenth-century science believes any longer in unchanging human nature. Modern humanistic thinkers who seek for a means by which society may transcend eternal conflict and rigid adherence to property rights as its integrating principles can expect no answer in the philosophy of balanced government as it was set down by the Constitution-makers of 1787." The implications are unmistakably harsh: "Modern humanistic thinkers" must turn away from the American idea of man and the political system based on it; those who want society to "transcend eternal conflict" must look elsewhere if they are to achieve their humanistic goals.[9]

At first blush, one might think that Hofstadter reaches this conclusion from something akin to the Aristotelian perspective. Hofstadter says more or less accurately that, rather than expecting "that vice could be checked by virtue," the American founders "relied instead upon checking vice with vice." This might suggest that Hofstadter takes his stand with the ancients in accepting the tension in human nature between virtue and vice and that he prefers, along with them, to make the difficult effort to help virtue to prevail over vice. But Hofstadter in fact sees no intrinsic difficulty in causing virtue to triumph, and this reveals how much he differs from both the ancients and an early modern thinker like Madison.

Both Aristotle and Madison agree that political life confronts a fundamental and ineradicable difficulty: human nature is unchanging, and there is a shortage in it of virtue or the "better motives." As we have seen, they disagree over what to do about this perennial difficulty; Aristotle sees in politics the necessity to "high tone" virtue as much as possible in any given circumstances, while Madison chooses the moderating system of opposite and rival interests. But against both of them Hofstadter believes that the perennial "defect" of virtue can simply be overcome by an "organic change" in human nature, which is promised in an unspecified way by "modern science." Hofstadter's entire criticism of the American Founding rests upon his apparent certainty that it is going to be possible "to change the nature of man to conform with a more ideal system." On the basis of what can only be called this utopian expectation, Hofstadter rejects both the Aristotelian and Madisonian views. Or, rather, one might speculate that he implicitly combines them, heedless of

---

9. To "transcend eternal conflict" means to end it, which means to solve all those human problems that have hitherto led to conflict. This is not humanism but utopianism, and it must not be permitted that humanism should thus be subsumed under the utopian perspective. Rather, it may be suggested, humanism means precisely to recognize as perennial those human sources of conflict and to face them reflectively and nobly.

their irreconcilabilities. He seems to take from the Aristotelian enterprise something of the elevation to which virtue is thought capable of reaching but strips it of its corollary severity and inegalitarianism; and this "high toned" expectation regarding virtue he apparently combines with the democracy and commodious well-being of Madison's enterprise, but strips it of *its* corollary, the foundation in the system of opposite and rival interests. Such complacent synthesizing or combining of irreconcilables is the hallmark of contemporary utopianism.

V

Hofstadter's characterization of the Founders' view of human nature, and of its potential for virtue, is of course not without justification. The political science of the American Founding does indeed have roots in the new political science of Hobbes, and it does seek to "check interest with interest...[and] faction with faction." And if that were the whole story—if Madison's "policy" were all that there is to the American political order, and all that there is to his political science—it would be difficult to defend the Founding from Hofstadter's harsh conclusions. We might still have to opt for Madison's apparently amoral "policy" against Hofstadter's utopian alternative, but it would be a most melancholy choice. Or to state this in a way that returns us to our main concerns: if this were all there is to the American political order, we might well have to conclude that, judging by Aristotelian standards, America is not a genuine political community. That is, in the light only of what we have said about the Madisonian foundation, America would seem to be little more than a clever new social arrangement, "an association of place and of not acting unjustly to one another, and for the sake of trade" among fellow residents, but not a regime that forms a common character among fellow citizens. Yet we all know in our bones that somehow there is more to the "American way" than that, that somehow we are fellow citizens within a political order, but one of a special kind. Whether what we feel in our bones is truly so is what we must now consider.

Since a regime reveals itself in the characters it forms, we must consider the American virtues or excellences, that is to say, the particular kind of human character formed among Americans. Now, the interesting thing is that however much we are not a regime in the ordinarily recognizable Aristotelian sense, we are emphatically so in one regard: We form a distinctive being, the American, as recognizably distinctive a human product as that of perhaps any regime in history. Something here turns out humanness in a peculiar American shape. What are those American virtues or excellences and how are they generated? While never forgetting its mooring in the Madisonian base, we may now consider briefly the height to which the formation of character in America reaches. This means, of course, to conclude our consideration of the particular American relationship of ethics and politics.

While the American Founders turned away from the classic enterprise regarding virtue, they did not thereby abandon the pursuit of virtue or excellence in all other possible ways. In fact, the American political order rises respectably high enough above the vulgar level of mere self-interest in the direction of virtue—if not to the highest reaches of the ancient perspective, still toward positive human decencies or excellences. Indeed, the prospect of excellences is opened up even within the very commercial interests, the unleashing of which is requisite to Madison's scheme. To see this, it is necessary to distinguish greed, or avarice, on the one hand, and acquisitiveness, on the other. The commercial society unleashes acquisitiveness; but this is by no means the same thing as to give vent to the avarice or covetousness that, traditionally, all philosophies and religious creeds have condemned. Both modern acquisitiveness and traditional avarice have perhaps the same source, namely, the desire, even an inordinate desire, for bodily things. But, as the roots of the two words suggest, in age-old avarice the emphasis is on the passion of *having*, whereas in modern acquisitiveness the emphasis is on the *getting*. Avarice is a passion centered on the things themselves, a narrow clutching to one's self of money or possessions; it has no built-in need for any limitation of itself, no need for moderation or for the cultivation of any virtues as instrumental to the satisfaction of the avaricious passion. But acquisitiveness teaches a form of moderation to the desiring passions from which it derives, because to acquire is not primarily to have and to hold but to get and to earn, and, moreover, to earn justly, at least to the extent that the acquisition must be the fruit of one's own exertions or qualities. This requires the acquisitive man to cultivate certain excellences, minimal ones perhaps from the classical perspective, but excellences nonetheless, as means to achieve his ends. He wants enlargement and increase and these require of him at least venturesomeness, and hard work, and the ability to still his immediate passions so as to allow time for the ripening of his acquisitive plans and measures. In short, acquisitive man, unlike avaricious man, is likely to have what we call the bourgeois virtues.

It is in this context that we must understand Hamilton's observation that a commercial society nurtures "the assiduous merchant, the laborious husbandman, the active mechanic, and the industrious manufacturer." Avarice, strictly understood, has no such salutary effects; acquisitiveness does. And it is not only excellences like assiduity, labor, activity, and industry that a commercial society nurtures. "Honesty is the best policy" is not acceptable prudence to the avaricious man, but it is almost natural law to the "assiduous merchant." Acquisitiveness may not be the highest motive for honesty, but if it produces something like the habit of honesty in great numbers, is not that a prodigious accomplishment? Similarly, the notion that "it takes money to make money," a maxim familiar to the acquisitive man, bears at least a relation to the ancient virtue of liberality; but the avaricious man simply cannot let loose his money to the extent that the commercial principle makes common practice. Scrooge was surely not less successful as a merchant after he acquired the liberal spirit of Christmas; indeed, the old Scrooge belonged to an older world of avarice, while the new Scrooge would perhaps be more at home in a modern commercial society. Finally, the acquisitive man is plunged by his passion into the give-and-take of society and must thus learn to accommodate himself to the interests of others. In this he is at least pointed toward something like justice. But the avaricious man is drawn by his passion wholly within the confines of his own narrow soul.

When Madison's "policy of opposite and rival interests" is understood in the light of this distinction between avarice and acquisitiveness, we can begin to see the ground for some of the excellences we all know to be characteristic of American life. We can then avoid thinking, as many have, that the vice of avarice peculiarly flourishes in America. On the contrary, we can claim that avarice here is peculiarly blunted by the supervening force of acquisitiveness and its attendant valuable qualities. No one understood this possibility more profoundly than Montesquieu, who argued that "frugality, economy, moderation, labor, prudence, tranquility, order, and rule" are virtues or excellences that are naturally generated in a "democracy founded on commerce."[10] These may be put down as merely "bourgeois virtues," but they are virtues, or human excellences, nonetheless. They reach at least to decency if not to nobility; they make life at least possible under the circumstances of modern mass society and seem more useful and attractive than ever now that they are in diminishing supply.

Tocqueville, who learned from Montesquieu, also teaches virtue in the same spirit but still more hopefully, and with him we may see a higher level to which the formation of American character reaches. The foundation, Tocqueville understands as does Montesquieu, is an acquisitive commercial order in which self-interest must be allowed to flourish; Tocqueville coolly accepts that it cannot be suppressed or transcended. Whatever might have been possible in earlier aristocratic ages, when men had perhaps been able to sacrifice self-interest for the "beauty of virtue,"

---

10. Montesquieu, *The Spirit of the Laws*, Book 5, Ch. 6.

this is now impossible. In the modern age of equality, "private interest will more than ever become the chief if not the only driving force behind all behavior." But this is not cause for despair; if there is no hope of transcending private interest, still much depends on how "each man will interpret his private interest."[11] What is necessary is that men learn to follow the "principle of self-interest properly understood." The Americans, Tocqueville says, have "universally accepted" that principle and have made it the root of all their actions: "The Americans enjoy explaining almost every act of their lives on the principle of self-interest properly understood. It gives them pleasure to point out how an enlightened self-love continually leads them to help one another and disposes them freely to give part of their time and wealth for the good of the state."

Oddly, and in a manner reminiscent of Madison in *Federalist 51*, Tocqueville interrupts his presentation at this point as if wishing to draw a veil over the harsh foundation of this "principle." But he forces himself, as it were, to a full statement of its implications.

> Self-interest properly understood is not at all a sublime doctrine.... It does not attempt to reach great aims, but it does... achieve all it sets out to do. Being within the scope of everybody's understanding, everyone grasps it and has no trouble bearing it in mind. It is wonderfully agreeable to human weaknesses and so easily wins great sway. It has no difficulty in keeping its power, for it turns private interest against itself and uses the same goad which excites them to direct the passions.
>
> The doctrine of self-interest properly understood does not inspire great sacrifices, but every day it prompts some small ones; by itself it cannot make a man virtuous, but its discipline shapes a lot of orderly, temperate, moderate, careful, and self-controlled citizens. If it does not lead the will directly to virtue, it establishes habits which unconsciously turn it that way.

One element in Tocqueville's account of these "habits," which are the common stuff of American political life, is especially worth noting. Not only does "self-interest properly understood" cause Americans to acquire certain personal excellences, and not only does it lead them regularly to help one another in their private capacities, but it also "disposes them freely to give part of their time and wealth for the good of the state." By this Tocqueville refers to the extraordinary extent to which Americans actually govern themselves; from the habit and practice of self-government, American character reaches up to the republican virtues. The imposing extent of American self-governance, and hence its character-forming significance, has been obscured in recent years because

---

11. Alexis de Tocqueville, *Democracy in America,* trans. George Lawrence (New York: Harper & Row, 1966). Unless otherwise noted, all references are to pp. 497–99.

observers have brought to the question a utopian expectation that degraded the reality. But Tocqueville, by making realistic comparisons and taking his bearings from the nature of things, was able to appreciate the astonishing degree in America of self-governing and self-directing activity in all spheres of life. In fact, he warns his readers that, while they could very well conceive all other aspects of America, "the political activity prevailing in the United States is something one could never understand unless one has seen it. No sooner do you set foot on American soil than you find yourself in a sort of tumult; a confused clamor rises on every side, and a thousand voices are heard at once, each expressing some social requirements."[12] This tumult, this clamor, is the sound of men and women governing themselves. And in presupposing and summoning forth the capacity of a people to govern themselves, the American political order advances beyond mere self-interest toward that full self-governance which is the very idea of virtue.

We may very briefly note two further aspects of American life which are, in a way, at the peak of the "ascent" we are sketching. First, American democracy as understood by its Founders, whether in the Declaration of Independence or the Constitution, made only a modest claim. It never denied the unequal existence of human virtues or excellences; it only denied the ancient claim of excellence to *rule as a matter of right*. Now this denial is of immense importance because, in contrast with the ancient justification of the political claims of the few, it deeply popularizes the very foundation of political life. But the American political order nonetheless still presupposed that an inequality of virtues and abilities was rooted in human nature and that this inequality would manifest itself and flourish in the private realm of society. The original American democratic idea thus still deferred to a relatively high idea of virtue, the while denying its claim to rule *save by popular consent*. Indeed, not only was the idea of unequal excellence acknowledged and expected to flourish privately, but it was the proud claim of American democracy to be the political system in which merit, incarnated in Jefferson's "natural aristocracy," was likeliest to be rewarded with public office, in contrast with the way "artificial aristocracy" flourished corruptly in other systems. Nothing is more dangerous in modern America than those subverting conceptions of human nature or of justice that deny that there are men and women who deserve deference, or deny democracy its aspiration to be that political system which best defers to the truly deserving.

Finally, and with a brevity disproportionate to importance, one should also note gratefully that the American political order, with its het-

---

12. *Ibid.*, p. 233.

erogeneous and fluctuating majorities and with its principle of liberty, supplies a not inhospitable home to the love of learning. This is at a respectable distance indeed from its foundation in a "policy of opposite and rival interests."

VI

We have examined the "policy" that is the restraining or ballasting base of the "American way," and now we have some idea of what are the distinctive and respectable American virtues or excellences that rise on and above the base. In the light of those distinctive virtues, we can claim that America manifestly qualifies as an authentically political community or regime, at least with regard to the production of an ethos, or of a distinctive human character or characters. But we still have not gotten a satisfactory handle on the political side of the ethics-politics relationship here: while American character is as much our distinctive ethical nurture as is the human character formed in any other regime, it still remains a puzzle as to how that character is politically generated here.

We cannot hope to explicate the matter fully, but it will help to recur to the Aristotelian understanding of a regime. In Aristotle's view, three elements together make a community authentically political rather than merely a social arrangement that lacks a regard for "what the qualities of the others are." A community is a political regime when: (1) it forms itself upon some particular idea of what is "advantageous and just" for human beings; (2) its citizens are molded into a particular human character on the pattern of that idea; and when (3) this is done by means of vigorous, comprehensive and penetrating laws, that is, by means of a political art that regulates—not just Madison's "various and interfering interests," but religion, education, family life, mores generally, economic behavior, and whatever helps bring into being the kind or kinds of human being contemplated by the central idea of the particular regime.

The puzzle in the American case is the discrepancy between the way we fully qualify as a regime regarding the second requirement, the forming of distinctive virtues or characters, but emphatically not qualify regarding the last requirement, namely, the use of governmental authority to form those virtues. It is in this respect, in the absence of the censorious and sumptuary laws and institutions characteristic of ancient political science, that America is most unlike an Aristotelian regime. As we saw earlier, this removal of government from the business of directly superintending the formation of character is central to the "new science of politics," on the basis of which the American republic was largely founded. And this narrowing of the range of political authority, we also saw, resulted from a lowering of the aims of political life. This meant a lowering of the idea of the "advantageous and the just." It is likely, then, that the explanation of the puzzling American discrepancy—character formation, but not by use of the laws—will be found in the status in America of the first of Aristotle's three regime requisites, that is, in the American idea of what is advantageous and right for humans.

By the "American idea" of the advantageous and just, we mean here the idea contained in the Declaration of Independence and the Constitution, the two linked founding documents of the American republic. This is not to deny that many other elements form part of the American idea in practice—elements like the Anti-Federalist "virtuous republic" tradition, or Puritanism with its original high-pitched piety, or the high-toned Anglicanism that long persisted in this country, or vestiges of the English aristocratic tradition, or, more recently, elements derived from powerful intellectual currents in the contemporary world, or from the many other possibilities that crowd into a particular national "idea" in practice. All of these elements must be given their due weight in a full account of the American relationship of ethics and politics. But they all become most intelligible in their operation when they are seen in tension with the central American idea, the idea derived from the new science of politics, the idea decisively embodied in the "frame" of the republic, that is, in the principles, institutions, and processes of the Constitution.

The central American idea of what is advantageous and just for humans, as we have seen, is clearly less elevated than that of the classical teaching. The ethical aim of the American political order being less lofty, the kinds of human characters to be politically formed are likewise less lofty and, hence, less difficult of formation. Such human beings may be produced by softer means, subterranean in their operation and indirect, thereby rendering unnecessary the strenuous and penetrating political authority characteristic of the ancient regime. It has in fact proved possible to raise human character to the American height in this gentler, less demanding fashion.

Consider what we have called the "bourgeois virtues." As Montesquieu observed, the "spirit of commerce" of itself entices these modest excellences into being. Their formation does not require the severity and constant statesmanship of the classical political outlook; it suffices that a modern regime generate that "spirit" and then the desired virtues tend naturally to form themselves. This fundamental difference is revealed in a superficial similarity between the ancient and modern ways of generating their respectively required virtues. In one interesting respect, the modern bourgeois virtues are formed politically the same way that the ancient teaching prescribed regarding its virtues, namely, by a decision regarding the size of the political community. The decisions are, of course, exactly opposite: The classical ethical-political teaching requires the small scale of the polis; the Madisonian "policy" with its attendant "bourgeois virtues" requires the scale of a very large republic. For the ancients, the polis had to be small so as to provide a constraining environment for the appetites; for the moderns, the republic had to be large so as to excite the acquisitive appetites whence the spirit of commerce arises. But for the ancients the size of the polis of itself accomplishes little regarding the right character formation; the polis was simply the requisite setting within which a high political art could be employed to generate the appropriate virtues. But once the modern republic has been organized on a large enough scale and, of course, once its fundamental laws have established the framework for the life of commerce, government need not be used thereafter closely to superintend the formation of the bourgeois character. The appropriate ethical consequences may be expected to flow. In this respect, the relationship of ethics and politics in America is more the work of the original Founding than of a demanding statesmanship thereafter; appropriate characters are formed by force of the original political direction of the passions and interests.

We have also pointed to the American republican virtues that arise from the habit and practice of self-government. Like the bourgeois virtues, these too are formed in the milder modern way. The American republican virtues arise primarily from political arrangements that accept and seek to channel the force of human passion and interest rather than to suppress or transcend them. And these republican virtues likewise arise primarily from the original Founding and not from subsequent statesmanship shaping the character of the citizenry. The Constitution, and, thanks to federalism, the state constitutions as well, establish a basic framework of institutions that elicit ethical qualities of citizenship such as independence, initiative, a capacity for cooperation and patriotism. Tocqueville teaches us the way these qualities are formed in the American character. He shows how, by means of administrative decentralization, the jury system, voluntary associations, and the like, self-interest is "unconsciously" drawn in the direction of republican virtue. Like the bourgeois virtues, these republican decencies in the American character do not depend decisively upon constant constraint or encouragement by statesmanship but tend to flow from the operation of the political institutions as originally founded. James Madison also teaches us about the character-forming possibility of the Founding, for example, in his understanding of the Bill of Rights. Madison justified the addition of the Bill of Rights to the Constitution in part on "declaratory" grounds. "The political truths declared in that solemn manner," he said, "acquire by degrees the character of fundamental maxims of free Government, and as they become incorporated with the national sentiment, counteract the impulses of interest and passion."[13] In this sense, the Founding becomes more than an arrangement of the passions and interests; when "venerated" by the people, it can serve as an ethical admonition to the people, teaching them to subdue dangerous impulses of passion and interest. This goes far in the direction of genuine republican virtue, but it still rests on the mild and merely declaratory tutelage of the Founding, not on the sterner stuff of ancient political science.

Finally, the American Founders seem simply to have taken for granted that the full range of the higher human virtues would have suitable opportunity to flourish, so to speak, privately. They presumed that man's nature included a perhaps weak but nonetheless natural inclination to certain virtues. Although they did not rely upon these "better motives," as we have here called them, as the basis for the political order, they were apparently confident that, privately and without political tutelage in the ancient mode, these higher virtues would develop from religion, education, family upbringing, and simply out of the natural yearnings of human nature. Indeed, they even accorded to these higher excellences a quasi-public status in the expectation mentioned earlier, that American democracy would seek out and reward the "natural aristocracy" with public trust. Whether these expectations of the Founders were reasonable then or remain so now is a grave matter for inquiry, but an inquiry beyond the scope of this essay.

We have suggested here a way through which Americans should inquire into, and go about, the ethical enterprise of politics. We have argued that there is a distinctive American way respecting the relationship of ethics and politics; and hence, while taking our bearings from the universal commands of the highest ethics, we must as political beings seek to achieve politically only that excellence of character that, to adapt a phrase from Tocqueville, "is proper to ourselves." That character largely remains the product of the subtle strategy of the American Founders, the understanding of which thus remains indispensable to us. We must accept that their political order had its foundation in the human interests and passions; but we must appreciate also that their political order presupposes certain enduring qualities that can and should be achieved in the American character. The preservation of that foundation and at the same time the nurturing of the appropriate ethical excellences remains

---

13. Madison to Jefferson, Oct. 17, 1788, in *Writings of James Madison* (New York: Putnam's, 1904), 5:273. I am indebted to my wife, Ann Stuart Diamond, for calling to my attention the appositeness of this passage to my purposes. Madison's view of how the Bill of Rights can acquire "the character of fundamental maxims of free Government" should be considered in connection with his discussion of "veneration" and public opinion in *Federalist* 49.

the compound political task of enlightened American statesmen and citizens. The easy error is to deal with only one side of that compound task. On the one hand, it is easy to be concerned only with the foundation and to settle for a form of liberty that consists only in the free play of raw self-interest. But this is to ignore the subtle ethical demands of the American political order. On the other hand, it is even easier today to make utopian demands upon the political system for unrealizable ethical perfections. But this is to ignore the limiting requisites of the unique American ethos, namely, the foundation in the passions and interests upon which it rests. Moreover, such utopianizing has the tendency inexcusably to ignore or depreciate the liberty and decencies which the American political order, resting on that foundation, continues to secure in an ever more dangerous world. In contrast to both these one-sided approaches, it is intellectually and ethically rewarding to grasp the compound ethical-political demands of the "American Way," and to seek within each day's budget of troubles "to attain that form of greatness...which is proper to ourselves" and even enclaves of other greatnesses as well.[14]

---

14. Tocqueville, *Democracy In America*, p. 679.

Chapter Nine

Democracy's Quiet Virtues

Sarah R. Adkins

The relationship between ethics, character and virtue in American society naturally engenders a discussion of American democratic mores. The term "mores" encompasses the values, character, morality and notions of virtue unique to an individual regime. Since the time of the Athenian democracy, it has been deemed both desirable and appropriate for organized governments to influence the mores of their society by encouraging particular characteristics in the citizenry. However, as Martin Diamond's essay "Ethics and Politics: The American Way" so eloquently illustrates, this approach was not incorporated into the framework of the American regime. American mores have been shaped by a political philosophy that sought to "[direct] man's passions and interests toward the achievement of those solid goods this earth has to offer: self-preservation and the protection of those individual liberties which are an integral part of that preservation."[1] Wilson is more direct when he asserts that, "human nature [was taken] pretty much as it was and [it was hoped] that personal liberty could survive political action if ambition were made to counteract ambition."[2] Yet scholars, political figures and the American public alike recognize a unique American character and to some degree attribute the past stability and success of the American regime to the mores of the people. Accordingly, some pertinent questions come to the fore: Is there indeed an "American character"? If so, has it existed historically? To what extent can it be said that the future of the American regime turns on the character of its citizenry?

Prophetically, Alexis de Tocqueville, a scholar whose works have been the subject of academic, political and popular commentary, was one of the earliest observers of American democratic society to identify the regime's mores as an integral component of its stability and success. In his mid-Nineteenth century analysis of the American democratic repub-

---

1. Martin Diamond, "Ethics and Politics: The American Way," in Robert H. Horowitz, ed., *The Moral Foundations of the American Republic*, 3rd ed. (Charlottesville, VA: University Press of Virginia, 1986), p. 83.

2. James Q. Wilson, "The Rediscovery of Character: Private Virtue and Public Policy," *The Public Interest* (Fall 1985): p. 14.

lic, *Democracy in America*, Tocqueville identifies the manners and customs of the people as one of three primary factors which contribute to the maintenance of the democratic republic in the United States. (The others being the providential situation of America at its founding and its laws.) Moreover, he notes that the mores of American society are unique historically. Tocqueville finds that the political revolution undertaken by the Americans was a social revolution as well. Democracy not only changed the nature of politics in America, "it has also created in their [the Americans'] minds many feelings and opinions which were unknown in the old aristocratic societies of Europe. It has destroyed or modified the old relations of men to one another and established new ones. The aspect of civil society has been as much altered as the face of the political world."[3]

Tocqueville took great care with his definition of what he understood customs and manners to encompass:

> I here use the word customs with the meaning which the ancients attached to the word mores; for I apply it not only to manners so called - that is, to what might be termed habits of the heart - but to the various notions and opinions current among men and to the mass of those ideas which constitute their character of mind. I comprise under this term, therefore, the whole moral and intellectual condition of a people.[4]

He dissects "the whole moral and intellectual condition" of the American people in Book III, Volume II of *Democracy in America*, "The Influence of Democracy on Manners So Called." Tocqueville's thesis in this commentary is that the equality of conditions which is unique to democracy finds mores guided by individual reason as opposed to legislated by the conventions of feudal society.[5]

> Every man therefore behaves after his own fashion, and there is always a certain incoherence in the manners of such times, because they are molded upon the feelings and notions of each individual rather than upon an ideal model proposed for general imitation.[6]

---

3. Alexis de Tocqueville. *Democracy in America*, ed. Henry Reeve (New York: Vintage Books, 1990), 2:v.

4. Tocqueville, *op. cit.*, 1:299.

5. An important distinction is aptly drawn by Raymond Aron. "In the majority of cases, Tocqueville uses the term democracy to signify a *state of society* and not a *form of government*. Democracy is opposed to aristocracy." His discussion of this may be found in *History, Truth, Liberty: Selected Writings of Raymond Aron*. (Chicago: University of Chicago Press, 1985), p. 165.

6. Tocqueville, op. cit., pp. 217-218.

For Tocqueville, this proved to be an uncertain foundation on which to rest the integrity of a nation. Thus, he sought to delineate that which might be gained and lost as democratic principles replaced the code of aristocratic convention. He also sought to examine the nature of the American character with the hope of ascertaining those qualities that had contributed to the success of the American nation to that date.

In order that he might better understand the situation of American mores, Tocqueville attempted to determine the genesis of American character; to identify and examine the guiding principles of American society; to analyze the method by which Americans are imbued with those principles; to describe the attributes of American manners; and to ascertain the relationship between American mores and the condition of the American nation. Tocqueville pursued his study of American mores by directly examining the founding situation, condition, and principles of the American nation and comparing its society with the only understanding of character formation with which he was familiar—that of European feudal society, most especially the French aristocracy. A thorough look at the product of Tocqueville's careful analysis offers valuable insight into the issues that are the subject of the contemporary discussion about ethics, character and virtue.

The Genesis of American Democratic Character

Tocqueville initiates Chapter 1 of Book III of *Democracy in America*, "Influence of Democracy on Manners Properly So Called," by drawing a basic distinction between social organization in an aristocracy and that in a democracy.[7] He defines an aristocracy as an artificial construct built upon the laws of a particular society of men which codifies inequality in the form of a caste system. The code that separates men into classes dictates the mores of each caste and molds unity of character among individual social groups. In an aristocracy of Tocqueville's understanding, "men are irrevocably marshaled... according to their professions, their property, and their birth[;] the members of each class, considering themselves children of the same family, cherish a constant and lively sympathy towards one another... But the same feeling does not exist between the

---

7. While Tocqueville acknowledges "that for several centuries social conditions have tended to equality" (Tocqueville, *op. cit.*, 2:162), one may assume after reviewing Book III in its entirety that he utilizes the contrasting principles of aristocracy and democracy to boldly illustrate the differing source and framework of American character as opposed to the constructs that continued to shape European society during his lifetime.

several classes towards each other."[8] Furthermore, because an aristocratic social organization is "driven by an instinct rather than a passion," an individual's societal concerns are more strongly attuned to "social duty" as opposed to the condition of "mere humanity."[9]

When Tocqueville turns to democratic society, he asserts that, where aristocracy is built upon artificial convention, democracy "originates in the law of nature."[10] The foundation of democracy in an equality of conditions reestablishes in a political society the human sensibilities that were a product of the state of nature. For Tocqueville:

> When all the ranks of a community are nearly equal, as all men think and feel in nearly the same manner, each of them may judge in a moment of the sensations of all the others; he casts a rapid glance upon himself, and that is enough.[11]

Thus, the source of American mores is rooted in a human nature which gives vent to the basic empathy that one man may have for all others. While it may not inspire the "lively sympathy" between men of a particular class or "the great acts of self devotion" that are true of an aristocracy,[12] democracy engenders in man "a general compassion for the human race" which may only occur when men view one another as alike.[13]

The Foundation and Situation of American Democratic Society

Tocqueville found that the source of American mores, an equality of conditions which reflects the natural human condition, works in concert with the structure and situation of the American nation to shape the manners of its citizenry. For Tocqueville, manners are the "outward form of human actions" that reflect the "very basis of character."[14] Thus, in his view, American manners proceed from the unique foundations of American character. It is in Tocqueville's discussion of honor in the American democratic republic that he illustrates his understanding of the unique American character. Tocqueville asserts that "honor signifies the

---

8. Tocqueville, *op. cit.*, 2:162.
9. *Ibid.*, pp. 163-164.
10. *Ibid.*, p. 163.
11. *Ibid.*, p. 165.
12. *Ibid.*, p. 163.
13. *Ibid.*, pp. 164-165.
14. *Ibid.*, p. 217.

aggregate of those rules by the aid of which...esteem, glory, or reverence is obtained."[15] Unlike the moral laws of mankind—"to the neglect of which men have ever and in all places attached the notion of censure and shame; to infringe them was to do ill; to do well was to conform to them"—honor is specific to an individual society and guides how the people of that society allot praise and blame.[16] Yet, Tocqueville finds that democratic honor does not completely conform to the concept of honor as he has presented it nor to how it has been understood historically. The aristocracy of feudal society, consisting of a class of people which "succeeded in placing itself above all others;...must especially honor those virtues which are conspicuous for their dignity and splendor and which may be easily combined with pride and the love of power." Furthermore, "feudal aristocracy existed by war and for war," so military courage was "foremost among virtues and in lieu of many of them."[17] In addition, the honor of the feudal aristocracy was associated with individuals. "In the feudal world actions were not always praised or blamed with reference to their intrinsic worth, but were sometimes appreciated exclusively with reference to the person who was the actor or the object of them."[18] For Tocqueville, American honor is wholly different from its predecessor. The American notion of honor proceeds from the nation's situation as a manufacturing and commercial power with boundless resources at its disposal.[19]

Tocqueville asserts that the "principal object of [the Americans] is to explore the [resources of the nation] for profit."[20] While one may not find "esteem, glory or reverence" in this purpose, he views it as "the principal characteristic that most distinguishes the Americans."[21] Since the virtues that a society extols are a product of the nature and structure of its organization,[22] the American concept of virtue must necessarily proceed from its foundation as a manufacturing and commercial nation. Thus,

> [a]ll those quiet virtues that tend to give a regular movement to the community and to encourage business will therefore be held in peculiar honor by that people...All the more turbulent virtues, which often dazzle, but

---

15. *Ibid.*, p. 230.
16. *Ibid.*, pp. 230-231.
17. *Ibid.*, p. 232.
18. *Ibid.*, pp. 233-234.
19. *Ibid.*, p. 235.
20. *Ibid.*
21. *Ibid.*
22. *Ibid.*, p. 233.

more frequently disturb society, will, on the contrary, occupy a subordinate rank in the estimation of this same people.[23]

Furthermore, Tocqueville finds that "certain propensities which appear censurable to the general reason and the universal conscience of mankind" are often encouraged in the American character. Propensities associated with the "love of wealth" that would have been "stigmatized as servile cupidity" by feudal society are considered the traits of "praiseworthy ambition" in order that the vast undeveloped territory of the American continent be made productive. It is this unique framework which draws the more traditional "quiet virtues" together with those attributes of character that are peculiar to the purpose of the American nation from which American honor flows.[24]

If the "principal object" of the Americans is to produce wealth, it follows that "the passion for wealth...is held in honor" because the drive which it creates is necessary to push men to transform the rich land of the nation into a productive resource. Tocqueville notes that the "boldness of enterprise" which springs from the passion for wealth "is the foremost cause of [America's] rapid progress, its strength, and its greatness." And, yet, American honor does not suffer in light of failure. The unlimited resources in need of development require that "boldness of spirit" which does not always lead to success but which will nevertheless persevere. The only restraint on this "energetic passion" is the concern for public security.[25]

In Tocqueville's view, courage is the highest virtue in American society and it is treated "as the greatest of moral necessities of man." Yet, this courage differs from the traditional understanding which associated it with military valor. The courage that is instead honored in America is associated with the creation of wealth. It is "the courage which emboldens men to brave the dangers of the ocean in order to arrive earlier in port, to support the privations of the wilderness without complaint...[It is] the courage which renders [the American] almost insensible to the loss of a fortune laboriously acquired and instantly prompts to fresh exertions to make another."[26]

Like courage, the "quiet virtues" that are honored in American society support the production of wealth. While Tocqueville gives passing reference to "strictly regular habits" and "uniform acts" as the type of "quiet virtues" which benefit the American commercial and manufactur-

---

23. *Ibid.*, p. 235.
24. *Ibid.*, p. 236.
25. p. 236.
26. *Ibid.*, p. 237.

ing nation, he gives them definition in an examination of the importance of personal morality. In his discussion of honor, Tocqueville asserts that:

> In America all those vices that tend to impair the purity of morals and to destroy the conjugal tie are treated with a degree of severity unknown in the rest of the world.[27]

Thus, while a strict morality may appear to contradict the relaxed notions of honor characteristic of American society, he finds that in fact a strong moral constitution contributes to the productivity of the nation. "The laxity of morals which diverts the human mind from the pursuit of well-being and disturbs the internal order of domestic life" distracts the American mind from its one true purpose, the creation of wealth.[28] In the chapter entitled "The Young Woman in the Character of a Wife," Tocqueville expands on this theme. He finds that the limitation of the American wife's life to her domestic duties and interests is in part a product of America's role as a commercial nation. The wife maintains and promotes the security and prosperity of the household so that the man may apply all his attentions and skills to the creation of wealth. By American women "[making] it a matter of honor to live chastely," they help to advance the purpose of the nation.[29]

In closing his discussion of those traits that the Americans esteem in the character of their people, Tocqueville finds that one particular point of dishonor in American society places the understanding of American honor in "stronger relief." He writes:

> In a democratic society like that of the United States, where fortunes are scanty and insecure, everybody works, and work opens a way to everything; this has changed the point of honor quite around and had turned it against idleness.[30]

Without the castes of feudal society to define and secure one's position, be it high or low, a man's position in society is distinguished by his abil-

---

27. *Ibid.*, p. 236.
28. *Ibid.*, p. 237.
29. *Ibid.*, p. 237. Related interpretations of Tocqueville's writing on the position and role of women in the American family and greater society are offered by Delba Winthrop, "Tocqueville's American Woman and the True Conception of Democratic Progress," *Political Theory*, 14, 2 (1986): 239-261; William D. Richardson and Brigitte H. Fessele, "Tocqueville's Observations on Racial and Sexual Inequalities in America," *Southeastern Political Review*, 19, 2 (1991): 248-277; and William Kristol, "Women's Liberation: The Relevance of Tocqueville," in Ken Masugi, ed., *Interpreting Tocqueville's Democracy in America* (Savage, MD: Rowman & Littlefield Publishers, 1991), pp. 480-494.
30. Tocqueville, *op. cit.*, p. 237.

ity to produce wealth. If "honor signifies the aggregate of those rules by the aid of which... esteem, glory, or reverence is obtained,"[31] then, in Tocqueville's view, American honor is a product of the nation's reverence for wealth. He concludes that "the notion of honor no longer proceeds from any other source than the wants peculiar to the nation at large, and it denotes the individual character of the nation to the world."[32]

The American Understanding of Character Formation

Tocqueville determines that democratic honor is "imperfectly defined." The equality of social conditions have made "its injunctions... less numerous, less precise, and... its dictates are less rigorously obeyed" than those of the aristocratic honor that was so familiar to him.[33] In the absence of feudal society's strict code of honor from which uniform manners flow based on one's station, Tocqueville sought to identify the method by which Americans adopt their society's principles and, in turn, how democratic society utilizes those principles to guide its citizens' behavior. His examination of the education and role of women in American society reveals his interpretation of the method by which Americans nurture the character of their citizenry.

Tocqueville opens his discussion of the "Education of Young Women in the United States" with the assertion that morals are the "work of women" in "free communities. Consequently, whatever affects the condition of women, their habits and their opinions, has great political importance."[34] Yet, he notes that the Americans understand the challenges that democracy presents to a girl when she reaches womanhood. American society is tumultuous. "The independence of individuals cannot fail to be very great, youth premature, tastes ill-restrained, customs fleeting, public opinion often unsettled and powerless, paternal authority weak, and marital authority contested."[35] He finds that the Americans have adopted a unique course of education for young women in their society in order that they may meet such a terrific obligation in the face of great societal challenges.[36]

Tocqueville asserts that, while the Americans are a very religious people, they do not depend on religion alone to imbue young women

---

31. *Ibid.*, p. 230.
32. *Ibid.*, pp. 241-242.
33. *Ibid.*, p. 238.
34. *Ibid.*, p. 198.
35. *Ibid.*, p. 199.
36. *Ibid.*

with virtuous behavior.[37] Furthermore, he posits that, from their understanding of human nature, the Americans felt that the "passions of the human heart" could not be repressed by convention alone. Therefore, they sought to nurture in women from early childhood the ability to restrain and control those passions in a tumultuous society which afforded no conventional guide for conduct.[38] Tocqueville observes:

> As they could not prevent her virtue from being exposed to frequent danger, they determined that she should know how best to defend it, and more reliance was placed on the free vigor of her will than on safeguards which have been shaken or overthrown. Instead, then, of inculcating mistrust of herself, they constantly seek to enhance her confidence in her own strength of character.[39]

An American girl's formative years are marked by great independence and a liberal education which together are meant to give her "a precious knowledge on all subjects." In this way, Americans seek to give a young woman the ability to reason and judge of life's situations for herself. Thus, she reaches maturity with the most valuable tool with which to enter democratic society - a sound judgment.[40]

The education an American woman receives in her formative years is meant to prepare her for her role in American society. Tocqueville interprets that role to be one of moral educator and arbiter; the strong center of the American family.[41] She is first given the opportunity to exercise this role in the choice of a husband.[42] The choice is an important one, for upon marriage the young American woman surrenders the independence she enjoyed during her formative years to enter the "cloister" of her husband's home. There her life will be limited to domestic duties and interests.[43] If the independence and education afforded the young American woman appears paradoxical when compared to the role she assumes at marriage, it is not in Tocqueville's analysis.[44] He finds that a woman's education and judgment lead her to choose a cloistered existence because "the sources of a married woman's happiness are in the home and husband."[45] Moreover, young American women have been prepared to meet and cope with "all the great trials of their lives." The independence and

---

37. *Ibid.*, p. 200.
38. *Ibid.*, p. 199.
39. *Ibid.*, p. 199 (emphasis added).
40. *Ibid.*, p. 200.
41. *Ibid.*, pp. 198, 202.
42. *Ibid.*, p. 202.
43. *Ibid.*, p. 201.
44. *Ibid.*, p. 201.
45. *Ibid.*, p. 202.

education afforded women permits them to be the strong foundation of their families and households, accepting the vicissitudes of fortune with "calm and unquenchable energy; it would seem their desires contract as easily as they expand with their fortunes."[46] Thus, though marriage may narrow their world, Tocqueville asserts that in the role of wife American women bring a purity of morals and a strength of character to their society.

Tocqueville's analysis of "How the Americans Understand the Equality of the Sexes" provides support and an explanation of a Nineteenth century woman's understanding of and pleasure in her role within American democratic society. He finds that the social changes that have accompanied the advent of an equality of conditions "will raise woman and make her more and more equal of man." Yet, he does not identify a natural equality of the sexes. Rather, he asserts that the Americans recognize wide differences between the physical and moral constitutions of men and women as appointed by nature. Nature's purpose was to divide labor and the Americans honor those appointments. If "morals are the work of women" in "free societies" as Tocqueville insists,[47] then he indirectly suggests that the "faculties" of men in a democracy are better suited to the spheres of business and politics which are characterized by the desire to acquire "property, power and reputation." [48] Tocqueville writes:

> The Americans have applied to the sexes the great principle of political economy which governs the manufacturers of our age, by carefully dividing the duties of man from those of woman in order that the great work of society may be better carried on.[49]

As such, he notes that American women do not participate in the outward concerns of the family, business or politics, nor are they required to complete tasks requiring physical labor.[50] Furthermore, while the woman may be the head of the household, the man retains his authority as "natural head of the conjugal association."[51] Although Tocqueville does not outline why man is the natural head of the family except to assert that the Americans "hold that every association must have a head in order to

---

46. *Ibid.*
47. *Ibid.*, p. 198.
48. *Ibid.*, p. 243. William Kristol, *op. cit.*, presents a similar analysis when he finds that Tocqueville identified the physical and moral faculties of American men and women as guiding the role of each in society - women in the home and men in the world.
49. Tocqueville, op. cit., p. 211.
50. *Ibid.*, pp. 211-212.
51. *Ibid.*, p. 212.

accomplish its object," he finds that American women accept this state of affairs with a sort of pride and that men and women understand that "the object of democracy is to regulate and legalize the powers that are necessary, and not to subvert all power."[52] He may provide some explanation for the understanding between the sexes when he notes that American men hold American women in great esteem. A man "displays confidence in the understanding of a wife and a profound respect for her freedom; [he] has decided that her mind is just as fitted as that of a man to discover the plain truth, and her heart as firm to embrace it."[53] Yet, Tocqueville's interpretation of this understanding, indeed his whole analysis of the American understanding of the equality of the sexes, is colored by his remarks regarding those who promote equality of the sexes in Europe. He avows that:

> It may readily be conceived that by thus attempting to make one sex equal to the other, both are degraded, and from so preposterous a medley of the works of nature nothing could ever result but weak men and disorderly women.[54]

Tocqueville recognized the state of affairs of American women to be very progressive and quite positive within the context of the times. When he compares the relation of men and women in America to that in France he notes that French women are "deprived of the greatest attributes of the human species and considered seductive but imperfect beings." Furthermore, French women often view themselves in the same light. In Tocqueville's view, the cloistered existence of the American women is a small sacrifice on her part if it means that she will be supposed to be "virtuous and refined."[55] Moreover, in the context of his interpretation of American democratic character, Tocqueville has afforded to women a more salutary role in society. He concludes his discussion of the American understanding of the equality of the sexes by further ameliorating his interpretation of it. Tocqueville finds that while the lot of men and women is different, it is considered of equal value. He asserts that "while they have allowed the social inferiority of woman to continue...they appear to me to have excellently understood the true principle of democratic improvement."[56] Most interestingly, Tocqueville identifies democratic improvement with the institutionalization of social inferiority for women in America, yet closes his examination of the rela-

---

52. *Ibid.*
53. *Ibid.*, p. 231.
54. *Ibid.*, p. 211.
55. *Ibid.*, p. 213.
56. *Ibid.*, p. 214.

tionship between the sexes in America by attributing the strength of the American nation to its women:

> If I were asked, now that I am drawing to the close of this work, in which I have spoken of so many important things done by the Americans, to what the singular prosperity and growing strength of that people ought mainly to be attributed, I should reply: To the superiority of their women.[57]

The American democratic principles that seek to imbue young women in America with strength of character and purity of morals and which constitute a role that "require[s] much abnegation on the part of woman and a constant sacrifice of her pleasures to her duties" are central to the continuing improvement of the American condition in Tocqueville's analysis.[58] He identified Americans to be at the "same time a puritanical people and a commercial nation."[59] While religious opinion constrained the role of women in American society, it was this precept—in conjunction with the commercial character of the nation—that led Americans to determine that women should support an environment that would provide "the highest security for the order and prosperity of the household."[60] As Tocqueville notes, there is great economy in this proposition. He identifies no system for the moral education of young men in American society aside from that which is imparted at their mother's knee. Therefore, women bring strength of character and purity of morals to the management of the household and the education of the children. In turn, men, free from the moral role and petty obligations required to nurture a family and manage the household, may give vent to "the passion for wealth," manning the engines of commerce.[61] For Tocqueville, it is this unique American understanding of the roles of the sexes that forms the foundation from which the American nation at large may progress.[62]

---

57. *Ibid.*
58. *Ibid.*, p. 201. Richardson and Fessele find that Tocqueville accepts inequality in the relationship between American men and women, because "compatibility between them...was most desirable for the common weal." *Op. cit.*, p. 271.
59. Tocqueville, *op. cit.*, II, p. 201.
60. *Ibid.*
61. Richardson and Fessele, *op. cit.*, and Kristol, *op. cit.*, find that Tocqueville recognized a restless, democratic spirit in American men which fueled their desire for material wealth. Conversely, American women possessed pure morals and followed a course of education that made their ability to reason strong, permitting them to accept the tumult of life's fortunes (Richardson and Fessele, p. 271).
62. Richardson and Fessele interpreted Tocqueville's analysis similarly. They suggest that Tocqueville found "...the relations between American men and women...[to be] one of—if not *the*—strongest supports of the regime" (p. 263).

American Manners: A Reflection of Democratic Character

An examination of Tocqueville's interpretation of the principles which guide American society and the framework which supports those principles illustrates his assertion that, founded in an equality of conditions, American democratic society is rooted in and reflects the natural condition of man. The purpose and structure of American democratic society gives vent to "the passion for wealth." Moreover, Tocqueville identifies this passion to be "the characteristic that most distinguishes the American people from all others."[63] In turn, he asserts that "the social and political state of a country" gives shape to the mores of its society. For Tocqueville, manners constitute "the outward form of human actions" and "are generally the product of the very basis of character" or mores.[64] Tocqueville utilizes this understanding of the source of manners in general and American manners in particular when he describes the attributes of American manners.

Tocqueville asserts that manners "are at once natural and acquired." While they are a product of character, they may also reflect "an arbitrary convention between certain men." Convention governed the manners of the citizens of European feudal society. Thus, whether a "peasant or a prince," each individual understood his "proper station [in society], neither too high or too low." For Tocqueville, such a code of behavior in a society produces manners that project "true dignity." In contrast, American manners are strictly a product of a national character. Free from the confinement of the conventions of a society in which men were socially and financially immobile, American manners are shaped by the nation's foundation in an equality of opportunity where every man may define his own station in life.[65] Yet, Tocqueville finds that manners suffer in an environment where conditions tend toward equality:

> In democracies all stations appear doubtful; hence it is that the manners of democracies, though often full of arrogance, are commonly wanting in dignity, and moreover, they are never either well trained or accomplished.[66]

The class mobility promoted by American society does not permit the conventions characteristic of a defined class system to become estab-

---

63. *Ibid.*, p. 235.
64. *Ibid.*, II, p. 217.
65. *Ibid.*
66. *Ibid.*

lished. Hence, "every man behaves after his own fashion."[67] "Nothing is more prejudicial to democracy,"[68] Tocqueville laments. American democracy exposes society to the tumultuous and true nature of human character. And, while American manners may be "neither brutal nor mean" and "are frequently more sincere" than those proffered by European feudal society, Tocqueville finds they do not present an image of human character that one may easily accept or respect.[69]

Tocqueville takes great care in illustrating his assertion that the manners embraced by American society "are generally the product of the very basis of character."[70] Animated by the "passion for wealth" with no guarantee of possessing it, he asserts that American character is founded in a drive to secure and maintain material comfort. As a result, Tocqueville finds that the manner of Americans is one that is serious in demeanor, yet hardly reflective.[71] Americans are possessed by a "craving and jealous" pride,[72] and are extraordinarily similar in personality, bringing little depth or breadth to the society in which they live.[73] The gravity of the Americans occurs naturally within the framework of their society. They are grave because "a large number of men are constantly occupied with the serious affairs of government." Those who are not are "wholly engrossed by the acquisition of a private fortune."[74] Yet, the causes which contribute to the serious nature of the American personality do not provide the opportunity for reflection. Never stationary nor secure, the financial and social position of the Americans obliges them "to do things which they have imperfectly learned, to say things which they imperfectly understand, and to devote themselves to work for which they are unprepared by long apprenticeship."[75] Furthermore, the possibility of improving one's social and financial position causes the American to be propelled through his existence by his wants and desires. "He therefore does everything in a hurry, and is always satisfied with pretty well, and never pauses more than an instant to consider what he has been doing."[76] It is this "habit of inattention" that Tocqueville most de-

---

67. *Ibid.*, II, p. 218.
68. *Ibid.*
69. *Ibid.*, II, p. 220.
70. *Ibid.*, II, p. 217.
71. *Ibid.*, II, p. 221.
72. *Ibid.*, II, p. 227.
73. Tocqueville, *op. cit.*, II, p. 228.
74. *Ibid.*, II, p. 222.
75. *Ibid.*, II, p. 223.
76. *Ibid.*

plores in American character.⁷⁷ Every man is a jack-of-all-trades and a master of none.

The same cause which promotes a "habit of inattention" in American manners contributes to a patriotism that is "troublesome" and "garrulous."⁷⁸ That Americans "appear impatient of the smallest censure and insatiable of praise,"⁷⁹ Tocqueville attributes to the equality of social conditions:

> When social conditions differ but little, the slightest privileges are of some importance; as every man sees around himself a million people enjoying precisely similar or analogous advantages, his pride becomes craving and jealous, he clings to mere trifles and doggedly defends them.⁸⁰

This vanity is further exacerbated by the uncertain grasp with which each man holds to his place in society. And yet, while each man seeks to differentiate himself, Americans are remarkably alike in Tocqueville's view. The variety of "fortunes, opinions and laws" in America is not reflected in the manners of its people. "All men are alike and do things pretty nearly alike."⁸¹ Once again, Tocqueville identifies American needs and desires associated with financial security as the cause. Unlike an aristocracy, where birth defines an individual's economic and social sphere, freeing men of all classes to pursue those passions within their reach, democracy narrows the scope of men's passions so that "most...either end in the love of money or proceed from it."⁸² For Tocqueville, each man in a democracy is independent. Nothing defines him but his ability to create wealth and nothing binds him to others but contracts of monetary value. He asserts:

> When the reverence that belonged to what is old has vanished, birth, condition, and professions no longer distinguish men, or scarcely distinguish them; hardly anything but money remains to create strongly marked differences between them and to raise some of them above the common level.⁸³

When Tocqueville suggests that "many men would willingly endure its [American] vices who cannot support its manners,"⁸⁴ it is the specter of human nature at the core of American character with which he is disillu-

---

77. *Ibid.*, p. 224.
78. *Ibid.*, p. 225.
79. *Ibid.*
80. *Ibid.*, p. 226.
81. *Ibid.*, p. 228.
82. *Ibid.*, p. 228.
83. *Ibid.*
84. *Ibid.*, pp. 218-219.

sioned.[85] The caste system and conventions of European feudal society established codes of behavior and defined the roles of every member of society. Where no opportunity for social or economic mobility exits, there is no foundation for "a craving and jealous pride." Furthermore, members of the upper class are free of "the petty interests and practical cares of life."[86] They may pursue individual passions in an environment which supports reflection. In Tocqueville's view, the manners of such a society "threw a pleasing and illusory charm over human nature; and though the picture was a false one, it could not be viewed without a noble satisfaction."[87] For Tocqueville, the equality of conditions upon which American democratic society is founded is a just reflection of the natural human condition. Yet, in its fair interpretation of that condition, democratic society narrows the scope of human endeavor to that of securing one's means, thereby exposing the more base characteristics of human nature. Moreover, American democracy replaced a strict societal code of behavior with the "mutable,"[88] "often unsettled and powerless"[89] specter of public opinion to guide the manners, and ultimately the mores, of American society.

The Mores of American Democratic Society

Tocqueville draws his analysis of the condition of American society and the manners of the American people together in the chapter, "Why So Many Ambitious Men and So Little Lofty Ambition are to be Found in the United States." Tocqueville asserts that the social condition and democratic manners of the American people work in concert to shape and reflect American mores. The equality of conditions and the manners that are a product of the unique American interpretation of democracy give the American people a desire to "acquire property, power, and reputation," yet do not give them cause to "entertain hopes of great magnitude or to pursue very lofty aims." Tocqueville can ascertain no limiting factor in the manners or laws of the Americans to temper these desires[90] but the equality of conditions which "gives some resources to all the members of the community, [yet also]...prevents any of them from having resources of great extent, which necessarily circumscribes their de-

---

85. *Ibid.*, pp. 220, 227, 229.
86. *Ibid.*, p. 217.
87. *Ibid.*, p. 220.
88. *Ibid.*, p. 242.
89. *Ibid.*, p. 199.
90. *Ibid.*, p. 243.

sires within somewhat narrow limits."[91] The distribution of resources in combination with the intellectual effort that must be applied daily to the pursuit of wealth tempers the situation of American ambition. Little creative energy remains for philosophical thought. The "range of view" of the Americans becomes limited; their power circumscribed.[92]

The American desire for short term gain further demeans ambition. Tocqueville notes that "the principal of equality, which allows every man to arrive at everything, prevents all men from rapid advancement."[93] It is easier to be satisfied with a series of small gains than to wait years for long term gratification. Furthermore, because there are only a few great fortunes to be made, and "the candidates appear to be nearly alike, and as it is difficult to make a selection without infringing the principal of equality, the first idea which suggests itself is to make all advance at the same rate and submit to the same trials."[94] Tocqueville does not identify an exception to this state of affairs. The humble background or "habits of prudence" that enable an American to amass a great fortune will reign in his ambition once he has attained great wealth and power.[95] He concludes his explanation of the dearth of American ambition with the following passage:

> Thus, in proportion as men become more alike and the principle of equality is more peaceably and deeply infused into the institutions and manners of the country, the rules for advancement become more inflexible, advancement itself slower, the difficulty of arriving quickly at a certain height far greater. From hatred of privilege and from the embarrassment of choosing, all men are at last forced, whatever may be their standard, to pass the same ordeal; all are indiscriminately subjected to a multitude of petty preliminary exercises, in which their youth is wasted and their imagination quenched, so that they despair of ever fully attaining what is held out to them; and when at length they are in a condition to perform any extraordinary acts, the taste for such things has forsaken them.[96]

It is the absence of lofty ambition which leaves an indelible mark on American society in Tocqueville's view. The absence of ambition in a democracy finds its citizens to be "less engrossed than any others with the interests and the judgement of posterity; the present moment alone engages and absorbs them."[97] Thus, for Tocqueville, the mores

---

91. *Ibid.*, pp. 244-245.
92. *Ibid.*, p. 245.
93. *Ibid.*
94. *Ibid.*, p. 246.
95. *Ibid.*, p. 245.
96. *Ibid.*, p. 246.
97. *Ibid.*, p. 247.

of democratic society are made mediocre. In American democratic society, great societal achievement will not be honored with lasting monuments; men will care more for success than fame; men will demand obedience and covet empire; manners will remain below men's stations; and because men's tastes do not rise with their fortunes, their power can never be put to valuable use.[98] Of the transformation of ambition in democratic society, Tocqueville writes:

> I confess that I apprehend much less for democratic society from the boldness than from the mediocrity of desires. What appears to me to be the most dreaded is that in the midst of the small, incessant occupations of private life, ambition should lose its vigor and its greatness; that the passions of man should abate, but at the same time be lowered; so that the march of society should every day become more tranquil and less aspiring."[99]

Tocqueville asserts that only pride, a vice in the view of the humble American, could give the citizens of a democracy "a more enlarged idea of themselves and their kind," elevating the ambitions of the American people, and ultimately, the achievements of their society.

Conclusion

In Tocqueville's view, the equality of conditions imbues "the whole moral and intellectual condition," or mores, of a society with a base self-interest that obscures consideration of a greater good. When he considered these effects of equality in conjunction with the unique situation and structure of democracy in America, he found that the attributes of the American democratic regime confound the problem of self-interest while ameliorating the more salutary effects of equality. For Tocqueville, equality requires that men provide for their needs. He finds that the American democracy promotes the desire to acquire much more: "property, power and reputation."[100] At the same time, however, the environment is characterized by a competition for limited resources.[101] Tocqueville asserts that these aspects of the American regime, in conjunction with the attributes of a condition of equality, define the unique character of the nation's mores.[102] The passion for wealth ties the citizen more closely to his self-interest, loosening the natural bond among men, while the competition for resources in an uncertain environment encourages

---

98. *Ibid.*, p. 247-248.
99. *Ibid.*, p. 248.
100. *Ibid.*, p. 243.
101. *Ibid.*, p. 223.
102. *Ibid.*, pp. 247- 248.

him to lower his aspirations.[103] Thus, while equality circumscribes the work of individuals and that of society at large within narrow limits, American democracy serves to diminish the natural affinity that exists between men. Moreover, Tocqueville can ascertain no structural prescriptive afforded by the American democratic regime to correct for the dilemmas of its societal organization. Instead, he attributes the stability and success of American democracy to the role and character of American women.

Tocqueville emphatically attributes "the singular prosperity and growing strength" of the American people "to the superiority of their women."[104] He ascribes their "superiority" to the American understanding of "the true principle of democratic progress."[105] For Tocqueville, this progress is defined by the role of women in American society and the education that is provided them in order that they may assume it. He asserts that women are the arbiters of morality.[106] Tocqueville finds that American women are amply prepared for this obligation by an education that affords them a strength of character informed by a trained reason that allows them to resist desire and accept "the vicissitudes of fortune."[107] In turn, they bring a morality to their circle of influence and a stability to their environment. Moreover, though he is not explicit, Tocqueville infers that, in the tumultuous environment of American democratic life, these attributes of American women imbue society with qualities that are not inherent to its constitution.[108] However, in Tocqueville's analysis, "democratic progress" is associated with the conventional inequality of women. Their circle of influence is limited to their family. Their environment is the home.[109] Therefore, in order that democratic society may enjoy the benefit of a woman's influence, her position in American life must be characterized by social inferiority.[110] Furthermore, when Tocqueville's analysis of American mores is considered in light of

---

103. *Ibid.*, pp. 215, 244-245.
104. *Ibid.*, p. 214.
105. *Ibid.*
106. *Ibid.*, p. 198.
107. *Ibid.*, pp. 199, 202.
108. Richardson and Fessele reached a similar conclusion when they found that Tocqueville accepts inequality in the relationship between men and women, because "compatibility between them...was most desirable for the common weal" ("Tocqueville's Observations", p. 271).
109. Tocqueville, *ibid.*, II, p. 214.
110. *Ibid.*, pp. 211-212. Kristol's analysis agrees on this point. He suggests that Tocqueville finds the mores of a society to be more fundamental to its success than laws that would establish gender equality ("Women's Liberation"., p. 485).

contemporary societal circumstances where the sphere of a woman's life mirrors that of society at large, the "superiority" he attributed to her character is undermined. Engaged in public and professional life, women are exposed to the mores of American democratic society. Thus, women are imbued with the more base desires promoted by the constitution of the nation. Their reason is informed by passion, weakening their morality. In turn, women can no longer bring a strong sense of morality to bear on their families, and their involvement in affairs outside of the home reduces the stability of that environment. Moreover, in the frame of Tocqueville's interpretation, the qualities of character that were afforded women by social inferiority are not only lost to them, but to all of American democratic society.[111]

The true equality of women in America represents the most influential societal change pertinent to Tocqueville's interpretation of the mores of the American democratic regime. Yet, his analysis remains entirely salient to an understanding of democratic character. Indeed, Tocqueville demonstrates that the essence of character for all citizens participating in the work of American society proceeds from the foundations of the nation. Perhaps he understood the implications of true equality for America, thus explaining his ardent defense of the inequality of women. In the absence of any convention to promote the betterment of men and the advancement of society, Tocqueville's analysis anticipates the encompassing effect of self-interest on the character of man. When he asserts that the success of the American regime is inextricably tied to the character of the citizenry, his analysis anticipates some of the contemporary scholarship about such societal problems as crime and welfare.[112]

In the absence of the qualities of character that the conventional inequality of women afforded American democratic society, Tocqueville's analysis of American mores suggests only one other prescriptive for the dilemma of character in American society: a defined course of citizen education. Indeed, it was their course of education that imbued early Nineteenth century American women with a strength of character.[113] Furthermore, when Tocqueville turns to the effect of democratic character on

---

111. Winthrop reaches a similar conclusion when she finds that Tocqueville's analysis reveals a "devastating critique of American, or modern democratic, life as a whole" ("Tocqueville's American Woman", p. 240). Winthrop finds that Tocqueville accepts the inequality of women because it is the only component of American life which is characterized by meaning and fulfillment (p. 253). Within the context of Tocqueville's analysis, Winthrop goes on to assert that should American women attain true equality, that meaning and fulfillment would be lost to American society.

112. See Wilson's discussion in Chapter 10.

113. Tocqueville, *op. cit.*, II, p. 199.

society at large, he asserts that, "to raise ambition and to give it a field of action," the proper course would be to give the American people "a more enlarged idea of themselves and their kind."[114] Moreover, he explicitly states that "freedom, public peace, and social order itself will not be able to exist without education" in his consideration of self interest. Yet, an education for democratic citizenship was not an attribute of American societal organization at the time Tocqueville considered the effects of democracy on individual and national character. Thus, when he closes his analysis of Democracy in America, he leaves the reader with this warning that illustrates his hopes and fears for a society founded in principles of equality:

> The nations of our time cannot prevent the conditions of men from becoming equal, but it depends upon themselves whether the principal of equality is to lead them to servitude or freedom, to knowledge or barbarism, to prosperity or wretchedness.[115]

---

114. *Ibid.*, p. 248.
115. *Ibid.*, p. 334.

Chapter Ten

The Rediscovery of Character: Private Virtue and Public Policy[1]

James Q. Wilson

The most important change in how one defines the public interest that I have witnessed—and experienced—over the last twenty years has been a deepening concern for the development of character in the citizenry. An obvious indication of this shift has been the rise of such social issues as abortion and school prayer. A less obvious but I think more important change has been the growing awareness that a variety of public Emblems can only be understood—and perhaps addressed—if they are seen as arising out of a defect in character formation.

The Public Interest began publication at about the time that economics was becoming the preferred mode of policy analysis. Its very first issue contained an article by Daniel Patrick Moynihan hailing the triumph of macroeconomics: "Men are learning how to make an industrial economy work" as evidenced by the impressive ability of economists not only to predict economic events accurately but to control them by, for example, delivering on the promise of full employment. Six months later I published an essay suggesting that poverty be dealt with by direct income transfers in the form of a negative income tax or family allowances. In the next issue, James Tobin made a full-scale proposal for a negative income tax and Virginia Held welcomed program planning and budgeting to Washington as a means for rationalizing the allocative decisions of government, a topic enlarged upon the following year by a leading practitioner of applied economics, William Gorham. Meanwhile, Thomas C. Schelling had published a brilliant economic analysis of organized crime and Christopher Jencks a call for a voucher system that would allow parents to choose among public and private purveyors of education. In a later issue, Gordon Tullock explained the rise in crime as a consequence of individuals responding rationally to an increase in the net benefit of criminality.

---

1. This chapter originally appeared as "The Rediscovery of Character: Private Virtue and Public Policy," *The Public Interest*, No. 81 (Fall 1985), pp. 3-16. Reprinted by permission.

There were criticisms of some of these views. Alvin L. Schorr, James C. Vadakian, and Nathan Glazer published essays in 1966, 1968, and 1969 attacking aspects of the negative income tax, and Aaron Wildavsky expressed his skepticism about program budgeting. But the criticisms themselves often accepted the economic assumptions of those being criticized. Schorr, for example, argued that the negative income tax was unworkable because it did not resolve the conflict between having a strong work incentive (and thus too small a payment to many needy individuals) and providing an adequate payment to the needy (and thus weakening the work incentive and making the total cost politically unacceptable). Schorr proposed instead a system of children's allowances and improved social security coverage, but he did not dissent from the view that the only thing wrong with poor people was that they did not have enough money and the conviction that they had a "right" to enough. Tobin was quick to point out that he and Schorr were on the same side, differing only in minor details.

A central assumption of economics is that "tastes" (which include what non-economists would call values and beliefs, as well as interests) can be taken as given and are not problematic. All that is interesting in human behavior is how it changes in response to changes in the costs and benefits of alternative courses of action. All that is necessary in public policy is to arrange the incentives confronting voters, citizens, firms, bureaucrats, and politicians so that they will behave in a socially optimal way. An optimal policy involves an efficient allocation—one that purchases the greatest amount of some good for a given cost, or minimizes the cost of a given amount of some good.

This view so accords with common sense in countless aspects of ordinary life that, for many purposes, its value is beyond dispute. Moreover, enough political decisions are manifestly so inefficient or rely so excessively on issuing commands (instead of arranging incentives) that very little harm and much good can be done by urging public officials to "think economically" about public policy. But over the last two decades, this nation has come face to face with problems that do not seem to respond, or respond enough, to changes in incentives. They do not respond, it seems, because the people whose behavior we wish to change do not have the right "tastes" or discount the future too heavily. To put it plainly, they lack character. Consider four areas of public policy: schooling, welfare, public finance, and crime.

Schooling

Nothing better illustrates the changes in how we think about policy than the problem of finding ways to improve educational attainment and student conduct in the schools. One of the first reports of the 1966 study on education by James Coleman and his associates appeared in this magazine. As every expert on schooling knows, that massive survey of public schools found that differences in the objective inputs to such schools — pupil-teacher ratios, the number of books in the library, per pupil expenditures, the age and quality of buildings — had no independent effect on student achievement as measured by standardized tests of verbal ability.

But as many scholars have forgotten, the Coleman Report also found that educational achievement was profoundly affected by the family background and peer-group environment of the pupil. And those who did notice this finding understandably despaired of devising a program that would improve the child's family background or social environment. Soon, many specialists had concluded that schools could make no difference in a child's life prospects, and so the burden of enhancing those prospects would have to fall on other measures. (To Christopher Jencks, the inability of the schools to reduce social inequality was an argument for socialism.)

Parents, of course, acted as if the Coleman Report had never been written. They sought, often at great expense, communities that had good schools, never doubting for a moment that they could tell the difference between good ones and bad ones or that this difference in school quality would make a difference in their child's education. The search for good schools in the face of evidence that there was no objective basis for that search seemed paradoxical, even irrational.

In 1979, however, Michael Butter and his colleagues in England published a study that provided support for parental understanding by building on the neglected insights of the Coleman Report. In *Fifteen Thousand Hours,* the Butter group reported what they learned from following a large number of children from a working-class section of inner London as they moved through a dozen non-selective schools in their community. Like Coleman before him, Rutter found that the objective features of the schools made little difference; like almost every other scholar, he found that differences in verbal intelligence at age ten were the best single predictor of educational attainment in the high school years. But unlike Coleman, he looked at differences in that attainment across schools, holding individual ability constant. Rutter found that the schools in inner London had very different effects on their pupils, not only in educational achievement but also in attendance, classroom behavior, and even delinquency. Some schools did a better job than others in teaching children and managing their behavior.

The more effective schools had two distinctive characteristics. First, they had a more balanced mix of children — that is, they contained a substantial number of children of at least average intellectual ability. By contrast, schools that were less effective had a disproportionate number of low-ability students. If you are a pupil of below average ability, you do better, both academically and behaviorally, if you attend a school with a large number of students who are somewhat abler than you. The intellectual abilities of the students, it turned out, were far more important than their ethnic or class characteristics in producing this desirable balance.

Second, the more effective schools had a distinctive ethos: an emphasis on academic achievement, the regular assignment of homework, the consistent and fair use of rewards (especially praise) to enforce generally agreed-upon standards of conduct, and energetic teacher involvement in directing classroom work. Subsequent research by others has generally confirmed the Rutter account, so much so that educational specialists are increasingly discussing what has come to be known as the "effective schools" model.

What is striking about the desirable school ethos is that it so obviously resembles what almost every developmental psychologist describes as the desirable family ethos. Parents who are warm and caring but who also use discipline in a fair and consistent manner are those parents who, other things being equal, are least likely to produce delinquent offspring. A decent family is one that instills a decent character in its children; a good school is one that takes up and continues in a constructive manner this development of character.

Teaching students with the right mix of abilities and in an atmosphere based on the appropriate classroom ethos may be easier in private than in public schools, a fact which helps explain why Coleman (joined now by Thomas Hoffer and Sally Kilgore) was able to suggest in the 1982 book, *High School Achievement,* that private and parochial high schools may do somewhat better than public ones in improving the vocabulary and mathematical skills of students and that this private-school advantage may be largely the result of the better behavior of children in those classrooms. In the authors' words, "achievement and discipline are intimately intertwined." Public schools that combine academic demands and high disciplinary standards produce greater educational achievement than public schools that do not. As it turns out, private and parochial schools are better able to sustain these desirable habits of work behavior—this greater display of good character—than are public ones.

Welfare

Besides the Coleman Report, another famous document appeared at about the time this magazine was launched—the Moynihan Report on the problems of the black family (officially, the U.S. Department of Labor document entitled *The Negro Family: The Case for National Action*). The storm of controversy that report elicited is well-known. Despite Moynihan's efforts to keep the issue alive by publishing in these pages several essays on the welfare problem in America, the entire subject of single-parent homilies in particular and black families in general became an occasion for the exchange of mutual recriminations instead of a topic of scientific inquiry and policy entrepreneurship. Serious scholarly work, if it existed at all, was driven underground, and policymakers were at pains to avoid the matter except, occasionally, under the guise of "welfare reform" which meant (if you were a liberal) raising the level of benefits or (if you were a conservative) cutting them. By the end of the 1960s, almost everybody in Washington had in this sense become a conservative; welfare reform, as Moynihan remarked, was dead.

Twenty years after the Moynihan Report, Moynihan himself could deliver at Harvard a lecture in which he repeated the observations he had made in 1965, but this time to an enthusiastic audience and widespread praise in the liberal media. At the same time, Glenn C. Loury, a black economist, could publish in these pages an essay in which he observed that almost everything Moynihan had said in 1965 had proved true except in one sense—today, single-parent families are twice as common as they were when Moynihan first called the matter to public attention. The very title of Loury's essay suggested how times had changed: Whereas leaders once spoke of "welfare reform" as if it were a problem of finding the most cost-effective way to distribute aid to needy families, Loury was now prepared to speak of it as "The Moral Quandary of the Black Community."

Two decades that could have been devoted to thought and experimentation had been frittered away. We are no closer today than we were in 1965 to understanding why black children are usually raised by one parent rather than by two or exactly what consequences, beyond the obvious fact that such families are very likely to be poor, follows from this pattern of family life. To the extent the matter was addressed at all, it was usually done by assuming that welfare payments provided an incentive for families to dissolve. To deal with this, some people embraced the negative income tax (or as President Nixon rechristened it, the Family Assistance Plan) because it would provide benefits to all poor families, broken or not, and thus remove incentive for dissolution.

There were good reasons to be somewhat skeptical of that view. If the system of payments under the program for Aid to Families of Dependent Children (AFDC) was to blame for the rise in single-parent families, why did the rise occur so dramatically among blacks but not to nearly the same extent among whites? If AFDC provided an incentive for men to beget children without assuming responsibility for supporting them, why was the illegitimacy rate rising even in states that did not require the father to be absent from the home for the family to obtain assistance? If AFDC created so perverse a set of incentives, why did these incentives have so large an effect in the 1960s and 1970s (when single-parent families were increasing by leaps and bounds) and so little, if any, such effect in the 1940s and 1950s (when such families scarcely increased at all)? And if AFDC were the culprit, how is it that poor, single-parent families rose in number during a decade (the 1970s) when the value of AFDC benefits in real dollars was declining?

Behavior does change with changes in incentives. The results of the negative income tax experiments certainly show that. In the Seattle and Denver experiments, the rate of family dissolution was much higher among families who received the guaranteed annual income than among similar families who did not—36 percent higher in the case of whites, 42 percent higher in the case of blacks. Men getting the cash benefits reduced their hours of work by 9 percent, women by 20 percent, and young males without families by 43 percent.

Charles Murray, whose 1984 book, *Losing Ground,* has done so much to focus attention on the problem of welfare, generally endorses the economic explanation for the decline of two-parent families. The evidence from the negative income tax experiments is certainly consistent with his view, and he makes a good case that the liberalization of welfare eligibility rules in the 1960s contributed to the sudden increase in the AFDC caseload. But as he is the first to admit, the data do not exist to offer a fully tested explanation of the rise of single-parent families; the best he can do is to offer a mental experiment showing how young, poor men and women might rationally respond to the alternative benefits of work for a two-parent family and welfare payments for a one-parent one. He rejects the notion that character, the Zeitgeist, or cultural differences are necessary to an explanation. But he cannot show that young, poor men and women in fact responded to AFDC as he assumes they did, nor can he explain the racial differences in rates or the rise in caseloads at a time of declining benefits. He notes an alternative explanation that cannot be ruled out: During the 1960s, a large number of persons who once thought of being on welfare as a temporary and rather embarrassing expedient came to regard it as a right that they would not be deterred from exercising. The result of that change can be measured: Whereas in 1967, 63 percent of the persons eligible for AFDC were on the rolls, by 1970, 91 percent were.

In short, the character of a significant number of persons changed. To the extent one thinks that change was fundamentally wrong, then, as Loury has put it, the change creates a moral problem. What does one do about such a moral problem? Lawrence Mead has suggested invigorating the work requirement associated with welfare, so that anyone exercising a "right" to welfare will come to understand that there is a corresponding obligation. Murray has proposed altering the incentives by increasing the difficulty of getting welfare or the shame of having it so as to provide positive rewards for not having children, at least out of wedlock. But nobody has yet come to grips with how one might test a way of using either obligations or incentives to alter character so that people who once thought it good to sire or bear illegitimate children will now think it wrong.

Public Finance

We have a vast and rising governmental deficit. Amidst the debate about how one might best reduce that deficit (or more typically, reduce the rate of increase in it), scarcely anyone asks why we have not always had huge deficits.

If you believe that voters and politicians seek rationally to maximize their self-interest, then it would certainly be in the interest of most people to transfer wealth from future generations to present ones. If you want the federal government to provide you with some benefit and you cannot persuade other voters to pay for your benefit with higher taxes, then you should be willing to have the government borrow to pay for that benefit. Since every voter has something he would like from the government, each has an incentive to obtain that benefit with funds to be repaid by future generations. There are, of course, some constraints on unlimited debt financing. Accumulated debt charges from past generations must be financed by this generation, and if these charges are heavy there may well develop some apprehension about adding to them. If some units of government default on their loans, there are immediate economic consequences. But these constraints are not strong enough to inhibit more than marginally the rational desire to let one's grandchildren pay (in inflation-devalued dollars) the cost of present indulgences.

That being so, why is it that large deficits, except in wartime, have been a feature of public finance only in the past few decades? What kept voters and politicians from buying on credit heavily and continuously beginning with the first days of the republic?

James M. Buchanan, in his 1984 presidential address to the Western Economic Association, has offered one explanation for this paradox. He has suggested that public finance was once subject to a moral constraint—namely, that it was right to pay as you go and accumulate capital and wrong to borrow heavily and squander capital. Max Weber, of course, had earlier argued that essential to the rise of capitalism was a widely shared belief (he ascribed it to Protestantism) in the moral propriety of deferring present consumption for future benefits. Buchanan has recast this somewhat: He argues that a Victorian morality inhibited Anglo-American democracies from giving in to their selfish desire to beggar their children.

Viewed in this way, John Maynard Keynes was not simply an important economist, he was a moral revolutionary. He subjected to rational analysis the conventional restraints on deficit financing, not in order to show that debt was always good but to prove that it was not necessarily bad. Deficit financing should be judged, he argued, by its practical effect, not by its moral quality.

Buchanan is a free-market economist, and thus a member of a group not ordinarily given to explaining behavior in any terms other than the pursuit of self-interest narrowly defined. This fact makes all the more significant his argument that economic analysts must understand "how morals impact on choice, and especially how an erosion of moral precepts can modify the established functioning of economic and political institutions."

A rejoinder can be made to the Buchanan explanation of deficit financing. Much of the accumulated debt is a legacy of having fought wars, a legacy that can be justified on both rational and moral grounds (who wishes to lose a war, or to leave for one's children a Europe dominated by Hitler?). Another part of the debt exists because leaders miscalculated the true costs of desirable programs. According to projections made in 1965, Medicare was supposed to cost less than $9 billion a year in 1990; in 1985, the bill was already running in excess of $70 billion a year. Military pensions seemed the right thing to do when men were being called to service; only in retrospect is their total cost appreciated. The Reagan tax cuts were not designed to impose heavy debts on our children but to stimulate investment and economic growth; only later did it become obvious that they have contributed far more to the deficit than to economic growth. The various subsidies given to special interest groups for long seemed like a small price to pay for insuring the support of a heterogeneous people for a distant government; no one could have foreseen their cumulative burden.

No doubt there is some truth in the proposition that our current level of debt is the result of miscalculation and good intentions gone awry. But what strengthens Buchanan's argument, I believe, is the direction of these miscalculations (if that is what they were) and the nature of these good intentions. In almost every instance, leaders proposing a new policy erred in the direction of understating rather than overstating future costs; in almost every instance, evidence of a good intention was taken to be government action rather than inaction. Whether one wishes to call it a shift in moral values or not, one must be struck by the systematic and consistent bias in how we debated public programs beginning in the 1930s but especially in the 1960s. It is hard to remember it now, but there once was a time, lasting from 1789 to well into the 1950s, when the debate over almost any new proposal was about whether it was *legitimate* for the government to do this at all. These were certainly the terms in which Social Security, civil rights, Medicare, and government regulation of business were first addressed. By the 1960s, the debate was much different: how much should we spend (not, should we spend anything at all); how can a policy be made cost-effective (not, should we have such a policy in the first place). The character of public discourse changed and I suspect in ways that suggest a change in the nature of public character.

Crime

I have written more about crime than any other policy issue, and so my remarks on our changing understanding of this problem are to a large degree remarks about changes in my own way of thinking about it. On no subject have the methods of economics and policy analysis had greater or more salutary effect than on scholarly discussions of criminal justice. For purposes of designing public policies, it has proved useful to think of would-be offenders as mostly young males who compare the net benefits of crime with those of work and leisure. Such thinking, and the rather considerable body of evidence that supports it, leads us to expect that changes in the net benefits of crime affect the level of crime in society. To the extent that policymakers and criminologists have become less hostile to the idea of altering behavior by altering its consequences, progress has been made. Even if the amount by which crime is reduced by these measures is modest (as I think in a free society it will be), the pursuit of these policies conforms more fully than does the rehabilitative idea to our concept of justice—namely, that each person should receive his due.

But long-term changes in crime rates exceed anything that can be explained by either rational calculation or the varying proportion of young males in the population. Very little in either contemporary economics or conventional criminology equips us to understand the decline in reported crime rates during the second half of the nineteenth century and the first part of the twentieth despite rapid industrialization and urbanization, a large influx of poor immigrants, the growing ethnic heterogeneity of society, and widening class cleavages. Very little in the customary language of policy analysis helps us explain why Japan should have such abnormally low crime rates despite high population densities, a history that glorifies samurai violence, a rather permissive pattern of child-rearing, the absence of deep religious convictions, and the remarkably low ratio of police officers to citizens.

In an essay in this magazine in 1983 I attempted to explain the counterintuitive decline in crime during the period after the Civil War in much the same terms that David H. Bayley had used in a 1976 article dealing with crime in Japan. In both cases, distinctive cultural forces helped restrain individual self-expression. In Japan, these forces subject an individual to the informal social controls of family and neighbors by making him extremely sensitive to the good opinion of others. The controls are of long standing and have so far remained largely intact despite the individualizing tendencies of modernization. In the United States, by contrast, these cultural forces have operated only in certain periods, and when they were effective it was as a result of a herculean effort by scores of voluntary associations specially created for the purpose. In this country as well as in England, a variety of enterprises—Sunday schools, public schools, temperance movements, religious revivals, YMCAs, the Children's Aid Society—were launched in the first half of the nineteenth century that had in common the goal of instilling a "self-activating, self-regulating, all-purpose inner control." The objects of these efforts were those young men who, freed from the restraints of family life on the farms, had moved to the boardinghouses of the cities in search of economic opportunities. We lack any reliable measure of the effect of these efforts, save one—the extraordinary reduction in the per capita consumption of alcoholic beverages that occurred between 1830 (when the temperance efforts began in earnest) and 1850 and that persisted (despite an upturn during and just after the Civil War) for the rest of the century.

We now refer to this period as one in which "Victorian morality" took hold; the term itself, at least as now employed, reflects the condescension in which that ethos has come to be regarded. Modernity, as I have argued elsewhere, involves, at least in elite opinion, replacing the ethic of self-control with that of self-expression. Some great benefits have flowed from this change, including the liberation of youthful energies to pursue new ideas in art, music, literature, politics, and economic enterprise. But the costs are just as real, at least for those young persons who have not already acquired a decent degree of self-restraint and other-regardingness.

The view that crime has social and cultural as well as economic causes is scarcely new. Hardly any lay person, and only a few scholars, would deny that family and neighborhood affect individual differences in criminality. But what of it? How, as I asked in 1974, might a government remake bad families into good ones, especially if it must be done on a large scale? How might the government of a free society reshape the core values of its people and still leave them free?

They were good questions then and they remain good ones today. In 1974 there was virtually no reliable evidence that any program seeking to prevent crime by changing attitudes and values had succeeded for any large number of persons. In 1974 I could only urge policymakers to postpone the effort to eliminate the root causes of crime in favor of using those available policy instruments—target hardening, job training, police deployment, court sentences—that might have a marginal effect at a reasonable cost on the commission of crime. Given what we knew then and know now, acting as if crime is the result of individuals freely choosing among competing alternatives may be the best we can do.

In retrospect, nothing I have written about crime so dismayed some criminologists as this preference for doing what is possible rather than attempting what one wishes were possible. My purpose was to substitute the experimental method for personal ideology; this effort has led some people to suspect I was really trying to substitute my ideology for theirs. Though we all have beliefs that color our views, I would hope that everybody would try to keep that coloration under control by constant reference to the test of practical effect. What works?

With time and experience we have learned a bit more about what works. There are now some glimmers of hope that certain experimental projects aimed at preparing children for school and equipping parents to cope with unruly offspring may reduce the rate at which these youngsters later commit delinquent acts. Richard J. Herrnstein and I have written about these and related matters in *Crime and Human Nature*. Whether further tests and repeated experiments will confirm that these glimmers emanate from the mother lode of truth and not from fool's gold, no one can yet say. But we know how to find out. If we discover that these ideas can be made to work on a large scale (and not just in the hands of a few gifted practitioners), then we will be able to reduce crime by, in effect, improving character.

Character and Policy

The traditional understanding of politics was that its goal was to improve the character of its citizens. The American republic was, as we know, founded on a very different understanding—that of taking human nature pretty much as it was and hoping that personal liberty could survive political action if ambition were made to counteract ambition. The distinctive nature of the American system has led many of its supporters (to say nothing of its critics) to argue that it should be indifferent to character formation. Friend and foe alike are fond of applying to government Samuel Goldwyn's response to the person who asked what message was to be found in his films: If you want to send a message, use Western Union.

Since I yield to no one in my admiration for what the Founders created, I do not wish to argue the fundamental proposition. But the federal government today is very different from what it was in 1787, 1887, or even 1957. If we wish it to address the problems of family disruption, welfare dependency, crime in the streets, educational inadequacy, or even public finance properly understood, then government, by the mere fact that it defines these states of affairs as problems, acknowledges that human character is, in some degree, defective and that it intends to alter it. The local governments of village and township always understood this, of course, because they always had responsibility for shaping character. The public school movement, for example, was from the beginning chiefly aimed at moral instruction. The national government could afford to manage its affairs by letting ambition counteract ambition because what was originally at stake in national affairs—creating and maintaining a reasonably secure commercial regime—lent itself naturally to the minimal attentions of a limited government operated and restrained by the reciprocal force of mutual self-interest.

It is easier to acknowledge the necessary involvement of government in character formation than it is to prescribe how this responsibility should be carried out. The essential first step is to acknowledge that at root, in almost every area of important public concern, we are seeking to induce persons to act virtuously, whether as schoolchildren, applicants for public assistance, would-be lawbreakers, or voters and public officials. Not only is such conduct desirable in its own right, it appears now to be necessary if large improvements are to be made in those matters we consider problems: schooling, welfare, crime, and public finance.

By virtue, I mean habits of moderate action; more specifically, acting with due restraint on one's impulses, due regard for the rights of others, and reasonable concern for distant consequences. Scarcely anyone favors bad character or a lack of virtue, but it is all too easy to deride a policy of improving character by assuming that this implies a nation of moralizers delivering banal homilies to one another.

Virtue is not learned by precept, however; it is learned by the regular repetition of right actions. We are induced to do the right thing with respect to small matters, and in time we persist in doing the right thing because now we have come to take pleasure in it. By acting rightly with respect to small things, we are more likely to act rightly with respect to large ones. If this view sounds familiar, it should; it is Aristotle's. Let me now quote him directly: "We become just by the practice of just actions, self-controlled by exercising self-control."

Seen in this way, there is no conflict between economic thought and moral philosophy: The latter simply supplies a fuller statement of the uses to which the former can and should be put. We want our families and schools to induce habits of right conduct; most parents and teachers do this by arranging the incentives confronting youngsters in the ordinary aspects of their daily lives so that right action routinely occurs.

What economics neglects is the important subjective consequence of acting in accord with a proper array of incentives: people come to feel pleasure in right action and guilt in wrong action. These feelings of pleasure and pain are not mere "tastes" that policy analysts should take as given; they are the central constraints on human avarice and sloth, the very core of a decent character. A course of action cannot be evaluated simply in terms of its cost-effectiveness, because the consequence of following a given course—if it is followed often enough and regularly enough—is to teach those who follow it what society thinks is right and wrong.

Conscience and character, naturally, are not enough. Rules and rewards must still be employed; indeed, given the irresistible appeal of certain courses of action—such as impoverishing future generations for the benefit of the present one—only some rather draconian rules may suffice. But for most social problems that deeply trouble us, the need is to explore, carefully and experimentally, ways of strengthening the formation of character among the very young. In the long run, the public interest depends on private virtue.

PART IV

Leadership and Virtue

Chapter Eleven

Military Ethics: An Aristotelian Tradition in a Democratic Society

Anthony J. Giasi

Introduction

For good or ill, the military plays a key role in the life of any nation. In authoritarian regimes, it can be an instrument of conquest and repression. The military can function as the shield of liberty in democracies — the "Safeguards of their nation."[1] What makes one military force a protector and the other a threat? Given that the military controls a nation's means of organized violence, what keeps the military from assuming a position of dominance in a free society? What prevents the protector from becoming the jailer?

Many professions, such as medicine and law, possess codes of ethics. The profession of arms as embodied in the United States military stands apart from these and other professions in two key respects. It is different from others because of what it is expected to do — nothing less than to employ the means of violence to deter, or if deterrence fails, to destroy the nation's enemies. It is also to a large extent self-regulating in that it maintains it own judicial system, its own communities, and ultimately, its own culture. One would assume that, given these differences, the civilian and military spheres would be constantly clashing, perhaps with disastrous results.[2] On this latter point Tocqueville, in his always relevant study of democracy in America, sounds two warnings. First, in commercial democracies, the army will seldom attract the "best and the

---

1. With apologies to Gilbert and Sullivan. See Buttercup's aria in HMS *Pinafore*, p. 10.

2. While it is acknowledged that relations between the civilian and military sectors in the U.S. have not been free of conflict, there has never been a military coup nor even a serious challenge to civilian authority. The same cannot be said of other democracies. See the discussion of the Revolt of the Generals during the Algerian War.

brightest," and will become a "small nation by itself"[3] where soldiers will have little commonality of interests with their civilian brethren. He writes:

> The opposite tendencies of the nation and the army expose democratic communities to great dangers. When a military spirit forsakes a people, the profession of arms immediately ceases to be held in honor and military men fall to the lowest rank of the public servants; they are little esteemed and no longer *understood*.[4]

Second, and more ominous, is Tocqueville's caution as to where these diverging interests and *cultures* may lead. He notes that the desire of the civilian sector for peace stands in stark contrast to the desire of a democratic military—especially its Non-Commissioned Officer (NCO) corps—for war. It is only through war that men of ambition, desirous of promotion, can advance in the army. Thus, democratic armies possess a "restless and turbulent spirit" that is one of their inherent evils.[5] While this makes revolution a real possibility, Tocqueville is quick to note that the officer corps will be restrained, seeking to protect what it has gained through its service.[6]

While I would vigorously dispute Tocqueville's argument that the military will not have its share of the "best and the brightest,"[7] as well as his notion that democratic armies desire war, his point on the danger of the divergence of culture and interests between the two sectors is well taken. More important, what keeps the U.S. military in check? Although civilian control of the U.S. military is guaranteed in the Constitution, it is the military, and not the civilian president, that is in possession of the means of violence. It is problematic whether the mere presence of a constitutional mandate requiring obedience by the military to the civilian president would be sufficient to deter a coup d'etat, *were the military predisposed to take power*. What prevents the U.S. military, or any democratic military, from acting like the Roman legions of old and placing in power rulers to their liking?

The answer, I believe, lies in the codes of *military ethics* that buttress the concept of civilian control while also ensuring that the military will

---

3. Tocqueville, Alexis de, *Democracy in America*. (New York: Vintage Books, 1990), p. 266.
4. *Ibid.* (emphasis added).
5. *Ibid.*, p. 269.
6. *Ibid.*, pp. 272-73
7. The great majority of all contemporary company-grade officers (second lieutenant to captain) have bachelor's degrees. Likewise, virtually all field grade officers (majors to colonels) and above obtain advanced degrees. Career Non-Commissioned Officers will normally obtain their Associates degree, and the bulk of recruits have been (at least until recently) high school graduates or the equivalent.

conduct itself in a manner that befits a democratic society. But unlike American civilian society, which follows the *utilitarian* ethical tradition, the U.S. military adheres to an *Aristotelian* code of ethics. The military's Aristotelian ethical tradition, which emphasizes adhering to moral absolutes or *virtues*, places it in a position of moral superiority to the society it serves, and prevents it from falling victim to moral decay.

This chapter will focus on the professional soldier—particularly the officer and the NCO—and how codes of ethics affect and help him ply his craft. Within that context, it will provide a working definition for military ethics, discuss its origins in the American military, and examine how codes of ethics are inculcated. The crucial relationship between ethics, character, and leadership will also be discussed. The chapter will then briefly examine the new pressures and threats to military ethics in the contemporary world, particularly the rise of unethical, ruthless foes that will challenge our commitment to ethics. It is here that the case study of the French experience in Algeria will serve as a cautionary tale. Lastly, it will provide some recommendations to cope with these new pressures and threats.

The Role of Military Ethics in Democratic Societies

It is the codes of ethics utilized by professional militaries in democratic societies (along with the tradition of civilian control that they reinforce) that act as safeguards against the military exchanging their role of loyal servants of society for that of its master. These codes of ethics—for no one code can fit the variety of situations that face military personnel in both peace and war—provide guidelines as to what is considered right and honorable behavior on the part of the custodians of the means of violence.[8]

Military ethics contains elements of two conflicting ethical traditions— *utilitarianism* and *Aristotelianism*. At the policy level, utilitarian considerations, in the form of cost versus gain calculations, enter into the ethical equation. Do we bomb the target, thus saving the lives of military personnel engaged in an operation, but at the cost of increased "collateral damage" (that is, greater civilian casualties)?[9] Or do we minimize collateral damage, accepting greater risk and greater casualties amongst our own forces, but maintaining our commitment to humanitarian ideals?

---

8. N. Fotion and G. Elfstrom. *Military Ethics* (Boston: Routledge & Kegan Paul, 1986). James H. Toner, *True Faith and Allegiance*. (Lexington: The University Press of Kentucky, 1995), p. 4.

9. A example of this is Truman's decision to drop the atomic bomb on Japan, thus ultimately saving hundreds of thousands of Allied and Japanese lives, but at a high price in civilian casualties.

At the level of the individual soldier, however, it is essentially an Aristotelian system, where one practices the military virtues, seeking to do the "harder right instead of the easier wrong," drawing strength from a reservoir of integrity and moral character.[10] Each soldier carries with him a moral compass that helps him make the difficult decisions that present themselves both in peace and, most especially, in war. These virtues are central to the practice of sound leadership and are taught by example. Indeed, the U.S. military stresses leadership by example—the modeling of desired behaviors, such as courage, integrity, devotion to duty, and loyalty by officers and NCOs. One needs only to observe the personnel of a military unit engaged in a difficult mission, such as peacekeeping, to see this moral compass at work. On the other hand, the breakdown of the soldier's moral compass became all to evident in the infamous My Lai massacre.

If military ethics and honor are key elements that help keep a democratic military in check, they are under stress from forces that are both internal and external. Internal pressures include elements such as shrinking budgets, an increased operations tempo, and experimentation with extraneous social policies, such as the integration of women in the force, and "Don't ask, don't tell." The latter is particularly worrisome, as the social experimentation desired by the utilitarian tradition of civilian society clashes with the military's Aristotelian tradition.

External forces include those stemming from the actions of the greater society, such as changes in mores and views of ethics, and the rise of new threats from abroad. In the case of the former, the increasing tendency of American society towards permissiveness creates an ever-widening chasm between the civilian and military cultures.[11] In the case of the latter, the emergence of new enemies, whose ruthlessness and disregard for the Law of Land Warfare and accepted norms of soldierly behavior are typified by the practices of both sides in the Bosnian conflict, place pressure on the ethically-oriented Western armies to "fight fire with fire."

Can notions of military ethics and honor weather these pressures? They must if both the military and the nation are to survive in their de-

---

10. John C. Bahnsen, and Robert W. Cone, "Defining the American Warrior Leader," *Parameters* (December 1990): 26; Lewis Sorley, "Doing What's Right: Shaping the Army's Professional Environment." *Parameters* (March 1989): 12.

11. The apparent tolerance displayed by the American public towards the scandals, wrongdoing and ethical ambiguity of its political officials stands in sharp contrast to the military's tradition of the vigorous enforcement of order and discipline. An example of this is the reaction (or lack of it) of the American public to the reports of illegal fundraising by the Clinton administration.

mocratic forms. There are examples of what happens when these codes of ethics break down, such as they did in the case of the French Army in the Algerian conflict and in our own Vietnam experience. What must we do to preserve military ethics and honor in a world where low intensity conflict, in the form of tribal/ethnic wars and terrorism, are the norm? I will argue that we, as a society, must make difficult choices as to what we will consider acceptable behavior in our military—and what price we are willing to pay on the battlefield for these choices.

Before these questions can be answered, the concepts of military ethics and honor, and their relationship to *character* and *leadership*, must be defined. Given the inherently "lawless" nature of military operations, where weapons of almost unbelievable lethality—from small arms to fuel-air explosives—are routinely employed, can there even be such a thing as military ethics?

The Nature of Military Ethics and Honor: Rival Concepts

Concepts of military ethics and honor have varied somewhat over time, and from country to country. While members of the profession of arms would take for granted that they follow codes of ethics, the concept does not go unchallenged. Unlike other professions, there is some question as to whether the military truly possesses a code of ethics. After all, if "all is fair in love and war," the notion of what constitutes ethical behavior seems, at first, a strange one.[12] Some would even argue that military ethics is little more than an oxymoron.[13]

If it exists, what is the nature of military ethics? The question of the existence of military ethics will be considered within the context of the discussion regarding the two rival models of military ethics: utilitarianism and Aristotelianism.

Fotion and Elfstrom: Utilitarianism as the Basis for Military Ethics

Even in war, do we ever really leave ethics behind? Fotion and Elfstrom argue that the answer to this question lies in examining the two

---

12. Fotion et al., op. cit., pp. 6-10; Toner, op. cit., p. xi.
13. Fotion, op. cit., pp. 1-2.

extreme positions of *realism* and *pacifism* regarding the existence of military ethics.[14]

The realist position, much like its international relations progenitor, maintains that war is a state of no rules—of "every nation/society for itself".[15] Thus, for realists, anything goes. Any weapon, including nuclear devices, can be used if it will ensure victory. Military ethics, per sé, do not exist, because ethics are not applicable in the interstate behavior known as war. The violence of war is thus essentially unrestrained, and in fact deemed uncontrollable.[16] In the realist view of warfare and ethics, there are no constraints placed on individual behavior, and therefore neither ethics nor honor apply.

The situation is reversed in the pacifist position, which holds that ethical concerns are paramount and, therefore, that the use of force can never be justified. "Military ethics," consequently, is a term that makes little sense because proper interstate relations cannot include the use of violence. An "ethical" military would therefore be one that operates without resorting to the use of force. Thus, the pacifist position is diametrically opposed to the essential role of the military, which is to engage with and destroy the enemy—a task which clearly implies the use of lethal force.

Fotion and Elfstrom reconcile these two extreme positions by arguing that military ethics exist somewhere between them.[17] They argue that codes of military ethics are pragmatic solutions to the problems faced by the military; a means of regulating the (potentially negative) behavior of soldiers, particularly under the stress of combat.[18] They note that military ethics can be seen as "paradigm examples of sets of ready-made rules" that take, to a large extent, the long deliberation and guesswork out of making difficult decisions, and operate on an intuitive level of moral thinking.[19] Military ethics are therefore a form of applied ethics, like law or medicine but containing special features such as the greater and more frequently exercised concern with life and death matters.[20]

---

14. This section draws heavily on the discussion of military ethics contained in Fotion and Elfstrom's *Military Ethics* and Toner's *True Faith and Allegiance*.
15. Fotion and Elfstrom, p. 6.
16. *Ibid.*
17. In essence, pacifism and realism are the opposite poles of what can be viewed as an ethical continuum.
18. Fotion and Elfstrom, p. 75.
19. *Ibid.*, pp. 67, 75
20. *Ibid.*, pp. 68-69.

Codes of military ethics set some limits, both on what happens in war and on the role of the military vis-á-vis society at large. Since the military is composed of different classes of warriors (officers, NCOs, and enlisted personnel) with different levels, types, and scopes of responsibility, more than one code is needed. Some codes, such as the Code of Conduct (Prisoner's Code),[21] the "fighting code,"[22] and the *creedal code* apply to all.[23] The creedal code forms the preamble to both the internal code (that is, how military professionals should behave towards each other; what they expect of each other) and such external codes as the fighting code. It serves two purposes. First, it is an inspirational call to duty,[24] stressing the need for self-sacrifice and dedication on the part of all. The second purpose of the creedal code is to paint a picture of the ideal fighting man. It this regard, it emphasizes such Aristotelian virtues as courage, honesty, valor, bravery, fairness, steadfastness, and leadership.[25]

Fotion and Elfstrom's construction of military ethics as being composed of a series of codes is supported by this author's own military experience. There are separate but related codes of ethical behavior for officers, NCOs, and enlisted personnel, which are grouped in the manner of a layer cake. On the bottom are the general codes which apply to all. The next layer would be more stringent and apply to NCOs — the "shop foremen" of the organized violence that is the military. They are the ones who, along with their enlisted charges, carry the burden of both the day-to-day work in peacetime and the fighting in wartime.

The top and most stringent layer is reserved for officers. They are the managers of violence, charged with the overall success or failure of military operations, and with the lives of the men under them. Because of these greater responsibilities, much more is demanded of officers than other ranks. This includes expecting them to possess habits and refinements normally associated with "gentlemen."

---

21. The Code of Conduct provides guidelines for the conduct of military personnel when captured or in imminent danger of capture by the enemy. It stresses the need to never surrender voluntarily, to keep faith with one's fellows, and so forth.

22. See Department of Defense, Department of the Army *FM27–10 The Law of Land Warfare* (Washington D.C., 1956). Fotion and Elfstrom's "fighting code" is essentially the Law of Land Warfare, which regulates behavior toward both the enemy and civilians. Based on a combination of customary international law and treaties, such as the Geneva and Hague Conventions, it has been made part of U.S. law, and violations can be punished under the Uniform Code of Military Justice (UCMJ).

23. Fotion and Elfstrom, op. cit., pp. 78-79.

24. The West Point motto of "Duty, Honor, Country" would fall into this category.

25. Fotion and Elfstrom, op. cit., p. 78.

Mere Guidelines or Absolutes? A Gentle Critique of Fotion and Elfstrom

While one finds much that is useful in Fotion and Elfstrom's approach, a number of issues arise from their assertion that military ethics are essentially *utilitarian* in nature. Simply put, the principles of utilitarianism maintain that ethical conduct produces the greatest *happiness* (or broadest benefit) for the greatest number.[26] It is clear that at some level, military and civilian authorities who promulgate policy make cost versus gain calculations. For example, principles minimizing "collateral damage" (that is, the destruction of non-military targets and/or civilians), and promoting the appropriate treatment of prisoners of war are not based solely on *humanitarian* principles. Rather, they reflect the desire to set an example for other powers and engender reciprocal behavior. This is particularly important for a nation such as the U.S., whose constitution mandates strict adherence to treaties.[27]

Fotion and Elfstrom criticize the Aristotelian school of military ethics, arguing that "rights-based or duty-based moral systems simply do not contain the means of accommodating future change or unexpected complication".[28] Adherence to absolutes would, they argue, preclude the necessary flexibility to redefine and/or clarify acceptable military behavior under changing situations and circumstances.[29]

American civil society is based in large part on the principle of enlightened self-interest as articulated by John Locke. In his *Second Treatise of Civil Government,* he argues that men are motivated by the desire for "life, liberty, and property" and give up their power of self-defense to

---

26. John Stuart Mill, *Utilitarianism*, ed. Oskar Piest (New York: The Library of Liberal Arts, 1957), pp. 16, 25; Leo Strauss and Joseph Cropsey, *History of Political Philosophy*. 3rd ed. (Chicago: The University of Chicago Press, 1987), pp. 789-90.

27. Article VI, paragraph 2 of the U.S. Constitution contains the Supremacy Clause, which states that treaties, along with other laws made pursuant to the Constitution, shall be the "Supreme Law of the Land." In essence, the Supremacy Clause requires that the U.S. adhere to the doctrine of international law known as *pacta sunt servanda* ("nations are bound to keep the promises they make") Burns H. Weston, Richard A. Falk, and Anthony D'Amato, *International Law and World Order*. 2nd ed. (St. Paul, Minnesota: West Publishing Co., 1990), p. 54.

28. Fotion and Elfstrom, op. cit., p. 280. An example of a rights-based moral system is the UN's *Universal Declaration of Human Rights*. It enumerates a set of basic rights and protections that signatory states must accord their citizens, such as freedom from arbitrary arrest, detention, or exile, the right to life, liberty, and the security of person, and so forth.

29. *Ibid.*, pp. 22-23

the civil government because of the greater protection that it offers.[30] Given our Lockean preferences, the promulgation and adherence to utilitarian codes of ethics fail to explain why men would willingly risk their lives for others. The desire for self-preservation is so strong that it is difficult to believe that military codes of ethics could be based solely, or even in large part, on "utility." At the level of the individual soldier, the idea that the sacrifice of his life may be necessary so that others might live may not convince him that the "gain outweighs the cost." A prominent military historian, S.L.A. Marshall, writing on the lessons learned from battle in World War II, concludes that men are motivated not by cost versus gain calculations but by the strong desire to "not let their buddies down." Marshall writes that "...personal honor is the one thing valued more than life itself by the majority of men."[31] But the desire not to let others down is countered by the ever-present element of fear. To defend himself against it, the soldier draws courage and strength from the comradeship of his fellows. The bond that cements this comradeship that is so crucial for fighting morale is provided by another virtue, loyalty.[32]

Indeed, while the creedal code may be based on the utilitarian need to regulate behavior, it is couched primarily in terms of an appeal to (Aristotelian) virtues such as honor, loyalty, duty, and so forth. Aristotle argued in the *Nicomachean Ethics* that man can achieve success in his endeavors by the use of *practical wisdom* (the how-tos of action). For the soldier, practical wisdom includes proficiency in the use of weapons, knowledge of tactics, such as how to properly assault a fortified enemy position, and so forth. Practical wisdom must be consistent with and based on moral virtue. While practical wisdom shows us the right *means* to achieve an end, it is virtue that shows us the correct mark or end at which to aim.[33] For the soldier, it is this set of inculcated virtues that serves as an internal moral compass and helps him find the wisdom and strength to do the hard right rather than the easy wrong.

While it is easy to see how these virtues can be transmitted to soldiers as part of the military's socialization process, does the soldier con-

---

30. John Locke, *Two Treatises of Government*. (New York: Hafner Press, 1947), p. 163.

31. S.L.A. Marshall, *Men Against Fire*. 1st ed. (New York: William Morrow & Company, 1947), p. 149.

32. Peter S. Kindsvatter, "Cowards, Comrades, and Killer Angels: The Soldier in Literature." *Parameters* (June 1990): 40.

33. Aristotle, *The Nicomachean Ethics*. Translated and edited by W.D. Ross. In *Great Books of the Western World*, vol. 9, ed. Robert Maynard Hutchins (Chicago: Encyclopedia Britannica, Inc. [page references are to reprint edition]), p. 393.

sciously embrace these Aristotelian virtues? Or is he just acting out of habit? From the time the civilian enters the military service, he is under the tight control of military professionals, such as drill sergeants, who tell him what to do, when to do it, how to behave, and so forth. By means of constant repetition and with the example of his superiors as a guide, he is, over time, *habituated* into the virtues required of the military professional. He learns to put the needs of the service first, to accomplish the mission (even at the cost of his life), to suffer hardships, and to sacrifice for others.

This is consistent with Aristotle's view of morality. Aristotle distinguishes between intellectual virtues and the moral virtues. Intellectual virtues are acquired by and nurtured in the individual by teaching. Intellectual virtues are distilled wisdom that comes from experience. In contrast, moral virtue is instilled in the individual by habit—by acting in a virtuous manner, even though one might not at first understand the reason why. In essence, one comes to understand virtue by doing what is virtuous.[34]

Fotion and Elfstrom are correct in maintaining that at least some aspects of military ethics are utilitarian, such as the practice of performing a cost versus gain calculation before deciding upon a course of military action. This leads me to conclude that the view one takes of the nature of military ethics is a function of the level of analysis being employed. Military codes of ethics may be seen as utilitarian at the societal level because they produce the public good of adherence to the principles of civilian control and international law, while fostering the indispensable public good of self-sacrifice on the part of the soldiery. At the level of the individual soldier—regardless of rank—military codes of ethics are Aristotelian. They are taught, enforced, and practiced in terms of soldierly virtues that must be emulated and high standards of conduct—both moral and professional—that must be maintained. It is at this level that codes of ethics are learned, practiced, lived, and sometimes fail. For these reasons, I maintain that the proper level of analysis with which to study military ethics is the level of the individual soldier.

The argument of Fotion and Elfstrom that military codes of ethics, especially the inspirational codes, are essentially utilitarian in nature is flawed, particularly in light of what we know about why men are willing to risk their lives for others. In this regard, Aristotle offers us a better model with which to study military ethics than does Mill. Two key arguments against a utilitarian model can be made. First, determining what constitutes the "greatest good for the greatest number" can be dif-

---

34. *Ibid.*, p. 348.

ficult (if not impossible) under conditions of great stress and personal danger. The soldier cannot know that putting his life at risk to save his fellows and/or accomplish the mission will actually result in success. In a purely cost versus gain calculation, the soldier may deem his life more valuable than those of his fellows or the completion of this particular mission, and err on the side of caution. Second, we know of many instances where soldiers fought on despite hopeless odds, and until the last man or round of ammunition.[35] Utilitarianism does not explain these situations, as they defy cold calculation or logic. It can only be explained by the strict adherence to Aristotelian virtues, such as courage, honor, and bravery, between choosing to do the hard right rather than the easier wrong.

Toner: An Aristotelian Model

In his thoughtful work, *True Faith and Allegiance*,[36] James H. Toner takes an Aristotelian approach in constructing his definition of military ethics. For Toner, military ethics is "...the study of honorable and shameful conduct in the armed services."[37] It is only by studying both the good and the bad that we will know the good. Ethics, in essence, is the study of virtue.[38] A military code of ethics based on virtue is neither blind obedience to absolutes nor purely situational. Rather, the soldier must reconcile *competing ethical demands* using reason and choice. Some ethical demands (the need to protect the lives of innocents) are more important than others (such as strict adherence to the lawful orders of superiors).

The Sources of Military Ethics

Military ethics has its roots in four sources. First, there are those norms of behavior that stem from *custom*. These include military practices such as respecting flags of truce or offering the "honors of war" to a beleaguered opponent. A second source is that of *rules* (deontology), such as those codified in international agreements and in the Law of Land Warfare. These rules are backed up by the force of military law as

---

35. For examples of soldiers practicing these Aristotelian virtues in desperate battles, see Robert Barr Smith, *To The Last Cartridge* (New York: Avon Books, 1994).
36. The title of the book is taken from a key phrase in the oath that soldiers—both officer and enlisted—take to support and defend the Constitution.
37. Toner, op. cit., p. 7.
38. *Ibid.*, p. 19.

found in the Uniform Code of Military Justice (UCMJ), which makes violations of the Law of Land Warfare violations of U.S. law as well. A third source of military ethics is *teleology*, which is comprised of the desired outcomes or goals of the military, the government, and society.[39]

A fourth source of military ethics involves *circumstances*. As Toner notes, the situation in which the soldier finds himself can affect his choice amongst competing ethical claims.[40] The effect of circumstances on the weight given to these competing claims is illustrated in the following example. A military unit is advancing into a town which contains a church from which an enemy artillery forward observer can direct bombardment against U.S. troops. Is it ethical to fire on the church if one knows that an enemy artillery forward observer is there directing fire on your troops? The Law of Land Warfare protects religious, historic and similar buildings and structures.[41] However, these protections are withdrawn if the building or structure is used for such military purposes as an observation post.[42] Since the enemy has shown bad faith regarding the protection given to these structures, the greater ethical claim is that of self-protection. Thus, the church could be attacked. Suppose, however, that the enemy also has civilians from the town in the church as hostages.[43] The greater ethical claim would be to prevent the loss of innocent life. Hence, the church should not be attacked. Circumstances do not take away the legitimacy of an ethical claim, but they can tip the scales in favor of one over the other.

The Soldier and Practical Wisdom

Aristotle defined *practical wisdom* as the capacity to act with regard to the things which are good or bad for man. It is a reasoned and true state of capacity to act with regard to human goods, to choosing right and ethical goals and the appropriate means to achieve them. For soldiers, the principles of practical wisdom include the knowledge of tactics, strategy, leadership, and so forth.[44]

How does the soldier know which of the competing ethical claims should carry the most weight in a given situation? By what means can he come to an ethical decision, especially given the chaotic and stressful

---

39. *Ibid.*, pp. 16-17.
40. *Ibid.*, pp. 16, 19.
41. Law of Land Warfare, FM 27–10, paragraph 45.
42. Law of Land Warfare, FM 27–10, paragraph 46 c.
43. Sadam Hussein's threatened use of "human shields" during the Gulf War is a more recent example of this type of violation of the Law of Land Warfare.
44. Aristotle, op. cit., p. 389.

nature of combat? Regarding the soldier's ethical duty, Toner makes an argument similar to Aristotle's about the nature of practical wisdom. It is essential that the soldier not only know what is right, but do right.[45] Most important, like Aristotle, Toner believes that only a moral soldier can be a good soldier. This does not mean that an unethical person cannot fight well or cannot demonstrate tactical and technical proficiency *in a particular engagement.* Such men, however, cannot be trusted with the command of others or with the control of the means of violence, for their true nature will sooner or later manifest itself.[46]

The Importance of Character, Integrity and Honor

Three concepts underpin Toner's Aristotelian model of military ethics. The first is *character*, which is the soldier's source of strength that enables him or her to follow an ethical path. Character can be defined as being "...the commitment to an admirable set of values, and the courage to manifest those values in one's life no matter the cost in terms of personal success or popularity."[47] Character is the essence of professionalism, particularly for the soldier.[48] Related to the concept of character is the notion of *integrity*, which can be defined as "knowing what to be."[49] The soldier, whether officer, NCO, or enlisted, cannot know what to do without a clear sense of his role, responsibilities, and obligations. The third concept—and a key element of the military profession—is that of military *honor*.[50] Honor is gained by the military professional by

---

45. Toner, op. cit., p. 19.
46. See Percival Christopher Wren, *Beau Geste* (New York: Permabooks, 1961). This novel of the French Foreign Legion at war in the North African desert contains an example of an unethical soldier, Sergeant-Major Lejaune, who is nonetheless proficient at his job. Lejaune is a cruel martinet, bent on obtaining a stolen emerald from the three Geste brothers who are assigned to his command at Fort Zinderneuf. When the fort is attacked by Bedouins, it is Lejaune's leadership and tactical proficiency that gets them through the battle. Once the danger is over, Lejaune's brutality and greed again put him on a collision course with his men. For those readers that remember the Hollywood version of *Beau Geste,* the name of the character of Sergeant-Major Lejaune (played by Brian Donlevy) was changed to Markov.
47. Sorley as quoted in Toner, p. 117.
48. Toner, op. cit., p. 117.
49. *Ibid.*, p. 117.
50. See Morris Janowitz, *The Professional Soldier* (The Free Press, 1960), pp. 215–25. Janowitz notes that military honor is "both a means and an end, " in that it

his gentlemanly conduct; loyalty to his command, the Constitution, and to the brotherhood of arms; and the pursuit of military glory.[51]

Why is honor so important to the soldier, given the urge for self-preservation? The answer to this question can be found in the theories of behavioral motivation, such as Maslow's *hierarchy of needs*.[52] For the military, honor is the highest of psychological rewards, corresponding to Maslow's need for *esteem*, and in many ways enables the soldier to be self-actualized. Whereas Maslow envisages a *hierarchy of needs*, with the motivation for the more primary needs such as self-preservation being dominant, the case of the military is one in which the need for honor may supersede that for self-preservation (that is, safety).

Given the importance of honor to the soldier [53] and Toner's definition of military ethics as being the study of honorable and shameful conduct in the armed services, it is necessary to define the parameters of both honor and its opposite, shame. This is done in terms of Aristotelian virtues, such as integrity, bravery, honesty, courage, faithfulness, loyalty, and so forth. Shameful conduct consists of violations of these virtues, such as disloyalty (disobedience) to the Constitution. By making obedi-

---

specifies not only how a soldier, particularly an officer, ought to behave, but serves as an objective towards which all must strive. When military honor is effective, it has considerable coercive power and acts as a self-correcting mechanism for military conduct.

51. Toner, op. cit., pp. 119-120.

52. Maslow envisages a pyramidal arrangement of needs that an individual seeks to fulfill. The most basic and important needs are *physiological*. That is, the need for food, shelter, clothing, etc. The next need to be satisfied is that of *safety*. This is the desire to remain free of the hazards of life — health hazards, personal safety, and economic instability—both in the present and future. The third need to be satisfied in the hierarchy is that of *social or affiliation* needs. Persons have a desire to belong to and be accepted by various groups, and this is particularly true in the military. The fourth need is that for *esteem*, both self-esteem and for the esteem rendered by others. The highest, and most important need is for *self-actualization*. Self-actualization is the need to maximize one's potential—to "be all that you can be." As a need is satisfied, it loses its motivational power, being replaced by the next higher need. Maslow's hierarchy of needs is not intended to be a precise predicator of behavior, but rather to provide clues to probable behavior (Maslow, 1970, 35-58; Hersey and Blanchard, 1993, 33-46).

53. In the nineteenth century, the concept of honor was deemed important to other professions, such as law or medicine. However, with the bureaucratization of these professions, honor was largely replaced by concepts of efficiency, business, and so forth. That the U.S. military has retained honor as a principal virtue is due to several factors. First, while the military has also been bureaucratized and has also embraced the concepts of efficiency and effectiveness, there is no profit motive. Psychological rewards, such as honor and esteem, are therefore more important to the soldier. Second, given that the military is in possession of the means of violence, honor and morality are essential to ensuring that these means are not misused.

ence to the Constitution and civilian authority a matter of honor and shame, military codes of ethics help keep the armed services subordinate to civilian authority.

Leadership and Military Ethics

In the Aristotelian model of military ethics, the military professional must blend competence (knowing how to do a task) with character and wisdom with virtue.[54] Effective military leaders are also ethical and moral military leaders, just as good soldiers are always also "good" (that is, ethical and moral) people.[55] Moral leaders serve as role models and are indispensable to an organization. It is they who, by their example, transmit these virtues to others. By modeling virtuous behaviors, such as selflessness, devotion to duty, and so forth, leaders foster the same behavior in their soldiers.

Building on Toner's model, ethical and moral military leadership can be thought of as part of a triad. Military leadership is underpinned by character, integrity, virtues, and professional competence. A leader who has character but lacks the virtue of competence is not an ethical leader because his failure to master the particulars of his profession can cost lives and success on the battlefield. Similarly, professional competency untempered by character and integrity can lead to bad outcomes, such as violations of the Law of Land Warfare or disloyalty to civilian authority.

Leadership is central to unit cohesion, which in turn is essential for combat effectiveness. Since character, integrity, virtue, and competence are the ingredients of effective leadership, they become functional imperatives for the military professional.[56] Leaders are shaped by a combination of forces. Among these are institutions, such as the service academies, the officer and NCO development courses; the units in which they mature and learn their trade; and, most important, the example set by other leaders.[57] It is for this reason that the principle of leadership by example receives so much emphasis.

George Washington: The Model for the American Military Leader

The tradition of American military leadership was shaped by George Washington. Washington took an essentially Aristotelian approach to

---

54. Toner, op. cit., p. 128.
55. *Ibid.*, pp. 82-85, 129.
56. *Ibid.*, p. 81.
57. *Ibid.*, p. 83.

military ethics and professionalism, becoming the exemplar for the officer corps.[58] He stressed efficient administration coupled with ethical conduct: the need for competence (such as proficiency in tactics, drill and ceremonies), impartiality and fairness, civilian control, discipline, and a sense of pride in being part of an effective fighting force.[59] His stress on the practice of military virtues was linked to an insistence that soldiers, particularly officers, conduct themselves with honor. In contrast to the European system in which officers purchased their commissions, Washington declared that officers are made by their actions, not their titles.[60]

Indeed, Washington's emphasis on leadership by example, particularly in regards to acting honorably at all times, shows how important he considered the task of establishing and maintaining the reputation of the fledgling Continental Army. Higginbotham quotes Henry Knox[61] in declaring that "wrongs and injuries" should be suffered to the utmost degree in preserving the "immaculate reputation of the American Army." The emphasis that Washington placed on honor and service to the nation also stemmed from the need to assuage the fears of the Continental Congress concerning the potential mischief that could be caused by a large standing army. The inculcation of the tradition of respect for civilian control of the military is among Washington's greatest contributions to his nation.[62]

Military Scandals: The Failure of Ethical Leadership

The recent sexual misconduct scandals that occurred at the U.S. Army's Aberdeen Proving Grounds training base can be explained on the basis of the Aristotelian tradition of military ethics as nothing less than serious failures of ethical leadership on the part of those involved. The pressuring of female enlisted trainees for sexual favors by their drill sergeants represents both an abuse of power and a breach of the bonds of trust that are necessary for unit cohesion and good order and discipline. This failure of leadership can be further traced to failures of character and integrity.

---

58. Don Higginbotham, *George Washington and the American Military Tradition*.(Athens, GA: The University of Georgia Press, 1985), p. 73.
59. *Ibid.*, pp. 16, 17, 19, 32-35, 115.
60. *Ibid.*, p. 71.
61. Major General Henry Knox was Washington's chief of artillery. After the Revolution, he later became the nation's first Secretary of War under the Articles of Confederation, and later under the Constitution.
62. Higginbotham, op. cit., p. 38.

The solution to these problems involves more than just punishing the guilty. The issue of women in the military aside, there is clearly a need to reinforce and reiterate the military virtues of honor, integrity, loyalty, and fairness throughout the force. A healthy dose of both reflective thinking and leadership by example is in order.

The Threats to Military Ethics in the Post-Cold War World

Threats to the state of health of military ethics are not confined to domestic sources, such as the changing mores of the society at large. In his thoughtful treatise on the future of warfare, Martin Van Creveld argues that large-scale conventional warfare has been rendered obsolete by nuclear weapons. Replacing conventional warfare as the predominant form of warfare since 1945 is *low intensity conflict* (LIC), waged primarily by such new non-state actors as ethnic and religious groups, terrorists organizations, and revolutionary movements. The state, armed with conventional forces constructed in the mold of Von Clausewitz's *Trinitarian Warfare*, in which war is used as an instrument of policy of *governments (states)* conducted by *armies* with the essential support (both moral and financial) of the *people,* will be unable to defend itself against these rising new forces for conflict and *will eventually succumb to them.*[63] Van Creveld sees these non-state actors as undermining the ability of the state to provide security to its citizens, eventually losing their loyalty as it dissolves into a state of anarchy. The death of the state will result in the birth of a "New Medievalism" in a world categorized by multiple centers of power.

Lieutenant Colonel Ralph Peters takes up Van Creveld's premise and describes "the New Warrior Class," which he sees as a significant threat to Western military ethics.[64] This new warrior class is made up of the fighting forces of Van Creveld's non-state actors recruited from four "pools".[65] All of them share a desire for loot and a total ruthlessness.

---

63. Martin Van Creveld. *The Transformation of War* (New York: The Free Press, 1991), pp. 35-36, 224-26.

64. Ralph Peters, "A Revolution in Military Ethics?" *Parameters* (Summer 1996): 105, 107.

65. Ralph Peters, "The New Warrior Class" *Parameters* (Summer 1994): 17-19. The four pools from which the New Warrior Class will be recruited are as follows. The First Pool warriors come from the underclass of society and are little better than armed thugs. The Second Pool is composed of men who have been failed by the institutions of society, and who see the warrior band as a source of camaraderie and loot. The Third Pool warriors are the patriots, freedom fighters, holy warriors, and the like. The Fourth Pool con-

The New Warrior Class has no use for ethics of any kind, and fights for the love of fighting, as well as for pillage and rapine. Examples of the New Warrior Class include the Somali gunmen who fought U.S. Army Rangers in Mogadishu. In many ways, the New Warrior Class is a throwback to the marauding bands of mercenaries that served on both sides in the Thirty Years War, with the alarming advantage of being far better armed than their seventeenth century counterparts.

The warning that both Van Creveld and Lieutenant Colonel Peters sound is that Western democracies, bound as they are by the codes of ethics and morality, *may not be brutal enough to defeat the New Warrior Class*.[66] The old saying about "fighting fire with fire" will take on a new and brutal meaning (at least for the twentieth century). The challenge to civil and military authorities that these authors pose is to answer the question, "How far are we willing to go to win?" It has been answered differently in other wars by other armies. One such army was that of France, which fought a war against a left-wing insurgency in Algeria between 1954–1962. In the next section, we will examine the effects of LIC on the military ethics of the French forces in two defining episodes: the Battle of Algiers and the Revolt of the Generals.

A Cautionary Tale: The French Army in Algeria

The Algerian War, 1954–62: Historical Background

Close upon the heels of their 1954 defeat at Dien Bien Phu in Indochina, the French found themselves faced with another left-wing insurgency, this time in the French colony of Algeria. The *Front de Libération Nationale* (FLN),[67] supported by neighboring Arab states such as Egypt and Tunisia, conducted a guerrilla campaign against French forces and civilians in both the countryside and the cities. The FLN initially enjoyed success against the French, who had not yet completed the buildup of their forces.[68] But the French had learned much from their bitter

---

sists of cashiered military men, who because of their experience and training, are the most dangerous (Peters, 1994, 17–18).

66. Van Creveld, op. cit., pp. 178, 202-203, Peters, "The New Warrior Class," op. cit., p. 24.

67. National Liberation Front. It was headed by Ahmed Ben Bella, a former Free French Army sergeant.

68. Robert B. Asprey, *War in the Shadows*, vol. 2 (Garden City, New York: Doubleday & Company, Inc.), 1975, pp. 911, and for a synopsis of the Algerian War, pp. 908-931.

defeat in Indo-China at the hands of the Vietminh. They developed a counterinsurgency strategy that was based on the successful Vietminh tactics, called *la guerre révolutionnaire*. This strategy, which required the army to rely heavily on psychological warfare, pre-supposed a fight to the finish with the Algerian Communists.[69]

Just prior to the Battle of Algiers at the end of 1956, French strength had grown to over 400,000.[70] The FLN terrorist cells in Algiers, operating out of the Arab Quarter (the Casbah), were conducting a bombing campaign against the Europeans. In late January 1957, the French government moved the 10th Parachute Division, under the command of Major General Jacques Massu, into Algiers to crush the FLN. The Battle of Algiers, which lasted until September 1957, had begun.

The Battle of Algiers

The French tactics used in the Battle of Algiers were shaped by the Vietminh and were simple in concept. They would fight fire with fire; terror with terror; torture with torture. In terms of casualties and brutality, the Battle of Algiers can be compared to the Warsaw Uprising of 1944. In essence, the French forces practiced the Machiavellian doctrine of the "end justifies the means." Suspected terrorists were made to talk by torture, and the information obtained was used to break up the terrorist cells. Asprey notes that French tactics were a reversion to medieval thinking.[71]

The Battle of Algiers represented a clear suspension of military ethics by the French—a reversion to the realist position. When French society finally learned of the widespread use of torture, they were shocked and revolted at the depravity of the military.[72] A paragraph from Lartéguy's *The Centurions*, a novel of the Algerian War, illustrates the "end justifies the means" mentality of the French. In it, a French officer, Marindelle, is replying to a taunt from an FLN terrorist that his code of military honor is holding back the French from winning the war.

> "No," Marindelle burst out. "Our *bourgeois* conception of honour, we left behind us in Indo-China in Camp One. We're out to win, and we're in too much of a hurry to saddle ourselves with such ridiculous conven-

---

69. *Ibid.*, pp. 912-913.
70. *Ibid.*, p. 917.
71. *Ibid.*, pp. 917–20. A favorite method of interrogation was the *gégêne*, in which field-phone wires were hooked up to the victim's genitalia and a current shot through them.
72. *Ibid.*, p. 919.

tions. Our diffidence, our indecision, our pangs of conscience are the best weapons you could use against us; but they won't work any longer."[73]

The French Army won the Battle of Algiers, but at the cost of its soul, and its honor.

The General's Revolt of April 1961

A second incident from the Algerian War that is relevant to our discussion of military ethics is the General's Revolt of April 1961. The war had dragged on and De Gaulle's promise of self-determination for the Algerians inflamed both the European Algerians and the French military in Algeria. The 1961 revolt was the third such serious challenge to civilian authority and was led by (retired) Generals Salan, Challe, Jouhaud, and Zeller. The leaders of the revolt hoped that once the operation was underway, French officers would join.[74] Approximately 40,000 officers and men eventually were involved in the revolt on the side of the rebel generals, but the majority of the conscripts either refused to join in the operation or committed acts of sabotage against the mutiners.[75] The revolt collapsed by the end of April 1961.

The Generals' Revolt serves as an illustration of what can happen when the tradition of civilian control of the military is abrogated. While many officers did violate their code of ethics and their honor by joining in the revolt, the great majority of the conscripts, who were closer to French civilian society, did not, and this made the difference.[76] The role played by the French conscripts—mostly lower-ranking enlisted soldiers—confirms Tocqueville's assertion that in democracies, it will be private soldiers that act as a brake against the revolutionary tendencies of democratic armies. They retain their connection with the civil society at large, and will therefore act more conservatively. Tocqueville also warned that, in contrast, it will be the NCOs and officers that pose the greatest threat, as these professional soldiers will be the least representative of the normally peaceful and orderly spirit of civil society.[77]

---

73. Jean Lartéguy, *The Centurions*. trans. Xan Fielding (New York: E.P. Dutton & Co., Inc., 1962), p. 458.
74. Edgar O'Ballance. *The Algerian Insurrection: 1954-62* (Camden, CT: Archon Books, 1967), p. 169.
75. *Ibid.*, p. 181.
76. In this latter regard, they were aided by the transistor radio, which kept them in contact with news broadcasts from metropolitan France regarding the course of the rebellion. *Ibid.*, p. 185.
77. Tocqueville, op. cit., pp. 272-74.

Conclusions and Recommendations

The cautionary tales from the Algerian War reinforce my belief in the importance of military ethics to both a healthy society and a capable military. While military codes of ethics may be viewed at the societal level as being essentially utilitarian in nature, at the level of the individual soldier these codes are Aristotelian. Although one can disagree with Fotion and Elfstrom's utilitarian formulation for military codes of ethics, their approach to the study of codes of ethics is nonetheless very useful.

The key issue facing military ethics today is how we are going to address the threat from the New Warrior Class and Low Intensity Conflict. Are we, as a society, willing to be as brutal as the French were in Algeria, in order to "win"? What adjustments will we need to make in our approach to military ethics? Peters is correct in arguing that it is time to reexamine our codes of military ethics.

This brief discussion of military ethics points to another, and equally disturbing, trend that is faced by America's contemporary military and the society that it defends. This is the growing gap in moral outlook between the civilian and military sectors. This gap is caused by the clash of two conflicting ethical traditions. On the one hand there is the military, with its Aristotelian virtues. On the other is the society at large, with its largely utilitarian tradition, and all too-frequent practice of "situational ethics." This lack of a common moral and ethical tradition between the military and the citizenry, which was not the case during even Tocqueville's time, may yet confirm Tocqueville's assertion that democratic armies are more revolutionary in spirit, and may pose a threat to the societies that they serve. Having little in common with their civilian brethren, the professional military may begin to question why they have to obey the orders of a civilian leadership that has proved itself to be its moral inferior. One need only look to the scandals of the current administration, to corporate executives who downsize workers while pocketing hefty bonuses, and to members of the clergy who disgrace their robes of authority to support claims of the ethical and moral degeneracy of the civilian sector.[78]

Toner is right in proposing that the military, with is Aristotelian tradition, serve as the wellspring that feeds the ethical rebirth of America. There is much that the civilian sector can learn from its military, and perhaps it is time that it did.

---

78. Toner, op. cit., p. 128.

Chapter Twelve

Administrators in a Democratic Republic: A Multivalent View of American Civil Religion

Ralph Clark Chandler

A prince whose character is thus marked by every art which may define a tyrant is unfit to be the ruler of a free people.
— Thomas Jefferson
A Declaration by the Representatives of the United States of America, in General Congress Assembled, 1776.

Every man, as long as he does not violate the laws of justice, is left perfectly free to pursue his own interest in his own way.
— Adam Smith
An Inquiry into the Nature and Causes of the Wealth of Nations, 1776.

The various modes of worship which prevailed in the Roman world were all considered by the people, as equally true; by the philosopher, as equally false; and by the magistrate, as equally useful.
— Edward Gibbon
The History of the Decline and Fall of the Roman Empire, 1776.

I

The Synchronicities of '76

I was once struck by the fact that the American Declaration of Independence and Adam Smith's *Wealth of Nations* were published in the same year. It is one of Jung's synchronicities, I thought, the conjunction of a powerful new economic theory and a governmental system in which the theory could be worked out. Jefferson spoke of that government governing best which governs least, and Madison did say, after all, that he and the other founders were designing a commercial republic in which interest would play the role of virtue. In one of the earliest commentaries on the place of public administrators in this new commercial republic, Madison wrote the following to the people of the state of New York on February 6, 1788:

> But the great security against a gradual concentration of the several powers in the same department, consists in giving to those who administer each department, the necessary constitutional means, and personal motives, to resist encroachments of the others. The provision for defense must in this, as in all other cases, be made commensurate to the danger of attack. Ambition must be made to counteract ambition. The interest of the man must be connected with the constitutional rights of the place. It may be a reflection on human nature, that such devices should be necessary to control the abuses of government. But what is government itself but the greatest of all reflections on human nature? If men were angels, no government would be necessary. In framing a government which is to be administered by men over men, the great difficulty lies in this: You must first enable the government to control the governed; and in the next place, oblige it to control itself. A dependence on the people is no doubt the primary control on the government; but experience has taught mankind the necessity of auxiliary precautions.[1]

For his part Adam Smith was openly contemptuous of public administrators who "pretend to watch over the economy of private people." Leave these private people alone, he advised, and they will serve the ultimate good of society. Speaking from the chair of moral philosophy at the University of Glasgow and with the authority that his widely acclaimed *Theory of Moral Sentiments* (1759) had earned him, Smith broke with the economic doctrines that had preceded him. Whereas the real source of a nation's wealth had been thought by the bullionists to be gold, by

---

1. *The Federalist*, No. 51 (Franklin Center, Pennsylvania: The Franklin Library, 1977), p. 374.

In recent American history "the necessity of auxiliary precautions" has included the Ethics in Government Act of 1978. A controversial provision of that Act now preoccupies the American people. It establishes the position of special prosecutor, a person who will investigate and, when necessary, prosecute high-ranking officials of the government for violations of federal criminal laws. The special prosecutor is chosen by a group of three federal judges, appointed by the chief justice for two years and known as the special division. The selection of special prosecutors and the description of the prosecutor's jurisdiction are the special division's only functions. It carries out these responsibilities after a preliminary investigation by the attorney general indicates that a special prosecutor is necessary. In *Morrison v. Olson* (487 U.S. 654, 1988) the Supreme Court held that the Ethics in Government Act did not infringe on the separation of powers.

the mercantilists to be manufacturing, and by the physiocrats to be agriculture, Smith said rather it was annual labor. The annual revenue of every society is always precisely equal to the exchangeable value of the whole annual produce of its industry. As every individual endeavors to employ his capital in the support of domestic industry, and so to direct that industry that its produce may be of the greatest value, so every individual necessarily labors to render the annual revenue of society as great as he can.

Smith said this private citizen neither intends to promote the public interest, nor knows how much he is promoting it. He intends only his own security. In this intention, however, he is "led by an invisible hand to promote an end which was no part of his intention. Nor is it always the worse for the society that it was no part of it. By pursuing his own interest he frequently promotes that of the society more effectually than when he really intends to promote it. I have never known much good done by those who affected to trade for the public good."[2]

The Declaration of Independence and the *Wealth of Nations* were not the only masterworks published in 1776. The synchronicity must also include Edward Gibbon's *The History of the Decline and Fall of the Roman Empire*. The connections between the early American republic and the Roman republic are universally recognized. *The Federalist* was published under the pseudonym Publius and the Antifederalist tracts were published under the names of such worthies of republican Rome as

---

2. *An Inquiry into the Nature and Causes of the Wealth of Nations*, Book 4, Chapter 2, Reprinted in Charles W. Needy, Ed. *Classics of Economics* (Oak Park, Illinois: Moore Publishing Company, Inc., 1980), p. 25.

In a recent visit to the People's Republic of China I was impressed by the extent to which my hosts in the People's Protectorate had read and pondered Adam Smith's work. The fate of most classics, of course, is to be much talked about but little read. The inexorable movement of the Chinese toward a capitalist economy is illustrated by John Leicester's Associated Press story of March 6, 1998:

> Breaking sharply from the era when communist bureaucrats ruled supreme, China's legislature began debate today on an ambitious government overhaul to catch up with two decades of market reforms.
>
> The restructuring—the most sweeping in 20 years—is intended to prevent government meddling in key industries, curb corruption, and reduce the burden of a bloated bureaucracy on the national economy, said Luo Gan, secretary general of the State Council.

The overhaul calls for the elimination of 11 out of 40 government ministries and commissions. Thus the Chinese continue to learn from the Soviet communist debacle of 1989, and as they continue to read their Adam Smith, they will also work on what I call their wild horse problem. "China is like a wild horse," a member of the politburo told me. "Sometimes it goes where it wants to go."

Brutus and Cato. The founders were close students of Roman institutions, particularly administrative ones, and the character necessary to sustain them was a matter of regular reflection during the founding period. The delegates to the Constitutional Convention of 1787 frequently mentioned Roman organizational arrangements, as Madison's notes tell us.

One example is the chartering of the first United States Bank in 1791. Alexander Hamilton was keenly aware that decentralized government under the Articles of Confederation had almost defeated the colonies in their bid for independence. Each colony had its own currency, raised money in its own ways, assumed responsibility for its own debts, and responded to national need such as equipping the Continental Army only when it was convenient. His close association with Washington during the war as the General's aide de camp taught Hamilton that if private financiers such as Robert Morris had not come forward, all would have been lost. After the war England was standing by for the new nation to be crushed under its debt to Dutch and French bankers. There must be a national currency, Hamilton argued, as well as national lines of credit, national forms of taxation, and national ways to help poorer states pay their Revolutionary War debts. Public administration in a Democratic Republic required a national bank.

During the debate in late 1787 over ratification of the Constitution, both Hamilton and Madison used the Greek Amphyctionic Council as their model for delegating administrative power upward.[3] The members of the council had general authority to propose and resolve whatever it judged necessary for the common welfare of Greece—to declare and carry on war, to decide in the last resort all controversies between members, to fine the aggressing party, to employ the whole force of the confederation against the disobedient, and to admit new members. The Amphyctions were also the guardians of religion, and, most important for Hamilton, they were the guardians of the immense riches belonging to the Temple of Delphos, the national bank of the united city-states of republican Greece.

There was another national bank which interested Hamilton even more. It was the Roman *Fiscus*, from the separate *fisci*, or chests, where public funds were kept. Until the ascendancy of Julius Caesar Octavianus in 29 B.C., Roman financial management and taxation policies were so dispersed in Italy and the provinces that no centralized banking

---

3. *The Federalist*, No. 18, December 7, 1787, *op. cit*. Both Hamilton and Madison later claimed authorship of this essay, as well as essays 19 and 20. Most authorities agree that the three came principally from the pen of Madison, but with ideas supplied by Hamilton.

organization was possible. Plutarch, for example, wrote of the experienced clerks and under-officials who habitually ignored the financial requests of the Roman Senate in much the same way that officials of the American colonies ignored Congressional requests under the Articles of Confederation. Even when such a worthy as Cato the Younger (95–46 B.C.), the great grandson of Cato the Censor, accepted magisterial office with announced intentions of bringing the bureaucracy to heel, Plutarch said, "Being bold, impudent fellows, they flattered the other quaestors, his colleagues, and by such means maintained an opposition against him."[4]

The main reason opposition could be maintained against Cato, as against the Continental Congress, was that no coercive state administrative apparatus was yet in place. Taxation was the local business of *publicani*, companies of rich men to whom tax collection was farmed for periods of five years or payment of a lump sum. The *publicani* were free to make as much profit from their business as possible, and extortion was frequently resorted to. By 27 B.C. when the Senate bestowed on Octavian the new cognomen "Augustus," he was finally free to do what his adoptive father, Julius Caesar, had been assassinated for trying to do.

---

4. Plutarch, *The Lives of the Noble Grecians and Romans*, trans. John Dryden and rev. Arthur Hugh Clough (New York: The Modern Library, 1949), p. 927.

Plutarch (46–120, A.D.) was a Greek essayist and biographer who lived as a priest in his native Boeotia. His *Lives* paired biographies of Greeks and Romans, concerned always with character and morality. He supplied most of the material for Shakespeare's *Julius Caesar* and *Antony and Cleopatra*. He employed a great deal of anecdotal material, of which we all have our favorites. One of mine is from *Lysander*:

A Roman divorced from his wife, being highly blamed by his friends, who demanded "Was she not chaste? Was she not fair? Was she not fruitful?" holding out his shoe, asked them whether it was not new and well made. "Yet," added he, "none of you can tell where it pinches me."

It is sometimes difficult for some of us to explain to our colleagues why we enjoy our classical roots. We can quote Woodrow Wilson and say, "a man's rootage is more important than his leafage," but the matter goes to the rhizome of the rootage, first to character and then to the words that character produces: appropriate, metered, and pleasing words. Of all those put together to commemorate a noble life, and 1296 pages of carefully researched history, among the most pleasing to me are the ones the Romans put on Plutarch's statue in the eternal city:

> Chaeronean Plutarch, to thy deathless praise
> Does martial Rome this grateful statue raise,
> Because both Greece and she thy fame have shared,
> Their heroes written, and their lives compared.
> But thou thyself couldst never write thy own;
> Their lives have parallels, but thine has none.

That was to centralize Roman public administration. Now bearing the title *Pontifex Maximus*, or chief priest, Augustus professionalized the Roman civil service, emphasizing an effective system of finance. The *Fiscus* was the linchpin of the system. Its revenues were now collected and transmitted by imperial agents of impeccable character who established and maintained a national treasury for the support and supply of the armed forces, the payment of public officials, and the cost of corn and wheat supplies, public roads, posts, and buildings. A typical agent of the *Fiscus* was Gracilis Turranius, formerly governor of Egypt, who as Commissioner of the Corn Doles chartered necessary shipping, looked after the storage of imported food, and punished private dealers who attempted to corner supplies. Turranius so demonstrated his organizing ability and steadfast character that he held his post for thirty years.

In the great battle between Hamilton and Jefferson, the Federalists and Antifederalists, over a national bank and the principle of centralized versus decentralized government, the examples from Greece and Rome were as operative as the founders' frequent reading of Livy, Cicero, and Plutarch. The neo-classical America of the founding period was acutely aware of what such words as "fame" meant in terms of the character traits of its magistrates. It meant self-satisfaction for work well done and the admiration of a few.

The synchronicity of the Declaration of Independence and the *Wealth of Nations* is much easier to understand than the third element of the dialectic of 1776, Gibbon's *Decline and Fall*. Yet Gibbon's contribution to our understanding of ethics and character in government is as critical as the first two. The first two are about equity and economic opportunity. The third is about religion and gives us some perspective for analyzing the American civil religion. Gibbon said religion, primarily the Christian religion, was largely responsible for the decline and fall of the Roman state. The sense in which this is true is profoundly important for modern America. The Greeks and Romans were amazingly tolerant of classical civil religion, the forms of worship, which made up the Greek Amphyctony and the Roman Pantheon. The Pantheon itself was a circular temple in the Campus Martius in Rome dedicated to all the gods and carrying their images. Its richly colored marble veneer and great bronze doors made it the most splendid building in a city of splendid buildings. The Pantheon said to the world, "We will tolerate the gods and goddesses of every nation living under the *Pax Romana*." At first only the Jews resisted this Roman civil religion, and then, in the middle of the first century A.D., the Christians came to resist it as well. Both Jews and Christians readily quoted Exodus 20:3, "You shall have no other gods before me."

For all its military and engineering exploits, Rome was above all else a religious community. From the earliest period the Romans cherished a powerful, pervasive, and peculiar religion. Centuries after the founding of Rome in 753 B.C., Cicero praised its continuing conviction that everything is subordinate to divine rule and direction. Roman religion was based on mutual trustfulness (*fides*) between the divine powers or gods, on the one hand, and men and women on the other. The trust accorded by the gods, and their benevolence—what was called the peace of the gods (*pax deorum*), a balance of nature in which divine powers and human beings worked in harmony—could be secured by meticulous ritual and not so much, as more recent religions would maintain, by good moral behavior. For centuries there was no prominent moral element in Roman religion. Nevertheless, the idea of the divine peace indirectly exercised a moral influence, since the respect that it induced for vows made to the gods was extended in the course of time to vows made to human beings as well.

The individual human being was not what mattered in Roman religion. Life among the Romans was a group affair, a matter for family, clan, and state. As in other Indo-European-speaking communities, the family or household, and the clan (*gens*) or group of households, were of overriding importance. The head of the family (*pater familias*), any male citizen who had no living ancestor in the main line, wielded absolute power. There is nothing in any other known culture as extreme as this long-lasting patriarchal assertion. Although the *pater familias* might call in a council of male relatives, and although he habitually left the running of his house to his wife, he monopolized all rights. In the home his word was literally the law, and, so long as he remained alive, his sons never came of age.

Thus he controlled the domestic cult, which played a conspicuous part in daily life. The household deities were worshiped every day and at every meal, and no important family event could take place without securing divine approval. Whether domestic or communal worship came earliest is disputed, but in any case the latter was a magnified version of the former. Vesta, worshiped by her Vestal Virgins beside the Forum in her round straw hut which later became a temple, was the hearth goddess of the Roman state. She was equally prominent in the family cult, symbolizing the solidarity of the home with the nation. Roman religion possessed no sacred writings except invocations and prayers, and its priests were not a caste set apart, but men following secular careers. "To understand the success of the Romans," declared the Greek historian Dionysius of Halicarnassus, "you must understand their piety."[5]

The Judeo-Christian religion stood in stark contrast to the Roman civil religion and to Roman ideas about what constituted civic virtue.

---

5. Quoted in Michael Grant, *History of Rome* (New York: Charles Scribner's Sons, 1978), p. 20.

Many of the founders of the American Republic were much closer to the Roman ideal than to what the Christian religion had become in 1776. While deists such as Benjamin Franklin, Thomas Paine, and Thomas Jefferson were sons of the enlightenment, they were also students of the phenomena Gibbon wrote about in the *Decline and Fall*. In the celebrated Chapter 15 of volume I of his work, Gibbon lamented the preoccupation with the self which Christianity encouraged at the expense of the general welfare. "It was the first but arduous duty of a Christian to preserve himself pure and undefiled," wrote Gibbon. The Christian with pious horror avoided civic responsibilities because they were infected with idolatry. He or she could not attend weddings or funerals because inhospitable deities were involved on those occasions; thus Christians were compelled to desert persons who were dear to them. "If a pagan friend on the occasion of sneezing used the familiar expression, 'Jupiter bless you,' the Christian was obliged to protest the divinity of Jupiter."[6]

Gibbon greatly admired the united reign of the Antonines, which he called, "the only period of history in which the happiness of a great people was the sole object of government." When the last of the Antonine emperors, Marcus Aurelius, died in 180 A.D., the strident fundamentalism of conservative Christianity bewitched the empire. Until that time the conduct of Roman magistrates had never been regulated by any serious conviction about the rewards or punishments of a future life. In fact that doctrine had been described by the orators of the civil religion as "an idle and extravagant opinion, which was rejected with contempt by every man of a liberal education and understanding."[7] Now, however, Christians were able to convince many Roman citizens to be contemptuous of their present existence for they "universally believed that the end of the world and the kingdom of Heaven were at hand." The strength of

---

6. *The Decline and Fall of the Roman Empire*, vol. 1 (New York: The Heritage Press, 1946), p. 359.

In the learned introduction to the Heritage edition of *Decline and Fall* we read, "Gibbon is now considered the greatest historian in the world's history, and this work the greatest historical composition existing in any language." It is certainly one of the wittiest books of scholarship in English. One of my favorite passages compares the martyr who "had renounced those temporal honors which it is probable he would never have obtained" with the saint who "once mistook a harmless funeral for an idolatrous process and imprudently committed a miracle." Over and over Gibbon betrays his dislike for the Church, as with the comment on an ecclesiastical authority that "his learning is to[o] often borrowed, and his arguments are to[o] often his own." His crowning judgment upon Constantine, whose conversion to Christianity he sorely doubted, was that "as he gradually advanced in the knowledge of truth, he proportionally declined in the practice of virtue."

7. *Ibid.*, p. 361.

the Christian movement and the numbing effect it had on civic virtue is attested by the fact that Constantine found it politically expedient to recognize the Church in the Edict of Milan in 313. "The problem with Christianity," wrote Gibbon, "was that its exclusiveness stood in the way of imperial unity."[8]

In the America of the late 1990s, a large and influential wing of the Christian Church again stands for exclusiveness. In Nancy Tatom Ammerman's phrase, "The world fundamentalists have constructed is by definition a world in opposition."[9] They oppose the same social policies their forebears opposed in the second and third centuries. They bring to discussions of the proper role of government in American life a kind of incivility and disdain for the opinions of others that the Roman policy of tolerance was designed to counteract. They have great difficulty accommodating either pluralism or doubt. The administrative institutions they often attack have evolved over decades to bring humane treatment for the economically disinherited who got the back of Adam Smith's invisible hand. They try to make a Christian state of one carefully designed both to avoid an establishment of religion and to encourage the free exercise of it. The character of the republic envisioned by the founders and based on classical models of toleration and administrative integrity is being challenged by influential citizens unfamiliar with the art of politics and the managerial usefulness of a civil religion. This was Plato's worst fear, Cicero's final warning, and the founders' reason for restricting the franchise.

The Ambiguities of American Civil Religion

Has democracy gone amuck? Have the synchronicities of 1776 somehow produced a Hegelian dialectic of despair? Is there some hidden order or hope in the apparent chaos of consuming America: "I shop, therefore I am"?

Civic virtue can be distinguished from the moral or religious virtues of the private individual, although it is not necessarily antithetical to them. The articulation of civic virtue presupposes a mutually agreed upon and rationally demonstrable conception of civic good. Without some consensus on "what is to be done," no agreement would be possible concerning which civic virtue should be developed to sustain the quest for the good, and which modes of conduct rejected as detrimental to it. So the positing of civic good guides an expression of civic virtue and a fashioning of civic character.

---

8. *Ibid.*, p. 363.
9. Nancy Tatom Ammerman, *Bible Believers: Fundamentalists in the Modern World* (New Brunswick: Rutgers University Press, 1987), p. 188.

In political thought the terms civic good and civic virtue are usually considered separately. While not all political theories emphasize civic virtue or advance a substantive conception of virtuous citizenship, nearly all have some implicit or explicit conception of a civic good at their core. Determining which civic good is paramount is a central issue in political theory and is as analytically open-ended as the history of ideas itself. *Whose* good is the civic good is narrowly circumscribed, especially relative to the notion of civic virtue. Although the civic good can be associated with the putative ruler of the community, in many political theories, especially democratic ones, the civic good is conceived of as the people's affair (*res publica*).[10] The virtues necessary for sustaining this good are attributes of the populace, not just the characteristics of nobility, gentry, or monarchy.

The *location* of virtue in a democratic republic was the fulcrum of Jefferson's great debate with Hamilton about the administrative forms of the new nation. In his famous letter to Madison from his post as minister to France on December 20, 1787, Jefferson wrote, "And say, finally, whether peace is best preserved by giving energy to the government, or information to the people. This last is the most certain, and the most legitimate engine of government."[11]

Jefferson advocated a strong system of public education. "Enable the people to see that it is their interest to preserve peace and order," he said, "and they will preserve them." The people are "the only sure reliance for the preservation of our liberty." There was a catch, however, one that Hamilton and the Federalists were cogently aware of. "This reliance cannot deceive us," Jefferson concluded, "as long as agriculture is our principal object, which will be the case while there remains vacant lands in any part of America. When we get piled upon one another in large cities, as in Europe, we shall become corrupt as in Europe, and go to eating one another as they do there." Can the closing of the frontier in 1890 be said to put an end to Jefferson's reliance on the people to preserve liberty?

Hamilton argued strongly for an "efficient constitution" in a letter to Washington on July 3, 1787. He was "seriously and deeply distressed" at the possibility that "anarchy and misery" would result from weak ministries of government. Washington agreed with him in a reply dated July 10, 1787. "The men who oppose a strong and energetic government

---

10. For an extended discussion of this subject see Ralph Clark Chandler, *Civic Virtue in the American Republic* (Kalamazoo, Michigan: The New Issues Press of Western Michigan University, 1987), especially chapter 7, "The Founders' Call for Virtue in Public Administration," pp. 103–117.

11. *Letters of a Nation*, ed. Andrew Carroll (New York: Kodansha International, 1997), pp. 79–80.

are, in my opinion, narrow minded politicians."[12] Washington never left any doubt about where he thought the virtue necessary to sustain the civic good was located. It was in the best people. It was in individual character, not the collective unnumbered. When Washington had to choose between Hamilton and Jefferson, both of whom he greatly admired and both of whom he insisted serve in his cabinet, his friends knew where his final loyalty lay. Hamilton's bravery in leading a charge at the Battle of Yorktown in 1781, thus turning the British left flank and allowing Washington the victory, was never forgotten by the man many people still called simply "the General."

It is easy to forget the kind of character it took to sign the Declaration of Independence. For the British such signing was an act of unpardonable treason. And at the time the document was announced, a military victory over Great Britain was anything but assured. One of the signers, Dr. Benjamin Rush of Philadelphia, remembered the testing time some twenty-five years later in a letter to his friend, John Adams, dated July 20, 1811. "Do you recollect your memorable speech upon the day on which the vote was taken?" Rush asked. "Do you recollect the pensive and awful silence which pervaded the house when we were called up, one after another, to the table of the President of Congress to subscribe what was believed by many at the time to be our own death warrants?"

In the kind of impudent humor that has characterized American life from the beginning, Rush remembered that Harrison of Virginia said to Gerry of Massachusetts on the same occasion, "I shall have a great advantage over you, Mr. Gerry, when we are all hung for what we are now doing. From the size and weight of my body I shall die in a few minutes, but you will dance in the air an hour or two." [13]

The kind of loyalty that existed between Washington and Hamilton and Rush and Adams and virtually every other member of the early American elite has come on hard times in the 1990s. Henry Louis Gates, Jr. begins a recent essay entitled "The End of Loyalty: Why has betraying Clinton—and everyone else—become a national pastime?" with the following words:

> There was a time when exemplary traits—thrift, honesty, temperance, what have you—were coupled with exemplary lives, when every virtue had a mascot. But these are the nineties, and Parson Weems is dead. Nowadays, George Washington and the cherry tree is a parable about the despoliation of the environment—the father of our nation as

---

12. *Ibid.*, pp. 74–75.
13. *Ibid.*, p. 89.

apprentice clear-cutter. Our virtues are faceless, and our faces are without virtue.[14]

Gates says that loyalty and other signs of character are essentially premodern for a large and simple reason: they bespeak partiality while our modernity was ushered in by trumpeting impartial principles, rights, and abstractions. As winding cow paths gave way to macadamized gridirons, the old codes of duty and honor gave way to the cool calculus of moral rationalism. This is both the gift and the curse of the enlightenment. In his "Enquiry Concerning Political Justice" (1793), William Godwin conjures up a situation where you are able to rescue only one person from a burning house. Do you save your mother or Archbishop Fenelon? For Godwin, it's an easy call: you go for the Archbishop, since he has the greater social contribution to make. "What magic is in the pronoun 'my' that should justify us in overturning the decisions of impartial truth?" Godwin demands. This tradition of liberal universalism has tended to send such virtues as loyalty into ethical exile. Moral modernizers prefer lofty abstractions to personal attachments, and, as Godwin saw, loyalty cannot be divorced from the pronoun "my." It is constituted by possessives: my mother, my friend, my partners, my lord, my dependents, my president.

Loyalty was still in vogue as late as the Kennedy Administration. The major Kennedy scandals, mostly about his sexual escapades, arose only posthumously, and the loyalists remain loyal today. Distinguished historian Arthur Schlesinger, Jr. says, for example, "I have the general feeling that questions which no one has a right to ask are not entitled to a truthful answer."[15]

The morality of the marketplace is a formidable thing. A book by a former insider—James Fallows, David Stockman, Donald Regan, Richard Darman, or George Stephanopoulos (the champion with a $2.8 million advance), for example—must be "candid." It must be forthcoming with compromising detail.

The idea that the great goods of truth and justice should sometimes bow to personal loyalty is something that a lot of Americans take for granted. It explains why most Americans admired Hillary Clinton's staunch display of solidarity with her errant, embattled husband, a display that high moral scorers know to be worthy only of derision. It explains why most Americans were sickened when Kenneth Starr com-

---

14. Henry Louis Gates, Jr., "The End of Loyalty: Why has betraying Clinton—and everyone else—become a national pastime?" *The New Yorker*, March 9, 1998, pp. 34–44.

15. *Ibid.*, p. 42.

manded Monica Lewinsky's mother to give testimony that might inculpate her daughter.

Gates and many others complain that in Kenneth Starr's America personal loyalty has no place. Starr is legally deputized by the Ethics in Government Act of 1978 to police his fallen countrymen as they struggle with the vexed exigencies of being human. Starr's righteousness offends our sense of humanity not because it is feigned but because it is not. "Ken Starr leaks that he stands by the river and listens to hymns," says presidential loyalist James Carville. Carville might have compared Starr, a teenage Bible salesman and son of a charismatic preacher, to Gibbon's second and third century Christian absolutists.

> I mean, come on: the river, the hymns, the cleansing.... Here's a guy on a mission to cleanse the Potomac of the fornicators and sodomites who inhabit its banks, and we're not going to have any dick-sucking around here, no sir. People say, "you gotta understand, Ken believes this." I know Ken believes it! He believes it right to the core. That's the problem![16]

One of Starr's favorite hymns has as its refrain, *"Purge me with hyssop, and I shall be clean: wash me, and I shall be whiter than snow."*

In modern America the moralist of the civil religion must distinguish politics from purification rites. We must admit that we might indeed rescue our own mothers from Godwin's burning house, and we might allow ourselves to theorize about why Godwin's daughter, Mary Shelly, wrote *Frankenstein*. Above all else, American public administrationists must define and defend a social ethics founded upon the intricately reciprocal character of life lived within community. In doing so, we will discover that the administrative policies of American government are sometimes an antidote to the principles of the enlightenment.

The enlightenment as the great liberating force of Western life began in the eighteenth century, was brought to the cutting edge of philosophical discourse in the nineteenth, and swept everything before it in the twentieth. The movement elevated skeptical reason, celebrated individual freedom, and anticipated material progress. It attacked convention, especially the conventions defended by revealed religion and prescriptive politics. It sought to emancipate man from a privileged church, an anointed king, and common opinion.

Although the great voices of the enlightenment were English—Bacon, Locke, Newton, Mill, Bentham—or French—Voltaire, Condorcet—the American environment made possible its fullest expression. Our most notable domestic apostles were Jefferson, Paine, and Franklin. Their failure to produce many great writings to defend their emancipating cause

---

16. *Ibid.*, p. 44.

reflected as much the absence of resistance to be overcome as any defect in the rhetorical powers at their disposal.[17] They had no privileged church to subdue, no resident monarch to overthrow, and, in the frontier conditions of a young republic, precious little conventional wisdom to defy.

By European standards the emancipation of American thought was easy, and so it was not obvious to us how much we took for granted in our new-found state of enlightened freedom. The magnitude of this assumption becomes clear if one asks what the founders did *not* put into the Constitution. Not only did the Constitution have to be amended to make clear that freedom of expression was guaranteed and no official church could be established, there was no positive grant of power to the national government to supervise education, to manage public welfare, or to attend to the health, safety, and morals of the people. There was, in short, no national police power. All of this power—anti-enlightenment activity—had to be focused in administrative agencies in the interest of the common good

Madison assumed that the citizenry would have "sufficient virtue" to make republican government possible.[18] Indeed, Republican government presupposes the existence of these qualities. Modern observers such as George Will disagree. "Presupposes?" he asks. "Qualities such as virtue must be willed."[19] The absence of any constitutional provision and political inclination for a tutelary state has led Will and others to consider the American nation "ill-founded."

Well-founded or not, the enlightenment basis of our popular regime has spread to cover our entire political and social landscape. We react with dismay and alarm at talk of character being a public problem rather than a private concern. Yet we express our dismay and alarm in well-modulated language that gives due regard to the feelings, and not just the rights, of others. There is a long-standing difference between what

---

17. The "great writings" of American political theory are not the carefully constructed essays and elaborate reasoning of the British and French models, but practical polemics and disputations called forth by immediate historical circumstances. Thus Americans look for their political theory in works such as Thomas Paine's *Common Sense* (1776), Thomas Jefferson's *Declaration of Independence* (1776), James Madison, Alexander Hamilton, and John Jay's *The Federalist* (1787–1788), John Marshall's *Marbury v. Madison* (1803) and *McCullock v Maryland* (1819), Henry David Thoreau's *Civil Disobedience* (1848), and Abraham Lincoln's *First Inaugural Address* (1861), *Gettysburg Address* (1863), *Second Inaugural Address* (1865).

18. *The Federalist*, No. 55, February 13, 1788.

19. George Will, *Statecraft as Soulcraft* (New York: Simon and Schuster, 1983), p. 156.

Americans profess and how we behave. As Alexis de Tocqueville wrote in the early 1830s:

> Americans are fond of explaining almost all the actions of their lives by the principle of self-interest rightly understood.... In this respect I think they frequently fail to do themselves justice; for in the United States as well as elsewhere people are sometimes seen to give way to those disinterested and spontaneous impulses that are natural to man; but Americans seldom admit that they yield to emotions of this kind; they are more anxious to do honor to their philosophy than to themselves.[20]

In trying to explain how Americans managed to maintain a democratic republic, Tocqueville noted the advantage providence had bestowed upon us as a vast and rich land. But many nations of Latin America have land nearly as vast and just as rich, yet democracy appears there only fitfully. Tocqueville observed that Americans have devised an ingenious constitution that separates the powers of government, preserves local rule, and created an independent judiciary.[21] But many nations, such as the Philippines, have faithfully copied our Constitution and laws, yet the people of these other countries are rarely free of tyranny. What distinguishes America from other nations are the customs of its people, the habits of our hearts. The habits are rooted in a kind of civil religion that asserts large claims of freedom, spontaneity, and self-expression but is rooted in character. Failures of character therefore preoccupy us.[22]

President William Jefferson Clinton has been surrounded by questions of character, his character, since his first presidential campaign in 1992. The author, as much a presidential loyalist in 1998 as he was over thirty-five years ago when he was a so-called whiz kid in the Kennedy Adminis-

---

20. Alexis de Tocqueville, *Democracy in America*, vol. 2, ed. Phillips Bradley (New York: Knopf, 1971), p. 122.

21. In *The History of Government From the Earliest Times*, S.E. Finer identifies what he considers to be the six great American inventions in the art of government. They are (1) the notion of a Constitutional Convention or Constituent Assembly to frame a constitution; (2) the written constitution; (3) the Bill of Rights which, *inter alia*, this constitution embodies; (4) the use of courts of law or specially constituted tribunals to signal breaches of the constitution and exercise powers to obstruct or cancel them; (5) the separation of powers on different lines from the mixed constitutions of the past; and (6) true federalism. The reviewer of Finer's three-volume work in the *Economist* of October 18, 1997 (p. 4) wrote: "If there were a Nobel Prize for political science Sammy Finer would deserve to win one for this extraordinary trilogy." It is the first major administrative history since E.N. Gladden's two volume *A History of Public Administration* (London: Frank Cass), published in 1972.

22. See James Q. Wilson, *On Character* (Washington, DC: The AEI press, 1995).

tration, recently wrote the following opinion piece for his local newspaper, the *Kalamazoo Gazette*:

> There is a crisis in the American presidency, all right, but it is not about the president's alleged sexual peccadilloes, the latest one unproved and probably unprovable. It is about the lengths to which Clinton-haters will go to discredit this president and with it the presidential office.
>
> When all is said and done the Clinton-Lewinsky affair, if indeed it ever happened, will take its place in the history books alongside George Washington and Sally Fairfax, Thomas Jefferson and Sally Hemmings, James Garfield and Rebecca Selleck, Grover Cleveland and Maria Crofts Halpin, Woodrow Wilson and Mary Peck, Warren Harding and Nan Britton, Franklin Roosevelt and Lucy Mercer, Dwight Eisenhower and Kay Summersby, John Kennedy and Judith Exner, and Lyndon Johnson and Alice Glass, to mention only a few presidential indiscretions. Many of these relationships were more interesting and morally challenging than the Clinton adventures, but they happened at a time when a president's personal life was considered off limits to reporting. Let's hear it for the good old days.
>
> What is different now is not only that the president's personal life is open to the closest scrutiny but that news reporters and commentators too often live on the edge of irresponsibility as they rush to publication and broadcast deadlines without checking their sources. Thus the "dress" Bill gave to Monica was in fact, as Monica's lawyer said, a long T-shirt like the one the president gave to all White House interns; the White House steward who saw a liaison was actually the speculation of a staff attorney of the Special Prosecutor; and the late night telephone call to Monica from Bill was still more speculation from the real villain of the piece, provocateur Linda Tripp. The clarifications do not get equal play, however, and the reputational damage has been done. It has not been one of the more admirable chapters in the history of American journalism.
>
> Yet the real constitutional crisis revolves around the role of the Special Prosecutor. When this position was created by the Ethics in Government Act of 1978 it was designed quickly to sort evidence of wrongdoing by senior public servants and expeditiously to gain indictments of them when the evidence so warranted. It is completely contrary to the intent of the legislation when a Special Prosecutor is able to exploit his position to harass a president for five years at a cost of over $30 million to American taxpayers. Mr. Starr is no closer to an indictment now than he was when he started. The evidence isn't there.
>
> The Monica Lewinsky affair has as little place to go as the Paula Jones affair and for the same reason. There were no witnesses. Whatever happened was between Paula and Bill and Monica and Bill. Given Paula's checkered personal history and her questionable association with the right-wingers of the Rutherford Institute and Monica's admission on tape that she lies a lot, both cases should be dispatched before the crocuses rise. The evidence isn't there.

Columnist William Safire is no friend of Bill Clinton's. Yet Safire has written, "It's hard to conceive of this deft politician being so reckless as to carry on an 18-month affair with a White House intern a few years older than his daughter, and then to raise it to the level of federal crime by suborning perjury." Even if one were completely cynical about the alleged relationship, this suborning would have been through Vernon Jordan and not directly by the president.

It is possible that the nation has grown up a little through all this. Dealing with moral ambiguity has always been a problem for us. Our puritan beginnings and our predisposition to reduce the moral to the sexual have caused a good deal of hypocrisy in both high and low places and not a few smiles of condescension from our friends in Europe.

Every year I await with some anxiety the discovery of some of my African-American graduate students that Martin Luther King, Jr. was something of a womanizer and did indeed plagiarize some of his academic work. The task of moral understanding begins here, I tell them. The fact that King could have these weaknesses *and* give his *I Have a Dream* speech is the reality of the human condition. The fact that George Washington could write passionate love letters to the wife of his neighbor *and* lead the Continental Army through the terrible winter at Valley Forge is the reality of the human condition. The fact that Lyndon Johnson could be unfaithful to Lady Bird *and* get the Civil Rights Act of 1964 passed is the reality of the human condition. Character cannot be reduced to sexual purity. As far as we know, Richard Nixon never slept with anyone but Pat.

Conservative Christians who feel outraged by this line of reasoning should consult the first eleven verses of the eighth chapter of John, the passage about Jesus and the woman caught in adultery.

If courage can be defined as grace under fire, then Bill Clinton is one of the most courageous presidents in American history. No president has ever so consistently been fired upon and yet performed so well under emotional pressure of the most debilitating kind. By any standard of professional performance William Jefferson Clinton has been a good, perhaps very good, president. Unless there is better evidence against him than the nation has seen, he deserves our respect. To withhold it on grounds of gossip writ large is to disrespect ourselves and the office that is the focal point of our national identity.[23]

The answers to this brief foray into old-style American civil religion came from Christian fundamentalists, six published in quick succession. They were straight out of Chapter 15 of volume one of Gibbon's *Decline and Fall*. Pastor Danny J. Janes of the Kalamazoo Wesleyan Church strongly objected to the sentence, "character cannot be reduced to sexual purity." Sexual purity is a *reflection* of character, he said, and if a man

---

23. The *Kalamazoo Gazette*, Kalamazoo, Michigan, February 16, 1998, p. A9.

will treat his marriage vows with trivial disregard, why should we assume he would be honest in other matters? Pastor Janes' response would have been more convincing if he had not misquoted the opinion piece he objected to six times.[24] He would not see his misrepresentations as a moral problem, because, as Gibbon said, preoccupation with personal values renders no public truth. Such a trained incapacity for dealing with moral ambiguity paralyzes much of the populace, especially when it reads uncompromised and uncompromising history. A case in point is the second volume of Taylor Branch's Pulitzer Prize-winning trilogy, *America in the King Years*. On the night of January 6, 1964, at the Willard Hotel in Washington, near the White House, FBI tape recorders picked up eleven reels and fourteen hours of partying in Martin Luther King's room. Over the clinking glasses and party babble and sounds of courtship and sex, Bureau technicians heard King's distinctive voice ring out with pulsating abandon, "I'm fucking for God!"[25] Eleven months later, in King's speech accepting the Nobel Peace Prize in Oslo, he said in sincerity, "I refuse to accept the idea that the 'isness' of man's present nature makes him morally incapable of reaching up for the 'oughtness' that forever confronts him."[26] Those who would engage the subtitle of the book in which this essay appears, *The Pursuit of Democratic Virtues*, must deal with the human phenomenon the King example represents.

The Despotism of the Petticoat

Tocqueville wrote of the American scene that "religion is often unable to restrain man from the numberless temptations of fortune; nor can it check that passion for gain which every incident of his life contributes to arouse, but its influence over the mind of woman is supreme, and women are the protectors of morals."[27] If that were true in Tocqueville's

---

24. The *Kalamazoo Gazette*, Kalamazoo, Michigan, February 25, 1998, p. A9.

25. Taylor Branch, *Pillar of Fire: America in the King Years, 1963–65* (New York: Simon and Schuster, 1998), p. 207.

26. Martin Luther King, Jr., "Speech Accepting the Nobel Peace Prize [December 11, 1964]," *Bartlett's Familiar Quotations* (Boston: Little, Brown and Company, 1980), p. 909.

27. Alexis de Tocqueville, "Indirect Influence of Religious Opinions Upon Political Society in United States." Quoted in Richard C. Sinopoli, ed., *From Many, One: Readings in American Political and Social Thought* (Washington, DC: Georgetown University Press, 1997), p. 354. This collection brings together in Part II, Gender and Politics: Citizenship, Equality, and Difference, an impressive assortment of writings by women authors such as Abigail Adams, Judith Sargent Murray, Elizabeth Cady Stanton, Lucretia Mott, Frances D. Gage, Susan B. Anthony, Emma Goldman, bell hooks, and Catharine A. MacKinnon. Among the writings is "The Sentiments of an American

observations of America, it was equally true that such protection could not yet be a public activity. Although the Constitution did not specifically bar women from federal office, it was clear that the election or appointment of women to fill administrative posts were ideas whose time had not yet come. Jefferson expressed the hope that "our good ladies... are contended to soothe and calm the minds of their husbands returning ruffled from political debate." When his Secretary of the Treasury, Albert Gallatin, suggested that President Jefferson might consider appointing women to public office, Jefferson responded sharply, "The appointment of a woman to office is an innovation for which the public is not prepared, nor am I."[28]

Although Jefferson and Hamilton agreed on little else, they made common cause about the problem of women serving in government. In the *Federalist*, No. 6, Hamilton warned of the perils posed to the safety of the state by the intrigues of courtesans and mistresses. The wiles women might exercise caused Jefferson at the age of seventy-five to write to his friend Nathaniel Burwell that the purest democracies would find it necessary to exclude women from the suffrage "to prevent deprivation of morals and ambiguity of issue."[29]

Such antifeminist prejudices lasted well into the early national era. So preeminent a bluestocking as Mercy Otis Warren, who corresponded on political issues with both Jefferson and John Dickinson, as well as the English historian, Mrs. Macaulay Graham, aroused the wrath of the irascible John Adams, whose literary jousts with his wife, Abigail, over women's rights are legendary. Adams did not take kindly to Mercy Warren's treatment of him in her *History of the Progress and Termination of the American Revolution*, published in 1805. "History is not the Province of the ladies," he observed caustically. In a letter to James Sullivan, Adams declared:

> Depend upon it, Sir. It is dangerous to open so fruitful a source of controversy and altercation as would be opened by attempting to alter the qualifications of voters; there will be no end to it. New claims will arise; women

---

Woman" (1780), taken from the Collection of the American Antiquarian Society. In the *Sentiments* an anonymous woman from Philadelphia told about how the women of her city raised contributions for American soldiers in the Revolution. The campaign was led by Esther DeBerdt Reed, wife of the president of Pennsylvania, and Sarah Franklin Bache, Benjamin Franklin's daughter. General Washington refused to let them give the money directly to the soldiers, so the women sewed shirts for them from linen purchased with the money. Each shirt was inscribed with the name of the seamstress.

28. From *The Writings of Thomas Jefferson*, vol. 9 Quoted in Richard B. Morris, *The Forging of the Union, 1781–1789* (New York: Harper and Row, 1987), p. 190.

29. *Writings*, vol. 10, *ibid*. Letter dated March 14, 1818.

will demand a vote, lads from twelve to twenty-one will think their rights are not enough attended to, and every man who has not a farthing will demand an equal voice with any other in all acts of state. It tends to confound and destroy all distinctions, and prostrate all ranks to the common level.[30]

In the republic of John Adams distinctions must not be destroyed and women must know their place.

The correspondence between Abigail and John Adams is justifiably famous as the first clarion call by a woman for the political rights of her gender in the language of rebellion and representation common among American revolutionaries. Abigail had been left alone to manage the family farm in Braintree, Massachusetts, while John was serving the new nation in a variety of political capacities. Abigail became a sound manager and maintained the farm in stable financial condition for over twenty years. The experience fostered a spirit of independence in her, as well as patriotism. Even before the war, when John was serving in the Second Continental Congress in Philadelphia, Abigail wrote him a blockbuster letter on March 31, 1776. She sent him news of Boston; she confessed that until the last few days she did not know if she could plant or sow with safety, or be driven by the British to seek shelter in the wilderness; she wondered what sort of defense Virginia could make against "our common enemy"; and she longed to hear that the Congress had declared for independence. Then she wrote:

> In the new code of laws which I suppose it will be necessary for you to make, I desire you would remember the ladies and be more generous and favorable to them than your ancestors. Do not put such unlimited power into the hands of the husbands. Remember all men would be tyrants if they could. If particular care and attention is not paid to the ladies, we are determined to foment a rebellion, and will not hold ourselves bound by any laws in which we have no voice or representation.
>
> That your sex are naturally tyrannical is a truth so thoroughly established as to admit of no dispute; but such of you as wish to be happy willingly give up the harsh title of master for the more tender and endearing one of friend.[31]

John replied two weeks later, on April 14, 1776. He told his wife the Virginians would make an able defense and their neighboring sister, North Carolina, "a warlike colony," would also offer a brave resistance to the British. The southerners, however, gave an aristocratic turn to all their proceedings because of the inequality of property. These southern patricians had a strong aversion to Paine's *Common Sense*. As for Abigail's declaration of independence, "I cannot but laugh," said another

---

30. From *The Writings of John Adams*, vol. 9 Quoted in Morris, *op. cit.*, p. 191.
31. The entire letter is quoted in Sinopoli, *op. cit.*, pp. 105–107.

kind of patrician. The struggling nation now aborning had loosened the bonds of government everywhere: children and apprentices were disobedient, schools and colleges had grown turbulent, Indians slighted their guardians, and negroes grew insolent to their masters. "But your letter was the first intimation that another tribe, more numerous and powerful than all the rest, were grown discontented." We know better than to repeal our masculine systems, concluded Adams. He and the other founders had no intention to be subject to "the despotism of the petticoat."[32]

It was hardly a despotism, but the petticoat elected William Jefferson Clinton president in 1996. It sits twice on the Supreme Court of the United States; it holds the offices of Secretary of State and Attorney General; it holds both seats in the United States Senate from the nation's most populous state, California, and it holds innumerable high-level posts in both federal and state governments. The petticoat has come a long way since the 19th Amendment was ratified in 1920. And always the words of Tocqueville haunt the nation, that women are the keepers of American morality.

The rise of notable women scholars in the past twenty years has frequently put traditional views of ethics, character, and virtue in such a different light that the rest of us must reimagine what we thought were verities. An example in theology is the work of Jane Schaberg, whose book, *The Illegitimacy of Jesus*, is so well researched that the burden of proof shifts to those who disagree with her. The information is there: in the gospels, in oral traditions, and in ignored history, but patriarchal understandings of the Jesus movement simply did not allow for such an interpretation.[33]

Other influential women theologians emerging in the past twenty years are Elizabeth Schussler Fiorenza, Paula Fredrikson, Susan Haskins, Ross Shepard Kraemer, Carol Meyers, Elaine Pagels, Uta Ranke-Heinemann, Karen Jo Torjensen, Phillis Trible, and Ann Belford Ulanov. Ulanov, for example, supports Schaberg by pointing out that only four of the female ancestors of Jesus were mentioned in Matthew's genealogy, and all four were guilty of some sexual irregularity. Tamar engaged in incest; Rahab was a harlot; Ruth seduced Boaz; and Bathsheba committed adultery with David. Yet each of them demonstrated character traits well beyond the requirements of sexual purity.[34] These women theologians

---

32. *Ibid.*, pp. 107–108.
33. Jane Schaberg, *The Illegitimacy of Jesus: A Feminist Theological Interpretation of the Infancy Narratives* (San Francisco: Harper and Row, 1987).
34. Ann Belford Ulanov, *The Female Ancestors of Christ* (Boston: Shambhala, 1993).

are united in their insistence that sex, understood either as the accident of gender or as a physical activity, cannot be the final commentary on one's character.[35]

This holding is of particular importance not only because of modern media attention to alleged sexual indiscretions by governmental leaders, but because of the tendency of modern historians to tell the whole truth. The distinguished Jefferson historian of a generation ago, Dumas Malone, could spend six volumes on Jefferson and never mention Sally Hemings. When woman historian Fawn Brodie first "broke the story" about Jefferson's long-standing liaison with his black slave, she was almost drummed out of the American Historical Association. Today, the publication of Annette Gordon-Reed's *Thomas Jefferson and Sally Hemings* by the prestigious University Press of Virginia settles the issue.[36] As one reviewer put it, "Short of digging up Jefferson and doing DNA testing on him and Hemings' descendants, Gordon-Reed's account gets us as close to the truth as the available evidence allows."

It is not just women theologians and historians who are forcing new thinking about character and practicing what Aristotle called *phronesis*, or intellectual honesty, in the *Nicomachean Ethics*. It is also women political theorists and public administrationists such as Kathryn G. Denhardt, Nancy K. Grant, Judith E. Gruber, Patricia Keehley, Carol W. Lewis, Rosemary O'Leary, Dorothy Olshfski, Beryl Radin, Judith N. Shklar, Camilla Stivers, and Margaret Wrightson. Of these, Judith N. Shklar (1928–1992), Cowles Professor of Government at Harvard, made a unique contribution in what we might call moral psychology. Shklar's favorite commentary on government was a couplet from Alexander Pope's *Essay on Man*:

> For forms of government let fools contest;
> Whatever's best administer'd is best.[37]

To know more about government and how it might be administered best, Shklar studied what she called "subversive genealogies." These genetic accounts include creation myths and conjectural histories of the human race, as well as narratives of founding a society and of its historical experience. Obviously not all the work of moral psychology is done in genealogies, but they are its epitome. Of myths of origins, she says:

---

35. See Carol A. Newsom and Sharon H. Ringe, Eds., *The Women's Bible Commentary* (Louisville, Kentucky: Westminster, 1992).

36. Annette Gordon-Reed, *Thomas Jefferson and Sally Hemings* (Charlottesville, Virginia: University Press of Virginia, 1997).

37. Quoted in Judith N. Shklar's, *Political Thought and Political Thinkers*, (Chicago: The University of Chicago Press, 1998), p. 194.

They are meant to make evident and clear what is often merely felt. Actuality is to be revealed, shown, and shown up by a review of its origins that does not delineate the causes, but the awful character of this aging world. This is neither pseudo-history nor pseudo-etiology nor primitive science. It is neither the rival nor the precursor of more rigorous forms of thought. It is psychological evocation, an appeal, with the aid of very familiar memories, to others to accept a picture of social man as a permanently displaced person.[38]

Thus in the myth of Adam and Eve in the garden, Old Testament man sees himself as the origin of evil. There is something inside Eve that responds to the serpent, so that it is not possible to blame that animal for the fall of man. Above all, evil is not primordial, coextensive with the generation of the divine being. The God of the Old Testament is the creator of everything except evil. Man is wholly responsible for his own unhappiness. He cannot look to God, as the rival Greek myth of Hesiod does, and see human evil as a mere mirroring of a cosmic pattern. In Greek psychology, human violence is justified by Olympian violence. There is no occasion or possibility for the fall of man in this scheme. The myth of Adam and Eve, in stark contrast, is wholly anthropological. A human ancestor, a being just like us, originates evil. In the Christian tradition this tension crystallized in the notion of original sin.

Apart from the Christian elaboration, however, the Adamic myth offers a totally different view of the origins of good and evil than the classical model does. A God so wholly outside the natural order, so wholly other as to be without any human features, can only receive humble obedience. And that is the response of Abraham and eventually of Job. Man cannot judge God or even comment intelligently upon his ways. Zeus neither invites, nor receives, such submission. These two creation myths, the biblical and the Hesiodic, offer archetypal alternatives upon which subsequent ethical systems have been built. On which does American morality rely? The answer, alas, is both. The admixture of the neoclassical constructs of the American enlightenment, built on the idea of civil religion, and the Bible-based commitments of American evangelicalism, built on the idea of personal piety, have competed for the soul of America from the beginning.

At this point Shklar and others offer a path of moral analysis different from that of political man in the *Declaration of Independence*, economic man in the *Wealth of Nations*, and religious man in the *Decline and Fall*. It is through artistic man in novels, drama, poetry, movies, music, art, and other forms of creative human expression. A century ago, people

---

38. *Ibid.*, p. xiii.

tended to get their moral lessons in weekly doses by attending religious services and listening to sermons. Today it is more likely that people will watch twenty movies a year as it is that they will listen to twenty sermons. Movies and other forms of popular entertainment are major contributors to such assumptions and images as are held in common in an increasingly diverse society.[39]

> In a nice way artistic man takes us back to Plato's aesthetics, where western ethical thought began. Plato held that moral principles serve the crucial psychological functions of controlling our appetites and harnessing our energies. Most people derive their moral priorities from social convention, and the most important task of political authority is to protect the common faith that maintains the community. Yet only those whose priorities are derived from knowledge, rather than convention, can be reliable interpreters of the common faith. Only they will be trustworthy guardians of its integrity. These guardians are lovers of wisdom. Being the most rational of humans, they are the most human, and they are the happiest of humans because knowledge of the real is meaningful in itself. Wisdom is the source of all real beauty, and the philosopher's ability to comprehend the ultimate nature of reality allows him or her

---

39. See Ralph Clark Chandler and Barbara A. K. Adams, "Lets Go to the Movies! Using Film to illustrate Basic Concepts in Public Administration," *Public Voices*, vol. 3, no. 2 (1997). This essay uses *Schindler's List*, *Crimson Tide*, and the Kenneth Branaugh production of *Henry V* to open up lanes of mental traffic in discussions of ethics and character. The interested reader should consult Charles T. Goodsell and Nancy Murray, eds, *Public Administration Illuminated and Inspired By the Arts* (Westport, Connecticut: Praeger, 1995) and Ralph Clark Chandler, "Public Administration Pedagogy: Another Look at Evolutionary Paradigms in Theory and Practice," Chapter 20 in Jack Rabin, W. Bartley Hildreth, and Gerald J. Miller, eds, *Handbook of Public Administration*, 2nd ed. (New York: Marcel Dekker, 1998). This piece discusses recent work in the literary and artistic environment of public administration in the areas of:

Architecture	Opera
Cartoons	Painting
Dance	Photography
Ethnic Art	Plays
Film	Poems
Legend	Quilting
Murals	Radio
Music	Sculpture
Native American	The Short Story
Cultural Traditions	Television
The Novel	

to experience the highest form of pleasure through such comprehension.[40]

Plato assumes that harmony is the source of lasting aesthetic value, and that harmony is an intellectual, rather than a sensual, characteristic. He would prefer Mozart, Beethoven, or Shostakovich to Frank Sinatra, Hank Williams, or the Beatles because classical music develops themes that can be appreciated regardless of how they are interpreted by different musicians. Because he was deaf when he composed it, Beethoven never heard his famous Ninth Symphony. Those who know musical theory can enjoy the beauty of the Ninth by *reading* it rather than listening to it. Thus it is in all artistic achievement. Beauty, like truth, is found in order, and all order is ultimately intellectual. Plato's philosopher loves wisdom because the abstract intellectual unity of reality provides the greatest possible aesthetic experience.

This is not as ethereal as it may sound. Aesthetics cuts across psychology, ethics, and politics in such a way that the quality of one's mind becomes also the predicate of one's being. Since being is a form of doing, a person's perception of reality can elevate him or her to a level of thinking that embraces universal truths. The reason the arts persist from generation to generation is that they fulfill a deep-seated need in us to understand ourselves and others. When that understanding occurs, as it did last term when one of my students finished her project on quilting, one ceases to scramble for places of honor or engage in activity for the sole purpose of appearing busy and important. One is less easily provoked into reacting to trivial matters and can display an open and honest demeanor when relating to others. One can measure actions. One can play. Through the arts one can lay hold of unconscious knowledge that is the wisdom of the race and that one has known from the beginning without knowing what one knows. One can be what Aristotle called an ornament of virtue.

The End of Classical Politics

Although the major tenet of classical republicanism, best stated by Cicero as *res publica est res populi* (*the people's good is the public good)*, has shown amazing resiliency in America, the fact is that we are at the end of classical politics. *Homo politicus,* emphasizing simply the partici-

---

40. Edward Bryan Portis, *Reconstructing the Classics: Political Theory From Plato to Marx* (Chatham, NJ: Chatham House, 1994), p. 18.

pation of (male) citizens in government, and *homo economicus,* emphasizing the property- owner and marketeer, have yielded to a vocabulary of representation, administration, and management. The civic good of government "of, by, and for the people" is now viewed in terms of particular interests, not as active participation by a virtuous citizenry in pursuit of a civic good.

There have been strong counterattacks, of course, notably by communitarianism, a doctrine in moral and political theory holding that the individual can flourish as a moral being and as a political agent only within the context of a community. But communitarianism, through such exponents as Alasdair MacIntyre, Charles Taylor, and Michael Walzer, has the same difficulty as the utilitarians and Kantians it criticizes, and that is a highly abstract and formal conception of community.[41]

So what is to be done? I believe that we would do well to realize that it will take a long time for the American civil religion to die. It is too well ingrained in us; we remember too well; and our institutions are too strong. Although my opinion piece in the *Kalamazoo Gazette* defending Slick Willy Clinton got a total of seven negative responses, it also received fifty-nine positive ones. We still want the facts. Tocqueville was right. We are a fairer and more just people than we let on sometimes. Our generosity of spirit is matched only by our broodings about a moral perfection in our public life that never was and never can be.

---

41. See "Communitarianism" in Lawrence C. Becker and Charlotte B. Becker, eds. *Encyclopedia of Ethics,* vol. 1 (New York: Garland, 1992), pp. 181–185; and Markate Daly, ed. *Communitarianism: A New Public Ethic* (Belmont, California: Wadsworth, 1994).

Chapter Thirteen

Moral Realism Versus Therapeutic Elitism: Christopher Lasch's Populist Defense of American Character

Peter Augustine Lawler

Christopher Lasch (1932–94), professor of history and the provocative, best-selling author of ten books, including *The Culture of Narcissism*, called himself a social critic, which means he was much more than a historian.[1] Such a critic, Lasch said, "holds a mirror to society, revealing patterns that might otherwise go undetected," and then he "passes judgment."[2] Lasch's judgments were in defense of the fact that human beings experience the truth about themselves and nature. They know, when they are not deluding themselves, that they are limited in many ways by their natures as embodied beings. They are self-conscious mortals, haunted always to some extent by death. So the need for character or virtue to live well with what we really know is ineradicable. The modern attempts to dispense with virtue by re-creating human identity are degrading illusions. They are also misguided, because human joy and love depend upon death. A genuinely truthful and morally responsible human being is grateful for the invigorating challenges his distinctive existence gives him.

---

1. This essay is based on Lasch's last five books, which contain his fully-developed views as a social critic: *The Culture of Narcissism: American Life in the Age of Diminishing Expectations* (New York: Norton, 1991, revised edition [original edition, 1979]); *The Minimal Self: Psychic Survival in Troubled Times* (New York: Norton, 1984, *The True and Only Heaven: Progress and Its Critics* (New York: Norton, 1991), *The Revolt of the Elites and the Betrayal of Democracy* (New York: Norton, 1995), *Women and the Common Life: Love, Marriage, and Feminism* (New York: Norton, 1997). The last book is an edited collection of Lasch's essays by his daughter, Elizabeth Lasch-Quinn, after his death. *The Revolt of the Elites* was finished while Lasch was very near death.

2. "History as Social Criticism: Conversations with Christopher Lasch," *The Journal of American History* (March, 1994), p. 1313.

Lasch's realism has two parts. He is a philosophical realist, convinced that human beings have knowledge of a natural and personal reality that exists independently of their making. He is also a "moral realist," opposing the fantastic efforts of modern utopians who aim to create a world where morality would be superfluous. There the distinction between good and evil would simply be replaced by the one between healthy and sick.

Lasch's realism makes him in one respect a Tocquevillian. He shared *Democracy in America's* perception that the Americans tend, in principle, to be Cartesian.[3] They are superficial rationalists who understand reality in terms of two rational systems, minds and bodies. So they divide human experiences into those of pure mind and pure body. Lasch agrees with the best Tocquevillian of our time, the novelist and philosopher Walker Percy, who called American theory a kind of therapeutic pop Cartesianism.[4] The elite or expert class incoherently describes human beings as nothing but animals well- or badly-adjusted to their environments and aims to reduce them to that subhuman condition.

The antidote to such Cartesianism, really an ignoble and fantastic diversion from the truth about fundamental experiences of the self-conscious mortal, is realism. Lasch, who never wrote as a believing Christian, approached Percy's twentieth-century Thomism almost in spite of himself. Like Percy, his study of the original or Socratic intention of psychoanalysis is the basis of both his criticism of the truth-denying intention of today's knowledge class and his turn to Christian psychology as a source expressing the ineradicable truth of human alienation. Lasch's distinctive and profound contribution to contemporary thought is his connection of class analysis to psychoanalysis, reminding us of Tocqueville's connection between Rousseau's history and Pascal's psychol-

---

3. Alexis de Tocqueville, *Democracy in America*, volume 2, part 1, chapter 1.

4. See Lewis A. Lawson and Victor Kramer, eds., *More Conversations with Walker Percy* (Jackson: University Press of Mississippi, 1995), pp. 232–33. The interpretation of Percy presented here and there in this essay is defended in my "Walker Percy's Twentieth-Century Thomism," *Perspectives on Political Science* 26 (Spring 1997): 70-76. Percy's novel *The Thanatos Syndrome* (New York: Farrar, Straus, and Giroux, 1987) presents a view of the development of psychoanalysis, including its original Socratic intention, which is uncannily similar to Lasch's; see my "Sex, Drugs, Politics, Love, and Death: The Political Teaching of Walker Percy's *Thanatos Syndrome*," *The Political Science Reviewer*, forthcoming. Percy's satiric mixture of literary forms *Lost in the Cosmos: The Last Self-Help Book* (New York: Farrar, Straus, and Giroux, 1983) is his social criticism which most closely corresponds to Lasch's work; see my "*Lost in the Cosmos*: Walker Percy's Analysis of American Restlessness," in *Poets, Princes, and Private Citizens*, ed. J. Knippenberg and P. Lawler (Lanham, MD: Rowman and Littlefield, 1996), pp. 168-89.

ogy.⁵ My intention here is to bring to light this philosophical dimension of his populism, his defense of what remains of the character of Americans.

Class Analysis

Lasch saw the Cartesian reduction of human reality to minds and bodies reflected in the development of the American class structure. His main concern was class analysis of American life. His analysis was not detached or nonpartisan. He thought one class is more admirable and lived more in light of the truth, and he encouraged that class to fight the "culture war" against those who would reduce its members to less than free and responsible beings.⁶ But Lasch was careful to present populism rightly understood. (He admitted, for example, that racism has been part of American populism, and he praised its ebbing as one of very few positive recent social developments.⁷)

The true goal of populism is "universal competence," or "a whole world of heroes." This "strenuous and morally demanding definition" of the good life is threatened by elites who aim to produce "a society of supremely contented consumers," people who live unmoved by the truth about their existence.⁸ The populist aims to universalize the practice of virtue, to make every human being an aristocrat of character. The elite aims to make virtue unnecessary or obsolete, by eradicating the difference between most people and thoughtless and readily controllable animals or machines.

Universal competence is the thoughtful, responsible, effective exercise of personal sovereignty. Lasch saw it as the devotion of the American founders and Lincoln. Lincoln embraced it through his description of the American goal of "universal education." He said "that [each] particular head...should direct and control the particular pair of hands." All "citizens of a free country" are "expected to work with their heads as well as their hands." So a free country is not divided into two classes, one that thinks for the other.⁹ The division of society into mental and physical laborers, Marx was right to say, is the end of democracy. "The American

---

5. See my *The Restless Mind: Alexis de Tocqueville on the Origin and Perpetuation of Human Liberty* (Lanham, MD: Rowman and Littlefield), 1993).
6. Lasch, Christopher, *The Revolt of the Elites*, p. 124.
7. *Ibid.*, pp. 90-91.
8. Lasch, Christopher, *The True and Only Heaven*, p. 530.
9. Lasch, Christopher, *The Revolt of the Elites*, p. 69.

revolution had made subjects into citizens," and the elite establishment of such a class system returns most citizens to subjection.[10]

In Lasch's view, the history of America has been away from democracy properly understood to a rather extreme separation of mental and physical laborers. It has been toward the welfare or therapeutic state. The mental laborers have compassion for those who have become dependent on their thought. They claim to work to alleviate the suffering of the others, but they cannot plausibly claim to have respect for them. Genuine respect only comes through "admirable achievements, admirably formed characters, natural gifts put to good use."[11] A society that does not expect everyone to be an admirable citizen is not a democracy.

Double-standards rooted in compassion create the paternalistic and degrading distinction between first- and second-class citizenship.[12] They make life too easy for everyone. There is nothing admirable in being a pitied victim. It is easier and otherwise self-serving for the elite to pity fellow citizens "than to hold them up to impersonal standards," the meeting of which really would entitle them to equal respect. The self-indulgence of compassion allows both classes to shy away from the hard work really required to raise the competence of everyone. Compassion-based toleration is really a form of apathetic indifference for the characters or souls of our fellow citizens.[13]

The virtue the pitying or "caring class" means to deny others is that exhibited by "those who refuse to exploit their suffering for the purposes of pity."[14] They fraudulently attempt to reduce virtue to words they know to be merely flattering, the rhetoric of indiscriminate self-esteem. But those words do not make people feel good, only cynical.[15] They cannot really mask the harsh reality of the absence of achievement. The absurd idea, for example "that a respect for cultural diversity forbids us to impose the standards of privileged groups on the victims of oppression" is "a recipe for... incompetence."[16]

A particularly absurd form of this dismissal of standards is Carol Gilligan's difference feminism. For women "to pit themselves against a demanding standard of perfection" is to "masculinize" themselves or engage in self-denial. Women, Gilligan contends, are too caring, coopera-

---

10. *Ibid.*, p. 58.
11. *Ibid.*, p. 89.
12. *Ibid.*, p. 88.
13. *Ibid.*, pp. 105–07.
14. *Ibid.*, p. 105.
15. *Ibid.*, p. 210.
16. *Ibid.*, p. 85.

tive, and compassionate, too concerned about relationships, really to regard such standards as "impersonal" or gender-neutral. Lasch responds that any argument for the equality of citizens concerns not the difference, but the similarity, in admirable human characteristics. Women, in truth, not only can be kind but have the same capacity for cruelty as men. So they are capable of being integrated into a world "where quality of ideas or workmanship counts for more than 'relationships.'" And they are capable of criticizing an excessive concern with the quality of relationships as petty and confining. If women can be equal citizens, it is because they can earn the respect of men, and not just their concern or support.[17]

For the caring class, "[c]ompassion has become the human face of contempt," which is why a genuine democrat or populist is "unambiguously committed" to the principle of respect justly accorded admirable deeds.[18] Lasch calls Martin Luther King, Jr., "a populist in his insistence that black people had to take responsibility for their lives and in his praise of petty bourgeois virtues: hard work, sobriety, and improvement."[19] Lasch opposes Marx on bourgeois virtue: It is what *keeps* an individual from functioning merely as a cog in a machine under capitalism. That virtue is what really protects the people from elite manipulation.

The utopia the compassionate or therapeutic elite claims to pursue is one with an abundance of agreeable jobs and a "life easy for everyone." But technological innovations and information revolutions have, in truth, mainly "widened the gap between the knowledge class and the rest of the population." Despite the unprecedented availability of information, "the public knows less about public affairs than it used to know."[20] People do not know because there is no reason for them to know. There is no national debate on public issues. There is almost no American common, political life.

The knowledge class does not believe it is possible to educate most people to be citizens. They deny the truth of the premises on which democratic citizenship is based. For Frederick Douglass, Lasch observes, "The power of speech—given through the equivalent of a classical education—gave him access to the inner world of his own thoughts and to the public world in which the fate of his people would be decided for better or worse." True and meaningful speech about his personal identity

---

17. Lasch, Christopher, *Women and the Common Life*, pp. 126-36.
18. Lasch, Christopher, *The Revolt of the Elites*, p 107.
19. *Ibid.*, p. 82.
20. *Ibid.*, pp. 161–62.

could ennoble his people. But our educators seem no longer "to believe in the reality of either the inner world or the public world, either in a stable core of personal identity or in a politics that rises above the level of platitudes and propaganda."[21] The knowledge class, ironically, no longer believes in the personal or political efficacy of the pursuit of knowledge, particularly self-knowledge. There is no self to know.

The knowledge class now holds that "personal identity" is an arbitrary and unstable personal construction, and that political speech is empty of any meaning but the pursuit of power. The truth about truth, freedom, and dignity is that they do not really exist. There is no point of view, no self, from which one can either know or defend one's own liberty or dignity. This therapeutic theory about personal emptiness both reflects and is the source of "a new kind of dependence, the dependence of the consumer on the market and the provider of expert services, not only for the satisfaction of their needs but for the definition of their needs."[22]

Lasch emphasizes that both corporate capitalism and the bureaucratic state engage in need creation. Their shared therapeutic theory is a sort of self-fulfilling prophecy. It both describes and creates beings whose seemingly materialistic or bodily needs really come from the manipulative minds of experts. The welfare or therapeutic state and corporate capitalism both work to have the knowledge class give content to the dependent class.[23]

So the elitist aim of the members of the expert class is to bring political life to an end. They describe and create beings incapable of being spirited and thoughtful citizens. Here Lasch seems to echo Tocqueville. The easy control of dependents solves the problem of "social discipline." But it also "makes it more and more difficult for political leaders to mobilize public support for their policies." The welfare or therapeutic state is, at heart, more weak than strong, because it excels at preventing, not doing. Interest in and sacrifice for the common good depends upon some participation in making public policy.[24] Lasch, again like Tocqueville, sees that the restoration of the public spirit of citizens requires considerable decentralization and voluntary involvement in political life. It also involves the freeing of personal experiences and intimate relationships from the reductionistic discipline of expert manipulation.[25] But the expert class is too full of easygoing contempt and aversion to risk really to

---

21. *Ibid.*, p. 180.
22. Lasch, Christopher, *Women and the Common Life*, p. 168.
23. Lasch, Christopher, *The Revolt of the Elites*, pp. 95-98; *The Culture of Narcissism*, pp. 232-34; *The True and Only Heaven*, pp. 518-19.
24. Lasch, Christopher, *Women and the Common Life*, pp. 182-83.
25. Lasch, Christopher, *The True and Only Heaven*, p. 532; *The Culture of Narcissism*, p. 238.

care for, much less act on behalf of, the souls of their fellow citizens.²⁶ So "to break the existing pattern of dependence and put an end to an erosion of competence, citizens will have to take the solution of their own problems in their own hands."²⁷

Psychoanalysis

For Lasch, the movement of the history of psychoanalysis from Socratic introspection to therapeutic "coping" mirrors the degradation of the knowledge class.²⁸ Originally, psychoanalysis was "linked to a long degree of speculation in which self-knowledge is seen as the beginning of wisdom." So its subject matter, the pursuit of the truth about the human soul or self, "drew it irresistibly toward the existential questions that have always defined religious discourse."²⁹ The original, Freudian psychoanalysts pursued a Socratic alternative to religious answers to those questions. They aimed to understand, not transform, human experiences. They "held out no cure for injustice or unhappiness," but they attempted to explain them as features of the normal human experience of alienation.³⁰ Psychoanalysis at its best is the discovery of a "moral realism that makes it possible for human beings to come to terms with the existential constraints to their power and freedom."³¹

The human experience of shame, the original psychoanalysts discovered, is in response to one's knowledge of "the contingency and finitude of the human condition, nothing less." That is why the suffering of shame "is so closely associated with the body," which necessarily escapes our effort at control and "reminds us, vividly and painfully, of our inescapable limitations, the inescapability of death above everything." What makes a human being ashamed, finally, is his knowledge of his "bondage to nature."³² The experience is that of a self-conscious mortal. So the original psychoanalysts saw a close connection between shame and curiosity.³³ To eradicate one would be to eradicate the other. The being who seeks knowledge or science is, among other things, ashamed.

---

26. Lasch, Christopher, *The True and Only Heaven*, p. 532.
27. Lasch, Christopher, *The Culture of Narcissism*, p. 235.
28. Lasch, Christopher, *The Minimal Self*, p. 58.
29. Lasch, Christopher, *The Revolt of the Elites*, p. 216.
30. Lasch, Christopher, *The Minimal Self*, p. 209.
31. Lasch, Christopher, *The Culture of Narcissism*, p. 209.
32. Lasch, Christopher, *The Revolt of the Elites*, 201.
33. *Ibid*, p. 212.

A world without shame would be one without scientists and philosophers.

But shame "refers, above all, to the irreducible element of mystery in human affairs."[34] Human beings do not know why they, alone among the animals, are alienated mortals. The truth about their own being necessarily eludes their comprehension and control. So shame is also "a kind of outrage in the face of whatever is mysterious."[35] It is a rebellion against the limits of philosophy or science, and so shame can lead to futile attempts to overcome those limits through science.

Human beings cannot help but long for a world without shame and without mystery. But the original psychologists knew that such an existence is both impossible and undesirable for human beings. The longing is really "to be free from longing." It is "a backward quest for absolute peace." The longing is for freedom from all that distinguishes human existence, from the alienation or "malaise" that characterizes the human condition as such.[36] Lasch's affirmation of "Nietzsche's connection between shame and mystery" is his affirmation of the greatness and misery of human existence against Rousseauean romanticism.[37]

The history of "the psychiatric profession" is its movement away from this affirmation. Its aim has become "behavior modification" and "management of symptoms," often with the help of drugs. It achieves "fast relief," not "deeper understanding." This change in approach, at first glance, seems both democratic and scientific. Introspective psychoanalysis "cost too much, last[ed] too long and demand[ed] too much intellectual sophistication from the patient." It also "often ended in failure, even after years of extensive self-exploration."[38] It culminated, at best, in the discovery of mystery and only the alleviation of anxious unhappiness. But symptoms can be managed with physiological certainty and without raising the unanswerable existential questions which occupy the soul.

If drugs can free us from the pain of shame and mystery, then is it unscientific or dogmatic to hold that mystery or the experience of ineradicable limits is intrinsic to human nature or the human condition? If it is, then shame can now be dismissed "as the vestigial remnant of an outmoded prudery."[39] The psychotherapists now say that shame is an unnecessary experience that gets in the way of a healthy and happy human existence.

---

34. *Ibid.*, p. 212.
35. *Ibid.*, p. 201.
36. Lasch, Christopher, *The Culture of Narcissism*, p. 240.
37. Lasch, Christopher, *The Revolt of the Elites*, p. 207.
38. *Ibid.*, p. 234.
39. *Ibid.*, p. 202.

The psychotherapeutic view is that what gets in the way of science and health is the human capacity to be moved by the truth about one's own death. So the new "technology of the self," which brought into existence "an elaborate network of therapeutic professions," is based on the "now-familiar insistence" that there is no depth or stability to human identity. So through technological transformation human beings can achieve a state of mind "beyond freedom and dignity,"[40] beyond shame and curiosity.

The original fear was that modern technology would enslave human beings to machines. The new "hope is that man will become something like a machine in his own right."[41] B.F. Skinner "scandalizes" twentieth-century liberal, therapeutic humanists by showing that the therapeutic goal is neither liberal nor humanistic. He simply thought through the implications of their assumptions and prejudices. The denial of moral responsibility in favor of the compassionate eradication of misery leads to the expert destruction of human liberty. So therapeutic democracy is actually "an oligarchy of experts, who claim no powers or privileges beyond the impersonal authority of science."[42] The technological experts on the self simply aim to eradicate all personal experiences, to make impersonal science wholly true. The conquest of nature is really the conquest of human nature, the reintegration of human beings into subhuman or unconscious nature.

Lasch connects the original psychoanalytic and the religious and existential objections to therapeutic pragmatism. The old psychoanalysis, by showing the intractability of human mystery and misery, leads human beings, against its scientific intention, to religion. Socratic philosophy, Lasch suggests, does the same.[43] The new psychotherapy, by treating human experiences as symptoms to be cured, more coherently attempts to replace religion by science. It aims to eradicate scientifically the experiences that brought religion into being.

But the problem remains that psychotherapy would eradicate the shameful, curious being who is the source of science. The new psychotherapy can neither account for nor affirm the experience of the scientist. The old psychoanalysis, unrealistically, pointed to the universalization of the introspective, scientific experience of Socrates. So one reason it failed is that it could not "satisfy the growing demand, in a world without religion, for meaning, faith, and emotional security."[44]

---

40. Lasch, Christopher, *The Minimal Self*, p. 58.
41. *Ibid*, p. 58.
42. *Ibid.*, pp. 215, 217.
43. Lasch, Christopher, *The Culture of Narcissism*, p. 248.
44. Lasch, Christopher, *The Minimal Self*, p. 209.

Psychotherapy aims to make emotional security easy by eradicating the needs for meaning and faith.

The therapeutic cure destroys "the very sense of moral responsibility." Human weakness and willfulness, manifestations of human individuality or "sin," become "sickness." No one is truly culpable or responsible. The being freed from responsibility is reduced from a citizen or sovereign individual to a "patient unfit to manage his own life." Therapeutic antimorality "delivers" the diseased "into the hands of a specialist for cure." So the populist Lasch notices the "close connection...between the erosion of moral responsibility and the erosion of the capacity for self-help."[45] The sick are not blamed but pitied; they cannot cure themselves.

Elite Self-Pity

The new psychotherapy seems to achieve the goal of science through its technological reduction of selves to readily manipulable machines or animals. Because human needs become nothing but a therapeutic creation, the therapist achieves human wisdom by knowing what he makes. The members of the dependent class become dependent on the knowledge class for their very identities. The aim is to reduce the dependent class to nothing but consumers of expertise. But the new psychotherapy is not, most radically, a tyranny of experts. It is a reflection of the moral weakness or self-denial of the knowledge class. The cure that class proposes for society as a whole it really imposes on itself. The pity its members claim to feel for others they really feel for themselves.

The foundation of this self-pity is today's extreme separation of mental and physical labor: "The thinking classes are fatally removed from the physical side of life." They only consume the results of but never do "productive labor." They are dependent on the manual labor of others. So their world is abstracted from "the palpable, immediate, physical reality inhabited by men and women." They too easily forget they are natural beings, or beings with bodies. But they also "have no experience of making anything substantial and enduring."[46] They have no experience of what beings with minds can really accomplish with their hands. Their Cartesian abstraction does not comprehend the limits, joys, and deserved pride in accomplishment of real men and women.

The knowledge class's largely successful creation of an artificial, controlled environment for itself is the source of its "central dogma" that all reality is socially constructed. All that exists is a willful, mental construc-

---

45. Lasch, Christopher, *The Culture of Narcissism*, p. 230.
46. Lasch, Christopher, *The Revolt of the Elites*, p. 20.

tion. This dogma is a denial of both the existence and the goodness of a reality that exists independently of human will. It comes from a class obsessed with control: "In their drive to insulate themselves against risk and contingency—against the unpredictable hazards that afflict human life—the thinking classes have seceded not just from the common world around them but from reality itself."[47]

The members of the thinking class actually aim to replace the harsh reality of conscious, embodied existence with their self-creation. Their separation of themselves from the working class is really a separation from their own embodiment. Their distinctive, "enlightened" values are really opposed to moral realism. Their therapeutic antimorality is really a way of attempting to escape the human necessity to come to terms with the existential limits to their power and freedom.

What usually passes for postmodernism really is "hypermodernism," the tendency toward unlimited exaggeration of the most unadmirable and seductive features of modern society. The attempt to dominate nature or reality becomes its artificial simulation. In "hyperreality" or virtual reality, human control is freed from "the intractable resistance of physical materials." Intelligence becomes "hyperintelligence," the purpose of which is not to understand "the real world" but "the world simulated by computers." Man himself becomes, Lasch emphasizes, "hyperman." This "pitifully shrunken, driven creature" is "subservient to the machines who demand his frantic attention." His artificial world never really comes under his control. There is nothing more contemptible than hyperman's futile, petty, fearful, anxious, antirealistic "hyperactivity."[48]

The thinking class denies the possibility of real perception of the world that human beings might share. So it denies the possibility of persuasion through rational public debate. On the basis of this dogma, it no longer tries to persuade the moral majority of the truth of its values. Its intellectual secession from reality is also from the moral and physical world occupied by most human beings. It is, as Richard Rorty says, secession for the creation of a private or class-based fantasy, which is the foundation for its "alternative" institutions, its gated communities.[49]

Therapy, in this light, becomes a way of protecting that fantasy from the reality of human beings who do not share it. Moral privatization or permissiveness means exempting not only the dependent class but the knowledge class from common moral standards. The extreme division of

---

47. *Ibid.*, p. 20.
48. Lasch, Christopher, "After the Foundations Have Crumbed," *Commonweal* 119 (November 20, 1992): 22–23.
49. Lasch, Christopher, *The Revolt of the Elites*, p. 20.

labor tends to make both classes too one-sided or unrealistic to live genuinely admirable and truthful lives. Both classes lose contact with the sense of continuity and permanence in human affairs that makes human excellence and civic life possible.[50]

Lasch dismisses communitarianism as it is usually understood as basically an elite construction, an implausible mixture of moral permissiveness and public trust and philosophy. The rejection of moral realism implied by moral privatization is destructive of all community. Communitarians are usually "more interested in the responsibility of the community as a whole than individual responsibility." But communal trust really depends upon the respect of one responsible individual for another.[51]

The Modern Project's Futility

The postmodern or hypermodern doctrine is incoherent. Rorty, for example, puts forward his version of the social construction of reality as a recognition of human contingency. Nothing human is stable; all human experiences are described into and may be described out of existence. But this assertion of radical contingency is meant to be the prelude to rational control of human identity through description and redescription. A genuine acknowledgment of contingency would be of what is beyond expert comprehension and control: God, nature, death, and so forth.

But the hypermodern assertion of control actually produces a deeper perception of genuine contingency, "a feeling of inauthenticity and inner emptiness," the absence of "a strong, stable sense of selfhood" that is the foundation of personal resistance to manipulation. One unacknowledged postmodern perception of the knowledge class is the emptiness of human and especially of one's own existence. The human self is a meaningless accident that is worthy of pity.[52]

The deepest perception of contingency is the futility of self-denial. Hypermodern man remains haunted by death, by what really cannot be conquered by talk or drugs. Hyperman cannot completely forget that he is not really hyperman at all. Human beings have not really mastered their environment until they have really comprehended and brought under their control "life's secret." So "the utopian possibilities of modern technology in its purest sense" depend on "a revolution in genetics" that could prolong life indefinitely.[53] But there is, in truth, no imaginable

---

50. Lasch, Christopher, *The Culture of Narcissism*, p. 249.
51. Lasch, Christopher, *The Revolt of the Elites*, p. 106–08.
52. Lasch, Christopher, *The Culture of Narcissism*, p. 239.
53. Ibid., p. 244.

way of postponing death forever, without bringing the whole universe under human control.

Accidental death will always remain a possibility, and eventual death will always remain a certainty. Turning death from an ennobling, challenging necessity into an unfortunate possibility makes human existence more accidental, or more determined by accidents, than ever before. Human beings surely become more risk-averse, or more ignobly defined by fear of death. The knowledge class is more progressive or pitiful than the working class, because it is less likely to accept the necessarily limited and tragic character of human existence. It will always be the case that "the shadow of death hangs over our pleasures and triumphs, calling them into question."[54]

Technological control, undertaken in the name of compassion, makes human beings more pitiful than ever before. They are more dependent than ever on forces beyond their control. Lasch applauds the ecological movement insofar as it makes clear the inescapability of our dependence on nature.[55] But the knowledge class is particularly badly-equipped to live well with that knowledge. It remains in rebellion against "the ancient religious insight that the only way to achieve happiness is to accept limitations in a spirit of gratitude and contrition." So it vacillates between the unrealistic, emotionally immature extremes "of attempting to annul those limitations and bitterly resenting them." The knowledge class childishly refuses to acknowledge the connection between human happiness and suffering.[56] So it is in rebellion against "the central paradox of religious faith: that the secret to happiness lies in renouncing the right to be happy."[57]

The Return to Superstition

The technological war against death is unwinnable. Its great but limited success makes us more aware of and more unwilling to come to terms with human limitations. Lasch observes that today it is "increasingly difficult to accept the reality of sorrow, loss, aging, and death." People, particularly members of the knowledge class, are more anxious than ever, and such experiences "have intensified the mechanisms of denial."[58]

So high technology is actually the cause of "the revival of ancient superstitions," particularly pantheism in the form of New Age spirituality.

---

54. Lasch, Christopher, *The Revolt of the Elites*, p. 243, *The True and Only Heaven*, p. 529.
55. Lasch, Christopher, *The Revolt of the Elites*, p. 244.
56. Lasch, Christopher, *The Culture of Narcissism*, pp. 242–46.
57. Lasch, Christopher, *The Revolt of the Elites*, p. 246.
58. Lasch, Christopher, *The Culture of Narcissism*, p. 245.

Pantheism is the illusion that opposes itself most radically to the truth about human alienation or individuality. It attempts "to restore the illusion of symbiosis, a feeling of absolute oneness with the world." That superstitious illusion grows as the technological fantasy of absolute mastery fades.[59]

Pantheism is the effort at "a complete surrender of the will" that comes with the failure of human willfulness.[60] Lasch agrees with Tocqueville that it is the most seductive modern doctrine because it denies most radically the truth about human individuality.[61] He also agrees with Percy that the self-denial of New Age/Eastern religion is most compatible with the impersonal claim for comprehensive truth of modern science.[62] Prideless individuals who attempt to lose themselves in pantheistic reveries deserve both our pity and our contempt.

Lasch explains that pantheism is the theological expression of the narcissistic solution to fear of death. The narcissist "does not acknowledge the separate existence of the self," and so "he lacks any conception of the difference between himself and his surroundings." He is unaware of his own death and so lacks even any "determination to stay alive." His particular existence has no significance; it is indistinguishable from the rest of existence.[63]

The narcissist or pantheist rebels against "the pain of separation" that constitutes individuality or selfhood by denying the truth of its existence.[64] Radical individualism, the modern assertion of unconstrained freedom, actually makes life so miserably contingent that it culminates "in the radical repudiation of individualism." Everyone and everything, the narcissist or pantheist says, is identical to everything else.[65] The radical repudiation of difference is really a repudiation of *the* human difference. Pantheism is the most rational of religions insofar as it describes a whole without incoherence or alienation. It describes a world without mystery, including the mysterious being who can really long for and know some of the truth about his own existence. Pantheism is the most unrealistic or untrue of religions for human or alienated beings.

---

59. *Ibid.*, p. 245.
60. Lasch, Christopher, *The Minimal Self*, p. 236.
61. Tocqueville, Alexis de, *Democracy*, volume 2, part 1, chapter 6. I take the term pantheism from Tocqueville, not Lasch. But Lasch is clearly describing what Tocqueville calls pantheism.
62. See the remarks about Buddhism in *Lost in the Cosmos* and throughout Percy's work.
63. Lasch, Christopher, *The Culture of Narcissism*, p. 240.
64. *Ibid.*, p. 240.
65. *Ibid.*, p. 70.

So science, contrary to its intention and expectation, has not really replaced religious superstition. Sophisticated twentieth-century life is a mixture of "hyper rationalism and a widespread revolt against rationality." The failure of rationalism really to produce hyperman, to purge the mystery of self-conscious mortality from human existence, has produced intensified "feelings of homelessness and deprivation." These feelings are largely in reaction to the contradiction between the promise of the modern project to bring nature under human control and the reality that the mysterious limitations of human existence persist.[66] Human beings have been deprived by the therapeutic language that describes only hyperreality of the words for articulating and coming to terms with what they really know about their existence.

The modern or postmodern knowledge class romantically aims to "recreate natural harmony in history." But the foundation of human or historical freedom, in truth, "is precisely the inescapable awareness of man's contradictory place in the natural order of things." So "[t]he distinguishing characteristic of selfhood...is not rationality but a critical awareness of man's divided nature." Selfhood necessarily includes "the painful awareness of the gulf between human aspirations and human limitations." Citing the Augustinian Reinhold Niebuhr, Lasch says that man is neither wholly rational hyperman nor wholly harmonious Rousseauean natural man, but an incoherent mixture of the two.[67] As the Pascalian Tocqueville said, man is the beast with the angel in him.[68]

Lasch never claimed to be a Christian, and he opposed using religion merely to achieve some social or cultural goal. The realist's concern is religion's truth. The Augustinian psychology of Christian realism is always true: "The modern world has no monopoly on fear of death or alienation from God. Alienation is the normal condition of human existence." What distinguishes "the modern temper" is the intensity and pervasiveness of the rebellion against this truth.[69]

Populism: The Working Class and the Culture War

Lasch's populism is rooted in his Socratic and religious moral realism. He opposes the modern elite's futile rebellion against nature and God, and he holds that human excellence is living well in gratitude with one's

---

66. *Ibid.*, p. 48.
67. Lasch, Christopher, *The Minimal Self*, pp. 257–59.
68. Tocqueville, Alexis de *Democracy*, volume 2, part 2, chapter 16.
69. Lasch, Christopher, *The Revolt of the Elites*, pp. 243, 245; *The Minimal Self*, pp. 257–59.

limitations. He observes that the therapeutic effort to reduce most human beings to thoughtless dependents has not succeeded completely. Lasch agrees with his fellow antitherapeutic thinker Philip Rieff that "the persistence of old-fashioned moralities among the 'less educated' " is a reason for hope for the future of guilt, moral responsibility, and religion.[70]

In our time, the people have a more truthful and morally demanding view of the good life than the elite. Although Lasch's class analysis owes much to Marx, he is not a Marxist because he sides with the "petit bourgeois" class's "deep reservations about the progressive scheme of history." Lasch accepts that class's populist critique of indefinite progress, therapeutic enlightenment and entitlement, and "unlimited ambition."[71] Generally, socialism was an elitist or intellectual movement, much more opposed to the morality of the herd or "bourgeois philistinism" than to capitalist elitism. Its attack on bourgeois or the ordinary person's culture was far more effective than its attack on capitalism.

Bourgeois virtues, in truth, are populist virtues, the qualities required of "active, self-respecting citizens."[72] Their ennobling practice is undermined by socialism's characteristically modern, therapeutic promise to dispense with virtue or self-restraint altogether. Socialist and capitalist elitism have had the same morally corrosive effects.[73] Both the capitalist market and the therapeutic state weaken "the character forming discipline of the family, neighborhood, school, and church." Both tend to transform all of human life in a standardized and degrading direction if not resisted. Lasch agrees with the Marxists about the market, and the conservatives about the welfare state.[74]

The knowledge class has identified working class's antiprogressive culture — its religion and morality — as "authoritarian prejudices." A preference for working over talking, the recognition of the limits of science, and the affirmation of honor are parts of the pathology called the authoritarian personality. Any choice for authority over unconstrained freedom is not primarily unenlightened but unhealthy. So moralistic or realistic positions need not be opposed by argument. They are symptoms of a disease that might be cured.[75]

---

70. Lasch, Christopher, *The Revolt of the Elites*, p. 223.
71. Lasch, Christopher, *The True and Only Heaven*, pp. 530–32.
72. Lasch, Christopher, *The Revolt of the Elites*, p. 82.
73. *Ibid.*, pp. 233–34, 83.
74. *Ibid.*, pp. 70, 95–98.
75. Lasch, Christopher, *The True and Only Heaven*, pp. 450–52.

The disease is a pathologically childish desire for security. The progressive theory of history shared by all versions of the modern knowledge class is a movement from childhood to maturity, a story of "emotional and intellectual growth." So all forms of "cultural conservatism" and "any respect for tradition" are dismissed as forms of clinging to childhood. The nonauthoritarian individual is the one who accepts without flinching "the burden of maturity."[76] His pride is in his disillusionment, his ability to live well without faith.[77] But in Lasch's own view, nothing is more childish than the modern effort to free human existence from all dependence, and premodern culture and tradition, whatever their shortcomings, tended to embody a largely lost moral maturity. "In an age that fancies itself as disillusioned," Lasch observes, "one illusion—the illusion of mastery—remains as tenacious as ever."[78]

Psychologizing social science is one weapon among many, and one that Lasch himself uses, in the moral or cultural war between the classes. Perhaps the key issue in this war today is abortion. The "working-class ethics of limits" affirms the dignity of motherhood and "a biological view of human nature" that includes fixed and desirable differences between men and women. The knowledge class's "enlightened ethic" opposes "biological constraints of any kind" with the "insistence that women ought to assume 'control over their own bodies.'" The separation of sex from reproduction makes it possible to bring both under human control, to liberate them both from illusion or mystery.[79]

The right-to-life movement is based on the perception that not only sex and love but being human itself are good and mysteries beyond our comprehension and control. The denial of the mystery of selfhood or personhood implicit in the pro-choice position leads logically to genetic engineering and other willful judgments about "the 'quality of life.'" The result could easily be the consignment of "whole categories of defective and superfluous individuals to the status of nonpersons." The elitism of the pro-choice position, which replaces the egalitarian recognition of the mystery of all human life with judgments concerning the quality of life, reflects the tendency of the extreme division of labor, as Marx said, to reduce the mass of people to nothing.[80]

---

76. Lasch, Christopher, *The Revolt of the Elites*, p. 237.
77. *Ibid.*, p. 242.
78. *Ibid.*, p. 246.
79. Lasch, Christopher, *The True and Only Heaven*, pp. 489–91.
80. *Ibid.*, pp. 490–91.

Lasch accepts completely the position of contemporary American Catholic Thomists such as Walker Percy that the unrealistic denial of human mystery and human goodness leads to tyranny and murder. The rule of law and limited democracy depend on respect for the personal mysteries of sex, love and death, and for the ordinary person's capacity to live well with them. So they also depend on the primacy of a kind of democratic moral responsibility over the willfulness of experts.[81]

With its acknowledgment of limits to choice, the working class is modest in its expectations for life. Its members accept the barrier the body poses to projects for nature's conquest and personal re-creation. They are more easygoing about exercise and diet, or more accepting of the inevitability of the body's decay. From the knowledge class's perspective, they are slackers when it comes to the body, but too tough when it comes to the soul or virtue. But for Lasch, they, because they accept the body, are more free to cultivate the soul.

The individual, ordinarily, is saved from the "crippling emotional conflict" that comes from self-obsession by love and work, meaning love of other, particular human beings and work that is challenging, somewhat spontaneous, and concrete or not purely mental or endlessly creative. But even love and work disappoint if we expect too much from them or give too little of ourselves to them. Both connect us with others and the world. Love is of particular men and women, not of humanity in general. So it, even more than work, is the foundation of our personal responsibility and moral realism. Abstract, Rortyan talk about solidarity and even the universal doctrine of rights is unrealistic, if taken to be a replacement for love as a foundation for responsibility.[82]

Bourgeois virtue or self-restraint on behalf of worthwhile work and one's familial and civic duties is indispensable for all lives worth living. Without the concrete, particular experiences associated with love and work, without especially the joys and longings connected with the many forms of eros,[83] the human experience of reality really is unstable and uncertain. So only someone well rooted in "particularism" can experience the "true cosmpolitanism" which is realism.[84] For hypermen, hyperreality or escapist self-denial seems better than what we really know about ourselves and the world.[85]

---

81. For this argument, see my "Sex, Drugs, Politics, Love, and Death."

82. See Jean Bethke Elshtain's nice summary of Lasch on love in "The Life and Work of Christopher Lasch: An American Story," *Salmagundi* (Spring, 1995), p. 154.

83. For an excellent account of Lasch on the therapeutic "domestication of eros," see Diana V. Schaub, "Girls Just Wanna Have Fun," *Public Interest* (Fall, 1997): 116–24.

84. Lasch, Christopher, *The Minimal Self*, p. 264.

85. Lasch, Christopher, *The Culture of Narcissism*, pp. 244, 249.

Lasch contrasts the ordinary or common world formed by love and work, which includes the political world, with Rorty's postmodern combination of private fantasies or narcissism and a limited, calculated public concern with protecting the space which makes equal-opportunity fantasizing possible.[86] Rorty, Lasch admits, is distressingly close to describing America's elite-dominated civic life as it actually exists today. What Lasch finds missing is "almost everything...that makes life worth living." The therapeutic erosion of the social joys of love and work may mean that we are losing the capacity not only to govern but even to amuse ourselves.[87] The knowledge class is so obsessed with control, or finally mere survival, and consumed with self-pity about the futility of its efforts, that it has no appreciation for the experiences that make merely human life good. Rorty's suggestion that the common human good become endless conversation divorced from real content is pitiful to anyone who has anything—love, work, politics nature, morality, death, or God—really to talk about.

The working class views the dominant knowledge class as whiny, self-indulgent, and needlessly unhappy. The elite's moral permissiveness or tolerance is really personal weakness, a lack of courage in one's convictions even within one's own family. Its members are "endlessly demanding of life," expecting more than anyone has a right to expect. And they expect so much without demanding much of themselves in return. They do not restrain their pursuit of happiness or self-fulfillment on behalf of, or in acknowledgment of, their dependence on others.[88]

From the working class's perspective, the knowledge class is unadmirable and unhappy because it believes it has a right to be happy. The working man can distinguish between a real man, a person of character, and a hyperman. He knows how thoughtful and courageous, how heroic, any human being must be who lives well. Lasch sided with the working man, finally, because he too was a real man. He worked, loved, and died well. In his life and in his writing, Lasch "made what was extraordinary seem ordinary."[89]

---

86. For a defense of the view of Rorty found here and there in this essay, see my "Bloom's Ineffectual Response to Rorty: Pragmatism, Existentialism, and American Political Thought Today," *Community and Political Thought Today*, ed. P. Lawler and D. McConkey (Westport, CT: Praeger, 1998).

87. Lasch, Christopher, *The Revolt of the Elites*, p. 128.

88. Lasch, Christopher, *The True and Only Heaven*, p. 493.

89. Lasch's daughter, Elisabeth Lasch-Quinn, quoted by Elshtain, 157. Elshtain was a good friend of Lasch, and her article contains many moving observations concerning his remarkable life and good death. See also the remarks by Lasch-Quinn in her introduction to *Women and the Common Life*, pp. xxv-xxvi.

Religion

The real but incompletely satisfying human joys of love and work both point in the direction of God. All of Lasch's thought points to the question of religion's truth, or the compatibility of truthful self-examination with revealed or biblical religion. Lasch holds that the tradition of introspection is in substantial agreement with Augustinian psychology. He agrees with the Christians that dialogic self-examination may not be enough to live well in light of the truth, which is not to say that religion is untrue. He rejected radically Freud's view that religion is merely a "hoax" to be perpetuated for the benefit of culture. For Lasch, "an honest atheist is always to be preferred to a culture Christian."[90]

Religion can function as a refuge, as a source of illusory security. But "the most radical form of religious faith," which is Christian, can also be "a challenge to self-pity and despair." Its affirmation of moral realism and responsibility opposes itself to victimization and resentment. Its understanding of human freedom as a limited, mixed, but genuine good opposes itself to the modern, atheistic extremes of the fantasy of self-sufficiency through control and apathetic passivity. By protecting the good which is human individuality, "[s]ubmission to God makes people less submissive in everyday life."[91]

The "deepest variety" of religion always "arises out of the background of despair." The "prelude to conversion" often is "black despair" or "melancholy." Faith is finally in "the goodness of being in the face of suffering and evil." It is not a negation of suffering and evil. Lasch's final word in his last book is that the future of the modern project is much more problematic than religion's future. The latter reflects the perennial human truth that "life and its negation" are "inextricably bound together." The acceptance of that truth and the practice of the "true virtue" it engenders is what separates a real man from a hyperman.[92]

The last section of that final book Lasch called "the dark night of the soul." It is composed of three chapters articulating in different ways the limits of secular views of the human soul. The phrase "the dark night of the soul" is taken from the American Catholic Thomistic writer Flannery O'Connor, who used it to show that even saints sometime experience "the truth as revealed by faith" as "hideous." Lasch adds "the whole world now seems to be going through a dark night of the soul."[93] But it

---

90. Lasch, Christopher, *The Revolt of the Elites*, p. 228.
91. Lasch, Christopher, *The Revolt of the Elites*, p. 245; *Women and the Common Life*, pp. 159–60.
92. Lasch, Christopher, *The Revolt of the Elites*, pp. 243–46.
93. *Ibid.* p. 246.

is reasonable to hope that the despairing awareness of the futility of that rebellion may be a prelude to faith based on a courageous and joyful affirmation of the goodness of being, including the alienated being who is mysteriously equipped to perceive that goodness.

It is only reaching a bit to say that Lasch's concluding use of the authority of O'Connor points to Thomism as the authentic postmodernism, or genuinely thoughtful, truthful reflection on the failure of the modern project. Lasch did write that a genuinely postmodern thinker would have to be "philosophically a realist." In light of the failure of modern and all human rebellion against nature, he "respects not only the 'intransigence' but the 'eloquence' of things."[94] And he sees the compatibility of philosophical and religious insight, and so he is open to the truth of revelation.

---

94. Lasch, Christopher, *After the Foundations*, p. 23.

References

Abel, Richard, 1981. "Why Does the ABA Promulgate Ethical Rules?" *Texas Law Review* 59: 639-688.
Adams, Bruce, 1984. "The Frustrations of Government Service." *Public Administration Review* 44 (January/February): 5-13.
Adler, Mortimer J., and Seymour Cain, 1962. *Ethics: The Study of Moral Values*. Chicago: Encyclopedia Britannica, Inc.
American Bar Association, 1983. *Model Rules of Professional Conduct and Code of Judicial Conduct*. Chicago: The American Bar Association.
American Society for Public Administration. 1985. *American Society for Public Administration Code of Ethics and Implementation Guidelines*. Supplement to *P.A. Times* (May 1).
Ammeran, Nancy Tatom, 1987. *Bible Believers: Fundamentalists in the Modern World*. New Brunswick: Rutgers University Press.
Appleby, Paul H., 1949. *Big Democracy*. New York: Alfred A. Knopf.
———, 1952. *Morality and Administration in Democratic Government*. Baton Rouge, LA: Louisiana State University Press.
Arendt, Hannah, 1972. *Crises of the Republic*. New York: Harcourt Brace Jovanovich.
Aristotle, 1975. *Nicomachean Ethics*. Translated by H. Rackham. Cambridge: Harvard University Press.
———, 1980. *The Nicomachean Ethics*. Translated by David Ross. Oxford: Oxford University Press.
———, 1986. *The Nicomachean Ethics*. Translated and edited by W.D. Ross. In *Great Books of the Western World*, Vol. 9, Robert Maynard Hutchins, ed. Chicago: Encyclopedia Britannica, inc (page references are to reprint edition).
———, n.d. *Politics*. Translated by Lawrence Berns (manuscript).
Aristotle, 1958. *Politics*. Edited and Translated by Ernest Barker New York: Oxford University Press.
Aron, Raymond, 1985. *History, Truth, Liberty: Selected Writings of Raymond Aron*. Chicago: University of Chicago Press.
Asprey, Robert B., 1975. *War in the Shadows*, Vol. II. Garden City, New York: Doubleday & Company, Inc.
St. Augustine, 1961. *Confessions*. Translated by R.S. Pine-Coffin. New York: Penguin Books.
Axtell, James L., ed., 1968. *The Educational Writings of John Locke*. Cambridge: Cambridge University Press.
Bailey, Stephen K., 1965. "Ethics and the Public Service." In Roscoe C. Martin, ed. *Public Administration and Democracy*. Syracuse: Syracuse University Press, pp. 283-298. Reprinted in Richard J. Stillman II, ed.

Public Administration: Concepts and Cases, 3rd ed. (Boston: Houghton Mifflin, 1984), pp. 480-489.

Bahnsen, John C., and Robert W. Cone, 1990. "Defining the American Warrior Leader." *Parameters* (December): 24-28.

Barthes, Roland, 1957. *Mythologies*. New York: Hill and Wang.

Becker, Lawrence C., and Charlotte B. Becker, eds., 1992. *Encyclopedia of Ethics*, Vol. I. New York: Garland.

Bennett, William J., ed., 1993. *The Book of Virtues: A Treasury of Great Moral Stories*. New York: Simon and Schuster.

———, 1995. *The Children's Book of Virtues*. New York: Simon and Schuster.

Bentham, Jeremy, 1948. *An Introduction to the Principles of Morals and Legislation*. New York: Hafner.

Biskowski, Lawrence, 1992. "Political Theory in the 1990s: Antifoundationalist Critics and Democratic Prospects." *Southeastern Political Review* 20 (Spring): 62-90.

Black, Henry Campbell, 1979. *Black's Law Dictionary*. 5th ed. St. Paul: West Publishing Company.

Blackstone, William, 1818. *Commentaries on the Laws of England*. 4 vols. Edited by David Christian. Boston: T.B. Wait and Sons.

Bok, Derek C., 1983. "A Flawed System of Law Practice and Training." *Journal of Legal Education* 33: 570-585.

Bork, Robert H., 1995. "Interpreting the Constitution." In Peter Augustine Lawler and Robert Martin Schaefer, eds. *Political Rhetoric*. Lanham: Rowman & Littlefield, Publishers. Inc., pp. 263-5.

Branch, Taylor, 1998. *Pillar of Fire: America in the King Years, 1963-65*. New York: Simon and Schuster.

Brennan, William J., Jr., 1985-86. "The Constitution of the United States: ContemporaryRatification." *South Texas Law Review* 27:433-445.

Cagle, M. Christine, J. Michael Martinez, and William D. Richardson, 1999. "Professional Licensing Boards: Self-Governance or Self-Interest?" *Administration & Society*, 30, 6 (January): 734-770.

Caiden, Gerald E., 1984. "In Search of an Apolitical Science of American Public Administration." In Jack S. Rabin and James S. Bowman, eds. *Politics and Administration: Woodrow Wilson and American Public Administration*. New York: Dekker, pp. 51-76.

Caldwell, Lynton K., 1944. *The Administrative Theories of Hamilton and Jefferson: Their Contribution to Thought on Public Administration*. Chicago: University of Chicago Press.

Carroll, Andrew, ed., 1997. *Letters of a Nation*. New York: Kodansha International.

Carter, Lief H., *Reason in Law*, 4th edition. New York: HarperCollins College Publishers.

Catron, Bayard L., and Kathryn G. Denhardt, 1994. "Ethics Education in Public Administration." In Terry L. Cooper, ed., *Handbook of Administrative Ethics*. New York: Marcel Dekker, pp. 49-61.

Chandler, Ralph Clark, 1983. "The Problem of Moral Reasoning in American Public Administration: The Case for a Code of Ethics." *Public Administration Review* 43 (January/February): 32-39.
———, 1987. *Civic Virtue in the American Republic*. Kalamazoo, MI: The New Issues Press of Western Michigan University.
——— and Barbara A.K. Adams, 1997. "Lets Go to the Movies! Using Film to Illustrate Basic Concepts in Public Administration." *Public Voices*, 3 (2).
——— 1998. "Public Administration Pedagogy: Another Look at Evolutionary Paradigms in Theory and Practice." In Jack Rabin, W. Bartley Hildreth, and Gerald J. Miller, eds. *Handbook of Public Administration*, Second Edition. New York: Marcel Dekker.
Chitwood, Stephen R., 1974. "Social Equity and Social Service Productivity." *Public Administration Review* 34 (January/February): 29-35.
Cody, W.J. Michael, and Richardson R. Lynn, 1992. *Honest Government: An Ethics Guide for Public Service*. Westport, CT: Praeger Publishers.
Conant, James B., ed., 1962. *Thomas Jefferson and the Development of American Public Education*. Berkeley, CA: University of California Press.
Cook, Brian J., 1992. "The Representative Function of Bureaucracy: Public Administration in Constitutive Perspective." *Administration and Society* (February): 403-429
Cooper, David E., 1996. *World Philosophies: An Historical Introduction*. Cambridge, MA: Blackwell.
Cooper, Phillip J., 1984. "The Wilsonian Dichotomy in Administrative Law." In Jack S. Rabin and James S. Bowman, eds. *Politics and Administration: Woodrow Wilson and American Public Administration*. New York: Dekker, pp. 79-94.
Cooper, Terry L., 1987. "Hierarchy, Virtue, and the Practice of Public Administration: A Perspective for Normative Ethics." *Public Administration Review* 47 (July/August): 320-328.
———, 1990. *The Responsible Administrator: An Approach to Ethics for the Administrative Role*. 3rd ed. San Francisco: Jossey-Bass.
———, ed., 1994. *Handbook of Administrative Ethics*. New York: Marcel Dekker.
Corwin, Edward S., 1969. "The 'Higher Law' Background of American Constitutional Law." In *American Government: Readings and Cases*. 3rd ed. Edited by Peter Woll. Boston: Little, Brown and Company, pp. 37-54.
Daly, Markate, ed., 1994. *Communitarianism: A New Public Ethic*. Belmont, California: Wadsworth.
Davis, Kenneth Culp, 1969. *Discretionary Justice*. Baton Rouge, LA: Louisiana State University Press.
Denhardt, Kathryn G., 1988. *The Ethics of Public Service: Resolving Moral Dilemmas in Public Organizations*. Westport, CT: Greenwood Press.
Derrida, Jacques, 1976. *Of Grammatology*. Translated by G. Spivak. Baltimore: Johns Hopkins University Press.

———, 1978. *Writing and Difference*. Translated by A. Bass. London: Routledge & Kegan Paul.

———, 1982. *Margins of Philosophy*. Translated by A. Bass. Chicago: The University of Chicago Press.

DeShaney v. Winnebago Department of Social Services, 489 U.S. 189 (1989).

Dershowitz, Alan M., ed., 1990. *The World's Most Famous Court Trial: Tennessee Evolution Case*. Birmingham, AL: The Notable Trials Library.

Devine, Donald J., 1972. *The Political Culture of the United States*. Boston: Little, Brown & Company.

Dewey, John, 1927. *The Public and Its Problems*. New York: Holt.

Diamond, Martin, 1976. "The American Idea of Man: The View From the Founding." In Irving Kristol and Paul Weaver, eds. *The Americans 1976, Critical Choices for Americans*, Vol. 2. Lexington, MA: Lexington Books; Washington: Heath and Co., pp. 21-22.

———, 1983. "The Federalist." In Morton J. Frisch and Richard G. Stevens, eds. *American Political Thought: The Philosophic Dimension of American Statesmanship*, 2nd ed. Itasca, IL: F.E. Peacock, pp. 51-70.

———, 1986. "Ethics and Politics: The American Way." In Robert H. Horowitz, ed. *The Moral Foundations of the American Republic*, 3rd ed. Charlottesville, Virginia: University Press of Virginia, pp. 75-108. A reprint of this essay is also found in *The Quest for Justice: Readings in Political Ethics*. 3rd ed. Edited by Leslie G. Rubin and Charles T. Rubin. Needham Heights, MA: Ginn Press, 1992: 295-315. It appears in the present collection as Chapter 8.

Dietze, Gottfried, 1960. *The Federalist: A Classic on Federalism and Free Government*. Westport, CT: Greenwood.

Dobel, J. Patrick, 1990. "Integrity in the Public Service." *Public Administration Review* (May/June): 354-366

Dworkin, Ronald, 1978. *Taking Rights Seriously*. Cambridge, MA: Harvard University Press.

Elshtain, Jean Bethke, 1995. "The Life and Work of Christopher Lasch: An American Story." *Salmagundi* (Spring).

Farrand, Max, ed., 1937. *The Records of the Federal Convention of 1787*. New Haven: Yale University Press.

Farrell, Daniel M., 1985. "Hobbes as Moralist." *Philosophical Studies* 48: 257-283.

Finer, Herman, 1990. "Administrative Responsibility in Democratic Government." *In Combating Corruption/Encouraging Ethics: A Sourcebook for Public Service Ethics*. Edited by William L. Richter, Francis Burke, and James W. Doig. Washington, DC: The American Society for Public Administration: 44.

Finer, S.E., 1997. *The History of Government From the Earliest Times*, 3 vols. New York: Oxford University Press.

Fiss, Owen M., 1981. "The Varieties of Positivism." *Yale Law Journal* 90: 1007-1016.

Fleishman, Joel L., 1981. "Self-Interest and Political Integrity." In Joel L.Fleishman, Lance Liebman, and Mark H. Moore, eds. *Public Duties: The Moral Obligations of Government Officials*. Cambridge, MA: Harvard University Press, pp. 52-92.

———, Lance Liebman, and Mark H. Moore, eds., 1981. *Public Duties: The Moral Obligations of Government Officials*. Cambridge, MA: Harvard University Press.

Fletcher, George P., 1981. "Two Modes of Legal Thought." *Yale Law Journal* 90: 970-1006.

Fortin, Ernest L., 1972. "St. Thomas Aquinas." In Leo Strauss and Joseph Cropsey, eds. *History of Political Philosophy*. 2nd ed. Chicago: The University of Chicago Press.

Foster, Gregory D., 1981. "Law, Morality, and the Public Servant." *Public Administration Review* 41 (January/February): 29-34.

Fotion, Nicholas G., 1990. *Military Ethics*. Stanford, California: Hoover Institution Press.

Fotion, N., and G. Elfstrom, 1986. *Military Ethics*. Boston: Routledge & Kegan Paul.

Foucault, Michel, 1972. *The Archaeology of Knowledge*. Translated by A. Sheridan. New York: Harper.

———, 1980. *The Order of Things: An Archaeology of the Human Sciences*. London: Tavistock.

Fox, Charles J., and Clarke E. Cochran, 1990. "Discretion Advocacy in Public Administration: Toward a Platonic Guarding Class?" *Administration and Society* (August): 249-271.

Frankena, William K., 1963. *Ethics*. New York: Prentice-Hall, Inc.

Frederickson, H. George, 1980. *New Public Administration*. University, AL: University of Alabama Press.

———, and D.K. Hart, 1985. "The Public Service and the Patriotism of Benevolence." *Public Administration Review* 45: 547-553.

———,1991. "Toward a Theory of the Public for Public Administration" *Administration and Society* (February): 395-417

Fried, Charles, 1976. "The Lawyer as Friend: The Moral Foundations of the Lawyer-Client Relation." *Yale Law Journal* 85: 1060-1089.

Friedrich, Carl J., 1972. *The Pathology of Politics*. New York: Harper & Row.

———, 1990. "Public Policy and the Nature of Administrative Responsibility." In William L. Richter, Francis Burke, and Jameson W. Doig, eds. *Combating Corruption/Encouraging Ethics: A Sourcebook for Public Service Ethics*. Washington, DC: The American Society for Public Administration: 43-44.

Gauthier, David, 1967. "Morality and Advantage." *Philosophical Review* 76: 460-475.

———, 1979. "Thomas Hobbes: Moral Theorist." *The Journal of Philosophy* 22: 547-559.

Gawthrop, Louis C., 1984. "Civas, Civitas, and Civilitas: A New Focus for the Year 2000." *Public Administration Review* 44 (March): 101-107.

———, 1984. *Public Management Systems and Ethics*. Bloomington, IN: Indiana University Press.
Gibbon, Edward, 1946. *The Decline and Fall of the Roman Empire*, Vol. I. New York: The Heritage Press.
Gideon v. Wainwright, 372 U.S. 335 (1963).
Gilbert, Sir William S., and Sir Arthur Sullivan, n.d. *The Complete Plays of Gilbert and Sullivan*. New York: The Modern Library.
Gladden, E.N., 1972. *A History of Public Administration*, 2 vols. London: Frank Cass.
Goldwin, Robert A., 1972. "John Locke." In Leo Strauss and Joseph Cropsey, eds. *History of Political Philosophy*. 2nd. ed. Chicago: The University of Chicago Press, pp. 451-486.
———, ed., 1980. *Bureaucrats, Policy Analysts, Statesmen: Who Leads?* Washington: American Enterprise Institute.
———, 1986. "Of Men and Angels: A Search for Morality in the Constitution." In Robert H., Horwitz, ed. *The Moral Foundations of the American Republic, 3rd ed*. Charlottesville, Virginia: University Press of Virginia, pp. 24-41.
Golembiewski, Robert T., 1965. *Men, Management and Morality: Toward a New Organizational Ethic*. New York: McGraw-Hill.
Goodsell, Charles T., 1983. *The Case for Bureaucracy: A Public Administration Polemic*. Chatham, NJ: Chatham House Publishers.
———, and Nancy Murray, eds., 1995. *Public Administration Illuminated and Inspired By the Arts*. Westport, Connecticut: Praeger.
Gordon-Reed, Annette, 1997. *Thomas Jefferson and Sally Hemings*. Charlottesville, Virginia: University Press of Virginia.
Gore, Albert, 1993. *Report of the National Performance Review: Creating a Government That Works Better and Costs Less*. Washington, DC: U.S. Government Printing Office (September).
Gortner, Harold F., 1991. *Ethics for Public Managers*. Westport, CT: Praeger Publishers.
Grant, Michael, 1978. *History of Rome*. New York: Charles Scribner's Sons.
Gulick, Luther, 1937. "Science, Values and Public Administration." In Luther Gulick and L. Urwick, eds. *Papers on the Science of Administration*. New York: Augustus M. Kelley Publishers, pp. 191-195.
Haakonssen, Knud, 1994. "Introduction." In David Hume *Political Essays*. Edited by Knud Haakonssen. Cambridge: Cambridge University Press, pp. xi-xxx.
Habermas, Jurgen, 1987. *The Philosophical Discourse of Modernity*. Cambridge: Polity.
Hamilton, Alexander, James Madison, and John Jay, 1961 and 1964. In C. Rossiter, ed. *The Federalist Papers*. New York: New American Library.
———, 1977. *The Federalist*. Franklin Center, PA: The Franklin Library.
Harmon, Michael M., 1974. "Social Equity and Organizational Man: Motivation and Organizational Democracy." *Public Administration Review* 34 (January/February): 11-18.

Hart, David K., 1974. "Social Equity, Justice, and the Equitable Administrator." *Public Administration Review* 34 (January/February): 3-11.
———, 1983. "The Honorable Bureaucrat Among the Philistines." *Administration and Society* 15 (May): 43-48.
———, 1984. "The Virtuous Citizen, the Honorable Bureaucrat, and 'Public' Administration" *Public Administration Review* 44 (March): 111-120.
———, 1989. "A Partnership in Virtue Among All Citizens: The Public Service and Civic Humanism" *Public Administration Review* (March/April): 101-105.
Hart, H.L.A., 1961. *Law, Liberty, and Morality*. New York: Vintage Books.
———, 1963. *The Concept of Law*. Oxford: Oxford University Press.
Hassner, Pierre, 1972. "Immanuel Kant." In Leo Strauss and Joseph Cropsey, eds. *History of Political Philosophy*. 2nd ed. Chicago: The University of Chicago Press.
Hayek, Friedrich A., 1944. *The Road to Serfdom*. Chicago: University of Chicago Press.
Hazard, Geoffrey C., Jr., 1991. "The Future of Legal Ethics." *Yale Law Journal* 100: 1239-1280.
Heckler v. Chaney, 470 U.S. 821 (1985).
Hejka-Ekins, April, 1988. "Teaching Ethics in Public Administration." *Public Administration Review* 48 (September/October): 885-891.
———, 1994. "Ethics in Inservice Training." In T.L. Cooper, ed. *Handbook of Administrative Ethics*. New York: Marcel Dekker, pp. 63-80.
Hersey, Paul, and Kenneth H. Blanchard, 1993. *Management of Organizational Behavior*. 6th ed. Englewood Cliffs, NJ: Prentice Hall.
Heywood, Andrew, 1994. *Political Ideas and Concepts: An Introduction*. New York: St. Martin's Press.
Higginbotham, Don, 1985. *George Washington and the American Military Tradition*. Athens, GA: The University of Georgia Press.
Hill, Robert S., 1972. "David Hume." In Leo Strauss and Joseph Cropsey, eds. *History of Political Philosophy*. 2nd ed. Chicago: The University of Chicago Press, pp. 509-531.
Hobbes, Thomas, 1958. *Leviathan*. Edited by Herbert W. Schneider. Indianapolis: Bobbs-Merrill.
Hofstadter, Richard, 1948. *The American Political Tradition*. New York: Vintage Books.
Holmes, Steven A., 1996. "Dick Morris's Behavior, and Why It's Tolerated." *The New York Times* (September 8): E5.
Horwitz, Robert H., ed., 1986. *The Moral Foundations of the American Republic, 3rd ed*. Charlottesville: University Press of Virginia.
———, 1986. "John Locke and the Preservation of Liberty: A Perennial Problem of Civic Education." In *The Moral Foundations of the American Republic, 3rd ed*. Charlottesville: University Press of Virginia, pp. 136-164.
Hume, David, 1977. *An Enquiry Concerning Human Understanding*. Indianapolis: Hackett Publishing.

Irwin, Terence, 1989. *Classical Thought*. Oxford: Oxford University Press.
Irwin, T.H., 1990. "A Conflict in Aquinas." *Review of Metaphysics* 14: 21-42.
Janowitz, Morris, 1960. *The Professional Soldier*. The Free Press.
Jefferson, Thomas, 1972. Edited by William Peden, *Notes on the State of Virginia*. New York: W.W. Norton & Co.
Jones, W.T., 1970. *The Classical Mind: A History of Western Philosophy*. 2nd ed. New York: Harcourt Brace Jovanovich.
———, 1970. *The Medieval Mind: A History of Western Philosophy*. 2nd ed. New York: Harcourt Brace Jovanovich.
Kant, Immanuel, 1987. *Fundamental Principles of the Metaphysics of Morals*. Translated by T. Abbott. New York: Prometheus.
———, 1990. "The Categorical Imperative." In William L. Richter, Francis Burke, and Jameson W. Doig, eds. *Combating Corruption/Encouraging Ethics: A Sourcebook for Public Service Ethics*. Washington, DC: The American Society for Public Administration: 27-29.
Karl, Barry, 1963. *Executive Reorganization and Reform in the New Deal*. Cambridge, MA: Harvard University Press.
Kavathatzopoulos, I., 1994. "Training Professional Managers in Decision-Making About Real Life Business Ethics Problems: The Acquisition of the Autonomous Problem Solving Skill." *Journal of Business Ethics* 13: 379-386.
Kindsvatter, Peter S., 1990. "Cowards, Comrades, and Killer Angels: The Soldier in Literature." *Parameters* (June): 31-49.
King, Martin Luther, Jr., 1964. "Speech Accepting the Nobel Peace Prize." *Bartlett's Familiar Quotations*. 1980. Boston: Little, Brown and Company, p. 909.
Kristol, William, 1984. "Libery, Equality, Honor," *Social Philosophy and Policy*, 2 (Autumn): 125-140.
———, 1991. "Women's Liberation: The Relevance of Tocqueville." In Ken Masugi, ed. 1991. *Interpreting Tocqueville's Democracy in America*. Savage, MD: Rowman & Littlefield Publishers, pp. 480-494.
Kuhn, Thomas S., 1970. *The Structure of Scientific Revolutions*. 2nd ed. Chicago: The University of Chicago Press.
Lane, Larry M., 1988. "Individualism, Civic Virtue, and Public Administration." *Administration and Society* (May): 30-45
Lartéguy, Jean, 1962. *The Centurions*. Translated by Xan Fielding. New York: E.P. Dutton & Co., Inc.
Lasch, Christopher, 1984. *The Minimal Self: Psychic Survival in Troubled Times*. New York: Norton.
———, 1991. *The Culture of Narcissism: American Life in the Age of Diminishing Expectations*. Revised edition. New York: Norton. Original edition, 1979.
———, 1991. *The True and Only Heaven: Progress and Its Critics*. New York: Norton.

———, 1992. "After the Foundations Have Crumbled." *Commonweal* 119 (November 20): 22-23.

———, 1995. *The Revolt of the Elites and the Betrayal of Democracy.* New York: Norton.

———, 1997. *Women and the Common Life: Love, Marriage, and Feminism.* New York: Norton.

Lawler, Peter Augustine, 1993. *The Restless Mind: Alexis de Tocqueville on the Origin and Perpetuation of Human Liberty.* Lanham: Rowman and Littlefield.

———, 1996. "*Lost in the Cosmos*: Walker Percy's Analysis of American Restlessness." *Poets, Princes, and Private Citizens.* Edited by J. Knippenberg and P. Lawler. Lanham, MD: Rowman & Littlefield, 1996.

———, 1997. "Walker Percy's Twentieth Century Thomism," *Perspectives on Political Science* 26 (Spring): 70-76.

———, 1998. "Bloom's Ineffectual Response to Rorty: Pragmatism, Existentialism, and American Political Thought Today." *Community and Political Thought Today.* Edited by P. Lawler and D. McConkey. Westport, CT: Praeger.

———, 1998. "Sex, Drugs, Politics, Love, and Death: The Political Teaching of Walker Percy's *The Thanatos Syndrome*." *Political Science Reviewer*, forthcoming.

Lawson, Lewis A., and Victor Kramer, eds., 1995. *More Conversations with Walker Percy.* University Press of Mississippi.

Lee, Harper, 1960. *To Kill a Mockingbird.* New York: Warner Books.

Levy, Michael B., ed., 1982. *Political Thought in America: An Anthology.* Homewood, IL: Dorsey Press.

Lewis, Anthony, 1991. *Gideon's Trumpet.* New York: Random House.

Leys, Wayne A.R., 1952. *Ethics for Policy Decisions.* Englewood Cliffs, NJ: Prentice-Hall

Lilla, Mark T., 1981. "Ethos, 'Ethics,' and Public Service." *The Public Interest* 63 (Spring): 3-17.

Locke, John, 1947. In T.I. Cook, ed. *Two Treatises of Government.* Edited by Thomas I. Cook. New York: Hafner Press.

———, 1964. *Some Thoughts Concerning Education.* Woodbury, NY: Barron's Educational Series, Inc.

———, 1975. *An Essay Concerning Human Understanding.* Edited by Peter H. Nidditch. Oxford: Clarendon Press.

———, 1996. *Some Thoughts Concerning Education and Of the Conduct of Understanding.* Edited by Ruth W. Grant and Nathan Tarcov. Cambridge: Hackett Publishing Company.

Lowi, Theodore, 1979. *The End of Liberalism.* 2nd ed. New York: W.W. Norton and Co.

Lowi, Theodore, 1969. *The End of Liberalism.* New York: W.W. Norton.

Luban, David, 1988. *Lawyers and Justice: An Ethical Study.* Princeton, NJ: Princeton University Press.

Lumbard, Thomas, 1981. "Setting Standards: The Courts, the Bar, and the Lawyers' Code of Conduct." *Catholic University Law Review* 30: 249-271.
Lyotard, Francois, 1986. *The Postmodern Condition: A Report on Knowledge.* Manchester: Manchester University Press.
Machiavelli, Niccolo, 1947. *The Prince.* Translated and edited by Thomas G. Bergin. Arlington Heights, IL: AHM Publishing.
MacIntyre, Alasdair, 1982. *After Virtue: A Study in Moral Theory.* London: Duckworth.
MacIver, Robert M., 1947. *The Web of Government.* New York: Macmillan Company.
Madison, James, 1904. *Writings of James Madison.* New York: Putnam's.
Marini, Frank, ed., 1971. *Toward a New Public Administration.* Scranton, PA: Chandler Press.
———, 1992. "The Uses of Literature in the Exploration of Public Administration Ethics: The Example of *Antigone*." *Public Administration Review* 52 (September/October): 420-426.
Marshall, S.L.A., 1947. *Men Against Fire.* 1st ed. New York: William Morrow & Company.
Marx, F.M., 1940. *Public Management in the New Democracy.* New York: Harper & Row.
Maslow, Abraham H., 1970. *Motivation and Personality.* 2nd ed. New York: Harper & Row, Publishers.
Masugi, Ken, ed., 1991. *Interpretting Tocqueville's Democracy in America.* Savage, MD: Rowman & Littlefield Publishers.
McCann, Michael W., and Gerald L. Houseman, 1989. *Judging the Constitution: Critical Essays on Judicial Lawmaking.* Glenview: Scott, Foresman.
McDonald, Forrest, 1985. *Novus Ordo Seclorum: The Intellectual Origins of the Constitution.* Lawrence: University Press of Kansas.
McGregor, Eugene B., 1974. "Social Equity and the Public Service." *Public Administration Review* 34 (January/February): 18-29.
Mill, John Stuart, 1947. *On Liberty.* Arlington Heights, IL: AHM Publishing.
———, 1957. *Utilitarianism.* Edited by Oskar Piest. New York: The Library of Liberal Arts.
Montesquieu, Charles, 1977. *The Spirit of the Laws.* Berkeley: University of California Press.
Morgan, Thomas D., 1977. "The Evolving Concept of Professional Responsibility." *Harvard Law Review* 90: 702-743.
Morris, Richard B., 1987. *The Forging of the Union, 1781-1789.* New York: Harper and Row.
Mosher, Frederick C., 1982. *Democracy and the Public Service.* New York: Oxford University Press.
———, 1987. "The Professional State." In Dean L. Yarwood, ed. *Public Administration: Politics and the People.* White Plains, NY: Longman, Inc.

Needy, Charles W., ed., 1980. *Classics of Economics*. Oak Park, IL: Moore Publishing Company, Inc.
Newsom, Carol A., and Sharon H. Ringe, eds., 1992. *The Women's Bible Commentary*. Louisville, KY: Westminster.
Nietzsche, Friedrich, 1966. *Beyond Good and Evil*. Translated by Walter Kaufmann. New York: Vintage Books.
Nozick, Robert, 1974. *Anarchy, State, and Utopia*. New York: Basic Books.
O'Ballance, Edgar, 1967. *The Algerian Insurrection: 1954-62*. Camden, CT: Archon Books.
Okun, Arthur M., 1975. *Equality and Efficiency: The Big Tradeoff*. Washington, DC: The Brookings Institute.
Osborne, David, and Ted Gaebler, 1992. *Reinventing Government: How the Entrepreneurial Spirit is Transforming the Public Sector From Schoolhouse to Statehouse, City Hall to the Pentagon*. New York: Addison-Wesley Publishing Company.
Ostrom, Vincent, 1974. *The Intellectual Crisis in American Public Administration*. University, AL: University of Alabama Press.
O'Toole, Jr., Laurence J., 1984. "American Public Administration and the Idea of Reform." *Administration and Society* 16 (August): 141-166.
————, 1987. "Doctrines and Developments: Separation of Powers, the Politics-Administration Dichotomy, and the Rise of the Administrative State." *Public Administration Review* 47 (January/February): 17-25.
Pangle, Lorraine, and Thomas Pangle, 1993. *The Learning of Liberty: The Educational Ideas of the American Founders*. Lawrence: University Press of Kansas.
Patterson, L. Ray, 1984. *Legal Ethics: The Law of Professional Responsibility*. 2nd ed. New York: Matthew Bender.
Percy, Walker, 1983. *Lost in the Cosmos: The Last Self-Help Book*. New York: Farrar, Straus, and Giroux.
————, 1987. *The Thanatos Syndrome*. New York: Farrar, Straus, and Giroux.
Peters, Ralph, 1994. "The New Warrior Class." *Parameters* (Summer): 16-26.
————, 1996. "A Revolution in Military Ethics?" *Parameters* (Summer): 102-108.
Plato. 1961. *The Collected Dialogues of Plato*. Edited by Edith Hamilton and Huntington Cairns. Princeton: Princeton University Press.
————, 1968. *The Republic*. Translated by Allan Bloom. New York: Basic Books.
————, 1979. *The Republic*. Translated and edited by Raymond Larson. Arlington Heights, IL: Harlan Davidson, Inc.
Porter, David O., and Teddie W. Porter, 1974. "Social Equity and Fiscal Federalism." *Public Administration Review* 34 (January/February): 36-43.
Portis, Edward Bryan, 1994. *Reconstructing the Classics: Political Theory from Plato to Marx*. Chatham, NJ: Chatham House Publishing Co.

Postema, Gerald J., 1980. "Moral Responsibility in Professional Ethics." *New York University Law Review* 55 (April): 63-89.
Powell v. Alabama, 287 U.S. 45 (1932).
Pratt, C.B., 1993. "Critique of the Classical Theory of Situational Ethics in U.S. Public Relations." *Public Relations Review* 19: 219-34.
Quine, Willard V.O., 1969. *Ontological Relativity and Other Essays*. New York: Columbia University Press.
Rawls, John, 1971. *A Theory of Justice*. Cambridge, MA: Belknap Press of the Harvard University Press.
Redford, Emmette S., 1958. *Ideal and Practice in Public Administration*. University, AL: University of Alabama Press.
———, 1969. *Democracy in the Administrative State*. New York: Oxford University Press.
Richardson, William D., 1984. "Thomas Jefferson and Race: The Declaration and *Notes on the State of Virginia*." *Polity* 16 (Spring): 447-466.
———, and L.G. Nigro, 1987. "Administrative Ethics and Founding Thought: Constitutional Correctives, Honor, and Education." *Public Administration Review* 47: 367-376. A revised version of this article is included in the present collection as Chapter 4.
———, and Brigitte Fessele, 1991. "Tocqueville's Observations on Racial and Sexual Inequalities in America" *Southeastern Political Review* 19 (2): 248-277.
———, 1997. *Democracy, Bureaucracy, and Character: Founding Thought*. Lawrence: University Press of Kansas.
Rohr, John A., 1976. "The Study of Ethics in the P.A. Curriculum." *Public Administration Review* 36 (July/August): 398-406
———, 1978. *Ethics for Bureaucrats: An Essay on Law and Values*. New York: Marcel Dekker.
———, 1986. *To Run a Constitution: The Legitimacy of the Administrative State*. Lawrence: University Press of Kansas.
———, 1988. "Bureaucratic Morality in the United States." *International Political Science Review* 1988: 167-178.
———, 1991. "Ethical Issues in French Public Administration: A Comparative Study." *Public Administration Review* (July/August): 283-297.
Rorty, Richard, 1982. *Consequences of Pragmatism: Essays 1972-1980*. Brighton: Harvester.
———, 1989. *Contingency, Irony, and Solidarity*. Cambridge: Cambridge University Press.
Rosenbloom, David H., 1989. *Public Administration: Understanding Management, Politics, and Law in the Public Sector*. 2nd ed. New York: Random House.
Rossum, Ralph A., and Gary L. McDowell, eds., 1981. *The American Founding: Politics, Statesmanship, and the Constitution*. Port Washington, NY: Kennikat Press.
Schaberg, Jane, 1987. *The Illegitimacy of Jesus: A Feminist Theological Interpretation of the Infancy Narratives*. San Francisco: Harper and Row.

Schiesl, Martin J., 1977. *The Politics of Efficiency: Municipal Administration and Reform in America*. Berkeley: University of California Press.

Schneyer, Ted, 1989. "Professionalism as Bar Politics: The Making of the Model Rules of Professional Conduct." *Law and Social Inquiry* 14: 677-737.

Schubert, Glendon A., 1960. *The Public Interest*. New York: The Free Press.

Shaffer, Thomas L., and Mary Shaffer, 1991. *American Lawyers and Their Communities*. Notre Dame, IN: University of Notre Dame Press.

Shakespeare, William, 1904. *Coriolanus*, Act IV, Scene vii. In *The Works of William Shakespeare*. New York: Oxford University Press, pp. 965-1006.

Shakespeare, William, 1904. *King Henry VI, Part II*, Act IV, Scene ii. In *The Works of William Shakespeare*. New York: Oxford University Press, pp. 31-64.

Shaub, Diana, 1997. "Girls Just Wanna Have Fun." *Public Interest* (Fall): 116-24.

Sheeran, Patrick J., 1993. *Ethics in Public Administration: A Philosophical Approach*. Westport, CT: Praeger Publishers.

Shklar, Judith N., 1998. *Political Thought and Political Thinkers*. Chicago: The University of Chicago Press.

Shuchman, Philip, 1968. "Ethics and Legal Ethics: The Propriety of the Canons as a Group Moral Code." *George Washington Law Review* 37: 244-269.

Simon, William, 1978. "The Ideology of Advocacy: Procedural Justice and Professional Ethics." *Wisconsin Law Review* 1: 29-143.

Sinopoli, Richard C., ed., 1997. *From Many, One: Readings in American Political and Social Thought*. Washington, DC: Georgetown University Press.

Smith, Adam, 1976. *The Theory of Moral Sentiments*. Indianapolis: Liberty Classics.

Sorley, Lewis, 1989. "Doing What's Right: Shaping the Army's Professional Environment." *Parameters* (March): 11-15.

Stillman, II, Richard J., 1984. "The Changing Patterns of Public Administration Theory in America." In Richard J. Stillman, ed. *Public Administration: Concepts and Cases*. 3rd ed. Boston, MA: Houghton-Mifflin, pp. 5-24.

Stivers, Camilla, 1990. "The Public Agency as Polis: Active Citizenship in the Administrative State." *Administration and Society* (May): 86-105.

Storing, Herbert J., 1980. "American Statesmanship: Old and New." In Robert A. Goldwin, ed. *Bureaucrats, Policy Analysts, Statesmen: Who Leads?* Washington, DC: American Enterprise Institute, pp. 88-113.

———, 1981. *What the Anti-Federalists Were For: The Political Thought of the Opponents of the Constitution*. Chicago: The University of Chicago Press.

Strauss, Leo, and Joseph Cropsey, 1987. *History of Political Philosophy*. 3rd ed. Chicago: The University of Chicago Press.

Streib, Gregory, 1992. "Ethics and Expertise in the Public Service: Maintaining Democracy in an Era of Professionalism." *Southeastern Political Review* 20 (Spring): 122-143.
Taylor, Henry, 1992. In D.L. Schaefer and R.R. Schaefer, eds. *The Statesman*. Westport: Praeger.
Thayer, Frederick C., 1973. *An End To Hierarchy! An End to Competition*! New York: New Viewpoints.
Tocqueville, Alexis de, 1966. *Democracy in America*. Edited by J.P. Mayer and Max Lerner, and translated by George Lawrence. New York: Harper and Row.
——, 1969. *Democracy in America*. Edited by J.P. Mayer. Garden City: Anchor Books.
——, 1971. *Democracy in America*. Vol. 2. Edited by Phillips Bradley. New York: Knopf.
——, 1990. *Democracy in America, Volumes I & II*. General editor Henry Reeve. New York: Vintage Books.
Toner, James H., 1995. *True Faith and Allegiance*. Lexington: The University Press of Kentucky.
Torp, Kenneth H., 1994. "Ethics for Public Administrators." *National Civic Review* 83 (Winter): 70-73.
Tribe, Lawrence, 1988. *American Constitutional Law*. Mineola: Foundation Press.
Tucker, David, 1981. "The Political Thought of Thomas Jefferson's *Notes on the State of Virginia*." In Ralph A. Rossum and Gary L. McDowell, eds. *The American Founding: Politics, Statesmanship, and the Constitution* Port Washington, NY: Kennikat Press, pp. 108-121.
Tusa, Ann, and John Tusa, 1986. *The Nuremberg Trial*. New York: Atheneum.
Ulanov, Ann Belford, 1993. *The Female Ancestors of Christ*. Boston: Shambhala.
U.S. Bureau of the Census, 1995. *Statistical Abstract*. 115th ed. Washington, DC: U.S. Government Printing Office.
U.S. Department of Commerce, 1995. *Statistical Abstract of the United States: 1995*. Washington, DC: U.S. Government Printing Office.
U.S. Department of Defense, Department of the Army, 1956. *Field Manual (FM) 27-10: The Law of Land Warfare*. Washington, DC
U.S. Office of Government Ethics, 1994. *Third Biennial Report to Congress*. Washington, DC: U.S. Government Printing Office.
Van Creveld, Martin, 1991. *The Transformation of War*. New York: The Free Press.
Van Riper, Paul, 1958. *History of the United States Civil Service*. Chicago: Row, Peterson.
Wakefield, Susan, 1976. "Ethics and the Public Service: A Case for Individual Responsibility." *Public Administration Review* (November/December): 661-666.
Waldo, Dwight, 1948. *The Administrative State*. New York: Ronald Press.

———, 1980. *The Enterprise of Public Administration*. Novato, CA: Chandler and Sharp Publishers.

———, 1984. "The Perdurability of the Politics—Administration Dichotomy: Woodrow Wilson and the Identity Crisis in Public Administration." In Jack S. Rabin and James S. Bowman, eds. *Politics and Administration: Woodrow Wilson and American Public Administration*. New York: Dekker.

———, 1984. *The Administrative State*, 2nd ed. New York: Holmes and Meier Publishers.

Wallace, James D. 1978. *Virtues & Vices*. Ithaca: Cornell University Press.

Wasserstrom, Richard, 1975. "Lawyers as Professionals: Some Moral Issues." *Human Rights* 5: 1-24.

Weber, Max, 1978. *Economy and Society*. Edited by G. Roth and C. Wittich Berkeley, CA: University of California Press.

———, 1992. "Selections from *Politics as a Vocation*." In Leslie G. Rubin and Charles T. Rubin, eds. *The Quest for Justice: Readings in Political Ethics*. 3rd ed. Needham Heights, MA: Ginn Press: 273-283.

Weisband, Edward, and Thomas M. Franck, 1975. *Resignation in Protest*. New York: Grossman Publishers.

Weston, Burns H., Richard A. Falk, and Anthony D'Amato, 1990. *International Law And World Order*. 2nd ed. St Paul, Minnesota: West Publishing Co.

White, Orion, and Bruce L. Gates, 1974. "Statistical Theory and Equity in the Delivery of Social Services." *Public Administration Review* 34 (January/February): 43-52.

Wildavsky, Aaron, 1980. *How To Limit Government Spending*. Berkeley, CA: University of California Press.

Will, George, 1983. *Statecraft as Soulcraft*. New York: Simon and Schuster.

Wilson, James Q., 1975. "The Rise of the Bureaucratic State." *The Public Interest* 41 (Fall): 77-103.

———, 1985. "The Rediscovery of Character: Private Virtue and Public Policy." *The Public Interest* (Fall): 3-16. This essay is reprinted in the present collection as Chapter 10.

———, 1995. *On Character*. Washington, DC: The AEI Press.

Wilson, Woodrow, 1987. "The Study of Administration." In Dean L. Yarwood, ed. *Public Administration: Politics and the People*. White Plains, NY: Longman, pp. 20-30. This essay originally appeared in *Political Science Quarterly* (June 1987); reprinted in 56 (December): 481-506.

Winthrop, Delba, 1986. "Tocqueville's American Woman and the True Conception of Democratic Progress." *Political Theory*, 14 (2): 239-261.

Wise, David, 1973. *The Politics of Lying: Government, Deception, Secrecy, and Power*. New York: Random House.

Wittgenstein, Ludwig, 1953. *Philosophical Investigations*. 3rd. ed. Translated by G.E.M. Anscombe. New York: MacMillan.

Wolfram, Charles W., 1978. "Barriers to Effective Public Participation in Regulation of the Legal Profession." *Minnesota Law Review* 62: 619-647.

Wolfson, H.A., 1956. *The Philosophy of the Church Fathers*. Vol. I. Cambridge, MA: Harvard University Press.

Wolin, Sheldon S., 1960. *Politics and Vision: Continuity and Innovation in Western Political Thought*. Boston: Little, Brown & Company.

Wren, Percival Christopher, 1961. *Beau Geste*. New York: Permabooks.

Contributors

Sarah R. Adkins received her M.A. in political science from Georgia State University. She is also the co-author of "Understanding Ethics Through Literature: Character, Honor, and the Corruption of Body and Soul in *King Rat*," which recently appeared in *Administration & Society*.

Ralph Clark Chandler is professor of political science and public affairs at Western Michigan University, where he is also Director of the School of Public Affairs and Administration. Dr. Chandler holds five academic degrees, including the doctorate in public law and government from Columbia University and ethics degrees from Union and Princeton Theological Seminaries.

Martin Diamond (1919–1977) was the Thomas and Dorothy Leavey Professor on the Foundations of American Freedom at Georgetown University at the time of his death. He had also taught at the Illinois Institute of Technology, University of Chicago, Claremont McKenna College and Graduate School, and Northern Illinois University. He wrote extensively on American political thought. Among his numerous publications are *The Democratic Republic: An Introduction to American National Government*, and *The Founding of the Democratic Republic*.

Anthony J. Giasi, Lieutenant Colonel, U.S. Army (Ret.) was commissioned as a Second Lieutenant (Armor Branch) in 1971, and has served in tank, cavalry and airborne units. His most recent troop assignment was from 1985–87, when he served as the Executive Officer of the 3rd Battalion (Airborne), 73rd Armor Regiment, 82nd Airborne Division. He is married and has four children. LTC Giasi was last assigned as the Branch Chief of the Implementation Branch of the Forces and Arms Control Division, of Headquarters, U.S. European Command, Stuttgart, Germany, where he was responsible for overseeing the implementation of conventional arms control treaties for the U.S. He retired in June 1994 at Fort McPherson, Georgia, and is currently pursuing his doctorate in political science at Georgia State University.

John C. Koritansky is professor of political science at Hiram College. He is the author of several articles on American politics and political philosophy and has authored a book, *Alexis de Tocqueville and the New Science of Politics*, published by Carolina Academic Press in 1986.

Peter Augustine Lawler is professor of political science at Berry College, Georgia. Among his many publications are *The Restless Mind: Alexis de Tocqueville on the Origin and Perpetuation of Human Liberty*, *American Views of Liberty*, and the forthcoming *Postmodernism Rightly Understood*. He is chair of the politics and literature section of the American Political Science Association.

Alasadair MacIntyre taught at several universities in England before emigrating in 1970. Since then he has taught at Brandeis University, Boston University, Wellesley College, Vanderbilt University, the University of Notre Dame, and Duke University. In 1989 he was a Luce Visiting Scholar at the Whitney Humanities Center of Yale University. His books include *A Short History of Ethics; After Virtue; Whose Justice? Which Rationality?* and *Three Rival Versions of Moral Enquiry*. His central interests are in the history of ethics, and more especially in the moral philosophies of Aristotle and Aquinas, and in the nature of practical rationality. He is a past President of the Eastern Division of the American Philosophical Association.

J. Michael Martinez currently works as an environmental/governmental affairs representative for a Fortune 400, privately-held plastics manufacturing company. He also serves as a part-time political science instructor at Kennesaw State University in Kennesaw, Georgia, and an adjunct instructor of law at John Marshall Law School in Atlanta, Georgia. A member of the Bar in Georgia and South Carolina, Mr. Martinez holds a B.A. in philosophy and political science from Furman University (1984), a J.D. from Emory University (1987), an M.P.A. from the University of Georgia (1991), and a Ph.D. in political science from Georgia State University (1995). Along with William D. Richardson and Ronald L. McNinch-Su, he is also co-editor of a forthcoming collection of essays, *'Old Times There Are Not Forgotten': Confederate Symbols in the Contemporary South*.

Lloyd G. Nigro is professor of public administration and urban studies at Georgia State University in Atlanta, Georgia. He received his Ph.D. in public administration from the University of Southern California in 1972. Before joining the GSU faculty in 1979, he taught at Syracuse University and the University of Southern California. He is the co-author of two widely read texts, *Modern Public Administration* and *The New Public Personnel Administration*. He has also published numerous book chapters and articles in the areas of public personnel policy, administrative ethics, and public administration and American political thought.

William D. Richardson is professor of political science, chair of the Department of Political Science, and director of the W.O. Farber Center for

Civic Leadership at the University of South Dakota. He received his Ph.D. from the State University of New York at Buffalo. His articles on aspects of American government, political thought and ethics have appeared in numerous journals and books, including *Administration and Society, Public Administration Review, Polity, Interpretation,* and *Public Voices*. His most recent book, *Democracy, Bureaucracy, and Character: Founding Thought,* was published by the University Press of Kansas in 1997.

Kerry R. Stewart received a B.A. in both history and philosophy from the University of Hawaii at Hilo. He received Masters degrees in both policy history and philosophy from Bowling Green State University in Ohio. He is currently pursuing his doctorate in political science at Georgia State University. He was assistant editor of *Cambridge History of Disease* and *Cambridge History of Nutrition*. He also has published several poems in *Kanilihua*, the UH-Hilo's literary magazine.

James Q. Wilson was a professor of government at Harvard University from 1961–1987 and a professor of management and public policy at UCLA from 1985–1997. He is the author or coauthor of 14 books, including *Moral Judgment, The Moral Sense, Bureaucracy, Political Organizations,* and his textbook, *American Government*. He has also written about crime and criminal justice (*Thinking About Crime* and *Crime and Human Nature*). He has been a president of the American Political Science Association and received its James Madison Award for a distinguished career.

Index

Abelard, Peter, 28
absolutes, 34, 43, 243, 248, 251
acquisitiveness, 185, 188, 193-194
Adair, Douglass, 183
Adams, John, 76, 82, 273, 281-282
administration, 7, 12-13, 37, 69-72, 74-75, 79-84, 86-91, 100-101, 103-104, 107-108, 110-111, 119, 122-131, 133-137, 139, 144-145, 147, 149, 154-155, 157, 244, 256, 261, 266, 268, 272, 274, 277, 286, 288
administrator, 70-71, 79, 81, 89, 107, 122, 125, 127-128, 130-131, 134-135, 139
Aesop, 6
After Virtue, 9, 25, 59, 87
Algeria, 243, 258, 260-261
Algiers, 16, 258-260
alienation, 290, 295-296, 302-303
ambition, 70, 74, 78, 80, 144, 183-184, 187-188, 203, 208, 218-220, 223, 235-236, 242, 264, 304
America, 5, 8, 14-15, 70, 76-77, 86, 95, 102, 104, 124, 136, 141-142, 145-149, 153-154, 156-159, 166-167, 177, 183, 189, 192-199, 201, 204-205, 208-209, 213-214, 217, 220, 222-223, 229, 241-242, 261, 263, 268, 271-272, 275, 277, 280-281, 285, 287, 290, 292, 307
American Bar Association, 113, 115, 121-122
American Political Tradition, The, 189, 244
American Society for Public Administration (ASPA), 37, 84, 126-127, 135
Amin, Idi, 95
Anglicanism, 198
Anti-federalists, 72-73, 76, 78, 85, 97

Appetites, 21, 23-24, 52, 188-189, 199, 286
Appleby, Paul, 70, 123
A Priori Judgments, 38
Aquinas, St. Thomas, 28-29
Arab, 258-259
Arete (excellence), 20, 173
aristocracy, 13, 77-79, 82, 103, 142, 146, 154-155, 161, 196, 200, 204-207, 217
Aristotelian, 5, 9-10, 16, 28, 47-49, 58-59, 62-64, 103, 120, 175, 183, 191-192, 197, 241, 243-244, 247-251, 253-256, 261
Aristotle, 9-10, 19, 24-29, 48, 51-52, 60, 62, 64, 102, 107, 109, 120, 134, 139, 151, 172-177, 182, 187, 191, 197-198, 236, 249-250, 252-253, 284, 287
ASPA Code of Ethics and Guidelines, 135
Augustine, St., 21
Aurelius, Marcus, 270
authority, 26, 30, 32, 57, 112, 114, 126, 136, 144-145, 147, 149-152, 154-156, 158-160, 163, 165-167, 176, 197-198, 210, 212, 241, 255, 260-261, 264, 266, 270, 286, 297, 304, 309
auxiliaries, 23

Babbitt, George, 174
Barthes, Roland, 42
Beard, Charles, 189
behavior, 8, 11, 15, 19, 25-26, 29-32, 34, 36, 69, 80-81, 84, 94-98, 100, 102, 104, 110-113, 118, 122, 125, 127, 130-132, 138, 144, 176, 181-182, 184, 188, 195, 197, 210-211, 215, 218,

226-228, 230, 232-233, 243-249, 251, 254-255, 269, 296
Bennett, William J., 6
Bentham, Jeremy, 39
Bill of Rights, 159, 164, 199-200, 277
Book of Virtues, The, 5-7, 17, 25-26, 149, 280
Bork, Robert, 163
bravery, 247, 251, 254, 273
Brutus, 266
Buchanan, James M., 231
bureaucrat, 75, 80, 135
bureaucratic, 82, 95, 112, 122-127, 132, 294
bureaucracy, 70, 74-75, 82-83, 102, 107, 132, 135-136, 144, 265, 267

capitalism, 232, 293-294, 304
Cartesianism, 290
Castro, 95
Casuistry, 114-115, 120-121
Categorical Imperative, The, 37-38
Cato, 266-267
character, 1, 5-17, 19-45, 48, 50, 52-54, 56, 58, 60, 62-64, 69-78, 80-82, 84, 86, 88, 90-92, 94, 96-98, 100, 102-104, 107-108, 110, 112, 114, 116, 118, 120, 122-124, 126, 128, 130, 132, 134-136, 138, 142, 144, 146-148, 150-154, 156, 158, 160, 162, 164, 166, 172-182, 184, 186, 188, 190, 192-200, 203-206, 208-218, 220-223, 225-237, 242-246, 248, 250, 252-256, 258, 260, 263-264, 266-268, 270-280, 282-286, 288-292, 294, 296, 298, 300-302, 304, 306-308
Christian, 16-17, 21, 27-28, 36, 109, 148, 177-178, 188, 268, 270-271, 275, 279, 285, 290, 303, 308
Christianity, 16-17, 27, 177, 270-271
Cicero, 60, 172, 268-269, 271, 287
citizenship, 62, 69, 75, 77, 85, 99-100, 199, 223, 272, 280, 292-293
civic, 16-17, 44, 74-76, 81, 104, 124, 132, 156, 176, 269-273, 288, 300, 306-307
Civil War, 164, 234

class, 16-17, 83-85, 87-88, 90, 137-138, 142-143, 155, 161, 167, 185-186, 189, 205-207, 215, 218, 228, 233, 257-258, 261, 290-295, 298-301, 303-307
classical, 6, 17, 20-21, 23, 27, 76-77, 103, 107, 124, 147, 165, 172, 176-179, 188, 193, 198-199, 267-268, 271, 285, 287, 293
Clinton, 7, 91, 113, 244, 273-274, 277-279, 283, 288
code, 12-13, 16, 34, 84, 109, 113-115, 119, 121-122, 125, 135-136, 138-139, 156, 205, 210, 215, 218, 243, 245, 247, 249, 251-252, 259-260, 282
Coleman Report, 227-228
Commedia, 53
commerce, 15, 86, 99, 175, 185, 194, 198-199, 214
commercial, 76-77, 79, 97, 175, 185, 188, 193-194, 207-209, 214, 236, 241, 264
community, 8, 10, 14, 16, 20, 22, 39, 51, 70, 73-76, 82, 85, 89-90, 104, 109, 117, 121, 144, 157, 165, 173-177, 179, 181-182, 192, 197-198, 206-207, 218, 227, 229, 268, 272, 275, 286, 288, 300, 307
competence, 17, 69, 80, 82, 103, 126, 144, 255-256, 291-292, 295
conduct, 12-13, 19, 22, 33-34, 36-37, 39, 80-81, 83, 85, 96-97, 101, 108-115, 118-122, 126-127, 134, 142-144, 147, 190, 211, 227-228, 236-237, 243, 247-248, 250-251, 254, 256, 270-271
Confessions (St. Augustine), 21
Congress, 101, 137, 256, 263, 267, 273, 282
conscience, 12, 31, 61, 70, 89, 121, 127, 133-134, 166-167, 208, 237, 260
Constitution, 71-75, 77-80, 82, 87, 89, 95-99, 129-130, 136, 142, 145, 159-160, 162-163, 166, 187, 190, 196, 198-199, 209, 221-222, 242, 248, 251, 254-256, 266, 272, 276-277, 281
Cooper, Terry L., 103, 122, 124, 130

correctives, 11, 69, 71, 73, 75-79, 81, 83, 85, 87-89, 124
courage, 7, 14-15, 20, 23, 26, 55, 61, 73, 173, 175, 184, 207-208, 244, 247, 249, 251, 253-254, 279, 307
crime, 15, 222, 225-226, 233-236, 279
cultural, 11, 91, 230, 234, 286, 292, 303, 305
culture, 11, 36, 43, 53, 59, 83, 91, 122, 241-242, 269, 289, 291, 294-298, 300-306, 308
Culture of Narcissism, The, 289, 294-302, 306

Darrow, Clarence, 117
death, 17, 27, 30, 37, 43, 116, 162, 166, 246, 257, 273, 289-290, 295, 297, 300-303, 306-307
death penalty, 116, 162, 166
decentralization, 13, 154-156, 199, 294
Declaration of Independence, 144, 146-147, 159, 165, 171, 179, 196, 198, 263, 265, 268, 273, 276, 282, 285
degeneracy, 261
democratic, 5-8, 10-13, 15-16, 20, 39-40, 43, 69, 71, 73, 75-77, 79, 81-85, 87, 89-91, 93-100, 103, 105, 107-109, 112, 116-117, 123, 125, 127-129, 131-132, 135-139, 141-142, 146-149, 151, 153-157, 161, 166, 172, 185-186, 188-189, 196, 203-207, 209-215, 218, 220-223, 241-244, 260-261, 263, 265-267, 269, 271-273, 275, 277, 279-281, 283, 285, 287, 293, 296, 306
democracy, 5-8, 11-12, 14, 16-17, 70, 75, 79, 86, 88, 93, 95, 97, 102, 107, 111, 116, 123-124, 126, 128, 132-133, 135-136, 138, 142-143, 146-156, 160-162, 164-167, 172, 180, 184-187, 189, 192, 194-196, 200-201, 203-207, 209-213, 215-221, 223, 241-242, 271, 277, 289-292, 297, 302-303, 306
Denhardt, Kathryn G., 103, 110, 124, 131, 284
Derrida, Jacques, 42

Descartes, Rene, 34
despotism, 77, 151, 155-156, 160-161, 163, 166, 280, 283
Diamond, Martin, 14, 25-26, 69, 73-74, 77, 109, 133, 143, 171, 203
discretion, 11, 69, 82, 87, 91, 96, 100-102, 104-105, 123, 125-127, 129, 132, 179
Douglass, Frederick, 293
duty, 37, 44, 74, 80, 87, 107, 113, 116, 121, 126, 128, 131, 139, 206, 244, 247, 249, 253, 255, 270, 274
Dworkin, Ronald, 109

education, 5-6, 8, 11, 20-22, 26, 33, 50-52, 54, 69, 74-75, 81, 84-89, 91, 98, 101-103, 107, 119, 124, 139, 142, 144, 157, 161, 167, 176, 179, 197, 200, 210-212, 214, 221-223, 225, 227, 270, 272, 276, 291, 293
egalitarian, 13, 146, 154, 165, 167, 176, 305
Eighth Amendment, 162, 166
elections, 88, 93-94, 100, 104
elites, 17, 84, 289, 291, 293-296, 298-301, 303-305, 307-308
elitism, 17, 289, 291, 293, 295, 297, 299, 301, 303-305, 307, 309
ends, 7-8, 41, 50-51, 60, 64, 78, 93, 147, 178, 193
England, 109, 156, 160-161, 227, 234, 266
Enlightenment, The, 19, 27, 29, 32, 36, 43-44, 270, 274-276, 285, 304
Epicureanism, 9, 27
Equality, 14, 95, 123, 146-149, 153-154, 156, 164-166, 172, 195, 204-206, 210, 212-213, 215, 217-223, 280, 293
Ergon, 26
ethical, 3, 8-13, 16, 19, 22, 24-26, 28-32, 34-41, 43-45, 71, 75-76, 79, 101-104, 108-111, 113-116, 119-120, 122-127, 129-136, 138-139, 173-174, 176-177, 179, 186, 190, 197-201, 243-248, 251-253, 255-256, 261, 274, 285-286
ethics, 1, 6, 8-14, 16, 19-45, 48, 50-54,

56, 58-60, 62, 64, 67, 69-70, 72-80, 82-84, 86, 88, 90-105, 107-139, 142, 144, 146, 148, 150, 152, 154, 156, 158, 160, 162, 164, 166, 171-201, 203-206, 208, 210, 212, 214, 216, 218, 220, 222, 226, 228, 230, 232, 234, 236, 241-261, 264, 266, 268, 270, 272, 274-276, 278, 280, 282-284, 286-288, 290, 292, 294, 296, 298, 300, 302, 304-306, 308
Ethics for Bureaucrats, 75, 79, 84, 103, 124, 129
Ethics of Public Service, The, 11-12, 70, 84, 89, 100-101, 107-108, 110-111, 122-123, 125-126, 128-135, 138
ethos, 5, 7-8, 96, 110, 133, 173-174, 177, 197, 201, 228, 234
Eudaimonia, 25
excellence, 20, 25-27, 51-52, 90, 173, 177, 190, 193, 196, 200, 300, 303
existentialism, 307

factions, 13, 98, 143, 152, 181-185
fairness, 101, 247, 256-257
federalism, 13, 33, 128, 156-159, 199, 277
Federalist, 14, 33, 72-75, 77-78, 80, 91, 112-113, 117, 141-146, 152, 179-180, 185, 187, 195, 200, 264-266, 276, 281
finance, 15, 157, 226, 231, 236, 268
Finer, Herman, 126-127
force, 5, 11, 14, 37, 39, 58, 91-92, 99, 138, 156, 158, 165, 183-184, 189, 194-195, 199, 236, 241, 244, 246, 251, 256-257, 266, 275
forms, 21-23, 25, 28, 40, 51, 103, 105, 146, 152, 165, 173-174, 179, 186, 192, 197, 214, 245, 247, 266, 268, 272, 284-286, 290, 305-306
Fortas, Abe, 118
Foucault, Michel, 42
foundation, 5, 11, 20-21, 29, 37, 69, 77-78, 83, 86, 89, 91-92, 96, 146, 165-166, 173, 177, 189-190, 192, 194-197, 200-201, 205-207, 212, 214-215, 218, 298-300, 303, 306

Founders, 11, 13-14, 17, 71-76, 79-80, 82, 85, 88-90, 94-98, 102, 135, 182, 189-193, 196, 200, 236, 264, 266, 268, 270-272, 276, 283, 291
Framers, 79, 141-142, 145-147, 152, 162-164, 166
France, 156, 213, 258, 260, 272
Frankena, William K., 132
Frederickson, H. George, 74, 86-87, 89, 101, 127
freedom, 39, 130, 146-150, 153-154, 156-158, 164, 189-190, 213, 223, 248, 257, 275-277, 294-297, 299, 302-304, 308
Friedrich, Carl J., 122, 125-126
fundamental, 5-8, 12, 16, 20, 30, 33, 35, 37, 40-41, 48-49, 54, 58, 78-79, 82-83, 90, 92-94, 100, 112, 134, 139, 145-146, 149, 159, 164-165, 173, 184, 191, 198-200, 221, 236, 290
Furman v. Georgia, 162

Garcia v. Metropolitan Transit Authority (MTA), 159
Gates, Henry Louis, 273-274
gentlemen, 85, 247
Gibbon, Edward, 263, 265
Gideon v. Wainwright, 118
Gilligan, Carol, 292
God, 21, 27, 29, 32, 92-93, 280, 285, 300, 303, 307-308
golden, 37
good, 8-10, 13-14, 16-17, 19-27, 29, 31, 34-35, 38, 40-41, 43, 47-57, 60-64, 73-75, 86, 93-94, 96, 102-104, 117, 120, 132, 134, 142, 144-145, 150-151, 154, 156-157, 164-165, 176-177, 180, 183, 187, 195, 220, 226-232, 234-235, 241, 250-253, 255-256, 264-265, 269, 271-273, 276, 278-279, 281, 285, 287-288, 290-292, 294, 304-305, 307-308
Goodsell, Charles, 82-83, 136, 286
Gorgias, 23
governance, 39, 70, 90
governors, 11, 69-70, 73-78, 88

Greeks, 19, 25, 27, 30, 34, 43-44, 107, 173, 267-268
Gregg v. Georgia, 162
guidelines, 84, 135, 138, 243, 247-248
Gyges's Ring, 21

Habermas, Jurgen, 42
habits, 7, 10, 15, 26, 61, 85-86, 98, 107, 110, 132, 148, 155, 195, 204, 208, 210, 219, 228, 236-237, 247, 277
habituate, 16, 97
Hamilton, Alexander, 72-73, 91, 113, 185, 266, 276
happiness, 9, 25-28, 36, 39-40, 60, 145, 147, 179, 185, 211, 248, 270, 301, 307
Hazard, Geoffrey C., Jr., 111, 116
Hobbes, Thomas, 30, 32-33, 109
Hofstadter, Richard, 189
honesty, 7, 11, 35, 117, 132, 144, 193-194, 247, 254, 273, 284
honor, 10, 14, 16, 20, 23, 25, 44, 52, 60, 69-70, 75, 77, 80-82, 84, 88-90, 124, 136, 165, 172, 175, 206-210, 212, 242, 244-247, 249, 251, 253-257, 259-260, 274, 277, 287, 304
humanism, 75, 191
Hume, David, 33-35
hyperman, 299-300, 303, 307-308

ideology, 114, 186, 235
Inclinationes, 50-51
inclinations, 13
individual, 8-10, 12, 14, 16, 19-20, 24, 31, 39-41, 44, 52, 59, 74, 76, 79, 81, 85, 90, 95, 97, 102, 107-113, 116, 119, 124-133, 135, 139, 146-147, 152, 162-164, 178-179, 185, 203-207, 210, 215, 217-218, 223, 227, 234, 244, 246, 249-250, 254, 261, 265, 269, 271, 273, 275, 288, 293, 298, 300, 305-306
individualism, 9, 75, 302
inequality, 16, 94-95, 149, 184-185, 196, 205, 214, 221-222, 227, 282

integrity, 16-17, 63, 74, 90, 205, 244, 253-257, 271, 286
interest, 8, 11, 25, 35, 64, 70, 72-74, 78-79, 82, 88-89, 99, 101, 110, 121, 123-124, 128, 138, 143, 150-151, 153, 155-156, 181-187, 189, 192, 195, 199-200, 203, 223, 225, 231-232, 237, 263-265, 272, 276, 294, 306
Irwin, T.H., 50

Jackson Administration, 147
Jackson, Robert, 118, 161
Japan, 141, 233-234, 243
Jay, John, 72, 91, 113, 276
Jefferson, Thomas, 86-87, 96, 98, 263, 270, 276, 278, 281, 284
Jones, Paula, 7, 278
justice, 21, 23, 26, 35, 40-41, 55, 61, 96, 109, 112, 114, 118, 122, 127-128, 132, 143, 145-147, 150, 152, 154-155, 159, 161-167, 185-186, 194, 196, 233, 247, 252, 263-264, 274, 277

Kant, Immanuel, 36-38, 49
Keynes, John Maynard, 232
King, Martin Luther, Jr., 279-280, 293
Knowledge, 10, 22-23, 30, 32-34, 42, 49, 87-88, 94, 102-103, 120, 156, 211, 223, 249, 252, 270, 286-287, 290, 293-295, 298-301, 303-307
Kuhn, Thomas, 42

Lasch, Christopher, 17, 289, 291, 293-309
law, 8, 11-13, 30-31, 33, 36-37, 47, 50, 54-56, 63, 65, 67, 75, 79, 81, 85-86, 88-97, 99-105, 107-117, 119, 121, 123-127, 129-131, 133-135, 137, 139, 142, 144, 151, 155-156, 161-166, 177, 194, 206, 241, 244, 246-248, 250-252, 254-255, 269, 277, 306
lawmakers, 92, 94
lawyers, 8, 11-13, 67, 111-119, 121, 124, 135-137, 141-145, 147-149,

151, 153-157, 159, 161-163, 165-167
leaders, 5, 7, 14, 16-17, 77, 85, 102, 110, 117, 119, 125, 135, 183-184, 229, 232, 255, 260, 284, 294
leadership, 8, 11, 16, 91, 102, 239, 243-245, 247, 252-253, 255-257, 261
legitimacy, 41, 70, 79, 92-93, 95, 104, 134, 136, 159, 165-166, 252
Leviathan, 30, 32, 109, 190
liberalism, 71, 125, 144, 146-147, 165-166
liberty, 31, 39, 41, 69, 74, 77, 79, 81, 85-87, 95, 98, 109, 112, 118, 135, 147, 152-153, 157, 179, 181-182, 197, 201, 203-204, 235, 241, 248, 272, 291, 294, 297
Locke, John, 32-33, 74, 81, 85-86, 92, 103, 109, 248-249
love, 14, 21, 28, 35, 80-82, 146, 148-149, 153-154, 156, 165, 172, 175, 184, 197, 207-208, 217, 245, 258, 279, 289-290, 305-308
loyalty, 16, 20, 244, 249, 254, 257, 273-275
Lyotard, Jean-Francois, 42

Machiavelli, Niccolo, 29
Machiavellian, 6, 259
Madison, James, 72, 91, 113, 179-180, 199-200, 276
majoritarian, 13, 93-94, 98, 104-105, 146, 151, 153, 155
majority, 13, 26, 40-41, 82-83, 93, 109, 117, 143, 146, 148-154, 160, 166, 180-181, 185, 204, 242, 249, 260, 299
Mao, 95
Marshall, S.L.A., 249
Mather, Cotton, 173
Marx, F.M., 126
means, 10, 12, 14, 30, 37, 39-41, 57-58, 78-80, 88-89, 93, 102, 112-113, 124-125, 127-128, 137-138, 145-146, 151, 160, 162, 164, 166, 176, 178-179, 184, 187-189, 191, 193, 197-199, 213, 218, 225, 241-243, 246, 248-250, 252-254, 259, 264, 267, 289, 292, 299
merit, 8, 20, 83, 102, 161, 196
meritocracy, 14, 24, 94
metaphysics, 30, 35, 37, 43, 50, 65
McCarthy, Joseph, 118
military, 16, 94, 103, 158, 173, 207-208, 232, 241-261, 268, 273
Mill, James, 39
Mill, John Stuart, 39, 62, 153, 248
Model Rules of Professional Conduct, 12-13, 113, 115, 118-119, 121-122, 134
monarchy, 77, 87, 146, 272
moral, 6-7, 9-10, 15-17, 22, 25-26, 31-40, 47-49, 51, 53-59, 61-65, 73-75, 77-79, 81, 84-85, 87, 89-90, 102, 104, 109-111, 114-116, 118-121, 123, 125-126, 130-135, 144, 147-148, 166, 171-173, 177, 187, 189, 203-204, 207-209, 211-212, 214, 220, 229-233, 236-237, 243-244, 246, 248-250, 253, 255, 257, 261, 264, 269, 271, 274, 279-280, 284-286, 288-291, 293, 295, 297-301, 303-309
morality, 3, 8, 32, 34, 49, 64, 72, 78, 85, 95, 109-112, 114-115, 118-120, 122-124, 130, 132-133, 138, 166-167, 172-173, 203, 209, 221-222, 232, 234, 250, 254, 258, 267, 274, 283, 285, 290, 304, 307
mores, 43, 148-149, 174, 179, 197, 203-206, 215, 218-222, 244, 257
motives, 8, 14, 20, 74, 187-188, 191, 200, 264
Moynihan, Daniel Patrick, 225

national, 5, 15, 38, 71, 77, 80, 85, 98, 100-101, 103-104, 124, 135, 137, 144, 157-159, 198-199, 215, 223, 229, 236, 258, 265-266, 268, 273-274, 276, 279, 281, 293
National Endowment for Democracy, 5
natural Law, 33, 47, 50, 54-56, 63, 109, 155-156, 194
natural rights, 33, 145, 147, 159, 172

nature, 9, 11, 13, 25-27, 30-31, 33, 37-38, 41-42, 50-52, 55, 57, 61, 63, 72, 77, 86-87, 92, 97, 100, 102, 104, 109, 112, 117, 121-123, 126, 133, 152, 165, 171, 174, 176, 178-182, 187, 190-192, 196, 200, 203-207, 211-213, 216-218, 232-233, 235, 245, 248, 250, 253, 261, 263-265, 269, 280, 286, 289, 295-297, 299-301, 303, 305-307, 309
Neo-Platonism, 21
Nicomachean Ethics, The, 23-26, 28, 51-52, 60, 64, 102, 107, 119-120, 133-134, 249, 284
Niebuhr, Reinhold, 303
Nietzsche, Friedrich, 22
noble, 9, 80, 120, 149, 154, 156, 218, 267
Nozick, Robert, 132
Nuremberg Trials, 117

O'Connor, Flannery, 308
opinion, 36, 39, 49, 77, 81-86, 90, 115-116, 127, 131, 153, 162, 180-184, 186-189, 200, 210, 214, 218, 234, 270, 273, 275, 278, 280, 288

pantheism, 301-302
parliament, 161
participation, 70, 105, 114, 119, 130, 137, 154, 288, 294
passions, 5, 13-14, 52, 61, 64, 69, 74, 77-78, 80-82, 141, 143, 145, 147, 149, 151, 153, 155, 157, 159, 161, 163, 165, 167, 178, 181-184, 187, 193, 195, 199-201, 203, 211, 217-218, 220
Percy, Walker, 290, 306
perspectivalism, 22
Peters, Ralph, 257
philosopher-kings, 23
philosophy, 9-10, 15, 20-24, 27-33, 35-37, 39, 42-44, 47, 49, 51, 53, 55, 57-59, 61, 63-65, 107, 115, 121, 123, 129, 131-132, 142, 145, 165, 172, 177-179, 188, 190-191, 203, 237, 248, 264, 277, 296-297, 300

Phronesis, 55, 284
Plato, 9, 19-26, 38, 44, 60, 107, 271, 286-287
Plutarch, 267-268
polis, 23-24, 75, 174-176, 180, 188, 199
politics, 6, 14, 17, 26, 29, 43, 45, 53, 62, 70-73, 75, 77-78, 83-84, 87-89, 91, 100, 104, 109, 112-113, 118-119, 121-127, 130, 133, 147, 159, 171-183, 185-191, 193, 195, 197-201, 203-204, 212, 234-235, 271, 275, 280, 287, 290, 294, 306-307
Politics, The, 6, 14, 17, 25-26, 29, 43, 45, 53, 61, 70-73, 75, 77-78, 83-84, 87-89, 100, 104, 109, 112-113, 118-119, 121-127, 130, 133, 147, 159, 171-182, 184-191, 193-194, 196-201, 203-204, 212, 234-235, 271, 275, 287, 290, 294, 307
polity, 42, 87, 125, 129, 179, 185
popularity, 6, 159, 253
populism, 17, 291, 303
post-enlightenment, 19, 44
postmodernism, 9, 41-45, 299, 309
Powell v. Alabama, 117
prejudice, 41, 157
prerogative, 161
Prince, The, 29, 215, 263
principle, 5, 30, 39-41, 52, 74, 78, 83, 94-95, 132, 146, 151, 183, 186-187, 194-195, 197, 212-213, 219, 221, 248, 255, 268, 277, 290, 293
profession, 10, 12, 84, 108, 111-119, 121-125, 129, 133-134, 136-139, 141, 154-156, 162, 165, 167, 241-242, 245, 253, 255, 296
professionalism, 70, 83, 111, 113, 118-119, 121, 123, 128, 135, 138, 161, 253, 256
progressives, 162
property, 12, 30, 35, 77, 86, 97, 117, 162, 179, 184-186, 191, 205, 212, 218, 220, 248, 282
psychoanalysis, 17, 290, 295-297
psychotherapy, 297-298
Publius, 72-75, 77-80, 112, 117, 265

338 · Ethics and Character

Puritanism, 198

Quine, Willard, 42

Radin, Margaret Jane, 162
Rawls, John, 40-41, 132
regime, 5-8, 10-17, 22, 27, 30, 39, 45, 69-80, 82-83, 85, 87-101, 103-105, 107-108, 111, 113-114, 116-119, 123, 125, 129-130, 132-133, 139, 141-147, 159-160, 172-175, 179, 183, 192, 197-198, 203, 214, 220-222, 236, 276
Reid, Thomas, 49
reinventing, 99, 137
religion, 11, 16-17, 29, 85, 91, 147, 159, 179, 183, 197, 200, 210, 263, 266, 268-271, 275, 277, 279-280, 285, 288, 297, 302-304, 308
representation, 114-115, 121, 137, 141, 143-144, 282, 288
representative, 31, 74, 110, 142-143, 147, 161, 260
Republic, The, 12-13, 16-17, 21-24, 38, 72-79, 81-82, 85, 89, 91, 96-97, 103, 107, 123, 129, 152, 171, 174, 177, 180, 185, 188, 197-199, 203-204, 206, 231, 235, 264-268, 270-272, 276-283, 286-287
republican, 29, 76-77, 79, 100, 103, 146, 180, 189, 195, 199-200, 265-266, 276
republicanism, 287
republics, 5, 91, 99, 180
reputation, 75, 77, 81-82, 90, 212, 218, 220, 256
Responsible Administrator, The, 122, 127, 130-131, 133-135
responsibility, 8, 15, 20, 23, 26, 36, 44, 79, 104, 111-116, 118-121, 125-128, 130, 133, 137, 142, 157, 164, 230, 236, 247, 266, 293, 297-298, 300, 304, 306, 308
Richardson, William D., 5, 12, 69-70, 75, 87, 91, 102, 107, 124, 132, 209
restraint, 78, 95, 208, 236
right, 14-16, 19, 22, 29-35, 38, 50, 54, 63, 90, 92, 109-110, 122, 139, 141, 146, 150, 152, 157, 159, 163, 176, 185, 196, 198-199, 226, 228, 230-232, 236-237, 243-244, 248-249, 251-253, 261, 274-275, 278, 288, 291, 297, 301, 307
Right, Divine, 92
Right-to-Life Movement, 305
Rohr, John, 75, 79-80, 82, 84, 95, 103, 124, 129, 136
Roman, 16-17, 29, 174, 242, 263, 265-271
Rorty, Richard, 42, 299
rulers, 5, 7, 23, 75, 93, 95, 97-98, 102-103, 152, 242
rules, 9-13, 27-28, 31, 34, 36, 43, 47, 50, 54-58, 62-64, 91, 93, 101, 108-115, 118-123, 126, 130, 133-134, 138, 150, 154, 207, 210, 219, 230, 237, 246, 251
ruthlessness, 244, 257

sacrifice, 16, 40, 117, 150, 194, 213-214, 249-250, 294
scandal, 142
Schlesinger, Arthur, 274
schooling, 15, 226-227, 236
Scopes , 3, 5-17, 19-45, 47-65, 69-105, 107-139, 141-167, 171-201, 203-223, 225-237, 241-261, 263-309
secular, 29, 94, 97, 269, 308
self-interest, 11-12, 16, 35, 40, 73-78, 80-81, 85-86, 89-90, 97-98, 100, 136, 163, 186, 190, 193-196, 199, 201, 220, 222, 231-232, 236, 248, 277
self-pity, 298, 307-308
Senior Executive Service, 137
Shakespeare, William, 19, 118
shame, 81, 97, 207, 231, 254-255, 295-297
Sheeran, Patrick J., 123, 131
Sidgwick, Henry, 49
skepticism, 9, 20, 27, 33-36, 44, 226
Skinner, B.F., 297
Smith, Adam, 81, 263-265, 271
socialization, 85, 249

Socrates, 21, 297
Socratic, 290, 295, 297, 303
soldiers, 16, 242, 246, 249, 251-252, 255-256, 260, 281
Sophists, 20-22, 44
Social Contract, The, 146
Stalin, 95
state, 11, 16-17, 25, 29-33, 36, 38, 70, 75, 79-80, 82, 84-87, 89, 95-96, 99, 101, 104-105, 120, 122-125, 132, 135-136, 141, 146, 148, 152, 164-165, 179, 182, 190, 192, 195, 199, 204, 206, 213, 215, 219, 246, 252, 257, 264-265, 267-269, 271, 276, 281-283, 292, 294, 297, 304
statesmanship, 69, 72, 74, 79-80, 87, 142, 198-199
statesmen, 72, 79-80, 201
Stoicism, 9, 27
Strauss, Leo, 29, 33, 36, 177, 248
Summa Contra Gentiles, 28
Summa Theologiae, 50, 52
Summa Theologica, 28
superstition, 301, 303

Taking Rights Seriously, 109
tastes, 15, 21, 210, 220, 226, 237
Telos, 10, 22, 53, 58
temperance, 13, 26, 35, 105, 141, 143, 145, 147, 149, 151, 153, 155, 157, 159, 161, 163, 165, 167, 234, 273
temperament, 79, 98
Teresa, Mother, 93
Tertullian, 27-28, 44
Thinking Class, 85, 299
Thomism, 290, 309
Thomistic Tradition, 47
To Kill a Mockingbird, 117
tradition, 3, 8, 19-20, 22, 24, 28, 32, 40, 42, 44-45, 47, 71, 76, 91, 107-108, 112, 130, 133, 156, 189, 198, 241, 243-244, 255-256, 260-261, 274, 285, 305, 308
transcendentalism, 9
Tocqueville, Alexis de, 8, 13-14, 86, 124, 148, 195, 203-204, 242, 277, 280, 290-291, 302-303

Toner, James H., 243, 251
trait, 35, 77
truth, 17, 22, 30, 32, 38, 43, 56, 62, 141, 151, 153, 204, 213, 232, 235, 270, 274, 280, 282, 284, 287, 289-291, 293-297, 299-300, 302-304, 308-309
tyranny, 13, 95, 150-155, 161, 166-167, 277, 298, 306

Ubermensch, 22
United States Code of Ethics of 1980, 135
utilitarianism, 33, 38, 40-41, 62, 243, 245, 248, 251
utilitarians, 9, 19, 39, 41, 57, 288
utopia, 132, 293
utopianism, 191-192

valor, 208, 247
vices, 6-8, 11, 20, 36, 53, 69, 71, 73, 75, 77, 79, 81, 83, 85, 87, 89, 169, 209, 217
virtue, 6-9, 11, 15-17, 19-23, 25-27, 29, 31, 33-37, 39, 41, 43-45, 50, 55, 59, 72-77, 80-83, 85-88, 90, 92-93, 98, 102, 109-110, 113, 122-123, 132, 134, 161, 173-174, 178, 186, 191-196, 199-200, 203, 205, 207-208, 211, 225, 236-237, 239, 249-251, 254-255, 264, 269-274, 276, 283, 287, 289, 291-293, 304, 306, 308
virtuous, 24-25, 27, 29, 33, 35, 50, 73-75, 77-78, 80-82, 85, 88-90, 97, 102, 151, 173, 186, 195, 198, 211, 213, 250, 255, 272, 288

Wakefield, Susan, 128
Waldo, Dwight, 70-71, 80, 84, 88-89, 123
Washington, George, 81, 114, 255-256, 273, 278-279
war, 30-31, 33, 38, 98, 132, 149, 164, 177, 190, 207, 232, 234, 241-249, 251-253, 256-261, 266, 282, 291, 301, 303, 305
wealth, 25, 52, 60, 108, 132, 185, 195,

208-210, 214-217, 219-220, 231, 263-265, 268, 285
Weber, Max, 80, 112, 122, 231
Welch, Joseph, 118
welfare, 15-16, 41, 73, 96, 105, 222, 226, 228-231, 236, 266, 270, 276, 292, 294, 304
White, Leonard, 144
Wilde, Oscar, 173
Will, George, 148, 276, 278
Wilson, James Q., 15, 123-124, 203, 225, 277
Wilson, Woodrow, 38, 70-71, 74, 81, 83, 88-89, 126-127, 267, 278

wisdom, 14, 23-24, 39, 74-75, 93, 102, 104, 120, 134, 139, 150, 161, 184, 249-250, 252-253, 255, 276, 286-287, 295, 298
Wittgenstein, Ludwig, 42
women, 15, 62, 130, 196, 209-214, 221-222, 230, 244, 257, 269, 280-284, 289, 292-294, 298, 305-308
workers, 23, 51, 62, 261